Lincoln

THE ROAD TO WAR

Lincoln

THE ROAD TO WAR

Frank van der Linden

Fulcrum Publishing
Golden, Colorado

Library of Congress Cataloging-in-Publication Data
Van der Linden, Frank.
    Lincoln : the road to war / Frank van der Linden.
       p.   cm.
    Includes bibliographical references and index.
    ISBN 1-55591-420-9
    1. Lincoln, Abraham, 1809–1865. 2. Political leadership—United States—History—19th century. 3. United States—Politics and government—1849–1861. 4. United States—Politics and government—1861–1865. 5. United States—History—Civil War, 1861–1865—Causes. I. Title.
E457.2.V36   1998
973.7'092—dc21   98–35214
                                             CIP

Printed in the United States of America

0 9 8 7 6 5 4 3 2

Fulcrum Publishing
350 Indiana Street, Suite 350
Golden, Colorado 80401-5093
(800) 992-2908 • (303) 277-1623
e-mail: fulcrum@fulcrum-books.com
website: www.fulcrum-books.com

To the memory of my brother, Harry,
Brigadier General William H. Vanderlinden,
United States Army Reserve, a brave soldier
and a fellow student of American history.

CONTENTS

PREFACE

Abraham Lincoln hated war. He repeatedly called himself a man of peace. A kindly, generous, great-hearted man, he yearned to lead a united people into an era of peace and prosperity. Yet he presided over a divided nation during its most catastrophic war, in which armies of Americans killed and wounded each other over political disputes that should have been settled by compromise, a "brothers' war" that his critics called unnecessary, unconstitutional, and a terrible waste of six hundred thousand lives.

Lincoln waged the war for the initial purpose of restoring the Union, broken by the secession of several Southern states; yet the evidence strongly indicates that, with more wisdom and patience and less political face-saving, the Union could have been saved by conciliation without the enormous cost in blood.

Senator George Pugh, an Ohio Democrat and bosom friend of Lincoln's arch-rival, Stephen A. Douglas, called Lincoln "the most obscure man ever elected to the presidency." "Ninety-nine out of a hundred" of the people who elected him had never heard of him before his debates with Douglas, Pugh declared.

Pugh exaggerated a little, but his main point was correct: Lincoln was simply a successful Illinois lawyer, a one-term congressman who had twice lost in bids for the United States Senate, a man with no executive experience whatever. In his debates with Douglas, Lincoln had shown his superior mind, his tenacious debating skills, and his iron determination to fight for the eventual end of slavery. As a wartime president, he wielded more power than any other man who had ever occupied the White House before. He used that power to attain his goal of freedom, but at tremendous cost.

The story of Lincoln's drive for power is a fascinating drama, enacted by an incredible cast of characters—conniving politicians, greedy financiers, ambitious senators, idealists, charlatans, and ruthless men who dreamed of a golden empire.

To present a complete and colorful picture of the American scene on the eve of the Civil War, this book tells not only of Lincoln's rise but of the Democrats' fall; how and why the Democrats fatally split into two warring factions and gave the presidency to Lincoln; how the Southern secessionists tried to make Washington, D.C., their own capital; how some wild men plotted to kill Lincoln; how he spurned all pleas for a compromise to avert bloodshed; and how, under intense political pressure, he cast the die for war.

1

"Spotty Lincoln"

When the Thirtieth Congress convened in early December 1847, a new House member from Illinois' Seventh District made his debut, a little awkwardly, on the stage of national politics. Abraham Lincoln, at thirty-eight, looked and acted like a man a few years older, solemnly attired in his new black suit.

He attracted attention chiefly because of his unusual height and the muscular physique that had made him a champion wrestler in his youth. Six feet, four inches tall, with long arms and legs and large hands and feet, the gray-eyed prairie lawyer made an impressive appearance.

"His eyebrows cropped out like a huge rock on the brow of a hill," said Billy Herndon, his law partner at Springfield. "His face was long, sallow, cadaverous ... wrinkled and dry. The whole man, body and mind, worked slowly, as if he needed oiling."

Lincoln's wiry black hair tumbled down over his big ears. His wide mouth, the lower lip protruding slightly, showed firmness and strength; it often opened wide for laughter, too, for he loved to tell funny stories, which were sometimes too ribald for polite company.

Within a few days after he and his wife, Mary, and their two little boys, Bob and Eddie, had moved into their single room in Mrs. Ann G. Sprigg's boarding house on Capitol Hill, "Abe" had become the most popular figure at the dinner table, regaling the other guests with his laughter and wit. At Caspari's bowling alley nearby, he amused the crowd with "the sport of narratives, some of which were very broad." In the House post office, where congenial yarn-spinners met, Lincoln would tilt back his chair by the open fireplace, with his long legs reaching over the chimney jamb, and soon he became acclaimed as "the champion story teller of the Capitol."

Lincoln longed to be taken more seriously as a statesman, not merely a comedian. The man who, years later, would tell Congress, "We cannot escape history," could see the clock above the desk of Speaker Robert Winthrop of Massachusetts. Above the clock sat the marble figure of Clio, the Muse of History, who seemed to be writing down the words of the Congressmen.

Three days before Christmas, the Illinois freshman made his bid to be remembered in history. He introduced a series of resolutions aimed at blaming President James Knox Polk for instigating the war against Mexico, now drawing to a close after nearly two years of conflict.

There was an air of partisan politics about this maneuver. Lincoln was the only Whig in the Illinois delegation, and President Polk was a Democrat. Hoping to win back the White House in the 1848 election, the Whigs were using their slim majority in the House to embarrass the President on the issue of war guilt.

Polk had won a declaration of war from Congress in April 1846 by charging that Mexico had started the fighting by attacking Americans and shedding their own blood on their own soil in Texas. Both countries claimed the disputed area between the Nueces River and the Rio Grande. Lincoln claimed that, by sending American troops to the Rio Grande, Polk had started the war.

Lincoln demanded that the President give Congress all the facts to show whether that particular "spot" where the fighting began really was American soil. He doubted that that "spot" had ever been legally part of Texas. Now the war was ending in an American victory and Polk proposed to seize the huge area of California and New Mexico as war indemnity.

On January 3, 1848, the Whigs narrowly won House approval of a measure asserting that the war had been "unnecessarily and unconstitutionally begun by the President of the United States." Lincoln voted with his party, and the Whigs won, 85 to 81.

In a speech on the House floor nine days later, Lincoln demanded that the President hurry up and answer all the questions in his "spot" resolutions. If Polk refused, the young Congressman said, "then I shall be fully convinced, of what I more than suspected, that the President is deeply conscious of being in the wrong in this matter; that he feels the blood of this war, like the blood of Abel, is crying from the ground against him."

Lincoln surmised that the President must have had some strong motive for involving the United States and Mexico in war and "had trusted to avoid the scrutiny of his own conduct ... by fixing the public eye upon military glory—that rainbow that rises in showers of blood—that serpent's eye that charms but to destroy; and thus calculating, had plunged into this war, until, disappointed as to the ease by which Mexico could be subdued, he found himself at last he knew not where."

Like a man in "the half-insane excitement of a fever dream," Lincoln charged, the President jumped around from one proposal to another—first calling for Mexico to give up half of its land as war indemnity and then suggesting possibly more. In his latest message to Congress, "he talked like an insane man," the Congressman said. "His mind, taxed beyond its power, is running hither and thither, like an ant on a hot stove."

If Lincoln expected his attack upon the President, coupled with his "spot" resolutions, would make him famous, he suffered a keen disappointment. The President never replied to the questions nor responded to the charge that he talked like a crazy man; he didn't even mention Lincoln in his diary. The "spot" resolutions never came up in the House for a vote. With his verbal shotgun blasts, Lincoln had simply shot himself in the foot.

Back home, where the war was popular and most people were proud of the fighting Illinois volunteers, especially since the victory would bring a huge area of Mexico under the American flag, the freshman Congressman found himself out of touch with the masses. Even Billy Herndon disagreed with his law partner's assault upon the President. Herndon considered it a mistake that would backfire and shatter his friend's dream of rapid advancement in national politics.

In a letter to Herndon, Lincoln said that Polk had acted like a king in starting the Mexican War. "Allow the President to invade a neighboring country whenever he shall deem it necessary to repel an invasion," he wrote, "and you allow him to do so whenever he may choose."

The Constitution gave Congress alone the power to declare war, Lincoln emphasized. He said this was done because "Kings had always been involving and impoverishing their people in wars," so the

Founding Fathers had deliberately framed the Constitution so that "no one man should hold the power of bringing the oppression on us."

Naturally, the Illinois Democrats leaped upon the issue with undisguised delight. They accused Lincoln of making an unpatriotic attack upon the administration's war policies and of insulting the brave men who had suffered wounds and death in battle. They noted that one of his predecessors in his House seat, John J. Hardin, had been killed at Buena Vista, and another, Edward Baker, had fought heroically at Cerro Gordo.

Referring to the "spotted fever" disease raging in Michigan, the _State Register_ said Lincoln had had an attack of it in Washington and it could prove fatal. With mock sympathy, the Democratic newspaper remarked: "What an epitaph: 'Died of Spotted Fever.' Poor Lincoln!"

At a series of rallies in his district, critics assailed the freshman Congressman as "Spotty Lincoln." The Morgan County assembly expressed "deep mortification" over his "base, dastardly and treasonable assault upon President Polk."

"Henceforth," it predicted, "will this Benedict Arnold of our district be known here as the Ranchero Spotty of one term."

Lincoln had earlier agreed to serve only a single term, in line with the Whigs' policy of rotation in office, but he was willing to take a second helping if the voters would give it to him. The Whigs made sure that their "Spotty" Congressman would come home. In 1848, they nominated Stephen T. Logan instead; and, in this previously safe Whig district, Logan lost to the Democrats' nominee, Thomas L. Harris, a war hero, by a margin of 106 votes.

Lincoln came home in despair, thinking his political career had ended forever. Herndon termed him "politically dead." Many acquaintances observed that he often fell into periods of depression, broken abruptly by fits of laughter, "black despondency and boisterous humor following one another like cloud and sunshine in a day of doubtful storm." Psychoanalysts of a later day might have diagnosed his case as one of "manic depression."

Lincoln picked up the pieces of his law practice and built it up steadily over the next five years, making no attempt to seek office again. Among his clients, he attracted several railroad companies engaged in extending a network of lines across Illinois and the Old Northwest.

Lincoln emerged from his self-imposed exile and returned to the political wars after Congress passed the Kansas-Nebraska Act, repealing the Missouri Compromise and permitting settlers in the new territories to vote slavery up or down as they pleased. The resulting explosion of voters' anger blew up the Whig Party, split the Democrats, and led to the birth of the new Republican Party, consisting chiefly of Whigs and "anti-Nebraska" Democrats. In the 1854 elections, the Democrats lost control of the Illinois legislature, thus assuring that they could not reelect Senator James Shields.

Lincoln perceived that, in a legislature composed of forty-one regular Democrats and fifty-nine "anti-Nebraska" men of various political hues, he would have a good chance of reviving his career by winning the Senate seat. He campaigned furiously for votes through personal appeals to lawmakers. When the state Senate and House met in joint session February 8, 1855, Lincoln led on the first round with 44 votes, Shields had 41, Lyman Trumbull, an "anti-Nebraska" Democrat, had 5, with others scattering.

The Democrats dropped Shields and consolidated their votes on Governor Joel A. Matteson. By the ninth ballot, Lincoln had sunk to 15 votes, Trumbull had risen to 35, and Matteson had 47, only 4 short of a majority.

To block Matteson, Lincoln tossed his remaining votes to Trumbull and gave him the victory. Once again, Lincoln suffered a crushing disappointment and, once again, he concentrated on his law practice.

Three years later, his hopes rose again. He became the overwhelming favorite of Illinois Republicans to challenge Democratic Senator Stephen A. Douglas for reelection. The Lincoln-Douglas debates that year made enduring history and brought the once obscure ex-Congressman into the national spotlight.

One hot, sultry evening during his 1858 campaign, Lincoln found himself caught in a thunderstorm at a lonely railroad station while waiting for a train to take him home to Springfield. From his latest speaking engagement, friends had brought him to the whistle stop in a buggy and left him there. Seeing no other shelter, the candidate took refuge from the rain by crawling into an empty freight car parked on a side track.

Inside he found another wet and weary traveler, Henry Villard, a young newspaperman. Villard, representing the German-language journal *Staats-Zeitung* of New York, had been covering the latest political meeting in Petersburg. The train, which was to carry Lincoln and Villard to Springfield, was late, and the rain was falling in torrents, so they squatted down on the floor of the boxcar like a couple of hoboes and talked about politics.

With his long legs pulled up, jack-knife fashion, and his chin resting on his knees, Lincoln recalled that he had been only a country store clerk whose first ambition had been realized when he won a seat in the state legislature. Although he had gone on to Congress, his single term had ended with the "Spotty Lincoln" fiasco. Now he was seeking a much higher goal, the United States Senate.

"I am convinced that I am good enough for it, but in spite of it all, I am saying to myself every day: 'It is too big a thing for you; you will never get it,'" he said. "Mary insists, however, that I am going to be senator and President of the United States."

Lincoln roared with laughter at the thought of his wife's prediction and he cried: "Just think of such a Sucker as me being President!"

The Illinois voters—who were nicknamed "Suckers"—already had a prospective presidential candidate, Senator Douglas, the dominant figure in the national Democratic Party. In the November election of 1858, they cast a plurality of their votes for the Republican state ticket, but they had no chance of placing Lincoln in the Senate because the senators were then chosen by the legislatures, not directly by the people.

Thanks to an out-of-date apportionment of the legislative districts in Illinois, the Democrats held a majority of the members on a joint ballot, and they reelected Douglas over Lincoln by 54 to 46. Thus Lincoln lost his second bid for a Senate seat, and he feared he had no political future left.

"Though I now sink out of sight and shall be forgotten," Lincoln told a friend, "I believe I have made some marks which will tell for the cause of civil liberty long after I am gone."

In his long and arduous struggle against Douglas, Lincoln had again neglected his law practice. So he was hard pressed to contribute money to the Republican Party's campaign costs. "I have been on expenses for so long," he wrote to Chairman Norman B. Judd, "that I am absolutely without money now for even household purposes."

At dusk one evening, shortly after the November election in 1858, Lincoln came out of the courthouse at Bloomington, Illinois, and met Jesse W. Fell, a landowner and railroad promoter, who had recently returned from a tour of the eastern states. Fell said people everywhere had been asking him, "Who is this man Lincoln?" They were favorably impressed by the way the tall prairie lawyer had traded blow for blow with the great debater, Douglas, and almost defeated him. Lincoln was gaining such a strong reputation, said Fell, that he might become a formidable presidential candidate.

"Oh, Fell, what's the use of talking of me for the presidency, when we have such men as Seward and Chase?" Lincoln protested. They were far better known and they deserved to head the Republican ticket as a reward for their years of leadership in the antislavery cause. Senator William Henry Seward of New York and Governor Salmon P. Chase of Ohio were entitled to the presidency, Fell agreed, but they had such a radical image, and had made so many enemies, that they could not be elected. To win in 1860, he insisted, the Republicans must choose a presidential nominee who was antislavery but with a more conservative image, a man who had come up from the working people.

Fell asked Lincoln to write a brief account of his life so that this could be printed in newspapers back East, to build up the public's awareness of his availability for the presidency. Lincoln replied that he would like to be President but he had to be realistic: his present aim was to take over Douglas's Senate seat in 1864.

"I must, in candor, say I do not think I am fit for the presidency," Lincoln wrote a few months later to Thomas J. Pickett, editor of the *Rock Island Register*, who offered to line up several other Republican editors in Illinois and have them endorse Lincoln for the White House. "I really think it best for our cause," Lincoln wrote, "that no concerted effort, such as you suggest, should be made."

Throughout 1859, Lincoln concentrated upon rebuilding his law practice and his bank balance. But he remained active in politics, corresponding with party leaders across the land and making speeches in Iowa, Missouri, Ohio, Indiana, and Wisconsin. Well aware of the rising importance of the German vote, he secretly purchased the *Illinois Staats Anzeiger*, a German-language newspaper published in Springfield. He gave Theodore Canisius, the former owner, a free hand to run it as editor as long as it would support the Republicans.

In December, a year after Jesse Fell had requested his autobiographical sketch, Lincoln finally provided it, along with a note: "There is not much of it, for the reason, I suppose, that there is not much of me. If any thing be made out of it, I wish it to be modest, and not to go beyond the material."

Lincoln also arranged for publication of his debates with Douglas, another way of promoting himself nationally; and he eagerly accepted an invitation to speak in New York City.

On the snowy night of February 27, 1860, fifteen hundred people came to the Cooper Union in Manhattan and listened to the rawboned Illinois lawyer introduced as the warrior who had battled the mighty Douglas. In his biography of Lincoln, Noah Brooks quotes an eyewitness of the event:

> When Lincoln rose to speak, I was greatly disappointed. He was tall—oh, how tall! and so angular and awkward that I had, for an instant, a feeling of pity for so ungainly a man. His clothes were black and ill fitting, badly wrinkled—as if they had been jammed carelessly into a small trunk. His bushy head, with the stiff black hair thrown back, was balanced on a long and lean headstalk, and when he raised his hands in an opening gesture, I noticed that they were very large.
>
> He began in a low tone of voice, as if he were used to speaking out of doors and was afraid of speaking too loud. He said "Mr. Cheerman," instead of "Mr. Chairman," and employed many other words with an old-fashioned pronunciation. I said to myself, "Old fellow, you won't do; it's all very well for the wild West, but this will never go down in New York."
>
> But pretty soon he began to get into his subject; he straightened up, made regular and graceful gestures; his face lighted as with an inward fire; the whole man transfigured. I forgot his clothes, his personal appearance and his individual peculiarities. Presently, forgetting myself, I was on my feet with the rest, yelling like a wild Indian.

Tracing the history of the slavery dispute back to the early days of the republic, Lincoln contended that the Founding Fathers did not forbid the federal government to control the institution in the territories.

Addressing "a few words to the Southern people," he denied that the Republicans were a sectional, radical, revolutionary party. He said they did not advocate slave insurrections; they simply wanted to keep the "wrong" of slavery from being extended to new regions.

"But you will not abide the election of a Republican president!" he exclaimed. "In that supposed event, you say, you will destroy the Union; and then, you say the great crime of having destroyed it will be upon us! That is cool. A highwayman holds a pistol to my ear and mutters through his teeth: 'Stand and deliver, or I will kill you, and then you will be a murderer!' "

It is difficult to convince the Southerners that the Republicans do not intend to disturb slavery in the states, he said. Nothing really will convince them, he added, unless "we cease to call slavery *wrong* and join them in calling it *right*."

His face aglow with emotion, Lincoln brought his listeners to their feet by declaring: "Neither let us be slandered from our duty by false accusations against us, nor frightened from it by menaces of destruction to the government nor of dungeons to ourselves. Let us have faith that right makes might, and in that faith, let us to the end, dare to do our duty as we understand it."

Lincoln's warm reception in New York City marked him as a rising star in the Republican Party, a challenger to Seward in the senator's own state. In a tour of New England afterward, he visited his son, Robert, who after failing his entrance examinations for admission to Harvard University, was studying at Phillips Exeter Academy and preparing for a second attempt. With a string of speeches in New Hampshire, Rhode Island, and Connecticut, Lincoln impressed more Republicans with the idea that he could be their nominee for the presidency.

Lincoln came home determined at last to make the big gamble for the highest stakes. When Senator Trumbull asked him to state, candidly, whether or not he really was a serious contender, he replied: "The taste *is* in my mouth a little."

Now, Lincoln ceased being coy and authorized several of his trusted friends to begin organizing a campaign for the nomination.

His unofficial manager was Judge David Davis, a three-hundred-pound lawyer, wealthy land investor, and mastermind of the Republican Party in Illinois.

Lincoln had to have the unanimous support of the Illinois delegation to the Republican national convention in Chicago in May. Seward had considerable support in the Chicago area, while conservatives in the southern counties backed Edward Bates, an old Whig from Missouri. Their followers wanted delegates chosen by districts, but the state central committee decided upon statewide election of delegates and they were all locked up for Lincoln under a binding unit rule.

To an Ohio delegate, Lincoln wrote: "I think the Illinois delegation will be unanimous for me at the start; and no other delegation will. A few individuals in other delegations would like to go for me at the start but may be restrained by their colleagues. It is represented to me by men who ought to know that the whole of Indiana might not be difficult to get."

"If I have any chance," he told another Ohio delegate, it consists mainly in the fact that the whole opposition would vote for me, if nominated. ... My name is new in the field, and I suppose I am not the first choice of a very great many.

"Our policy, then, is to give no offense to others—leave them in a mood to come to us if they shall be compelled to give up their first love."

When the Illinois Republicans met at Decatur May 9 at their state convention, Lincoln's cousin, John Hanks, and a companion marched in, carrying a strange banner tied between two old fence rails, and bedecked with flags and streamers.

"Abraham Lincoln the Rail Candidate for President in 1860," the banner proclaimed. "Two rails from a lot of 3,000 made in 1830 by Thos. Hanks and Abe Lincoln—whose father was the first pioneer of Macon County."

In response to cheers and shouts of "Speech, speech," Lincoln told the rowdy crowd: "I cannot say that I split these rails ... That was a long time ago. ... Well, boys, I can only say that I have split a great many better-looking ones."

So the myth of "Old Abe Lincoln, the rail splitter" was born. Bringing in the rails was a master political stroke, which paid off handsomely.

JUNE 2, 1860.]   M O M U S.   61

THE LAST RAIL SPLIT BY "HONEST OLD ABE."

This cartoon is from the collections of the Library of Congress.

It led many voters to view "Old Abe," who had risen from among the poor working people, as their champion.

Lincoln also benefited from another coup when the Republican national committee selected Chicago as the convention site instead of rival St. Louis, where Bates would have had an advantage.

Before they could assemble in May, however, the Republicans had to see how their opposition would shape up. They cast anxious eyes toward Charleston, South Carolina, where the Democrats would meet in late April to choose their national ticket. Lincoln's foe, Senator Douglas, clearly was the front-runner, "the man to beat." But the Little Giant had a host of enemies, one of the most vicious being his own fellow Democrat, President James Buchanan. The scene of the action must now shift, first to Washington, D.C., and then to Charleston.

2

HE "HELD THEIR HEARTS
IN HIS HAND"

Hundreds of happy, thirsty Democrats from all over the Northern states jammed a suite in the National Hotel in Washington
on the night of April 16, 1860, swilling barrels of free whiskey and
cheering like wild men for their hero, Stephen Arnold Douglas. Stopping over in the nation's capital for rest and refreshment on their
long journey by rail to the Democratic national convention at
Charleston, they joined the jovial senator from Illinois in a round of
festivities at his campaign headquarters—a rambling old hotel on
Pennsylvania Avenue, at the foot of Capitol Hill.

They vowed, by God, to storm the barricades and stay in Charleston until they had won for their "Little Giant" the grand prize he had
been seeking for a decade, the nomination for the presidency.

"Tonight," the *New York Herald* reported, "there was a jolly time at
the ranche, and speeches were made by senators and representatives.
Whiskey was drunk and stories told but nobody committed unless ver-
dant gentlemen of the press were induced to believe that everybody who
spoke there would shout and vote for Douglas at Charleston. Not a bit
of it. Good whiskey drinkers are not caught that way."

"The Douglas fever is so high that the hectic flush appears and
death is certain," the *Herald*'s man reported. "Much of the Douglas
fever today is the result of poor whiskey."

Douglas's own stentorian voice boomed with confidence as he
inspired his followers with "the wildest enthusiasm and the more reso-
lute determination to nominate him at all hazards," one reporter said.
"The Douglas men," said another, "vow that, unless Douglas is nominated, defeat is certain. ... They will try force, bullying, and perhaps
threaten a bolt unless the South yield to them."

No man of his time could cast such a spell over his followers as Douglas could, and he was at the peak of his powers on this riotous night when it seemed that, with such an army of devoted friends and camp followers to apply outside pressure on the convention, he could not possibly fail. A Republican senator, Jacob Collamer of Vermont, once said that Douglas had won "the sympathy and affection of the great body of the masses" of the long-dominant Democratic Party "and held their hearts in his hand."

Douglas dominated the crowd by the power of his personality, not by his physique. He did not tower above the throng. He stood only five feet, four inches tall. When he was seated, his stubby legs dangled above the floor, and he had tiny feet. But even his enemies were impressed by his enormous head, crowned by a mass of dark brown hair.

Douglas's dark blue eyes were sunk deep in their sockets. His nose was red and bulbous, his cheeks like a side of raw beef, and he had a double chin, from too much good eating and drinking. His barrel chest required a large vest and his waist had lately ballooned to match it.

Douglas looked, talked, drank, and smoked cigars like a typical politician of the Old Northwest—the region embracing Illinois, Michigan, Wisconsin, Minnesota, Iowa, Indiana, and Ohio. These states formed the core of his political strength. He was a rough customer, quite unlike some of his stuffy Senate colleagues who looked down upon him, considering him a coarse, crude demagogue obsessed with getting ahead, politically and financially, by hook or by crook.

This hard-driving, back-slapping politician had a huge appetite for good living and for making money. He speculated heavily in railroads and real estate in his booming region. He could often be found in a barroom, throwing his arms around his drinking buddies and chuckling over schemes for big profits.

"There are at least fifty runners and drummers for the nomination of Sen. Douglas shinning up and down Pennsylvania Avenue," the *Washington Evening Star* reported.

> So loose do his principles set upon him that the plunder-mongers of all parties—for every mother's son of them is a notorious lobbyist—have pitched upon Douglas as the proper candidate to suit their views of governmental things financial. ...

If there remains anybody here wanting the good things which the next administration will give out, we advise them to call on Senator Douglas or his squads at the hotels. From the vice presidency to cabinet places, down to messengerships in the departments, any aspirant may have promised whatever he desires, the only condition is attendance at Charleston and continuous legging for the nomination of Douglas.

It was hard to realize that this breezy Illinois politician was a native of the cold New England hills, where modesty and reticence were considered cardinal virtues. Born in Vermont, he left home as a slim, sickly youth of twenty to seek his fortune farther west. While studying law in Cleveland, Ohio, he came down with inflammatory rheumatic fever that prostrated him for months. With only a few dollars left in his pocket, he migrated farther west to St. Louis and finally settled in Jacksonville, Illinois. Like "a scrappy bantam cock," he flung himself into law practice and politics, becoming a state supreme court justice at twenty-eight, a congressman at thirty, and a United States senator at thirty-three. For the rest of his life, friends called him "Judge."

At thirty-four, Douglas married Martha Martin, twenty-two, the daughter of Col. Robert Martin of Rockingham County, North Carolina. Martha was small, hazel-eyed, in delicate health. A son, Robert, was born in 1849 and a second son, Stephen Arnold, the following year.

Now Douglas seemed to have everything he needed for happiness— a lovely wife, two young sons, prosperous investments, a promising career in the Senate, and prospects of even the presidency. Early in his career, he acquired the presidential "bug" and it never left him until his dying day.

At thirty-nine, the precocious Illinois senator began his first campaign for the Democratic presidential nomination. He plunged into a field crowded with older men who resented his impudence. His opponents professed to be offended by the lobbyists who flocked around him, while his admirers saw him as the champion of "Young America," against the "old fogies" of the past. Senator Andrew Johnson of Tennessee painted this word picture of Douglas and his cronies: "Their arms thrown about his neck along the street—reading pieces to him in the oyster cellar, of a complimentary character, to be sent off to some

*Senator Stephen A. Douglas, who defeated Lincoln in their
Illinois Senate race in 1858 but lost to him in the presidential
contest two years later. From the collections of the Library of
Congress.*

subsidized press for publication, then a drink, a haugh, haugh, then
some claim to be discussed by which they expect to practice some swindle
upon the government." They were better suited, Johnson said, to "occupy places (or cells) in the penitentiary than places of state."

At the Baltimore convention in 1852, Douglas became trapped in
a deadlock with Lewis Cass, James Buchanan, William L. Marcy, and
others. Finally, on the forty-ninth ballot, the exhausted delegates chose
a "dark horse," the amiable Franklin Pierce of New Hampshire. In
the November election, Pierce easily defeated the Whig nominee,
General Winfield Scott.

The following year Douglas's wife and baby daughter died, plunging him into the depths of despair. He rallied from his depression by throwing himself into his grand design for a railroad to run all the way from Chicago to the Pacific coast. Jefferson Davis, the Mississippian who dominated Pierce as his secretary of war, promoted a southern route for the Pacific railway, stressing an army engineers' survey that called this the easiest way to cut through the mountains. Through the Gadsden Treaty with Mexico, the United States acquired a strip of land north of the Gila River, an area needed for that route.

Alarmed by the rapid progress of the southern project, advocates of rival northern and central routes rallied their forces in Congress. Douglas introduced a bill in early 1854 to organize the Nebraska Territory, so that a railroad could be built through that region. Southern senators demanded that the bill repeal the Missouri Compromise, which barred slavery north of the 36° 30' line. They prevailed. President Pierce signed the Kansas-Nebraska Act, and Douglas predicted, correctly, that it would "raise a hell of a storm." It was this storm of protest that created the new Republican Party and brought Lincoln back into the political arena.

Rival gangs of Missouri slaveholders and abolitionist settlers from the North fought a civil war in Kansas. "Bleeding Kansas" made President Pierce so unpopular that the Democrats despaired of reelecting him. So a fierce fight ensued for the nomination in 1856, the chief contenders being Pierce, Douglas, and Buchanan.

Senator John Slidell of Louisiana became the mastermind of the campaign for Buchanan, who had the good fortune of being the minister to Great Britain and thus far away from the turmoil over Kansas. Merchants and bankers in the eastern cities and executives of railroads felt their interests would be safe in the hands of the "Old Public Functionary."

Buchanan also favored territorial expansion. As secretary of state, he had urged President Polk to grab all of Mexico as the fruits of the Mexican war. In London, he joined in the Ostend Manifesto advocating that the United States must acquire Cuba, by purchase or by force.

An energetic recruit for the Buchanan camp was the apostle of "Young America," George Nicholas Sanders, the Kentucky-born promoter who had been a drum-beater for Douglas. As Pierce's consul to

London, Sanders became an intimate friend of Kossuth, Garibaldi, Mazzini, Louis Blanc, and other radicals promoting revolution against the monarchs on the Continent.

However, the Senate disapproved of his activities and some of his newspaper articles criticizing certain senators, and he failed to receive confirmation. Sanders blamed his rejection on Douglas, who actually had tried to help him, and the two friends became estranged.

Upon his return to New York City, Sanders became recognized as a peerless political operator. Robert J. Walker, a former treasury secretary now promoting railroad and real estate speculations, praised him as "the Warwick of America."

When another friend asked what job he would like to have in the future, a cabinet post or a foreign mission, Sanders replied: "Nothing but money. I had an office without political influence and yet the Senate took it from me."

Staking his future on Buchanan, whom he had known in London, Sanders mobilized his forces in New York. "Mr. Sanders feels that it is a crisis in his political career," his wife confided in her journal. "He has taken the management of the Buchanan campaign and will feel it much if it fails."

Senator Slidell of Louisiana, Senator Jesse Bright of Indiana, and the wealthy Washington banker W. W. Corcoran provided money and influence for Buchanan. Before the Democrats opened their nominating convention at Cincinnati on June 2, 1856, they entertained delegates and others at a lavish suite in the principal hotel, the Burnet House. S.L.M. Barlow, a powerful New York lawyer involved in railroad promotions, occupied a temporary home in Cincinnati where Democrats opposed to Pierce and Douglas met and mapped their strategy.

Sanders energetically managed the Buchanan forces on the convention floor. President Pierce started out as the chief challenger to Buchanan but the fight narrowed down to a duel between Buchanan and Douglas. Sanders feared the anti-Buchanan forces could combine and win, and his wife found him "deeply agitated." However, when Buchanan achieved a bare majority—but not the two-thirds required under party rules—Douglas sent a message urging all of his friends to unite and make the old Pennsylvanian's nomination unanimous.

"Today Mr. Sanders triumphed," his wife recorded. "His good judgment in conducting a campaign is vindicated and fully acknowledged. Mr. Buchanan is nominated by acclamation."

As a favor to the "Young America" forces, Buchanan's managers let the vice-presidential nomination go to John C. Breckinridge, a tall and handsome Kentuckian, at thirty-five the youngest man ever nominated for that office.

The Democrats prevailed in a close campaign, chiefly by winning the state elections in October in Pennsylvania, Indiana, and Ohio. In November, Buchanan won 174 electoral votes to 114 for the Republican nominee, General John Charles Fremont, while former President Millard Fillmore, on the American ticket, carried only the 8 votes of Maryland. Buchanan polled about 45 percent of the total popular vote; Fremont, 33 percent, and Fillmore, 22 percent.

Buchanan combined 112 electoral votes from the almost-solid South with those of Pennsylvania, Illinois, Indiana, New Jersey, and California. Fremont swept all of the other Northern states—an ominous sign for the Democrats' future.

Mrs. Sanders proudly wrote in her journal on November 17 that her son, Reid, working with his father in New York, recorded: "His father generaled the first men in the country in his room at the New York Hotel during the canvass. They called him 'Marat,' 'tyrant,' etc., but did as he said. They bent all their energies to gaining the October election in Pennsylvania and succeeded. This ... contributed largely to the glorious election of Mr. Buchanan. ... Thus, what was dimly thought of in 1854 in London becomes a historic reality in 1856."

James Buchanan had occupied the White House less than a year when he and Stephen A. Douglas began a bitter feud that split the Democratic Party and led eventually to the secession of the South and the totally unnecessary Civil War. Besides being Democrats, the two rivals had one thing in common—their birthday, April 23. But they were a generation apart. Buchanan was born in 1791, when George Washington was president. As a young lawyer, he served with volunteer troops that marched from Lancaster, Pennsylvania, to the relief of Baltimore when that Maryland city was besieged by the British in 1814. At that time, Douglas was a year-old baby in Vermont.

At twenty-eight, in 1819, Buchanan was engaged to Ann Coleman, a black-haired, dark-eyed girl who was the belle of Lancaster, the daughter of Robert Coleman, a millionaire ironmaster. But she came to believe the gossip that "Jimmy was just after her money." When he visited another girl in town one day, she sent him an angry note releasing him from their engagement. Ann became depressed and suddenly died.

Thereafter Buchanan endured vicious rumors that she had killed herself and the tragedy was all his fault. Some people even branded him her "murderer." Apparently, he never recovered emotionally from her death.

There is no record showing Buchanan's serious interest in any other woman for the rest of his life. An essentially lonely man, he devoted his life to politics and to the care of his many nieces and nephews who often were guests at his "Wheatland" home near Lancaster. His niece, Harriet Lane, served as his White House hostess.

Through his long career in Washington as a member of Congress and a cabinet minister, the Pennsylvanian cultivated close personal and emotional ties with conservative lawmakers from the South. For several years he shared a suite of rooms in a capital boarding house with Alabama's prissy Senator William Rufus Devane King, a fellow bachelor nicknamed "Miss Nancy." One politician referred to the pair as Buchanan and "his wife." Although his foes might joke that Buchanan had a limp wrist as well as a wry neck, and that he was an "old maid in pantaloons," the evidence on that disputed topic is inconclusive.

At sixty-six in 1857, the President seemed even older. In outward appearance, his tall, stately figure concealed a timid soul within.

He had a mass of white hair that long ago had been blond and he wore a high collar with a flowing white neckerchief, partially to conceal a wry neck. He had bright blue eyes but one eye had a defect and, to make up for the flaw, he would tilt his head forward and sideways. So he always seemed to be listening with rapt attention to the person speaking to him. This habit caused many men to imagine that he agreed with their views, but often they were sadly mistaken.

One fellow Democrat denounced him as "that damned old wry-necked, squint-eyed, white-livered scoundrel who disgraces the White

House with his presence." A New York society woman commented, after meeting him: "That poor, almost imbecilic man! Surely no woman would have been crazy enough, had he been in the profession of medicine, to entrust him with the health of her favorite poodle."

Senator Thomas Lanier Clingman, a North Carolina Democrat, once said: "Mr. Buchanan was, like most timid, insincere men, very malicious and bore an intense hatred to Douglas. ... His powers of deception were very great and his capacity for personal intrigue was extraordinary." Douglas said of Buchanan: "He likes to have people deceived in him. He enjoys treachery, sir, enjoys it as other men enjoy a good cigar. He likes to sniff it up, sir, to relish it."

Douglas, having clinched Buchanan's nomination at the Cincinnati convention, expected some sign of appreciation. But the President froze him out of the patronage for the Old Northwest states and gave it all to Senator Bright. Thus the feud began.

"By God, sir," Douglas is said to have exclaimed, "I made Mr. James Buchanan and, by God, I will unmake him."

Their open rupture came about after Buchanan tried to bring Kansas into the Union as a slave state, as his Southern friends expected as their benefit from Douglas's Kansas-Nebraska Act. Robert J. Walker, who had worked hard with George Nicholas Sanders in winning the election for Buchanan, had hoped to become secretary of state. Instead, Lewis Cass received that coveted job and Sanders was sent out to Walker's house to persuade him to become the governor of the Kansas Territory. At first, Walker was quite indignant, but he calmed down when assured that he would get an important foreign mission, or perhaps even succeed the aged and infirm Secretary Cass, if he succeeded in quieting the disturbances in "bleeding Kansas."

Walker accepted the tough assignment and Buchanan sent him out to Kansas with instructions to obey the people's will. Sanders received from the President a lucrative assignment as the navy agent for New York.

Walker reported back that most Kansas settlers were antislavery and the bitterly cold winters would make it impossible for many Negroes to live there, anyway. So, he advised, Buchanan should let Kansas come in as a free state—Democratic, of course—and concentrate upon annexing Cuba, which could become one or more slave states, also for the Democrats. Walker tried to give the Kansas voters a fair chance to adopt a constitution without slavery, but the free-state settlers boycotted the election and the referendum on slavery. So the proslavery Lecompton constitution was ratified by a vote of only a fraction of the population.

In late 1857, Douglas went to the White House and urged the President not to submit the Lecompton constitution to Congress. "If you do," the senator warned, "I will denounce it the moment your message is read."

Buchanan, who considered Kansas "as much a slave state as Georgia or South Carolina," insisted upon sending up the Lecompton document and making it a test of party loyalty. He would expect every Democratic senator to vote for it. Douglas refused.

"Mr. Douglas," the President said, staring down at the Little Giant, "I desire you to remember that no Democrat ever yet differed from an administration of his own choice without being crushed. Remember the fate of Tallmadge and Rives." (These were two Democratic Senators who crossed President Andrew Jackson and he destroyed their careers.)

"Mr. President," Douglas retorted, "I wish *you* to remember that General Jackson is dead."

In open revolt, Douglas sided with the Republicans in opposing the admission of Kansas as a slave state. The Senate approved Lecompton, 33 to 25, but the House, by 120 to 112, substituted another bill that allowed a second referendum and offered five million acres of government land to the Kansans as a reward for approving the deal. In August 1858, the Kansas voters turned down the offer, which the Republicans called a bribe.

Thus, the furious fight resulted in a defeat for the President and the South, a split in the Democrats' ranks, and a relentless campaign by Buchanan and the Southern senators to read Douglas out of the Democratic Party as a renegade. Douglas found himself hailed as a hero by several leading Republicans, who hoped he would join their party. Horace Greeley, the influential editor of the *New York Tribune*, urged the Illinois Republicans to send Douglas back to the Senate, without an opponent. But they resented his interference and united behind Lincoln.

Douglas's victory over Lincoln in the vote by the Illinois legislature kept the Little Giant in the 1860 presidential race. He soon began a drive to take command of the Democratic Party machinery in the Northern states.

"Douglas will be laid up in lavender unless he shall appeal from the convention to the people," the *New York Herald* said. "He is well aware that his political capital, resulting from his flare-up over the Lecompton constitution, is of fancy stock and if he should wait until 1864, new issues and new men will come to the fore and leave him as thoroughly fossilized as poor Pierce, Fillmore or Captain Tyler," three ex-presidents with little influence left.

So it was "now or never" for Douglas in 1860.

With the help of the tireless intriguer, George Nicholas Sanders, who was once more his bosom friend, Douglas tried to rebuild his support in the South. But only a few allies there could stand up against the militant Ultras, who branded him an unfaithful friend.

Southern nightmares of slave rebellions intensified after John Brown's abortive raid at Harper's Ferry, Virginia, in October 1859. Brown's attack revived old memories of the blacks' insurrections on the island of Santo Domingo, where the white people were virtually exterminated amid frightful atrocities. Thousands of Southerners, who had scoffed at the idea of disunion before, now began to fear that they would not be safe if the Black Republicans should come to power.

The Senate chieftains wanted to keep on running the country as they had been doing since 1853, with the Southern Democrats dominating the Senate and an obedient Northern "doughface" like Pierce or Buchanan residing quietly in the White House and carrying out their orders. Douglas definitely did not fit the description of a "doughface" any more. Lacking a single strong candidate to beat him at Charleston, they encouraged a host of favorite sons, backed by their individual states, in the belief that, after Douglas failed to win the required two-thirds majority, some safe and sound man could be trotted out as a compromise "unity" candidate.

Georgia's organ-voiced Senator Robert Toombs commented: "The old fogies in the Senate are all candidates for the presidency, from highest to lowest, and are as silent, sanctimonious and demure as a whore at a christening." The Democrats jockeying for the presidency reminded him of "the officers of ships being engaged in cheating one another at 'Three Up' in the forecastle while the vessel is labouring among the breakers."

The *New York Herald* recognized that a clique of Democratic senators arrogated the power to choose the party's ticket. "This clique first began its operations in the Pierce administration and really brought about the nominations of Buchanan and Breckinridge at Cincinnati," the paper said. "Its most active and influential men are: Hunter of Virginia, Slidell of Louisiana, Bright of Indiana and Gwin of California. The head of the clique is Mr. Slidell."

While Douglas had the biggest bloc of convention votes pledged to him, he fell short of the two-thirds required to win. Boomlets were going on for Vice President Breckinridge, Senators Joe Lane of Oregon, R.M.T. Hunter of Virginia, and Andrew Johnson of Tennessee, each with a coterie of backers whooping it up at a Washington hotel, while Douglas's followers shouted for him at the National.

The "Douglas fever" displayed by his cheering delegates from the North, and the hundreds of friends and lobbyists imbibing his free whiskey in Washington, awakened the senatorial cabal to the horrifying idea that the Little Giant might have enough strength to seize the prize at Charleston after all.

Having seen the fervor of his fans, they rallied their forces to stop him at all hazards. They rolled out their biggest guns—Senators Slidell, Bright, and James Bayard of Delaware—and sent them, posthaste, to Charleston. There, the senators intended to apply their muscle to wavering delegates with offers of juicy plums of patronage and other rewards.

The Douglas forces, fearing Slidell as a "matchless wire-worker" who would wage "war to the knife," spread a tale on the telegraph lines that the Louisiana Machiavelli was bringing along a satchelful of money—the rumors ranged from a hundred thousand to half a million dollars—to be spent in bribing delegates. Buchanan administration sources denounced the charge as "an infamous lie."

So the battle of Charleston began.

2

Double Dealing
at Charleston

Charleston, with her charm and grace and her lazy, luxurious life as the epitome of Southern aristocracy, slumbered by the sea in the balmy days of late April 1860. Then suddenly a host of politicians burst in: Toughs from Tammany Hall and the Irish wards of Boston and Philadelphia, brawlers from Chicago and the Northwest; hot-tempered fire-eaters from the Deep South, most of them drinking heavily and spoiling for a fight.

These were the legions of the Democratic Party, eager for fun, frolic, and fisticuffs. Some of the gentlemen from New York, Pennsylvania, and Massachusetts arrived by boat; everyone else by the rickety trains with frequent stops for changes along the way. The boys from Gotham brought an amusing entourage of "amiable females," along with card-sharps, gamblers, and Faro bank operators—the most flashily dressed of all.

The hotels in the city of fifty thousand, unaccustomed to accommodating such huge throngs, were jammed to the eaves, and the air everywhere was thick with tobacco smoke and rumors.

Murat Halstead of the *Cincinnati Commercial* observed "great portly fellows with protuberant stomachs and puffy cheeks, thin hair and grizzly, dressed in glossy black and fine linen with the latest style of stovepipe hats and ponderous gold-headed canes."

Here is another newspaperman's description of the scene:

> Imagine a crowded barroom, a hundred people present. Huge bowls of claret punch and brandy punch are loading down the counter. Ten expert blacks assist the white bar princes in turning out cocktails, sherry cobblers, mint juleps. ...
>
> Loud declarations, secret conclaves, soft and hard whisperings, plotting and counter plotting, stratagems, pipelaying give a zest to

a social drink that no other excitement can produce. Yet the bright and fragrant roses you see through yonder window seem to weep and bow their heads sorrowfully in the gentle south wind as each drink is swallowed.

The conversations are heated though the drinks are cooling. Perspiration pours from many a brow.

"Douglas will sweep the entire Northwest," says one. "He will set the prairies a-burning and all Hell can't put the fire out."

"He is a true friend of the South, let the South say what they please."

A Californian says Dickinson of New York is his man; a Pennsylvanian says "Guthrie," another says "Breckinridge."

A fire-eating Louisianan appears. He curses both loud and deep. He comes to Charleston to expose both Slidell and Benjamin, U.S. Senators from that state. He says they are a brace of wicked men.

But behold! A gray-bearded defender of Slidell appears. Says Slidell is a good and true man, true to his friends as steel is to the magnet.

More drinks.

A Northerner's orthodoxy is questioned. He becomes enraged: "It's a damned lie!"

No challenge, no duel.

More drinks.

Two Southern young bloods, with nothing to do but to spend money, get into a quarrel. They are somewhat elevated. An epithet is uttered—a blow to the breast. Hatchets and bowie knives are spoken of. Friends intervene. Reconciliation. They shake hands.

More drinks.

So it goes, for hours. They jabber-jabber, drink and drink.

Of the Charleston hotel owners, the *New York Tribune* said: "With a proper appreciation of the habits of their Democratic patrons, they have discreetly removed all the best furniture temporarily."

Douglas's friends from the Northwest milled about the Mills House while his foes, the Southern fire-eaters, swarmed about the Charleston House. Also, the Douglas forces hired the Hibernian Hall, where the second floor was arranged like an army barracks. Several hundred cots, with white sheets and pillows, stood in rows, numbered and marked by states. Some delegations brought along their own supplies of whiskey, anticipating a long convention amid the summerlike heat of the South Carolina Low Country spring.

Slidell and his fellow senators, who had rushed to Charleston to head off Douglas, set up shop in a mansion on King Street, overlooking an ice cream parlor that was usually full of visitors, even on Sundays. This house became the nerve center of the "Stop Douglas" movement. Here, striving to keep cool on a very warm day, were the men of the Senate cabal: James A. Bayard of Delaware, a full-faced lawyer with long brown curling hair, parted in the middle; William Bigler of Pennsylvania, a ruddy-faced former governor, mopping his brow with a handkerchief; and Jesse D. Bright, boss of the Indiana Democrats, a beefy-faced, coarse-featured man with a yellow vest open to any breeze that might drift in from the Battery.

Indiana Democrats, in state convention, had instructed their delegates to Charleston to vote in a bloc for Douglas, whom Bright despised. Bright defied the Douglas men, saying that "Anti-Lecompton Democrats" were just rotten abolitionists. "I court and defy the opposition of every one of them," he said, "from the lying hypocritical demagogical master Douglas, down to the scurviest puppy in the kennel."

All the men in the parlor of the King Street house centered their attention upon their leader, universally regarded as the power behind the throne in the Buchanan regime: John Slidell. The Louisiana senator personally exerted almost hypnotic power over the effeminate President. As tall as Buchanan but much more forceful, Slidell had a hatchet face with a straight nose, thin lips, and the jaw of a prizefighter. Long strands of snow-white hair fell on either side of his massive forehead and framed his cherry red face. His locks were so thin and silky that the top of his head glowed like the pink shell of a boiled lobster. His eyes, set closely together, wore a cold and stern expression. Slidell correctly called himself "a man of strong will, with some tact and discretion."

Slidell customarily wore an expensively tailored black broadcloth suit, the attire befitting one of the wealthiest stars of the New Orleans bar, the chief of the Democratic Party in Louisiana and Washington. He spoke, not in the dulcet tones of a drawling Southerner, but with an accent marked by the sharp cadence of New York City. For he was born in Manhattan and grew up in a modest house on lower Broadway, where his father maintained a shop beneath the sign: John Slidell/Soap Boiler and Tallow Chandler.

Soon after finishing college, young John also began work as a candlemaker. A romantic youth of violent temper and strong affections, he fell in love with an actress and clashed with her theater manager, who also sought her favors. One morning, on a dueling ground outside Manhattan, the rivals exchanged pistol shots and the theatrical manager fell, seriously wounded.

So, at twenty-six, in 1819, Slidell fled from the police, and his creditors, by skipping out of town. Like many another Northern youth, he sought to make his fortune far away in the booming port city of New Orleans.

Slidell soon became a powerful figure in the Democratic Party by mobilizing the city's gangs into a machine that would not shrink from ballot box stuffing, "repeater" voting, and other tricks to win elections in a state that has long had the reputation of harboring political corruption like a banana republic.

Likewise, by sharpening his wits, Slidell made a steady climb to the top rank of New Orleans lawyers and amassed a fortune. He learned to speak French like the high-and-mighty Creoles who dominated the city's society; and finally, at forty-two, he achieved his ultimate goal: He married Mathilde Deslonde, a lovely Creole only half his age.

In the Senate, Slidell consolidated his power in the Democratic caucus. He served as an older brother to Judah P. Benjamin, his junior colleague, who had also come to New Orleans as a friendless youth and rapidly advanced to high rank in the city's bar.

Slidell used his influence to guide Buchanan into the presidency. He expressed confidence that his protégé could "build up and consolidate a sound, homogeneous National Democracy, that can defy the fanatics North and South."

Slidell was no "fire-eater." He would prefer to continue the Union under the control of the Democratic Party, which, in turn, would be directed by the Southern senators seeking to dictate the nominee at Charleston. Following their strategy of holding their votes on favorite sons and then trading for an acceptable nominee—almost anybody except Douglas—the Southerners began their chats with wavering delegates.

Slidell himself was Louisiana's candidate, but early in the game he released a letter to his state's delegation, withdrawing his name and saying he would support any of four prospective standard bearers. Two were New Yorkers, former Governor Horatio Seymour and former Senator Daniel S. Dickinson; the others were Vice President Breckinridge and Senator Joe Lane of Oregon. Lane, a North Carolina native and longtime Indiana resident and hero of the Mexican war, strongly sympathized with the South's demand for federal protection of slavery in the territories.

Senator Jefferson Davis likewise withdrew as Mississippi's favorite son and offered to back the men on Slidell's list as well as James Guthrie of Kentucky, a railroad executive who had been his companion in the Pierce cabinet as secretary of the treasury.

Senator Wigfall wrote a similar letter to his Texas delegation, opposing Douglas and calling him "the candidate of the pothouse politicians."

Because neither Douglas nor his enemies could muster the two-thirds majority required under the party's rules, New York's big delegation played a pivotal role in the Charleston convention. Its thirty-five votes could prove decisive. New York sent two rival delegations, each claiming to be the regular "simon pure" faction, chosen at a riotous state convention in Syracuse the previous September.

Their rivalry began in 1848, when a Free Soil, antislavery faction backed former President Martin Van Buren for the White House on a third-party ticket. He carried enough votes to take New York away from the Democrats and thus defeat their nominee, Lewis Cass, and elect his Whig opponent, General Zachary Taylor, a hero of the Mexican war.

Men in the Free Soil faction of New York Democrats were nicknamed "Barnburners," and compared to the farmer who burned down his barn to get rid of the rats. The conservatives were called "Hunkers," apparently a Dutch term meaning "conservative." Many "Barnburn-ers" later became Republicans. The "Hunkers" divided into two camps, the "Hard Shells" who opposed allowing the rebels to come back into the Democratic Party, and the "Soft Shells," willing to welcome the prodigals. The nicknames were shortened to "Hards" and "Softs," and New York's seats in the 1856 convention were equally divided between them.

Undisputed boss of the Softs, and head of their delegation to Charleston, was Dean Richmond, a tough, portly, broad-shouldered Buffalo businessman. He had come up from poverty, built a prosperous shipping business on the Great Lakes, and then become a successful railroad executive. Although he never could write or speak with perfect grammar, the often profane, intimidating chieftain achieved great power in both business and politics.

Richmond consolidated seven upstate railroads into the New York Central system, lobbying the legislature—by fair means and foul—into making it all legal. In 1858 he became the vice-president of the corporation and a few years later, president. At forty-seven, this shrewd, adroit, and dictatorial entrepreneur stood at the peak of his powers. He combined the old Albany Regency clique upstate with the Tammany Hall politicians in New York City, his lieutenants including Peter Cagger, Albany lawyer and secretary of the state committee, and William Cassidy, editor of the party's newspaper, the *Albany Atlas and Argus.*

Richmond's great authority as vice-president of the New York Central Railroad was acknowledged by the *New York Herald*, which compared him to the French emperor Napoleon III, saying: "Dean Richmond is as potent at Albany as Louis Napoleon among his French legislators."

Against Dean Richmond's Softs were arrayed the mayor of New York City, Fernando Wood, and his Mozart Hall boys, Tammany's rivals, and his mouthpiece, the *New York Daily News.* Tall and handsome, with keen blue eyes and a thick shock of light brown hair, Wood had a fascinating personality that enabled him to rise swiftly in politics. He became a congressman at twenty-eight and his later maneuvers made him an influential figure in Manhattan. However, De Alva Alexander, in his definitive study of New York's labyrinthine political maze, said this of Wood: "As a politician he was as false as his capacity would allow him to be, having no hesitation, either from principle or fear, to do anything to serve his purpose."

His purpose, in April 1860, was to have his delegates seated at Charleston, or, at least, to win half of the seats. Mild and bland in manner, the mayor told the credentials committee that his followers had won their right to the seats at the Syracuse convention, which turned into a riot. If a thirty-two-pounder had been fired in that hall full of brawlers, he said, the gun could not have been heard above the tumult.

Wood arrived early at the Syracuse hall, bringing along a gang of roughs, headed by John C. Heenan, "the Benicia Boy," the champion American prizefighter. They organized the convention, selecting their own chairman and committees. When the Soft delegates came in later, Peter Cagger mounted the platform and declared John Stryker temporary chairman. In the ensuing melee, Stryker was pushed off the platform and "an intimidating array of pistols" appeared.

The Soft delegates marched out to various saloons and Wood's Mozart boys completed their organization and adjourned. Then the boys of Tammany and the Albany Regency returned from their refreshment hour and welcomed a speech by the last of the Hard leaders, Daniel Dickinson.

Dickinson—often called "Scripture Dick" for his many Bible quotations—wore his white hair in long, flowing locks and wrote poetry. He believed that his long advocacy of the South's side in the battles over slavery would endear him to the anti-Douglas forces and, perhaps, even propel him into the presidency. In pursuit of his dream, he listened to the siren song of Dean Richmond and his allies. They promised him that, although they would first vote for Douglas, they would switch the delegation over to Dickinson if, at any time, it would assure the nomination to the white-haired gentleman from Binghamton.

Richmond was quoted as having told "a former U.S. Senator" (Dickinson, of course) that "I would in no case go for Douglas"; but the truth was that he had secretly promised to back Douglas and, in case of a deadlock, to bring out a New York compromise candidate— not Dickinson but Seymour.

One day in Wall Street, Richmond crowed: "We've got that damned fool of Binghamton all right."

To make sure that his delegates won all the New York seats at Charleston, Dean Richmond played a double game. He agreed to vote with the Douglas forces on such major issues as the platform. At the same time, he made a solemn promise to Senator Slidell and the Southerners that he would go along with them in nominating an acceptable presidential candidate who would unite the party.

By his double dealing, he persuaded the Southerners to go along with seating all of his delegates instead of letting half of them go to the forces of Mayor Wood, who promised to vote with the South.

"We have got to start, first, to toss that damned smart fellow, Wood, overboard," the portly railroad mogul was quoted as saying in the midst of the credentials fight. "Haw, haw, haw! When we get rid of him, there will be time enough to talk."

Some credentials committee members proposed dividing the New York seats evenly between the Hards and the Softs. But, in the end, Dean Richmond got them all. The Southerners, who went along with the decision, found out too late that they had been tricked. Douglas would hold New York.

In the convention, the states each had their electoral votes, totaling 303, so a winning two-thirds would be 202. Douglas had a bloc of about a hundred sure to stick with him to the bitter end. Having lost practically all of his Southern friends, he had to pick up many votes from the Northeast. Without New York, he had no chance.

New York's seventy delegates, each with half a vote, were divided, forty for Douglas, thirty against him: a Douglas edge of twenty to fifteen. Under the unit rule enforced by Boss Richmond, all thirty-five New York votes would be cast for Douglas. As one reporter expressed it, "Richmond had the delegation in his pocket."

The Pennsylvania delegation had an anti-Douglas majority including several postmasters and others in federal jobs. They proposed to slap on the same kind of unit rule but the pro-Douglas men, in the minority, rebelled and threatened to walk out, so the proposal was dropped.

Chief of the Little Giant's convention forces was William Richardson, a former Illinois congressman, a large, coarse, powerful man with broad shoulders, "shaggy head and broad-axe nose," whose harsh voice could be heard "like a fire bell over the clatter of engines in the street." Close to Richardson were several other Illinois men: Congressman "Black Jack" Logan, with his dark, narrow face, black hair and eyes, "his hands in his pockets and his mouth full of tobacco"; Congressman John McClernand, with a peaked face and a hooked nose; and Usher F. Linder, an Old Line Whig, now a Douglas Democrat.

Linder acquired the nickname of "For God's Sake Linder" because Douglas once sent him, at the height of a close election race, a telegram saying: "The hell hounds are on my track. For God's sake, Linder, come and help me fight them."

In the Ohio delegation, solidly for Douglas under the unit rule, were Henry B. Payne, a lawyer and railroad builder; Daniel P. Rhodes, a coal and iron capitalist; and George Pugh, Douglas's lone defender in the Senate.

Also working for Douglas, and speaking up for him in the hotels and barrooms of Charleston, were numerous friends eager to share in the spoils of the next Democratic administration in Washington. These lobbyists, one newspaper reported, "believe that, if he is made President, his motto will be that of Tittlebat Titmouse [something for everybody] an open Treasury for all comers. All sorts of fat jobs and contracts, a snug office for every occupant, open house and free rations at the White House all the year 'round—a four-year carnival in Washington and all over the land, and oceans of money and lawless speculations that will each be a fortune to all concerned; in fact, a perfect millennium to the lobby, which will throw into the shade all the railroad land grants of poor Pierce.

"Shall all this be spoiled at Charleston? Saints and angels forbid!"

A hostile South Carolinian, writing from Charleston, sniffed that the Douglas men "came here like a gang of wolves, or a flock of vultures, bent on spoil, without compromise or alternative; their howlings are for blood."

Determined to stop Douglas, Slidell and his Senate cabal pinned their hopes on the key committees: credentials, permanent organization, and resolutions. Each had one member per state, or thirty-three. The fifteen slave states, plus California and Oregon, made a thin majority, seventeen to sixteen. Besides seating Dean Richmond's New York delegation, the credentials committee admitted the regular Douglas delegation from Illinois, barring an irregular faction of Buchanan officeholders.

On Monday, April 23, when the delegates entered the hall of the South Carolina Institute on Meeting Street for their opening session, everyone knew that the delegates from several Southern states had agreed in caucus that, unless the platform protected slavery in the territories, they would walk out. Since Douglas had vowed that he would not accept the nomination of any such "slave code" platform, its sponsors hoped he would have to refuse it.

The Southern hotheads were not the only ones threatening a walkout if they failed to get their way. Douglas himself was figuring that two could play the game of bluff and bolt. The *New York Herald* thus revealed his plans for his followers to march out of the hall if defeated: "Now, then, you may depend upon it," the article said in part, that if the platform has a "slave code" in it, the Douglas delegates will walk out; he will run as an independent for the presidency and be "taken up by the Whig Americans" when they meet at Baltimore May 9. This was the outline of Douglas' dream of a conservative Union party.

The anti-Douglas forces at Charleston scored a point with the selection of the convention's permanent chairman, Caleb Cushing of Massachusetts. This former Whig, a respected lawyer and one time U.S. attorney general, could be relied upon by the Buchanan-Senate cabal to rule as ordered on major points of dispute.

On the next round, the Douglas forces prevailed with the adoption of a new rule. It provided that individual delegates could vote as they pleased for presidential candidates unless their state convention had specifically imposed the unit rule. The Douglas men had clamped the unit rule tightly on all the delegations in which they had a majority; but, in states where they were outnumbered, they insisted upon their right to vote as individuals. So Douglas had it both ways, by this "Douglas dodge," which was worth about thirty or forty extra votes.

Everyone sweltered in the extremely hot weather; it was like New York City in August. The bake-oven heat, "plus over-indulgence in fruits and vegetables, causes dysentery and diarrhea affecting quite a number of Northerners," the *Washington Evening Star* reported.

By Friday, the weather had turned cold and rainy, causing everyone to shiver in a chilling wind. On that day, the worn and haggard resolutions committee members trooped at last into Institute Hall. By a 17 to 16 margin, they reported a platform which said that Congress had no power to abolish slavery in the territories, nor would a territorial legislature, and "that it is the duty of the federal government to protect, when necessary, the rights of person and property on the high seas, in the territories, or wherever else its constitutional authority extends."

In clear contrast, the pro-Douglas minority report said that "all questions in regard to the rights of property in states or territories arising under the Constitution of the United States are judicial in character" and the Democratic Party would "faithfully carry out" the Supreme Court's decisions on these questions, past and future.

Douglas's friend, Henry B. Payne of Ohio, pleaded for adoption of the minority report as the only platform on which the Democrats would have a chance of carrying any free states. Why, he asked, should the South throw away party victory for a mere abstraction?

Ah, but the South's demand for protection of slavery in the territories was not a mere abstraction. W. W. Avery of North Carolina made that clear in presenting the majority report. Although few slaves might be taken into such places as Nebraska or the Far West, the Democratic Party, North and South, had long been pledged to acquire new lands in the warmer climes to the south. Unanimously, the resolutions committee advised enlarging the nation's limits. Avery said Cuba, Mexico, and Central America inevitably would be brought into the American empire; and if the "popular sovereignty" doctrine prevailed, no slaveholder would dare to bring his property into the new lands. Douglas himself favored acquiring Cuba.

Without expressly saying so, Avery revealed the Southerners' grand dream of creating several more slave states around the "golden circle" of the Gulf of Mexico and the Caribbean. With two senators apiece, the new states could maintain the South's control of the United States Senate, which otherwise would surely slip away as more free states entered the Union. That was the real crux of the battle over the territories—not the arid and rocky spaces of the West but the tropical climes of the new states where cotton and sugar could be cultivated by slave labor most profitably.

Avery stressed that the majority report represented 127 electoral votes considered sure to be cast for the Democratic presidential candidate, while the minority report was drafted by men whose states were largely Republican. But Payne insisted that the party must stick with Douglas's "popular sovereignty" doctrine. "We never will recede from that doctrine, sir," Payne shouted, "never, never, never, so help us God!"

Late Friday, the premier orator of the Cotton Kingdom, William Lowndes Yancey, took the stage amid a storm of applause, cheers, "hi-hi's and cock crows."

"Yancey burst into tears," one observer noted, so strong were his emotions. He appealed to the Northerners to understand why the Southerners must have a platform that recognized their rights. "Ours," he said, "is the property invaded; ours are the institutions which are at stake; ours is the peace that is to be destroyed; ours is the honor at stake—the honor of children, the honor of families, the lives, perhaps, of all—all of which your course may ultimately make a great heaving volcano of passion and crime."

By "the great heaving volcano of passion and crime," Yancey referred to the Southerners' nightmare that the abolition of slavery would mean turning loose four million blacks to roam about in idleness and crime, and to threaten white people's lives. The prospect of a social revolution, even a race war, was no idle fancy; it filled the Southerners' minds with horror.

Before Yancey closed his long oration, darkness had fallen and the gas lamps in the hall had been lit. It was in this brilliant atmosphere that Douglas's devoted Senate champion, George Pugh, arose and made a scathing reply.

The Ohio senator blamed the South for the downfall of the once-dominant Democracy in the Northern states. One by one, Democrats had lost Senate and House seats and governorships while fighting bravely in defense of Southern rights, he said, and what was their reward? Now, taunted with being in the minority, the Northerners were "thrust back and told in effect they must put their hands on their mouths and their mouths in the dust."

"Gentlemen of the South," Pugh exclaimed, "you mistake us—you mistake us—we will not do it!"

The telegraph wires between Charleston and Washington crackled with urgent messages. Southern senators told their delegations to insist upon the majority platform or walk out. George Nicholas Sanders, the irrepressible manipulator, sent President Buchanan a long telegram begging him to give up and accept the nomination of Douglas, just as Douglas had graciously clinched "Old Buck's" victory at the Cincinnati convention. Sanders had labored successfully for Buchanan in 1856; now, although still his navy agent in New York, he had switched his allegiance to Douglas.

The *New York Times* said Sanders drove the President "nearly frantic" by advising him, in these words: "Send for Douglas immediately. Lose no time in making friends with your successor. All the past shall be forgiven, and your particular friends shall be retained in office. From one who differs from you in opinion but never deceives you, George Sanders."

Sanders' telegram was not only "inconceivably impudent"; it was expensive and he sent it collect. Buchanan had to pay $26.80 for it. He was not amused.

New York's delegation came under furious attack by Senator Slidell for lining up with the Douglas forces in the platform dispute despite Chairman Dean Richmond's solemn pledge to cooperate with the Southerners and the Senate cabal. Slidell and Senator Bright, through S.L.M. Barlow, tried to induce a majority of the New Yorkers to sign a paper releasing themselves from the unit rule, but the effort failed.

Richmond decided to cast the entire bloc of thirty-five New York votes in favor of Douglas on every issue, including the platform. Slidell, roaring that he had been betrayed, personally confronted the burly railroad mogul and cursed him out as a double-crosser. The *Washington Evening Star*, in a Friday dispatch from Charleston, observed: "Mr. Slidell, who is an imperious man, ... cursed Dean Richmond 'up hill and down dale' today as an unmitigated scoundrel, better fitted to grace a penitentiary cell than a position in control of the New York delegation.

"Slidell is furious because Richmond kept New York with Douglas after his New York delegation was seated on a pledge to vote with the South."

The crowds milling about in the lobby of the Mills House were also treated to an exciting spat between Dean Richmond and Congressman John Cochrane, "the brains of the Cagger-Cassidy delegation" from New York. Cochrane, a tall, nearly bald man with a sandy beard and a sonorous voice, was a bachelor and a high-living man about town. He was frustrated because Richmond, as Slidell charged, was refusing to promote harmony with the South.

"Cochrane denounced Richmond as a faithless man, without personal character or principle," one newsman reported. "Richmond retorted with curses against the South and the national administration. Richmond, losing his temper, broke out in a furious tirade, cursing the South and damning the President."

Richmond favored "a platform to suit the North so as to make a great Northern Democratic party and gain a majority of the representatives in Congress and let the South go to the devil."

"What the hell do we care about the South?" Richmond shouted. "What we want, by God, is a Democratic party at the North. Damn the South! ...

"Our people won't stand this God-damned agitation. They want somebody they can elect. They can elect Seymour and, notwithstanding his squatter sovereignty, they can elect Douglas. ... The people in the rural districts are all for him because they hate the administration and they admire pluck."

Despite Dean Richmond's diatribe against the South, Douglas's managers kept trying to woo some Dixie delegates by hinting that the Little Giant would choose a running mate from their region. His personal favorite was Alexander H. Stephens, but the wizened little Georgian declined. No one could count how many Southern politicians were told that, if they would just deliver some votes for Douglas, they might be his choice for the vice-presidency. Even South Carolina's Senator James Hammond, a wealthy slaveholder, listened to a siren song by the persuasive George Nicholas Sanders, who insinuated that "lightning might strike" Hammond if he would help Douglas to break the nearly solid Southern bloc against him.

"The vice-presidency has been held out as bait to North and South Carolina, Tennessee, Virginia, and Georgia," the *New York Tribune* said.

The Douglas men became alarmed at signs of "shakiness" in some of their delegations, Murat Halstead told his Cincinnati readers. "Slidell & Co. were willing to buy all such fellows on the platform question."

To counteract the tempting lures of jobs and money dangled by Slidell, the Douglas managers offered promises of their own to delegates who might wish to become cabinet officers, judges, postmasters, marshals, or diplomats. The weekend passed with furious trading by both sides.

Douglas lost a large part of his cheering squad in the galleries, as many of his friends, who had spent the week in Charleston, had nearly run out of money—and in some cases, whiskey—and they had to bid farewell to the lovely little city by the sea. On Monday, another sunny day, a crowd of South Carolinians rushed into the convention hall and took over the seats vacated by the Yankee spectators. Now the convention "wears a Southern aspect," wrote reporter Halstead, who added this note of comic relief about the vile habits of tobacco-chewing guests: Just before the decisive votes on the platform, "an old gentleman declared on the floor that the gentlemen in the galleries were respectfully requested not to use the heads of the gentlemen below them for spittoons."

In the first test of the platform, a version simply reiterating the language of the 1856 Cincinnati document, lost 198 to 105. In the most crucial decision, the slave code demanded by the majority of the resolutions committee went down to defeat by 165 to 138. New York's bloc of thirty-five votes clinched the victory for the Douglas forces.

In a series of roll calls, the various planks were hammered into the platform and thus the decision became irrevocable: defeat for the Southerners and for the senators seeking a compromise. Yancey, the king of the Alabama fire-eaters, was observed at this time "smiling as a bridegroom."

Then former Senator Charles Stuart of Michigan, a Douglas loyalist, whose "round, bald head glowed like the full moon," irritated the Gulf State delegates with a fiery speech accusing them of demanding too much in the platform. Some delegates suggested that he was really baiting the Southerners on purpose, to drive out a few of them so that Douglas's bare majority could reach the magic figure of two-thirds of the votes that would remain after the walkout.

If that was his game, Stuart miscalculated. Instead of igniting a little explosion to chase out a small part of the Gulf squadron, he touched off a dynamite blast in which "the very citadel and heart of the Democracy was blown away."

Throughout Stuart's speech, a tall Southern gentleman with a high forehead and a long, pale face, stood on a chair, asking recognition. It was Leroy P. Walker, the Alabama chairman. He announced that his state convention had instructed the Alabama delegates to walk out if they did not get a platform plank protecting slave property in the territories. So the Alabama men were bound to bolt—and they did. A year later, Walker would become the Confederacy's first secretary of war.

The Mississippians were the next to go out—after delegate D. C. Glenn, "his face pale as ashes," proclaimed that, within sixty days, there would be a united South. Louisiana, South Carolina, Florida, Texas, and Arkansas followed. The next day, twenty-six of the thirty-four Georgians left, too.

That night, an enormous crowd assembled before the courthouse, cheered Yancey and Mississippi's L.Q.C. Lamar, and hailed the idea of a great, free Southern republic. "Perhaps even now," cried Yancey, "the pen of the historian is nibbed to write the story of a new revolution!"

The bolters met in St. Andrew's Hall, with Senator Bayard as their chairman. Bayard charged that Dean Richmond's New Yorkers "came here professing a desire to join in such a nomination as would suit the South, but just as soon as they were given the seats, they turned their backs upon the South."

The next day, the Douglas men, who had first welcomed the Dixie bolt, suffered a shock. The delegations of Virginia, North Carolina, Tennessee, and Kentucky had reached an agreement with the New Yorkers to have Chairman Cushing decree that, to win the presidential nomination, a candidate must receive, not merely two-thirds of the remaining votes, but two-thirds of the original 303 votes. The Border State men promised that, if this were done, they would stay in the convention and fight the seceders to the bitter end. The New Yorkers, in a stormy caucus, hesitated to take the deal. But Sanford Church shouted, "In God's name, let us sacrifice all we can for peace and harmony," and the majority agreed.

On Tuesday morning, Howard of Tennessee moved that Chairman Cushing make the ruling that the winning nominee must receive "a number of votes equal to two-thirds of the votes of all the electoral college." Richardson, Douglas's hard-charging floor manager, was furious. He moved to table the motion. But he lost, 141 to 111½, with the New Yorkers voting, for the first time, against Douglas's interests. The final vote sustaining the rule, said one observer, had the sound of "clods falling on Douglas' coffin."

The Douglas managers' calculations, said the *Washington Evening Star*, have been "knocked into the middle of next week. After their boasts and bluster, they are now as mute as mice."

At last, the delegates turned to the business of trying to choose a presidential nominee. Within a few minutes the names of six men were presented: Douglas, Dickinson, Guthrie, Hunter, Lane, and Andrew Johnson. The first ballot gave Douglas 145½, with Hunter and Guthrie trailing. After a dozen ballots, Douglas stood at 150½. On the twenty-third ballot, Douglas reached his peak: 152½. This amounted to a bare majority of the 303 electoral votes, nowhere near the 202 required.

On the thirty-sixth ballot, Tennessee withdrew Senator Johnson's name and the Buchanan administration's forces pooled their strength on Guthrie, lifting him to 64½. Why Guthrie, who was not a popular hero among the masses? He had a great reputation as an executive, being president of the Louisville & Nashville Railroad. He was the favorite of the railroad and iron interests in Pennsylvania and New Jersey. "Guthrie would be a very strong candidate in Pennsylvania and would be formidable in the West," the *New York Times* said.

"Caleb Cushing and Jefferson Davis, who served in Pierce's cabinet as colleagues of Guthrie, have also struck hands for him," the *New York Herald* said. "Gen. Butler of Massachusetts, who has been counted for Douglas, would prefer Seymour of New York but would take Guthrie."

To the practical politicians, it was a matter of simple arithmetic: If Guthrie could combine Pennsylvania and New Jersey with the 120 electoral votes of the South, the Democrats could elect him against any Republican, just as they had put over Buchanan in 1856. Douglas, they figured, could not possibly be elected because he had lost his popularity in the South. Some observers said Douglas could not even be sure of a single electoral vote. (This prediction came close: He won twelve.)

After fifty-seven ballots continued the deadlock, the New York delegates made a fateful move. Peter Cagger, their secretary, speaking for Dean Richmond, gave the bad news to Douglas's floor manager, Richardson. If Douglas could not clinch the nomination by the sixtieth ballot, the New Yorkers would consider that their bargain with him was at an end, and they would feel free to swing their big bloc of votes to someone else.

"The Douglas men were caught in a trap," said the *Washington Evening Star.* "New York, which they had bought and paid for, now has sold them and only awaits the right moment to join the Guthrie forces."

Quickly, the word raced around the convention hall that New York would switch to Guthrie and boost him to about a hundred votes on the next ballot, while slashing Douglas to about 115, making the Little Giant "a dead cock in the pit." If Guthrie could not succeed, rumors held, the next likely favorite would be Joe Lane, the Oregon senator and Mexican war veteran. Dean Richmond also harbored a hope that, in the end, the nominee would be his personal favorite, former Governor Seymour. In any case, Douglas would be politically dead.

Realizing their peril, the Douglas forces quickly staged a coup d'état. They adjourned the convention, to meet again at Baltimore on June 18. They figured that, in the intervening weeks, they could drum up competing pro-Douglas delegations from Alabama, Georgia, Louisiana, and perhaps other Southern states. In that way, they might manufacture a two-thirds majority and block such compromise candidates as Seymour, Dickinson, Guthrie, and Lane.

In the *New York Herald's* view, "the Douglas leaders feared that, after the loss of New York, the Northwest would drop off by degrees in favor of Lane, and they agreed to adjournment to save themselves from utter rout." "The Republicans are jubilant," the *Herald* reported, quoting their leaders as saying: "We owe everything to Douglas. He founded the Republican party with his Kansas-Nebraska bill. He will now consolidate the Republican party."

"A new deal will be dealt," continued the *Herald*, "yet who will turn up jack?"

Douglas, who had remained in Washington and followed the Charleston sessions by telegraph, relying on his loyal lieutenants to take care of his interests, felt deep disappointment over their failure. Nervous and close to despair, he sought solace in his old friend, the bottle.

On May 4, the day after the Democrats adjourned, California's young Senator Milton Latham saw him under the influence of liquor.

Douglas's dark eyes flashed fire when he denounced his enemies as "bloodhounds after his life."

Latham told him "there was too much fire in his eye for a great man and he showed too much passion—so keep cool and it would come out all right."

Resuming his Senate seat a few days later, the Little Giant looked pale, as if rallying from a hangover, clasping and unclasping his hands and drumming his fingers nervously on the arms of his chair. His lips were drawn tightly as if he could "bite a pin in two."

On May 9, at Baltimore, the survivors of the ship-wrecked Whig Party convened under the new name of "Constitutional Union." They selected former United States Senator John Bell of Tennessee for president and the Massachusetts orator Edward Everett for vice-president. Instead of wrangling over a platform, the old Whigs simply said they supported "the Constitution, the Union, and the enforcement of the laws."

The Southern delegates were elated over their prospects of carrying Kentucky, Tennessee, Virginia, and Maryland, where the Republicans were weak and the Democrats in disarray. There were confident predictions that no candidate would achieve a majority of the 303 electoral votes in November, so the final decision would be made by the House.

Delegate G. A. Henry of Tennessee evoked roars of laughter by describing the last stragglers he had seen returning from the Democrats' "busted up" convention at Charleston. "I never saw a more broken down and desponding set," he said. "They were tired, sleepy and disheartened—and unwashed."

One doleful Democrat said, "I have not slept a wink for four nights."

"Perhaps a little good brandy would cheer you up," Henry suggested.

"No," said he, "even burnt brandy wouldn't save me now."

* 4 *

"Lincoln Ain't Here"

While the Democrats were bitterly split and the remnant of the Whigs aimed at carrying the border states, the Republicans converged on Chicago for their national convention, opening May 16, full of hope for victory. Thousands, by special trains and excursion steamers, jammed the booming young metropolis on Lake Michigan, where an ever-expanding network of railroads made Chicago the throbbing heart of the commercial West. From the lakefront docks and the railway stations, the visitors swarmed through the plank-paved streets, competing with horse-drawn wagons and carriages; the crowd filled all of the city's forty-two hotels.

Hordes of Illinois "Suckers" were there, chanting and cheering for Lincoln as the spokesman for the plain people of the West against the party bosses of the East, who sent out trainloads of boosters for the front-running candidate, Senator Seward.

One special train carried thirteen cars loaded with New York "irrepressibles," all shouting for Seward. Murat Halstead, the eagle-eyed writer for the *Cincinnati Commercial*, arrived on the same train and reported that these strange eastern Republicans acted like Democrats by guzzling more whiskey than had been consumed on any train that had entered Charleston during convention time.

The New Yorkers would slap each other on the back and call out, "How are you?" or "How are you, hoss?" in a style, said Halstead, "that would do honor to Old Kaintuck on a bust." At night, they liked to be out "raising hell, generally."

One morning, at his hotel, the reporter was awakened by a vehement debate among his roommates, who were playing cards to see who should pay for gin cocktails all around.

Some other delegates were aroused from bed with even less decorum. They were caught in Mayor "Long John" Wentworth's weekly raid on Chicago's many bawdy houses.

At the Richmond House, the air was blue with cigar smoke and echoing with the laughter of politicians drinking free champagne as guests in the palatial headquarters suite of Senator Seward, who expected to be nominated for the presidency on the first or second ballot. Seward himself stayed demurely at his home in Auburn, just as Lincoln remained at Springfield, observing the quaint custom that required candidates to pretend that they weren't really seeking office, just responding to the call of the people.

Seward's alter ego, Thurlow Weed, the snowy-haired New York State Republican boss, greeted delegates personally with a warm handshake at the door.

However, Seward had won the reputation of being a "radical," and that frightened some conservatives whose votes the Republicans had to win, especially in the four "battleground" states—Pennsylvania, New Jersey, Illinois, and Indiana. Buchanan had carried all four states, along with the South, in beating the Republicans' first presidential nominee, John C. Fremont, in 1856; then the anti-Buchanan vote had been split between Fremont and the Whig, former President Millard Fillmore.

Indiana and Pennsylvania had special significance as "October" states, which elected state officials in October. Whichever party could win in October could use this psychological boost toward victory in the presidential balloting in November.

Henry Lane, the Republican candidate for governor of Indiana, said he would be dragged down to defeat if he had to carry the dead weight of a radical candidate for president. Andrew Curtin, running for governor of Pennsylvania, despondently said he might as well withdraw if Seward led the ticket.

Illinois delegates "agonized" over the mention of Seward's name, predicting that he could cause them to lose control of their legislature to the Democrats.

Horace Greeley, the eccentric editor of the *New York Tribune*, long a partner in the political firm of Seward, Weed, and Greeley, had broken with his former allies and was relentlessly sabotaging Seward at Chicago. Having wangled a seat as a proxy from Oregon,

*David Davis, Illinois lawyer who masterminded Lincoln's
campaign for the Republican presidential nomination.
Lincoln rewarded him with a seat on the U.S. Supreme
Court. Photo courtesy of the Chicago Historical Society.*

the editor roamed around the hotels, warning delegates that Seward
would lead the party down to certain defeat.

Greeley was promoting Bates as a conservative who could pull
the old Whigs over into an alliance with the more liberal Republicans; but the Missouri lawyer had never been a Republican and had little
appeal for younger antislavery voters, or to the German Americans.

Pennsylvania held its fifty-four delegates for its own Senator Simon
Cameron, while Ohio's forty-six were pledged to Governor Salmon P.
Chase, both converts from the Democrats. New Jersey backed its former
senator, William L. Dayton, Fremont's running mate.

Lincoln's friends among the Illinois Republican politicians began
working hard to parlay their little bloc of 22 votes into a majority of
the 465 votes in the convention. On Sunday, May 13, Judge David
Davis shoe-horned his three hundred pounds into a chair behind a
large table in Illinois' Tremont House headquarters and discussed
strategy with others of the Lincoln clique.

Around the table he could see the familiar faces of trusted lieutenants, dedicated to Lincoln: Leonard Swett of Bloomington; Richard Yates of Jacksonville, who had just won the nomination for governor by beating Swett and Judd at the state convention; Stephen T. Logan, Lincoln's one-time law partner; Jesse K. Dubois, the state auditor; Ozias M. Hatch, the secretary of state; William Butler, the state treasurer; State Senator John M. Palmer; Orville H. Browning, a future U.S. senator; Jackson Grimshaw of the state central committee; former lieutenant governor Gustave Koerner, a leader of the German vote; and Joseph Medill and Charles Ray, editors of the *Chicago Press and Tribune.*

Judge Davis paid for the Tremont House headquarters suite out of his own pocket. Judd arranged for the railroads to give special cheap excursion rates from communities all over Illinois so that plenty of Lincoln boosters would flock to Chicago and pack the "Wigwam," the huge wooden convention hall. Lincoln himself remained in Springfield, anxiously awaiting his friends' bulletins from the battle front. On Sunday night, Jesse K. Dubois sent him the first message:

> Dear Lincoln
> We are here in great confusion things this evening look as favorable as we had any right to expect. Indiana is very willing to go for you, although a portion are for Bates. ... Eight of the Ohio men are urging you on with great vigor. ... Pennsylvania says Cameron or nobody, but that starch must be taken out of them. Horace Greeley is working for Bates. Judge Davis is furious; Never saw him work so hard and so quiet in all my life.

The next day, delegate N. M. Knapp of the Springfield district reported to Lincoln:

> Dear Sir:
> Things are working; keep a good nerve—be not surprised at any result—but I tell you that your chances are not the worst. We have got Seward in the attitude of the representative Republican of the East—*you* of the West. We are laboring to make you the second choice of all the Delegations we can where we cannot make you the first choice. We are dealing tenderly with delegates, taking them in detail, and making no fuss. Be not too expectant but rely upon our

discretion. Again I say brace your nerves for any result.
truly your friend

N. M. KNAPP

Davis and Dubois telegraphed Lincoln on Tuesday, May 15: "We are moving heaven & earth nothing will beat us but old fogy politicians the heart of the delegates are for us."

The next day Dubois telegraphed: "Prospects fair friends at work night & day tell my wife I am well."

On Wednesday morning, May 16, ten thousand people crammed into the Wigwam, the huge wooden barn at the corner of Lake and Market Streets, especially built as the convention hall. Twenty thousand more swarmed in the streets outside, providing the largest force of "outside pressure" ever seen in a political convention. The enthusiasm of the Republicans, and their hopes for victory, inspired a wave of partisan oratory both on Monday and on Tuesday, when the platform was adopted with none of the vitriolic feuding that had wrecked the Democrats at Charleston.

Since they had only a few delegates from the South and the Border States, the Republicans had no split on the slavery issue. They simply agreed that the natural state of the territories was for freedom; they promised not to interfere with the domestic institutions inside the states; and they approved a rather moderate plank favoring a protective tariff, as demanded by the iron interests in New Jersey and Pennsylvania.

The real work of choosing a presidential nominee had begun in the hotel rooms of the delegates as the crowds began arriving on Sunday; and the furious wheeling and dealing, offers of offices and campaign funds in exchange for votes, mounted to a crescendo by Thursday.

In their suite at the Tremont House, Judge Davis and his Illinois cohorts tallied up their prospects. They first picked up the twenty-six votes of neighboring Indiana, whose party chairman, Caleb Smith, aspired to be the secretary of the interior. Charles Ray of the *Chicago Press and Tribune* brought the good news to this partner, Joseph Medill:

"We're going to have Indiana for Old Abe, sure!"

"How did you get it?" asked Medill.

"By the Lord, we promised them everything they asked."

By picking up two or three delegates among various states, the Lincoln men could add up possibly a hundred votes on the first ballot. But where could they add enough to reach the magic winning number, 233?

Judge Davis considered the Pennsylvania delegation, with its fifty-four votes, a fertile field for the harvest. Although pledged to their wily Senator Cameron on the first ballot, many of the Keystone delegates wanted to go to someone else. Cameron had little strength outside of his home state. He had too notorious a reputation as "the prince of stock and claim jobbers," a man who made politics pay.

The judge met with the Pennsylvania delegates, begging them to come over to Lincoln. He soon found that Thurlow Weed had also been there, offering favors and campaign funds if the state would go for Seward. Davis discovered that Cameron wanted to be secretary of the treasury.

Davis telegraphed the word to Lincoln, who wired back: "I authorize no bargain and will be bound by none." Davis tried again to pull the Pennsylvanians over to Lincoln, despite a new telegraphed order from his candidate at Springfield: "Make no contracts that will bind me."

While his Illinois allies wondered what to do about this, the judge handed down his verdict: "Lincoln ain't here, and don't know what we have to meet, so we will go ahead as if we hadn't heard from him, and he must ratify it." To Lincoln he wired: "Am very hopeful don't be excited nearly dead with fatigue telegraph or wire here very little."

After midnight, delegates from the four "battleground" states—Pennsylvania, Indiana, Illinois, and New Jersey—caucused to decide which candidate could best stop Seward. Judge Davis estimated that Lincoln's vote of about one hundred on the first ballot made him the strongest bet. New Jersey's men agreed that, after their complimentary vote for Dayton, they would switch to Lincoln.

But the Pennsylvanians stalled until after breakfast, holding out for their price. In the predawn hours, the Lincoln agents made a last appeal to them. Joseph Medill is the authority for this story:

Judge Davis and Charles Ray went to the Pennsylvanians' rooms to close the deal. Medill waited in the lobby. He knew that Lincoln had said, "I want that big Pennsylvania foot brought down on the scale." But he had refused to be bound by any contract.

Before daybreak, Davis and Ray came down the stairs, smiling in triumph.

"Damned if we haven't got them," the judge crowed.

"How?" Medill asked.

"By paying their price," Davis replied.

Ray put in, "We promised to put Simon Cameron in the cabinet. They wanted assurances that we represented Lincoln and that he would do what we said."

"What have you agreed to give Cameron?" asked Medill.

"The Treasury Department," Ray calmly replied.

"Good heavens! Give Cameron the Treasury Department? What will be left?"

"Oh, what's the difference?" Ray shrugged his shoulders. "We are after bigger things than that; we want the presidency and the Treasury is not a great stake to pay for it."

Seward's "irrepressibles" still felt highly confident on Friday morning, before the balloting began. They suffered a rebuff when, upon arriving at the Wigwam, they found most of the seats inside had been grabbed by Lincoln men, who used "duplicate" tickets which had been conveniently printed for them the night before. So, the Lincoln cheering section had an edge in the battle over which claque could issue the loudest yells and whistles.

On the first ballot, Seward led with $173^1/2$, Lincoln had 102, Bates 48, Cameron $50^1/2$, Chase 49, Dayton 14, Supreme Court Justice John McLean of Ohio 12, and Senator Jacob Collamer of Vermont 10, leaving 6 scattered among minor candidates.

When the second round began, Vermont switched to Lincoln, and Seward's New Yorkers jumped "as if a bomb had exploded." Then Boss Cameron's whole Pennsylvania delegation swung to Lincoln. When the ballot ended, Seward had risen to $184^1/2$ but Lincoln had soared to 181.

On the third ballot, Lincoln rose to $231^1/2$, only one and a half votes short of a majority. D. K. Cartter of Ohio rose—a big man, with a mop of black hair, bright eyes, a face marred by smallpox, and an impediment in his speech.

"I rise (eh), Mr. Chairman (eh)," he stammered, "to announce the change of four votes of Ohio from Mr. Chase to Mr. Lincoln."

"Fire the salute," cried a tally clerk. "Lincoln is nominated!"

The cannon on the Wigwam roof thundered and the thousands in the hall shouted with such tremendous fury that the cannon's roar could hardly be heard by those on the stage. Some Seward men cried like children. Lincoln's friends seemed mad with joy.

As a consolation prize, the anguished Seward supporters could have had a chance to name Lincoln's running mate, possibly New York's Senator Preston King, but they were too crushed to care. So another former Democrat, Senator Hannibal Hamlin of Maine, was chosen. He and Lincoln had never met.

Waiting in his Springfield law office, Lincoln received the news of his triumph in telegrams from his faithful friends in Chicago:

"We did it, glory to God."

"God bless you, we are happy, and may you ever be."

"City wild with excitement, from my inmost heart I congratulate you," wired Jesse W. Fell, the man who had months before suggested that the skeptical Lincoln should seek the presidency.

Judge Davis's promises—although based on his personal word alone and unauthorized by Lincoln—nevertheless proved a binding contract, in the eyes of Cameron's men who made the deal; and those tough Pennsylvania politicians collected a cabinet post for their boss despite howls of outrage from the reformers in the Republican Party. When he found out about his manager's trading tactics, Lincoln complained: "They have gambled on me all around, bought and sold me a hundred times. I cannot begin to fill the pledges made in my name."

As President, Lincoln paid all the political I.O.U.s. Judge Davis also received a justly deserved reward—a seat on the United States Supreme Court.

Overjoyed by his nomination, Lincoln felt a strong desire to go to Chicago at once, to thank the delegates, congratulate Hannibal Hamlin, and to do whatever he could to ease the pain of the poor New Yorkers, who were miserable over the surprise defeat of their hero, Senator Seward. On the face of it, this move might look like good politics, for, if Seward's admirers would sulk in their tent, the Republicans might lose New York in the November election.

But his managers were dead set against allowing Lincoln to surface anywhere. They intended to keep him under wraps throughout the entire campaign.

"Don't come here for Gods sake," Judge Davis telegraphed. "Write no letters and make no promises till you see me." Lincoln followed orders, stayed at home, and kept his mouth shut.

On May 19, ex-Congressman George Ashmun of Massachusetts led a delegation from the convention to Lincoln's house in Springfield and officially notified him of his victory. The meeting, that Saturday evening, began stiffly as Lincoln stood erect before the parlor fireplace, with his eyes downcast. After the formal speeches were over, however, the lanky candidate put the strangers at ease with his quaint good humor.

Most of the visitors had never seen Lincoln before; indeed, they had never beheld any man exactly like this towering country fellow with enormous hands and feet. Charles Carleton Coffin of the *Boston Journal* was impressed by "the lines upon his face, the large ears, sunken cheeks, enormous nose, shaggy hair, the deep-set eyes, which sparkled with humor."

Despite his wife's insistence upon serving liquor, according to the custom in her family's home in Kentucky, Lincoln offered only a pitcher of ice water to cool his guests. They did not seem to mind.

Most Republicans seemed pleased to have a standard-bearer— even one as strange as this one—who could be presented to the voters as a plain American from the West, who had been born in a log cabin, split rails, come up from poverty to a respected place as a lawyer, and a strong campaigner against the "Slave Power." Yet some sour notes in the chorus of praise were sounded by envious Democrats.

In James Gordon Bennett's *New York Herald*, a Chicago correspondent wrote: "Lincoln was known as 'Old Abe' among the roughs, for whose ears he always had the roughest kind of stories. ... As a capital teller of smutty stories he is ... regarded as cunning rather than sagacious." Dipping his poison pen for an attack on Lincoln's running mate, the *Herald* writer charged: "I knew Hamlin twenty years ago when he first came green into the legislature of Maine ... He was then a Democrat and was called 'Negro Hamlin' in consequence of his complexion and features. While he was running for office, the opposition asserted, and tried to prove, that he had negro blood in his veins."

The *Herald* also branded Lincoln as "a vulgar village politician" and predicted that, as President, he would use "the whole power of the army and navy" to free the slaves.

Alarmed by the *Herald*'s hostile propaganda, Editor Joseph Medill of the *Chicago Tribune* hastened to New York to see Bennett and "dicker" with him about the price he would demand for changing his tune in the campaign. Norman Judd, the Illinois Republican chairman, followed Medill for a chat with "His Satanic Majesty," Medill wrote to Lincoln June 19.

"We deem it highly important to spike that gun," Medill continued. "We think his terms will not be immoderate. He is too rich to want money. Social position we suspect is what he wants. He wants to be in a position to be invited with his wife and son to dinner or tea at the White House, occasionally and to be 'made of,' by the big men of the party. I think we can afford to agree to that much."

Lincoln's men also courted the leaders of the old Whig Party by assuring them that Lincoln, a Henry Clay Whig, would follow a conservative course, so there was no point in throwing votes away on John Bell, the presidential nominee of the Whigs under their new name of "Constitutional Union."

Whig Representative Horace Maynard of Tennessee, where Bell was running strong, said Lincoln, if elected, would be "a mere wisp in the hands" of the men who really ran the Republican machine, "a party that holds no other doctrine in common than antagonism to the South and to the institution of slavery." These, he said, were the wildly contradictory elements of Lincoln's party:

Old Whigs and old Democrats; followers of Thomas Jefferson, admirers of Alexander Hamilton; friends of Jackson, friends of Clay; Masons, Anti-Masons; "barnburners," "hunkers," "renters," "anti-renters," "woolly heads," "silver grays"; Know Nothings, Americans, foreigners, Catholics, protective tariff men, free trade men; bank men, bullion men; radicals, conservatives; men of strict construction, and men of no construction; men of unquestionable political honesty and men whose honesty I will not venture to call into question; men of all grades of political sentiment, all shades of political opinion, all bedded together, heads and heels, covered by a single blanket, and that woven of African wool.

❧ 5 ❧

A DOUGLAS-YANCEY TICKET?

Lincoln's triumph over Seward delighted the closest friends of Stephen A. Douglas. George Nicholas Sanders said the embittered backers of Seward, who controlled a lot of money, would "not pay a dollar" to help Lincoln in the fall election campaign. Sanders predicted that, if Seward's men would remain unhappy, Douglas could carry New York City by fifty thousand votes. William Richardson, Douglas's broad-shouldered floor manager at Charleston, who was preparing to ram his nomination through the Baltimore convention in June, assured him: "With you, we can carry New York and the Northwest entire."

Douglas's enemies renewed their war against him in May by seeking Senate approval of Jefferson Davis's resolutions that would affirm, as official Democratic Party doctrine, the Southerners' demand for congressional protection of slavery in the territories. Davis, gaunt-faced and haggard, expressed dismay over the breakup of the Democrats at Charleston. "I hope this is, however, the mist of the morning, and that the party will reunite upon sound and acceptable principles" as "the only conservative element which remains in our politics," he said.

Deploring John Brown's raid as the first "overt act" of the North against the security of the South, Davis warned that "if a party hostile to our institutions shall gain possession of the government," the South must leave a Union which no longer protects it.

Douglas, replying to Davis several days later, appeared weary and far beneath his usual standard of rough-and-tumble debate. A recurrence of a throat ailment, he explained, "has severely affected my voice and impaired my physical strength."

He charged that the bolters of Charleston had followed Yancey in his "mad scheme to break up the Democratic party" when they lost their demand for a platform plank protecting slavery in the territories.

Now, he proclaimed, "I am no longer a heretic. I am no longer an outlaw from the Democratic party. The Charleston convention repudiated this new test, contained in the Senate caucus resolutions, by a majority of twenty-seven, and affirmed the Cincinnati platform in lieu of it."

Davis retorted that the vote of 165 to 138 did not represent an actual majority of the delegates if "each had been left to his own will to choose." The Douglas men won that test by casting all thirty-five New York votes on their side although fifteen anti-Douglas votes were locked in under the unit rule.

Anyway, the Mississippi senator said, "I would rather have an honest man on any sort of rickety platform you could construct, than to have a man I did not trust on the best platform that could be made."

"Why did you not tell us," Douglas fired back, "that the whole fight was against the man, and not upon the platform?"

Totally exhausted, Douglas disappeared from the Senate for several days amid reports that he was slowly recovering the use of his croaky voice. There were also rumors that he was drinking again.

"It is impossible for any one of us to say when he will be here again," Senator Judah P. Benjamin said in detailing the indictment of Douglas as a turncoat. Before 1857, the Louisiana orator said, Douglas had "the cordial friendship" of all Democrats but now he "finds himself separated from every Democratic state in the Union" and nearly all the Democrats in both houses of Congress.

The key to the change, said Benjamin, was this: When Congress passed Douglas's Kansas-Nebraska bill, he agreed to let the courts decide whether or not the Constitution carried slavery into the territories. But when the Supreme Court decided that it did so, in its 1857 Dred Scott verdict, Douglas went back on his bargain and said that, regardless of the decree, the people of a territory could block slavery by unfriendly local laws.

Douglas backed out from his promise when he found himself "going down in Illinois" in his reelection campaign against Lincoln, Benjamin said. "His knees gave way, his whole person trembled ... he faltered." Douglas barely saved his Senate seat but the presidency would slip from his grasp, Benjamin said. "He is a fallen star."

The Senate cabal's machine ground smoothly and the Davis resolutions were adopted in another defeat for Douglas. But Douglas looked to the Baltimore convention to vindicate him, the *New York Herald* said. "The friends of the plucky little man say they do not despair. ... They will nominate him regardless of the two-thirds rule."

Now, Douglas had cause for deep despair from another source—his private life.

Three years after the death of his beloved Martha, he had found new happiness by marrying a second time. His new bride was Adele Cutts, a brown-eyed, chestnut-haired beauty half his age. Her mother was a member of the notable Roman Catholic family, the Neales, in Maryland; her father, James Madison Cutts, a government clerk, was a nephew of Dolley Madison.

Adele reigned as a new queen of Washington society, rivaling President Buchanan's niece, Harriet Lane, in the popularity of her receptions. But Adele became critically ill after the birth of a daughter, Ellen, in September 1859, and for some time her life was in danger. Eventually she recovered but in June 1860, little Ellen died. Thus a new burden of sorrow was added to the return of Douglas's throat infection and fatigue at the crisis of his fight for the presidency.

Shortly before the Democrats were to reconvene at Baltimore, where Douglas's friends were determined to nominate him at last for the presidency, the politicians buzzed in excitement over an astounding report: That second place on his ticket would be offered to none other than William Lowndes Yancey. At first, this sounded incredible, for Douglas had repeatedly denounced the Alabama orator as the instigator of the "mad" Southern walkout at Charleston.

Yancey would accept the offer as the price for withdrawing his opposition to the Little Giant, on the basis of a secret interview, according to the rumors, "and many were the winks given by ardent Douglas men as they prophesied the speedy and unanimous nomination of their political favorite."

Outlandish though the tales might seem, Douglas had earlier made friendly remarks about Yancey, telling the Senate: "We are old personal friends. We met as members of Congress seventeen years ago. Our social relations have always been uninterrupted. I have as much admiration as any man living for his brilliant, his surpassing ability ... boldness and nerve."

The revelation of Yancey's hour-long meeting with Douglas at the senator's home in Washington sent a current of excitement through the Baltimore convention. "This visit set all sorts of rumors afloat that Yancey was going to run as a candidate for Vice-President with Douglas," the *New York Times* reported on June 19.

"Yancey and Douglas have been intimate and dear friends in the past, and Yancey says that it was from principle, and not from any personal dislike, that he opposes his old friend," the *Times* added.

Douglas may have been desperate enough to consider placing Yancey on his ticket. They would not be the first, or the last, "odd couple" to be paired by politicians in quest of victory. Douglas sorely needed to build up his weak forces in the South, which could provide 120 electoral votes in November, all almost certain to go against Lincoln. If Douglas, somehow, could win them back and then carry only a couple of states in the North, he could win the grand prize of all his hopes and dreams. But he could obtain the Southerners' votes only by patching up the rift with some powerful leader such as Yancey, so the offer to him must certainly have seemed worth a try.

Official denials of the strange alliance flew thick and fast from the Douglas camp, but the Charleston, S.C., *Courier* later let the cat out of the bag by saying: "We are authorized to state, positively and distinctly, and on responsible evidence which can be furnished to a proper demand, that the nomination for the vice-presidency on the Douglas ticket was offered to William L. Yancey of Alabama. The offer was made through or by George N. Sanders, of New York, and with the knowledge of Stephen Arnold Douglas, and but a few days before the meeting of the adjourned convention at Baltimore."

Sanders, the bearded wire-puller who sought to enlist leading Southerners in Douglas's cause, fired back at the Charleston paper with a letter that looked like a denial but really amounted to a confession that he had, indeed, made the offer to Yancey—but only in fun, "in a spirit of good-humored political raillery."

Sanders said he uttered his "playful words" at a private dinner party the Thursday before the opening of the Baltimore convention on Monday, June 18. Among those present were the host, J. D. Hoover; Vice President Breckinridge; J. W. Forney of the *Philadelphia Press*, a former Buchanan acolyte keenly disappointed by his failure to receive high political office as a reward from the President; General John Cunningham of Charleston and Albert Pike of Arkansas.

Sanders recalled that, when Buchanan had defeated Douglas for the presidential nomination at Cincinnati in 1856, "the Douglas party demanded and obtained the nomination of Major Breckinridge as vice president"; and thus it was the Democrats' custom to give second place to "the minority" at the convention.

There was no question that Yancey was the minority chief now, Sanders went on; "Douglas had, in his last speech, signally pointed out Mr. Yancey; and I felt authorized to say that the majority, with whom I had the honor to act, would generously follow the wise acknowledgement in '56 of that precedent, and allow the minority again to indicate the vice-president."

Furthermore, Sanders said "that Mr. Yancey had bravely won the position by breaking up the convention at Charleston, and that he had gained everything possible in that direction; that his star would now lead him to harmony and to preventing any more breaks in the Democratic party." Also, the New York promoter proposed to support a new platform plank on the slavery question, a compromise "which Mr. Yancey and his followers could honorably accept."

"Before leaving Mr. Hoover's, Mr. Yancey came to me and said he would like to make a complimentary visit to Mr. Douglas with me at a time when he would be most at leisure," Sanders continued. Sanders set up the date and called for Yancey at his rooms at ten o'clock the following night for the ride to Douglas's home in Washington. Sanders said: "I asked Mr. Yancey significantly if he had been considering the vice-president project. He archly indicated in his reply that he had higher aspirations."

Then Sanders recalled "the speedy annihilation" of Presidents William Henry Harrison and Zachary Taylor, who had died in office, and added this cryptic remark: "As Douglas's friends were much more numerous and enthusiastic than theirs, he could certainly count on his being killed off in six months."

Yancey's biographer, John Witherspoon Du Bose, wrote that Sanders made these remarks in the apartment of Alabama Congressman James L. Pugh, where Yancey was staying while visiting Washington, and in the presence of "a number of gentlemen." Du Bose said Sanders asked, in effect: "Would Yancey, now the confessed leader of a minority, very powerful, accept the second place, with the assurance of the majority that he should be put forward for first place in 1864? Mr. Sanders even held out the precarious state of Mr. Douglas' health as promise that the Vice President, elected with him, would receive promotion as the term expired."

Actually, had the Douglas-Yancey ticket been elected, the vice-president could have moved into the White House even earlier, for Douglas in June 1860 was ill with more than throat trouble. His health was wrecked by drink and exhaustion, and he had only one year left to live.

Sanders recalled that, when he and Yancey arrived at Douglas's home, hoping for a private talk, they found him surrounded by friends, "and spent a pleasant hour without a word on the vice-presidency" being uttered by anyone.

So the fantastic dream of a Democratic unity ticket faded into the mist of the might-have-been. The offer seemed "so preposterous that the Douglas forces in the ensuing campaign vehemently denied that it had ever been made," wrote Dwight Lowell Dumond in *The Secession Movement, 1860–61*. "That the offer was made, however, and that Douglas' illness and probable death at an early date were urged as an inducement, there seems to be little doubt," Dumond concluded, noting that Congressman Pugh was one of several witnesses to the conversation at his apartment.

Now Douglas faced a new threat from his old enemies, President Buchanan and the Democratic senators' cabal. They tried to undermine the Little Giant's support in the North, especially in New York. They sent word to Dean Richmond that, if his delegation would stop casting its thirty-five votes for Douglas, and switch them to another man, the Southerners would join in securing the nomination of the compromise candidate.

The most promising prospect for this role of "unity" nominee was New York's former Governor Horatio Seymour.

Seymour was acceptable to the South because he was no abolitionist. "To destroy the United States because of slavery," he once said, "would be as mad as to drag all Europe into war in order to abolish serfdom in Russia or polygamy in Turkey." He saw no reason for any "irrepressible conflict" between the North and the South. "But for the

looms of New England and Old England," dependent upon cotton produced by the slaves in the South, he said, slavery "could not live a day."

Even the cynical editor of the *New York Herald* had a good word
for Seymour: "Genial and fascinating, modest and generous in his
manners," said James Gordon Bennett, "he quietly wins his way as a
politician and can wind about his fingers, somewhat after the
fashion of Thurlow Weed, the more noisy and rampant managers
of his party."

"Tall, immaculately dressed, with golden voice and large, luminous
eyes," Seymour loomed as a formidable competitor if he could be
persuaded to run.

Dean Richmond liked the idea; he had privately favored Seymour,
even while carrying out his promises to back Douglas at Charleston.
Now, however, the railroad boss had concluded that Douglas could
not be elected.

So what would be the point of choosing a sure loser? Seymour, he
believed, could combine the strength of New York and the South for
at least 155 electoral votes—enough to beat Lincoln. It was a matter
of simple arithmetic.

Furthermore, many New York Republicans, disappointed because
of Seward's defeat by Lincoln, could turn to Seymour and award the
presidency to New York after all. "Considering the effect of Seward's
humiliation," wrote one reporter, "I am assured that the New York
American rump will support Seymour. ... Then New York and the
South can elect Seymour."

"We get this information," he added, "from a Democrat of some
authority in the Northern party camp, and when we look over the
whole course of the Dean Richmond delegation at Charleston we can
discover now that it was *not* to nominate Douglas but to use him to
bring about the nomination of Seymour. Why else was the vote of New
York given for the rule requiring two-thirds of the whole electoral vote
in the Union to nominate after eight states had left the convention?"

"The Regency in the New York delegation is split about Douglas,"
the *New York Herald* reported from Baltimore as the quarreling
Democrats reassembled there. "Cagger, Cassidy and Church go to
Douglas at all hazards. Richmond wants to drop him and take up
Seymour, if the South will only offer him.

*Horatio Seymour, former governor of New York, the personal
choice of his state's Democratic boss, Dean Richmond, for the
presidency. From the collections of the Library of Congress.*

"Richmond, who is a practical man, wants to secure the ascendancy in New York state. He says Douglas cannot be elected while
Seymour can. Yet Richmond and the majority of the New York
delegation will continue to vote for Douglas until the South, or the
convention, offers them some man they can accept.

"'This,' says the Dean, 'is my stand point and I will stick until the
South comes to terms.'

"It is well understood now that there is hardly one-fourth of the
delegation original Douglas men."

A minority in the delegation favored Daniel Dickinson, and
contended that Richmond had promised the white-haired former
senator the bloc of thirty-five votes if Douglas faltered. Upon finding
out that the boss now was scheming to give the prize to Seymour, the
Dickinson men did all they could to block the deal.

The Republicans, eager for a Democratic Party split that would benefit Lincoln, said "Pooh! Pooh!" to the scheme of naming Seymour as a
unity candidate to carry the Democrats to victory, the *Herald* reported.

"The Republicans," it said, "say 'Dean Richmond and his railroad
gang have shown their hand too soon. Douglas will not be humbugged
that way. He will hold his ground. We shall have two Democratic
tickets, for Douglas will be Caesar or nothing.'"

The *New York Times* correspondent reported from Baltimore that Dean Richmond's delegation consisted of four factions, three of them hostile to Douglas: "The first is the monied interest—the Guthrie interest—headed by Erastus Corning. The second interest is for Daniel Dickinson, headed by Edwin Crowel. ... The third interest is for Horatio Seymour, headed by John Stryker ..."

The fourth interest, the *Times* man wrote, was for Douglas and included Richmond, Church, Cagger, et al. The reporter visualized Boss Richmond "as a political coachman, with any quantity of red capes and a frizzled white wig, sitting on the box seat of the New York organization, and attempting to make one team of sixty-nine horses obey his will." (The seventy New Yorkers cast a half-vote each.)

"Pennsylvania talks of Dickinson—so does Georgia—but New York has no confidence that the Sage of Binghamton could beat Lincoln, and he will not be nominated against the opinion of his own state." Dickinson, the *Times* added, "is brought up now and then only to be dropped like a hot poker."

Years later, John Cochrane of the New York delegation wrote that he witnessed an offer by Senator Slidell, at the Baltimore convention, to nominate Seymour with the assurance of support by the South, if the Northerners would drop Douglas. Richmond put the issue to a vote; and by 20 to 15, New York's answer was "No."

Seymour ended his own presidential boom by publishing a letter, on the advice of his physician, taking himself out of the race. "All during his life," wrote his biographer, Stewart Mitchell, the former governor "seems to have suffered from some organic trouble which probably caused his fatigue and attacks of low spirits."

"It is now concluded that Seymour cannot be substituted for Douglas," the *Herald* reported from Baltimore. "His health, both of mind and body, his friends say, is not sufficient for the task."

The *New York Times* editorially blistered the jealous men inside the New York delegation who blocked the nomination of Seymour who, it said, could have won the required two-thirds vote of the convention. "The united New England and Southern delegations," it said, "made a direct offer of this to the gentlemen in control of the 35 votes of New York, with a promise that Pennsylvania, under Senator

Bigler's management, should wheel in line after having cast two or three complimentary votes for Mr. Breckinridge."

The draft-Seymour proposal was defeated, the *Times* said, by "the personal animosity, or rather angry jealousy which Peter Cagger and Sanford Church have always shown towards former Governor Seymour. Thus the first choice of a great portion of the New York delegation and the second choice of seven-eighths of the members of the party was not only defeated but denied expression."

Thus ended, said the *New York Herald*, the Albany Regency's plan "to lift Seymour out of the mire of their dirty Albany politics into the presidential chair."

"For once," the *Herald* gloated, "the wily, plotting Dean Richmond is in water beyond his depth. He finds that all the beautiful arrangements perfected at Syracuse last September for dictating the candidate of this convention fall short."

Abraham Lincoln was lucky, indeed, that the envy of some New York politicians against Seymour effectively blocked the deal whereby the Democrats could have united behind the one Democrat who would have had a chance of carrying New York in the presidential race in November. Without New York's 35 electoral votes, Lincoln would have fallen short of the 152 needed to clinch his victory. Seymour might have won outright, or a third contender, John Bell, could have carried enough states to throw the final decision into the House of Representatives.

Seymour's biographer, Mitchell, concluded: "A two-man contest between Abraham Lincoln and Horatio Seymour might have changed the course of American history."

If, indeed, Dean Richmond's calculations had proved correct, and if Seymour had carried New York State and the solid South, he would have won the presidency in 1860. If Lincoln had been defeated, there would have been no excuse for the South's secession and, therefore, no Civil War. The nation would have saved the six hundred thousand men whose lives were thrown away in that totally unnecessary war.

It is true that, without the war and the destruction of the South, the abolition of slavery would have been delayed by a number of years. But, Mitchell asked:

"Just how much blood and treasure and good will were free soil, abolition and emancipation worth?"

❧ *6* ❧

DEBACLE AT BALTIMORE

When the Democrats reconvened in the Front Street theater in Baltimore on Monday, June 18, they quickly fell into a dispute over the question of admitting most of the Southern bolters or replacing them with new pro-Douglas delegations. (South Carolina sent no one; Florida sent only observers.) A real fight loomed over the rival delegations from Alabama, Georgia, Louisiana, and Arkansas. The credentials committee took over the burning issue and deliberated for three days, while "Hotspurs" of the North and the South wrangled and made fiery speeches, on the floor and in front of their hotels, and fist fights often occurred in the city's many saloons.

A typical newspaper dispatch reported: "Mr. Whiteley of Delaware is confined to his room. His face was hurt by the falling of a spittoon at his hotel during a fight." The *New York Herald* deplored the "ruffianism," largely blamed on hard-drinking ward-heelers from the Northern cities, and called the violence a sign that "the days of the demoralized Democratic party are numbered; it is in the agonies of death."

George Templeton Strong, the New York diarist, recorded: "The worst temper prevails; delegates punch each other and produce revolvers." He deplored the "scandalous, shameful brutalities and indecencies that disgrace the whole country."

"If one half of its bullies and blackguards and Southern gentlemen will make free use of their revolvers on the other half ... and will then get themselves decently hanged for homicide, the country will be safe," Strong wrote.

The three senators who headed the anti-Douglas forces at Charleston—Slidell, Bayard, and Bright—were hard at work again at Baltimore, with the help of two Buchanan cabinet members, Treasury

Secretary Howell Cobb of Georgia and Interior Secretary Jacob Thompson of Mississippi.

Their foes in the Douglas camp vowed "to break down the oligarchy of the Senate, consisting of Gwin, Slidell, Bigler, Bright, Fitch, Davis, Benjamin, Clay, Green, and company," the *New York Times* observed.

On the fourth day, Thursday, June 21, the Front Street theater shook with a tremendous crash. The front of the stage and the section covering the orchestra pit had dropped three feet in the center, tossing the seats, and everyone sitting on them, into a jumbled mass. They all crawled out, as best they could, and ran off in all directions, amid the "wildest excitement." No one was seriously hurt. To some, the collapse seemed an ominous sign, symbolizing the collapse of the Democratic Party.

At noon that day, the credentials committee submitted a majority report recommending that the new, pro-Douglas delegations from Alabama and Louisiana be seated—a blow clearly aimed against Yancey and Senator Slidell. The newcomers from Georgia and Arkansas were to be admitted, along with the old bunch, the votes to be divided equally between them. The original delegates from Mississippi and Texas were to be allowed to regain their seats.

This compromise was unacceptable to most Southerners, and a second walkout loomed. Douglas, waiting anxiously in Washington, received telegrams warning him that the convention would surely break up unless he withdrew his name and let the party unify behind another candidate.

With a heavy heart, Douglas wrote a letter to his floor manager, Richardson, saying there was "danger that the Democratic party will be demoralized if not destroyed by the breaking-up of the convention." The nation would never be safe from the perils of sectional strife, he said, unless the principle of congressional nonintervention in the territories could be maintained.

"If, therefore, you and other friends who have stood by me with such heroic firmness at Charleston and Baltimore shall be of the opinion that the principle can be preserved and the unity and ascendancy of the Democratic party maintained, and the country saved from the perils of Northern abolitionism and Southern disunion by withdrawing my name and uniting upon some other non-intervention and Union-loving Democrat," he concluded, "I beseech you to pursue that course."

Richardson put the letter in his pocket and stubbornly denied persistent rumors that it even existed. On Friday, Douglas sent a telegram to Dean Richmond, repeating the offer of withdrawal.

Slidell, as spokesman for the Senate cabal, also warned Richmond that, unless Douglas withdrew, even more Southerners would leave the convention floor. The New Yorker asked Richardson to drop Douglas, but the loyal floor manager refused.

On Friday morning, the New Yorkers joined in finally rejecting the effort to readmit Yancey and his bolters. The vote was 150 to 100½. The regular Alabama delegation, following Yancey, and the original Louisiana delegates, loyal to Slidell, were excluded. In their places sat the pro-Douglas men from Alabama, led by John Forsyth, and the Louisiana substitutes, also ardently pro-Douglas, and their leader, the mercurial former Senator Pierre Soulé, the mortal enemy of Slidell.

When the Douglas forces moved to begin the balloting for the presidential nomination, delegate Charles Russell arose as spokesman for Virginia. He "stood up straight as a ramrod, pale as a sheet, and nervous as a witch."

Russell solemnly announced that the Virginians would walk out.

In quick succession, most of North Carolina, half of Maryland, plus Tennessee, California, and Oregon followed. The next day, most of the Missouri, Arkansas, and Kentucky delegations left. Then Caleb Cushing stepped down as the presiding officer, followed by those in Massachusetts who were loyal to the Buchanan administration. Douglas men cheered the departure of Cushing as good riddance and welcomed his replacement in the chair, David Tod of Ohio.

Delegates representing about a third of the original 303 votes in the convention were gone. So the hard-core Douglas men could reign supreme over the remains of the wrecked assembly. Naturally, Douglas led in the balloting and thus he finally won the great prize—for whatever it might be worth.

Meanwhile, the seceders trooped into the Maryland Institute at Baltimore and chose Cushing as their chairman. They quickly adopted

Vice President John C. Breckinridge of Kentucky, backed by the Southern Democrats as their nominee for the presidency with the support of incumbent President James Buchanan. A scheme to kidnap Buchanan in December 1860 and thus place Breckinridge in the White House fizzled. From the collections of the Library of Congress.

the platform, rejected at Charleston, which declared that it was the federal government's duty "to protect, when necessary, the rights of persons and property in the Territories."

Vice President Breckinridge was nominated for the presidency over Daniel Dickinson, 81 to 24. Senator Lane of Oregon was unanimously selected for the vice-presidency.

Back in the Front Street theater, the remaining delegates gave Douglas a southern running mate, as he requested: Senator Benjamin Fitzpatrick of Alabama, a former governor whose young wife was eager for him to receive the honor.

But Fitzpatrick's Senate colleagues solemnly warned him that he would wreck his career by being the tail of the Douglas ticket. Georgia's fiery Senator Bob Toombs enlisted Senator Gwin's wife and others to say the same thing to Mrs. Fitzpatrick. They "told her the Governor would be eternally ruined if he accepted—got her to crying unless he promised to decline," J. Henly Smith reported from Washington to Stephens. Torn between his weeping wife and the threatening senators, Fitzpatrick declined.

The convention having adjourned, the Democratic National Committee filled the vacancy by handpicking Herschel V. Johnson, a former senator and governor of Georgia. Yancey told this fanciful story of the scene when Johnson was drafted to receive the consolation prize:

> The committee went into the barroom at the National Hotel in Washington, and there they found Johnson. ... They patted him on the shoulder and said to him: "To be sure, you are pretty much of a fire-eater. You used to eat hot coals with Yancey, but still we are pretty hard-pressed for a vice president and we will elect you."
>
> The convention had all gone home but they said, "We will make you vice-president," and he said, "Oh, yes, I will accept.".... Now they claim he was nominated by two-thirds and he never got a vote in any convention.

Now, there were four major contenders for the White House, and Breckinridge—tall, arrow-straight, blue-eyed—was easily the most handsome. At thirty-nine, the Kentuckian was also the youngest man yet nominated for the presidency. Yet Breckinridge, who would gladly have been the nominee of a united party, felt reluctant to head a faction with no hope of victory. Senator Toombs, who had persuaded Fitzpatrick to get off the Douglas ticket, now went to work to make Breckinridge accept. Toombs told him that Breckinridge "would carry the whole South like a storm, and that in less than forty days he would have the field clear for himself—Douglas being withdrawn."

Jefferson Davis made a dramatic proposal for Douglas, Bell, and Breckinridge all to withdraw, so that the elements opposed to Lincoln could unite behind a single nominee, perhaps Seymour or Guthrie. Breckinridge's biographer, William C. Davis, dates the proposal as having been made in the last week of June, when the Mississippi senator and the three nominees were all in Washington at the same time. Bell and Breckinridge agreed to step down, if Douglas would, too. But Douglas refused.

Dean Richmond's New Yorkers went along with Douglas's refusal and came under fire for their tricky tactics at the two conventions. "The Albany Regency," said the *New York Herald*, has "slaughtered Dickinson, butchered Seymour, and made minced meat out of Douglas. They have cheated every man who put his trust in them. The word 'New York' to the Southern men is a synonym for 'rascality.'"

"On the whole," the *Herald* said sarcastically, "the Albany Regency have reason to feel proud ... Like harlots, they glory in their shame."

The *New York Times* blamed Buchanan and Douglas as "the joint authors of the disruption of the Democratic party."

True to his "cold and clammy nature," Buchanan fired several of his officeholders whom he considered traitors for backing Douglas. Most notable of the victims was George Nicholas Sanders, the well-paid navy agent in New York.

Sanders had done more than any other Northern man to organize the Douglas forces in the southern states, the *Times* said. It recalled his reckless record when, as the American consul in London, he became the trusted friend of the young radicals promoting revolution in Europe. He even advocated the execution of the French emperor, Napoleon III.

"He was a Red Republican in Europe" and just as reckless in promoting Douglas, the editorial noted.

Sanders struck back at Buchanan by publishing a sensational open letter to the President, accusing him of treachery and insinuating that Old Buck, nearly seventy, had sunk into senility or even insanity.

Editorially, the *Times* chided Sanders for wasting his time in flagellating the President, whose career was nearly over. "Sanders forgets that he is dealing with the dead," it said. "He is fighting a political ghost."

A colorful word picture of the doddering, wry-necked old President was painted by a reporter who covered New York Mayor Fernando Wood's visit to the White House in quest of a share of the federal jobs in return for organizing a Breckinridge-Lane ticket in the city:

He found Mr. Buchanan at his desk ... the old dressing gown wrapped more tightly than usual around his figure, the old velvet slippers a little more down-at-heel than heretofore, and the knot of his cravat twisted around several half-inches beyond the left ear. ... The head of Mr. Buchanan had a more active fit of shaking and jerking than is common at this hour of the morning.

Mr. Buchanan addressed him as "Alderman Wood." Wood commenced by deploring the nomination of Douglas, assuring Mr. Buchanan that, if his delegation had been admitted, they would have retired, almost unanimously, with the seceders. ...Wood said he could not run a successful Breckinridge organization without "some of your patronage in the city."

"Could you succeed if you did have such patronage?" asked Mr. Buchanan. "They tell me all New York is for Douglas, Mozart Hall included."...

Giving a vigorous suck, between each word, to his unlighted cigar, and sending his hands up either dressing gown sleeve in vain pursuit of his shirt cuffs [he added], "I—cannot—afford—to—turn—the last—days of my—administration into—a slaughter house. General Dix [the postmaster] cannot be removed. Collector Schell—is master of his own—patronage. You have your answer, Alderman."

With these words, Old Public Functionary wheeled around, caught the bellrope which dangled over his head. ... "Mr. Wood wishes to leave," the President told James, pretending to bend over some manuscripts on his desk. "Show him out."

The customs house and post office employees were out in full force when Daniel S. Dickinson harangued a rally of New York Democrats at the Cooper Institute, ratifying the Breckinridge-Lane ticket. "Scripture Dick," the ex-senator with his mane of billowing white hair, poured out the bitter resentment he felt over being denied any chance for the presidential nomination.

In an evident shaft at Dean Richmond, Dickinson accused the party boss of falsely promising to support any presidential candidate acceptable to the South but then resisting "each and every one" favored by the Southerners—including himself.

Dickinson's diatribe mirrored the venomous hostility that had led to the breakup of the once all-conquering Democratic machine. Now the Democrats were split into two warring camps and each would rather see Lincoln win than to have its rivals triumph. They virtually assured a Lincoln victory.

The Democrats' rancorous feuding delighted lucky Lincoln, who realized that it improved his prospects for sweeping the Northern states. He had to win almost all of them, because he had no chance whatever in the fifteen slave states.

His portrayal as an old-fashioned Henry Clay Whig helped him to gain many votes from Whigs who had feared Republican John C. Fremont as too radical in 1856, and had given the conservative ex-President Fillmore 22 percent of the popular vote, thus enabling Buchanan to win the presidency.

Now Lincoln could rejoice over the news from an Ohio reporter in late June, who wrote: "Every Fillmore paper in the Northwest has come out for Lincoln. In Illinois and Indiana the same thing is true."

In Pennsylvania and New Jersey, the desire for a high tariff to protect the local iron industries played a larger part in the Republican campaign than the slavery issue. Lincoln's supporters also heavily stressed their charges of widespread corruption in the Buchanan administration, through the awards of federal contracts to presidential pets, the misuse of bribery to shove bills through Congress, and the influence of corporate money to achieve political benefits.

Congressman John Covode, the Pennsylvania Republican whose investigating committee had dug up evidence of corruption in the Buchanan regime, told a Philadelphia rally for Lincoln that "offices were bought and sold in the ante-room of the Senate and the Executive Mansion was open as a butcher shop." "Slavery, corruption and fraud," he said, "were the motto of the Democracy."

Another speaker at the same late June conclave joked that Lincoln, the rail splitter, "is at it again. He has already split the Democratic party, split it all to pieces. Douglas is so short he can't split rails; but make whiskey barrel staves of him and he can hold all the whiskey in the country."

Republicans loved to ridicule Douglas about his short stature and his capacity for booze. Richard Yates, the party's candidate for governor of Illinois, addressed a rally in Lincoln's hometown in June and the Springfield Glee Club sang a parody of Stephen Foster's popular song, "The Camp Town Races." Witnesses said "it brought down the house." It went like this:

There's an old plow "hoss" whose name is "Dug,"
    Du da, du da,
He's short and thick, a regular "plug,"
    Da, du, da, day.
The little "plug" had had his day,
    Du da, du da,
He's out of the ring by all fair play,
    Da, du da, day.
His legs are weak, his wind unsound,
    Du da, du da,
His "switch tail" is too near the ground,
    Da, du da, day.
Old Abraham's a well-bred nag,
    Du da, du da,
His wind is sound, he'll never lag,
    Da, du da, day.
The Lincoln "hoss" will never fail,
    Du da, du da,
He will not shy at ditch or "rail,"
    Da, du da, day.
Chorus:
We're bound to work all night,
We're bound to work all day,
I'll bet my money on the Lincoln "hoss,"
Who bets on Stephen A.?

Isaac N. Morris, a Democratic congressman from Illinois, leaped to the defense of his friend, the "plug hoss," Douglas, by publishing a reply to the Springfield Republicans' "glee club" in some verses written by himself. Here are a few samples of his doggerel:

Old Abe, good soul, split rails
And made the best cock-tails,
    Hurrah! Hurrah! Hurrah!
He worked his way on "Broad Horn."
Loaded down with Wabash corn,
    Hurrah! Hurrah! Hurrah!
He is the chap to gain the race,
An awkward boy with flat-boat grace,

Hurrah! Hurrah! Hurrah!
We tell you what is strictly true
Abraham can "maul" 'em through,
   Hurrah! Hurrah! Hurrah!
He fought with "Dug" and got some fame
Reflected on his unknown name,
   Hurrah! Hurrah! Hurrah!

("Broad Horn," in an earlier verse, meant "flat boat.")

Morris jeered at the Republicans for calling their candidate "Uncle Abe," "Old Abe," "Honest Old Abe," "the rail-splitter," and "the flat boat man." "The terms simply signify," he said, "that he is a good natured, easy, good-for-nothing sort of a man. ... But everyone who knows him, knows full well he is not qualified, either by talents, force of character, or experience, to guide the ship of state."

Washington Barrow, a former Whig Congressman from Tennessee, campaigning in New York for the Bell-Everett ticket, recalled having served in the House with Lincoln, and said: "He had the biggest mouth, the longest nose, and the most ungainly appearance of any man I have ever seen in all my life."

Lincoln, immured in Springfield, paid no attention to such attacks and remained as silent as the Sphinx. On July 4, he wrote to an old friend, Dr. A. G. Henry, in Oregon: "Today, it looks as if the Chicago ticket will be elected. I think the chances were more than equal that we could have beaten the Democracy united. Divided as it is, its chance appears indeed very slim. But great is Democracy in resources; and it may yet give its fortunes a turn. ...

"The signs now are that Douglas and Breckinridge will each have a ticket in every state. They are driven to this to keep up their bombastic claims of nationality, and to avoid the charge of sectionalism which they have so much lavished on us."

❧ 7 ❧

DOUGLAS DENOUNCES "DISUNIONISTS"

While Lincoln, as early as the Fourth of July, was confidently predicting his own victory, Stephen A. Douglas sounded equally sure of a sweep for his Democratic ticket. Douglas expected to run ahead of Lincoln in various states; indeed, he said he could have beaten Lincoln in every state except Vermont and Massachusetts if separate slates of electors had not been offered for Breckinridge.

Douglas predicted that Breckinridge would carry only South Carolina, and perhaps Mississippi, while Douglas and Bell would divide the rest of the South.

To believe these rosy forecasts, Douglas must have been intoxicated by something—perhaps his dreams of at last reaching his cherished goal of the White House. But some of his best friends, who did not believe in pipe dreams, were much more sober than that.

Alexander H. Stephens, a great admirer, said Douglas's managers must have been crazy to have rammed his nomination through after the Border States had joined in the Southern walkout at Baltimore. "Madness and folly," said the little Georgian, "seemed to have ruled the hour."

"Anyone who has got sense enough to get out of a shower of rain" should know that is impossible for Douglas to carry the Border States after their bolt, Stephens asserted. "And when it is apparent that he will lose the entire South, thousands of men at the North, some for spite and some to get on the winning side, will quit his standard then, and thus leave him perhaps without the vote of a single state."

Why was Douglas making such a hopeless race? Daniel Dickinson asked rhetorically in a Baltimore speech on August 2. "It can only be," he said, "in the hopes of building up a great Northern party which will swallow up Republicans in its ranks and create a new party which will eventually override the Constitution and trample underfoot the rights of the Southern states." Dickinson and other Breckinridge-Lane supporters in New York harangued a state convention at Syracuse on August 7 and called upon Democrats to carry the state for "the Old Line National Democracy."

A week later, the faction headed by Dean Richmond, combining the Albany Regency and Tammany boys, met at Syracuse and puffed for Douglas. Here are a newspaper reporter's candid glimpses of the brethren:

> Old Dean Richmond rolls round like a super-annuated porpoise, milking his nose and patting his protuberant stomach. Free passes for "bearer and family" on the Central [railroad] are plenty for all who will vote for the P. Cagger programme.
>
> Peter himself buttons his single-breasted frock coat more tightly and plays delicately—using the forefinger and thumb of his left hand—with the little gold watch chain worn outside his coat, which he seems to mistake for the Legion of Honor. Poor John Stryker, of Rome ... hurled off the platform at the last state convention, limps round, supporting himself on a stick.

Following the will-o-the-wisp of votes in the East, Douglas first made a tour of solidly Republican New England. The only possible explanation for this strange choice was that he imagined the Yankees would prefer himself, a native Vermonter, to such a crude westerner as Lincoln. Douglas sought out his father's grave at his birthplace, Brandon, Vermont, swung through several Vermont and New Hampshire towns, and reveled in a big clambake on Narragansett Bay near Providence, Rhode Island. For twelve days in August, he relaxed at Newport, attending balls, talking politics, and bathing in the surf.

But at Newport he finally had to come out of the surf and face some grim realities. Four of his campaign officials—his national chairman, August Belmont, George Nicholas Sanders, A. D. Banks, and F. O. Prince, a Boston supporter—met him there and brought bad news. Belmont, the Rothschilds' New York agent, had to report that his pleas for campaign funds from other rich men were meeting stiff resistance. William A. Aspinwall and George Law, major steamship line owners, who had backed the Little Giant financially before, were

*Senator Joseph Lane of Oregon, the running mate of
John C. Breckinridge of Kentucky, the presidential
candidate of the Democratic faction backed by the South
and by President Buchanan's administration. From the
collections of the Library of Congress.*

holding back now. Manhattan merchants, who carried on a profitable
trade with the South, were afraid of angering their best customers
there by giving money to Douglas.

By exerting pressure on certain rich men in New York and Boston, Belmont raised enough money to finance a desperate effort by
the Democrats in Maine, where the state elections in September could
be a portent of the national outcome in November. "As Maine goes,
so goes the nation," the politicos believed.

Heeding his managers' appeals, Douglas made speeches in Portland, Bangor, and Augusta, Maine, although he must have known
that New England was really a Lincoln stronghold.

A New York newspaper writer, seeking Douglas's real motives in
an interview, reported from Newport in mid-August: "He cares nothing
about his own personal success and comparatively little for the
success of the Democratic party, as it stands at present. *But he intends*

to crush out utterly and forever the Disunion Party. ... I do not believe he has any hope of his own election and I am quite sure that he would prefer Lincoln's success to any result which should carry Breckinridge into the House as one of the three highest candidates and thus give the Senate a chance of electing Lane."

This discerning writer, who signed his dispatch simply "O," put his finger precisely upon the Southerners' hopes of keeping Lincoln from winning a clear majority of the electoral votes and thus throwing the contest into the House of Representatives. These were the statistics behind their strategy, which Douglas was determined to block:

- To win the presidency, a candidate must collect a majority of the 303 electoral votes, or 152.
- Lincoln had no chance of picking up any of the 120 in the fifteen slave states, and did not even try.
- Therefore, he must sweep nearly all of the 183 electoral votes in the eighteen free states.
- Should he lose even 32, he would fall short of a clear majority; he would have only 151.
- Then, the Constitution required that the House must choose the President from among the three candidates polling the most electoral votes. Each state, large or small, would have only one House vote. The winner must carry seventeen of the thirty-three House delegations. If Breckinridge could carry all the fifteen slave states, plus California and Oregon, he would have seventeen.

Of the thirty-three state delegations in the House, fifteen were counted as sure for Lincoln, thirteen for Breckinridge, one for Bell, and four uncertain—usually because the members were equally divided and thus would have to cast a blank ballot.

Conceivably, then, the House could deadlock and be unable to elect anybody before Inauguration Day, March 4. In that case, the vice-president would be elected by the Senate, which was dominated by the Democrats. They would choose Breckinridge's running mate, Joe Lane, and the pro-Southern Oregon Senator would move into the White House. Therefore, some Republican campaigners told Northern voters they really must choose "Lincoln or Lane."

Although he boasted that Breckinridge could carry only one or two Southern states, Douglas knew better than that. So he decided upon a bold move: He would campaign in the South, denounce the Breckinridge men as "disunionists," and try to swing the electoral votes to Bell, if he could not win them for himself. He directly sought an alliance with the former Whigs who could be strong enough to make Bell the winner in Virginia, Kentucky, Tennessee, Maryland, and North Carolina, while Missouri and a few Northern states might go to Douglas.

In that way, Douglas hoped to chop Breckinridge down to fourth place, so that the House contest—if one occurred—would involve himself, Bell, and Lincoln.

The Douglas-Bell coalition bore its first fruit in a special election in August, humiliating Breckinridge in his own home state. Leslie Combs, a Whig-American, won a Kentucky state office—clerk of the court of appeals—by a margin of 22,000 votes. Combs, in a letter to the *Louisville Journal*, thanked the Douglas men for their help, saying: "The patriotic National Union Democracy have cooperated with us manfully and we must hereafter consider them as brethren. The Yancey-Breckinridge Democrats ... are doomed."

Encouraged by the glad tidings from Kentucky, Douglas carried his campaign into Virginia, speaking first on August 25 from the steps of the Norfolk city hall.

Midway in his speech denouncing the Breckinridge men as "disunionists," a slip of paper was handed to him, relaying two questions from a Breckinridge elector:

"If Abraham Lincoln is elected President of the Union," read the first, "will the southern states be justified in seceding from the Union?"

"No!" Douglas emphatically replied, evoking great applause.

The second question: "If they secede from the Union upon the inauguration of Abraham Lincoln, before he commits an overt act against their constitutional rights, will you advise or vindicate resistance by force to the decision?"

Amid shouts of "No, No!", Douglas answered:

"It is the duty of the President of the United States, and all those in authority under him, to enforce the laws of the United States, passed by Congress, and as the courts expound them, and I, as in duty bound by my oath of fidelity to the Constitution, would do all in my power to aid the Government of the United States in maintaining the supremacy of the laws against all resistance to them, come from what quarter it might."

If Lincoln were elected, it would all be the fault of the "secessionists" backing Breckinridge, who are splitting the Democrats, Douglas charged. Now, he said, they were asking him, in case of a Lincoln victory, "if I will help them to dissolve the Union ... I tell them, No, never on earth!"

Douglas kept hammering away on the same theme in Raleigh, N.C., Petersburg, and Richmond. When he reached the Virginia capital, where Bell supporters helped to swell the crowd, the Little Giant was thus described by an eyewitness: "He was roughly dressed, his enormous head being covered by an old slouch hat, and his general appearance more like that of a weary, war-worn backwoods traveler, seeking repose from the toil and the dust of the road, than like that of a distinguished statesman. ... He was very hoarse and seemed to suffer much in speaking."

Douglas won praises in the North for boldly invading the slavery kingdom—which Lincoln refused to do—but he wiped out the last hope of carrying any states in the Deep South, where his Norfolk speech touched off a firestorm of denunciation.

"This man calls himself a Democrat!" cried the *Charleston Mercury*. "He is a regular old John Adams Federalist and consolidationist. He is a faithful disciple of John Brown, who inaugurated the policy of force, to rule the South."

"It is the culmination of his treachery and of his alliance with the Black Republican party," thundered the *Natchez Mississippian*.

The *Richmond Enquirer* printed a sizzling letter signed by forty prominent Southern men who interpreted Douglas's remarks as offering to help President Lincoln in subduing the Southern states if they should secede. Judge Douglas, they said, is "volunteering his aid to wage war upon our people and to slay them in battle as rebels, or hang then in cold blood as traitors, if they shall render obedience to state rather than federal authority."

Isaac Stevens, chairman of the pro-Breckinridge National Democratic Executive Committee, charged that Douglas was traipsing around the country like a "traveling mountebank," and that he was in cahoots with the Republicans in the North and the Bell forces in the South.

In September, the returns from the state elections in Maine and Vermont proved the futility of Douglas's barnstorming in New England. Maine elected a Republican governor by an 18,000-vote margin, and Vermont did the same by a majority of 22,000.

Douglas and his running mate, Herschel V. Johnson of Georgia, spoke to thirty thousand at a "grand political carnival and ox roast" on September 12 at Jones Wood outside New York City. A crowd of freeloaders came early and ran off with most of the barbecued meat, leaving many loyal Democrats hungry.

Douglas fed them the raw meat of his oratory, denouncing secessionists as traitors and declaring: "There is no excuse, no pretext whatever, for secession."

If Lincoln is elected, he must be inaugurated, he said. But if Lincoln should "make war on the rights and interests of any section of the confederacy, I will aid ... in hanging him higher than Virginia hanged John Brown."

"There's plenty of rope in New York for them traitors," shouted a voice in the crowd and others chimed in: "Go it, Little Giant! Go it, Doug!"

At the beginning of his long speaking tour, Douglas had tried to disguise his political campaigning by saying he longed to see his dear old mother again and he would visit her soon in upstate New York. As the weeks went by, and he wandered over New England, Pennsylvania, and the upper South, Republican newspapers jeered him and the Republicans printed handbills, signed "S. D.'s Mother," pleading for news about her wandering boy. This was a sample handbill:

A BOY LOST!

Left Washington, D.C., some time in July, to go home to his mother. He has not yet reached his mother, who is very anxious about him. He has been seen in Philadelphia, New York City, Hartford, Conn., at a clambake in Rhode Island. He has been heard from at Boston, Portland, Augusta, and Bangor, Me.

He is about five feet nothing in height and about the same in diameter the other way. He has a red face, short legs, and a large

Former Governor Herschel V. Johnson of Georgia, the
running mate of Senator Stephen A. Douglas of Illinois,
presidential standard bearer of the Northern
Democrats. From the collections of the Library of Congress.

belly. Answers to the name of Little Giant, talks a great deal, very loud, always about himself. Has an idea that he is a candidate for President.

At long last, on September 15, the Little Giant and his lovely Adele arrived at Clifton Springs, near Canandaigua, New York, and in a carriage drawn by six horses rode to the residence of his patient, loving mother for a reunion. Later in the day, while addressing fifteen to twenty thousand people in a grove opposite the Clifton Springs Hotel, Douglas expressed pleasure that he could relieve the anxiety of his Republican friends by announcing that he had finally found his mother.

"The old lady, God bless her, was in fine health," one newspaperman reported, "and in no wise annoyed by the comments of the partisan press."

When Douglas spoke in Ohio in the early autumn, Artemus Ward of the *Cleveland Plain Dealer* skewered him with his own peculiar brand of spelling. "Mister editor," the humorist began:

> I seez my quil to inform the public, through the medium of your column, of the great addishun I have gest made 2 mi grate metropolitician sho bizness and darin slak rope & gymnastic Sirkus. Last nite I had an intervu with Stephen A. Duglas, the renounced politikal ambidexter & proprioter and Cheef Kloun of the grate popler sovrenty show. Mr. Duglas is generally kald the littil jiant from his havin performed the grate feet of walking the whole length of Mason's and Dixon's close line, the dred scot decisshun in one hand and his hole popler suvrenty sho in the other.

Pursuing his own wicked brand of humor, Ward went on:

> Says I, how do yu like the sho business?
> Sez he, it don't pa.
> Sez I, Douglas, whattle yu tak for your popsovrenty?
> Sez he, ile sel it cheep.
> I tole him I diddint no how to manig his tricks; but I wood go into partnership with him in the sho business.
> Sez he, its a bargain.
> I then axt him what he thaut of takin along some darkies 2 sing songs and dans the hornpipe.
> Sez he, I wont have ennything to do with the nigger bizness agin; it don't pa.
> He sed he went into the nigger bizness in 1854 and had bin goin down hil ever since; he said it had nerly rooined him. ...
> One of Abe Lincoln's rales was next browt in and duglas was set on it and rode out thru the oak dors. Duglas is about 5 fet hi and a thunderin grate man for wun for his size.
> I maid a frenological examination of him. He is a man of tremendous power. ... His bump of humbuggin is as big as a goos eg.

Douglas campaigned in Ohio's major cities—Cleveland, Columbus, Cincinnati—but at the risk of further damaging his throat. He kept a supply of lemons on hand and, as his voice diminished to a croak, he would squeeze a lemon and pour its juice down his throat.

Despite his exhaustion, he addressed a large crowd at Indianapolis and thirty thousand at Louisville before going home to Chicago to rest and to rally his followers for a final effort to save Illinois from Lincoln.

Douglas was barnstorming in Iowa when he received telegrams informing him that the Republicans had swept both Indiana and Pennsylvania in the state elections of October 9, virtually assuring Lincoln's election. The winners were the two candidates for governor who had helped to clinch Lincoln's nomination at Chicago by swearing that he, and not Senator Seward, would enable them to triumph: Andrew G. Curtin carried Pennsylvania by a 32,000 majority; Henry S. Lane won Indiana by a margin of 9,759.

"Mr. Lincoln is the next president," Douglas commented to his secretary. "We must try to save the Union. I will go South."

While Douglas roamed all over the land—the first presidential candidate to indulge in such an exhausting tour—Lincoln remained quietly at home in Springfield. He followed the traditional policy, which required that the candidate must be surprised to find himself chosen by his party for high office and then must modestly remain above the undignified hurly-burly of dirty politics. He did keep in close touch with Republican leaders in such major states as New York and Pennsylvania, sometimes offering private advice about individuals or factions to be kept safely within the fold of the party, which was a coalition of all sorts of elements. Meanwhile, Republican speakers by the score stumped for the ticket in rallies before large crowds, everywhere except the South, where it was deemed unsafe for a "Black Republican" to venture, lest he be roughed up or worse.

Youthful marchers, called "Wide-Awakes," carrying torches and wearing oilcloth capes to shield themselves from the drippings, marched in the Northern city streets and drummed up a tremendous amount of enthusiasm for the Republican ticket. One moonlit night in October, a *Times* reporter wrote a rapturous description of a colorful, "Wide-Awake" parade in New York City.

Here are some samples of his enthusiastic account:

We observe Fourteenth Street solidly paved with flaming torches. Turning round towards the North river, a similar magnificent spectacle ... a long line of flaming light moving down Fifth Avenue, thus forming a fiery cross at the intersection. ... The whole of this stately avenue, with its solid brown-stone fronts, plate glass windows and blinds of polished woods, is illuminated by the artificial daylight of more than ten thousand torches. Solid and steadfast men ... of many states are ranged here under their respective banners, all dressed in shiny capes and caps, all bearing flaming torches. ...

Wheeling into the Washington Parade ground at the foot of Fifth Avenue, fresh discharges of grand fireworks take place. ... Roman candles, whizzing rockets, blazing blue lights and effervescent rosy effulgences.

The reporter for the *Times,* a strong advocate of Lincoln, observed that the Republicans, marching on the streets of Democratic New York, were bound to encounter some hostility from their political rivals in the crowds. "One company, while giving cheers in front of the Tribune, provoked a retort of groans from a crowd of Douglas Democrats, who had assembled on the steps of Tammany Hall. ...

"One young friend of Douglas called for cheers for the Little Giant and repeatedly shouted in the face of the younger members of the Wide-Awakes:

'Here's another boy voter.'

'Have you got a vote, bub?'"

The reporter also heard various "brutal, blasphemous, ribald, and obscene remarks ... too strong for publication."

At the Lafarge House, the proprietor was "strongly Democratic and the guests mostly of the Southern stripe," so there were a few exchanges of insults. "One Georgian lamented that he did not have his rifle with him. He said it would afford him especially to pick off the leaders of battalions singly—one portly captain in particular. He would experience grim satisfaction in perforating his abdomen with a leaden bullet. He inclined to regard the 'Wide Awakes' as an organization designed to coerce the South into obedience and quell the first rising symptoms of rebellion."

At the Metropolitan Hotel one Southerner said, "As for that cuss, Hamlin, he has nigger blood in him, and everybody knows it."

At the St. Nicholas Hotel, another Georgian accosted the procession, saying: "You're a pretty lot of suckers. ... You can shoulder your lamps now, but we'll make you shoulder muskets before next Spring. How would you like that? Do you think you can fight, eh?"

A bystander broke in: "My friend, for God's sake, shut up."

Senator Hannibal Hamlin of Maine, the Republican candidate running with Abraham Lincoln. From the collections of the Library of Congress.

"No, siree, I don't shut up," replied the Georgian. "I'm in a free country and shall speak what I like."

Bystander: "You *are* in a free country because you are not in Georgia."

The argument ended without a fight. One man told the "Wide-Awakes" they were good boys and had better go right home now and let their "mammies" put them to bed.

A footnote: The police had expected many pickpockets would be busy, working the vast crowd of spectators. Usually, there would be at least fifty on such an occasion, but on this night no more than seven "well known rogues" were found, and none was caught in the act. The suspects were just pulled in "to keep them from temptation" and, when the procession ended, after midnight, they were all set free.

❧ 8 ❧

LINCOLN AND
REPUBLICANS TRIUMPH

The Republicans' victories in the October elections—a clear portent of a Lincoln victory in November—shattered conservative Southerners' last hope of keeping an antislavery administration from seizing power in Washington; and a doleful chorus of prophecies arose from the press.

"All hope for a speedy arousal of the boasted conservatism of the North is well-nigh vanished," said the Columbia, South Carolina, *Guardian*. "It is powerless to stop the rushing tide of aggressive fanaticism."

The *Atlanta Locomotive* interpreted the October election results as showing that "Abe Lincoln must be our next President." But, it added, "the true inhabitants of the South ... have written upon their hearts with clenched teeth: Abe Lincoln, so help us Heaven, shall never be *our* President!"

"We believe now that the Union will be dissolved if Lincoln is elected," said the Columbus, Georgia, *Cornerstone*. It called for South Carolina, Alabama, or Mississippi to lead the secession parade and promised that Georgia would follow.

"If a financial pressure of continuous and general character follows the election of Lincoln, the days of the Union are not only numbered but they will be very few," said the *Richmond Examiner*.

All through the unusually hot, dry summer, the South had seethed with reports of towns being burned in Texas, and slave insurrections plotted by abolitionists there and in other states. The *Houston Telegraph* reported the burning of Dallas and the discovery of "a diabolical plot" to devastate North Texas. "Our jail is filled with the villains, many of whom will be hung, and that right soon," the paper said.

An 1860 Republican campaign banner for the Lincoln-Hamlin ticket. Note that Lincoln's first name is misspelled, "Abram." From the collections of the Library of Congress.

Texas Congressman John H. Reagan, who had good reason to have firsthand knowledge of events in his own back yard, said: "There now lie in ashes near a dozen towns and villages in my district."

Reagan, who was not a "fire-eater," blamed certain members of "the Methodist church, North" for advocating abolition and organizing a society called "The Mystic Red." "Under its auspices, the night before the last August election, the towns were to be burned and the people murdered," he told the House. The poisonings "were only arrested by information which came to light before the plan could be carried into execution."

In South Carolina, the former Speaker of the U.S. House of Representatives, James Orr, who was also a moderate Democrat, joined in sounding the alarm about the horrible future. In Texas, he said, "the incendiary torch of the slaves, lighted by abolition traitors, has reduced to ashes one million dollars' worth of property, and the timely discovery of the hellish scheme alone saved the lives of thousands of men, women, and children."

Orr predicted that Lincoln and Hamlin would be elected and, therefore, "the honor and safety of the South will require the prompt secession of the slaveholding states."

To South Carolinians, the awful prospect of Lincoln as President was even surpassed by the idea of Hamlin as vice-president, because the *Charleston Mercury* editor, R. Barnwell Rhett, told them that Hamlin was a "mulatto."

Hamlin, it was true, had a swarthy face; a schoolmate remembered him as being "as tall, straight, supple and dark as a young Indian." Colleagues in Congress nicknamed the gentleman from Maine "that black Penobscot Indian" and "the old Carthaginian." A New Yorker, upon meeting Hamlin, remarked: "His complexion is so swarthy that I cannot wonder at the demented South for believing him a mulatto."

Among the race-conscious South Carolinians, a secret organization of "Minutemen" was formed, its recruits including some members of the legislature and sundry "fire-eaters." Each man paid a one-dollar initiation fee and promised to stand ready, with a rifle and a revolver loaded, "and be prepared to march to Washington at a moment's notice, to block Lincoln's inauguration."

The *New York Times* editorially denounced a reported scheme for an army of "restless and idle vagabonds" from Dixie "to tramp into Washington, murder Mr. Lincoln, turn Congress out of doors, plunder the treasury and put an end to the United States." A hot-headed Virginia Congressman, Roger Pryor, "has publicly announced his willingness to play the part of an assassin," the *Times* observed—this

*Edward Everett of Massachusetts, the vice-
presidential nominee of the Constitutional
Union party, which chose former Senator John
Bell of Tennessee for the presidency. From the
collections of the Library of Congress.*

was four years before John Wilkes Booth carried out the insane idea—
and Pryor's boast brought forth jeers from Unionists in his own state.

John Minor Botts, a strongly antisecessionist Whig ex-Congress-
man, excoriated the disunionists in a speech at a Bell-Everett rally in
Richmond. "His scathing ridicule of Mr. Pryor and his threat to play
Brutus," said one newsman, "brought down the house."

A former Virginia governor, Henry A. Wise, also prattled about
the notion of leading an army into Washington and preventing
Lincoln's inauguration. In reply, the sharp-tongued Pennsylvania
Congressman Thad Stevens told a Republican audience in New York
City: "Governor Wise and his co-workers will not take possession of
the Capitol and prevent the inauguration. If they tried that, the calm,
brave Lincoln would split them like a rail. (Applause and laughter.)"

Senator Douglas confided to friends his firm conviction that some
southern "fire-eaters" were involved in a deep conspiracy to carry out a

coup d'état, which would place Breckinridge in the White House. That was why Douglas barnstormed across Virginia, Maryland, North Carolina, and elsewhere, denouncing Breckinridge's followers as "disunionists" and working openly with the pro-Union Whigs in the Upper South particularly, to throw their electoral votes to the Bell-Everett ticket.

Every slave state that could be carried by either Bell or Douglas would frustrate the Buchanan-Ultra scheme to have Breckinridge carry all fifteen of those states, plus California and Oregon, where their friends controlled the Democratic Party machinery. Such a victory would give him seventeen states—a majority of the thirty-three. If Douglas would pick up enough Northern states to keep Lincoln from a clear triumph, the election would be thrown into the House. There Breckinridge could claim a majority of the states and the presidency.

If their plans should go awry, the plotters backing Breckinridge had another, more daring, alternative, according to the story that Douglas told his old Whig friend from Illinois, Orville Browning, who was destined to succeed him in the Senate. It might have explained why the bolters at Baltimore chose the youthful vice-president as their standard-bearer. The key was the fact that the vice-president would move into the presidency at once if the office should, for any reason, become vacant.

Douglas relayed to Browning his absolute conviction that there was a secret deal involving Buchanan, Jefferson Davis, and Bob Toombs and others whereby, if Breckinridge ran as well as they hoped, Buchanan would resign immediately after the election and turn the presidency over to Breckinridge. It would all be legal because the young Kentuckian was vice-president. Then Breckinridge would control the army and navy as the new commander-in-chief.

Breckinridge would "seize upon the government and complete the revolution by deposing Lincoln or rather by preventing his inauguration," Browning confided to his diary. "Douglas says he *knows* this to be a *fact*."

Douglas confided his concerns about the possible coup d'état to Charles Francis Adams, a Republican Congressman from Massachusetts, who recorded them in his diary. Adams, the son and grandson of presidents, shared Douglas's alarm and believed the disunion plots were real.

A Washington dispatch to the *Philadelphia Press* gave credence to the Douglas story. "The plan of the seceders," it said, "is to make Breckinridge President at all hazards—i.e., if not of the whole United States at least of a southern Republic. Mr. Buchanan is initiated in that movement and he is to make over to Mr. Breckinridge the public archives, Treasury, buildings, army and navy ... for the seceders still hope to carry all the slave states next November."

A *New York Times* correspondent reported in late October that the seceders planned to have their state legislatures meet immediately after Lincoln's election, "declare the Union dissolved and proclaim Mr. Breckinridge President." The scheme, it said, "has its headquarters in the Treasury Department."

Under the headline, "Treason at Washington," the *Louisville Journal* said "a former judge and Congressman," a high treasury official very close to Secretary Howell Cobb, was instigating this plot. Its description of the unnamed "subaltern" precisely fitted one man: Junius Hillyer, fifty-three, a Georgian like Cobb, a circuit judge, 1841–1845, a Congressman 1851–1855, a Democrat, and solicitor of the U.S. Treasury under Cobb, 1857–1861.

R. J. Lackey, a treasury employee who would have been termed, in a later era, "a whistle-blower," told the press that Judge Hillyer "is a rampant fire-eater, and if not for smashing things up generally, goes in at least for armed resistance to Lincoln, if elected." Lackey said he was "shocked" when he heard the good judge expressing such treasonous views, and said so. Soon, Lackey was fired.

Actually, in the golden days of Indian summer, preparations laying the groundwork for a new Southern confederacy were under way. South Carolina's Governor William H. Gist sent letters on October 5 to all of the slave-state governors except Sam Houston of Texas, who was pro-Union. Gist asked their advice about the next move they should make after Lincoln's election. His brother, General States Rights Gist, delivered the letters and listened to the governors' views.

Governor Gist also called the South Carolina legislature into a special session, to begin November 5, to name electors and to act "if deemed advisable for the safety and protection of the state." On October 25, most of the South Carolina congressmen, along with Governor Gist, ex-Speaker Orr, and former Governor Adams, met with U.S. Senator

James Henry Hammond in the magnificent new manor house on his plantation, "Redcliffe," near the Savannah River. They agreed that secession must follow Lincoln's victory. Hammond preferred that Georgia or some other state should take the lead; but, if necessary, little South Carolina would go out first and challenge the others to follow.

Warnings about the certain secession of some Southern states caused panic among New York investors and merchants having a multimillion-dollar interest in the Southern trade. Treasury Secretary Cobb came to Manhattan for the sale of some government bonds and said the bonds would become worthless if the Union should be broken up as a result of a Lincoln triumph. Stock prices slumped in late October, causing the diarist George Templeton Strong to observe that, if the panic had happened sooner, it might have affected the election, "for comparatively few Republicans love niggers enough to sacrifice investments for their sweet sake."

The fears of financial disaster resulting from a Lincoln victory stimulated one last desperate effort to carry New York State for a "Fusion" ticket, cobbled together by the two Democratic factions and the Bell-Everett forces. They offered a slate of electors representing all three, with some private understandings that the thirty-five electoral votes would be thrown to whichever candidate had a chance of winning.

Former Governor Washington Hunt explained the crisis succinctly to Senator John J. Crittenden in asking the old Kentucky Whig to come in and help the Fusionists. "The presidential problem," Hunt wrote, "is reduced to a single point: If the vote of this state can be turned against Lincoln and Hamlin, they are defeated; otherwise, in all human probability, they will be elected. It is *the* battleground—the turning point in the campaign. ... The Republicans are alarmed and very ferocious towards me personally, but I meet them in the spirit of knightly defiance."

Douglas himself did nothing to encourage Fusion. He hoped to carry New York on his own. He was quoted as saying: "By God, sir, the election shall never go into the House. Before it shall go into the House, I will throw it to Lincoln." Douglas's followers in New York fought on, however, for Fusion.

George Nicholas Sanders summoned the strong men of the state and of New York City to a strategy session, at which it was agreed to raise ample funds by appeals to the wealthy merchants, whipped into line by August Belmont.

Blithely ignoring the storm warnings from the South, the Republicans dismissed the threats of secession as merely some more of the same old "bluff" and "humbug" that had proved, in the past, to be political scare tactics. They ridiculed Douglas's denunciations of the disunionists as just gasconade to help the Democrats. They laughed at the "fire-eaters" who regularly threatened walkouts if thwarted in their demands.

"Every year the Southerners have been dissolving the Union and yet it is not dissolved," said Congressman John Sherman of Ohio in a typical Republican campaign speech. "If so harmless-looking an individual as myself had been chosen Speaker, they were going to dissolve the Union. If Abraham Lincoln is elected President, they will dissolve the Union, they say. These threats are as idle wind. ... We are going to elect Old Abe, and then let them try disunion."

Salmon P. Chase, addressing a Republican ox roast and clam bake on Long Island, October 24, laughed at the Democrats' desperate efforts to combine forces with the Bell-Everett people. "They are reduced to going about like a beggar," he jeered, "seeking the crumbs that fall from the rich man's table of the Bell and Everett party." Chase predicted that "peace" would follow the Republicans' triumph.

Haranguing the Republicans of Kings County, New York, October 29, Senator Benjamin Wade of Ohio said Douglas had been repudiated by the Democratic leaders of the Senate and had one lone defender left there, Senator Pugh of Ohio. "Did you ever see an old hen scratching around with one chicken?" Wade asked. "Douglas has but one chicken left and that chicken is Pugh." "Douglas thought himself alive," his old foe said, "but politically he was dead."

The Democrats' hopes that Senator Seward's friends would be lukewarm in support of Lincoln proved wrong. Seward rallied his followers to turn out a big vote for the man who defeated him for the presidential nomination. Discarding his old talk about the "irrepressible conflict" between free and slave labor, he called for national harmony in the happy new Republican regime.

Lincoln himself viewed all the "disunion" talk in a most light-hearted way, as if totally unaware that the secessionists were much more than a disgruntled set of politicians soon to lose power. Don

Piatt, an Ohio newspaperman who visited him during the campaign, wrote: "He considered the movement south as a sort of political game of bluff, gotten up by politicians, and meant solely to frighten the North. He believed that, when the leaders saw their efforts in that direction unavailing, the tumult would subside." Piatt quoted Lincoln as telling him: "They won't give up the offices. Were it believed that vacant places could be had at the North Pole, the road there would be lined with dead Virginians."

Lincoln "could not be made to believe that the South meant secession and war," the journalist added. "When I told him ... that the Southern people were in dead earnest, meant war, and I doubted whether he would be inaugurated at Washington, he laughed and said the fall [in the price] of pork at Cincinnati had affected me."

Senator Douglas, who knew all too well that the leaders of the Deep South were planning secession in the event of a Lincoln victory, made one final swing through the region in hopes of reducing the vote for the "disunion" candidate, Breckinridge. He drew friendly crowds in Tennessee, Georgia, and even Alabama. But many Southerners distrusted him. Rotten eggs and tomatoes were hurled at him in Montgomery, but missed.

When Douglas and his beautiful Adele boarded a river steamboat to carry them to Selma, a huge crowd stormed onto the vessel, collapsing the upper deck and throwing the Douglases to the lower deck. The senator suffered a leg injury and was badly bruised; his wife was so shaken that she could not continue the trip.

On election night, the Little Giant and his secretary, James Sheridan, watched the telegraphed election returns in the *Register* office at Mobile with its loyal editor, John Forsyth. When the dispatches showed that Lincoln had crushed him throughout the North, while Douglas had lost every slave state except Missouri, the bad news did not come as a great surprise. Then the defeated campaigner and his secretary walked to their hotel, the Battle House. Sheridan said later that Douglas seemed "more hopeless than I had ever before seen him."

Abraham Lincoln spent most of the election day—Tuesday, November 6, 1860—in the governor's room of the State House in

Springfield, greeting visitors. In the afternoon he strolled to the court-house across the way and voted the straight Republican state and local ticket, tearing off the electors' names at the top so that he would not be voting for himself. Then he returned to the State House which, by nightfall, was packed with a crowd of excited Republicans, eagerly receiving the returns that pointed to their certain victory.

Later, in the nearby telegraph office, where bulletins were pouring in from everywhere, Lincoln read this wire from Senator Simon Cameron: "Pennsylvania 70,000 for you. New York safe. Glory enough."

Lincoln and several associates walked across to a nearby hall where the Republican women welcomed him to a long table loaded with food and cried out merrily: "How do you do, Mr. President?" Moments later, a messenger rushed in with a telegram confirming that Lincoln had carried New York—he would soon learn that his statewide majority was an amazing fifty thousand—and everyone rejoiced by joining in the campaign song: "Ain't you glad you joined the Repub-licans?/Joined the Republicans—joined the Republicans!"

The Republicans mobbing the State House were still cheering and laughing when Lincoln walked home and said: "Mary, we're elected."

The final returns showed that Lincoln had won 180 electoral votes, or 28 more than the 152 required to keep the election from being thrown into the House, while Breckinridge polled 72, Bell 39, and Douglas only 12.

Lincoln swept all the free states except for three votes in New Jersey that went to Douglas on a Fusion ticket. Douglas carried only Missouri's nine votes plus the three in New Jersey. Bell carried Ken-tucky, Tennessee and Virginia; Breckinridge swept all the rest of the slave states except Missouri.

In popular votes, Lincoln would be definitely a minority presi-dent, as his three opponents together piled up about a million more votes than he did. The precise totals are in doubt, but most authori-ties say they look like this: Lincoln, 1,866,452; Douglas, 1,376,957; Breckinridge, 850,082; and Bell, 588,879.

Douglas's large popular vote showed him to be the favorite of the Democratic masses in the North. But, despite his campaigning, which left him exhausted, he ran behind Lincoln all across the board, com-ing close only in their home state, Illinois. There, Lincoln polled about 50 percent; Douglas, 47 percent; Bell, 2 percent; and Breckinridge, 1 percent.

Lincoln thus earned a clear title to a majority of the electoral votes, as required by the Constitution, and he would be officially elected in February, assuming that the electors' ballots would be counted and accepted by Congress then. Nevertheless, he was the choice of only 39 percent of the voters, so it could not be said accurately that the American people had chosen him as their overwhelming favorite. In fact, many had never heard of him before his nomination and knew little about him. His managers kept him incommunicado in Springfield throughout the campaign and he purposely said virtually nothing.

Although his victory has been interpreted as a solemn decision by the American public to place slavery within bounds and on the road to ultimate extinction, the truth is that Lincoln's past comments in that vein were deliberately played down by the Republicans in their efforts to paint him as an old-fashioned Henry Clay Whig and thus pick up the votes of the Whig-Americans so vital to his success in such doubtful states as Pennsylvania, Indiana, and Illinois.

They succeeded triumphantly in capturing those former strongholds of "the Democracy," and sweeping the North. But Lincoln polled only a few thousand votes in the South and not a single one in ten slave states.

To a great degree, Lincoln owed his victory to the Democratic Party's split and to voters' disgust with President Buchanan and his administration, which many considered narrowly partisan, incompetent, and corrupt.

August Belmont, the New York financier and chairman of the Democratic Party, or faction thereof loyal to Douglas, pleaded with Southern friends to realize that Lincoln's election really *did not* show "overwhelming anti-slavery feeling at the North." "We owe the election of Lincoln only to the misrule of the present administration and to the unfortunate dissensions in our own party," he wrote to John Forsyth, the *Mobile Register* editor.

Despite the Buchanan administration's treachery and a shortage of campaign funds, Belmont said, "we polled 317,000 votes in our state for the fusion ticket, 30,000 more than were ever given before by the united Democratic party," and, if they had carried New York State, Lincoln could not have won. He would have fallen short of the necessary 152 electoral votes, so the final decision would have been made by the House of Representatives.

"In a vote of 700,000, a change of 26,000 votes, less than four percent, would have given us the state," the Rothschilds' representative continued. "More than four percent were made up of men who voted for Lincoln because they were disgusted with the administration, while thousands and thousands were led into the mistake of voting with the Republicans ... because they knew that Lincoln was the only candidate who could be elected by the people, and considered that the greatest evil which would befall the country would be an election by the House. ...

"I meet daily with men who confess the error they have been led into and, almost with tears in their eyes, wish they could undo what they helped to do."

Another close friend of Douglas, Senator George Pugh of Ohio, also tried to assure the South that, contrary to its fears, most Northern people did not desire to abolish slavery in the states: "I do not believe that ninety-nine hundredths of the men who voted for Mr. Lincoln thought anything about the subject of slavery in the states, or had any policy on the subject. They were opposed to the introduction of slavery into the territories. They were in favor of a general division of the offices and the plunder."

Many Republicans wanted tariff protection for iron but "most of them were animated by a thorough hatred of the Democratic party," Pugh said, "not by any desire to interfere with the domestic institutions of the states."

Francis Granger, white-haired leader of the "Silver Gray" Whigs in New York State, said they would have helped a conservative Democrat to carry the state. If the Democrats had not split, and if they had nominated such a "good conservative Democrat, there were seventy-five thousand good Old Line Whigs who would have buckled on their armor and would have won the battle for him," said Granger, who had been the Whigs' unsuccessful candidate for the vice-presidency in 1836.

This was an echo of the New York Democrats' plan to name Horatio Seymour for the presidency, in the belief that he could have combined New York's 35 electoral votes with 120 from the South and beaten Lincoln.

But those 75,000 Old Line Whigs could not support their old foe, Douglas, or Breckinridge, so some voted for John Bell and most of them backed Lincoln.

Lincoln's victory gave the secessionists exactly the excuse they needed to stampede their people into secession. It also marked the end of the Democrats' long domination of the federal government, an era that had begun with Andrew Jackson's inauguration in 1829. The "Democracy" had reigned in the White House except for the two brief periods marked by the Whigs' election of two military heroes, William Henry Harrison in 1840 and Zachary Taylor in 1848. Both died in office.

James Buchanan might linger on, like a ghost, in the White House until March 4, and then the Republicans would usher in their new era with their promises of reform and peace.

❧ 9 ❧

A Golden Dream
of Empire

"Lincoln elected. Hooray!"

That was George Templeton Strong's reaction when the New York diarist heard the news of the Republicans' sweeping triumph.

"Hooray!" could also sum up, in a single word, the response of the secessionists in the Deep South. They had been counting on a Lincoln victory to frighten their timid friends into joining them in leaping into the great unknown, secession.

In South Carolina especially, those who had been making the direst predictions of ruin to result from the Black Republicans' antislavery rule rejoiced that at last it was really coming, so the South must escape it by pulling out of the Union. Crowds of delighted secessionists roamed through Charleston's streets, the palmetto flag floated above the *Mercury's* newspaper office, while the people cheered the news that Federal Judge A. G. Magrath and Collector W. F. Colcock had resigned. Both U.S. Senators, James Chesnut and James Hammond, gave up their seats and Hammond commented: "I thought Magrath and all those fellows were great asses for resigning and have done it myself. People are wild. The scenes of the French Revolution are being enacted already."

Fire-eating Congressman Laurence Keitt, in response to a midnight serenade by a crowd in South Carolina's capital, Columbia, declared that President Buchanan "was pledged to secession and would be held to it." Keitt's claim was received in Washington with great astonishment, because the President had not made such a pledge in any public statement. But Keitt knew that Buchanan was the virtual captive of the Southern Democrats who were his closest friends and advisers.

At a long cabinet meeting on November 9, Buchanan conceded that South Carolina seemed determined to secede and he stressed that she would be let alone by the present administration. He was quoted in the press as saying that "it would be madness to attempt coercion, as the slightest collision would disrupt the whole country, and involve us in irretrievable ruin."

He suggested calling a convention of the states to consider some way of compromising the issues fueling the Southerners' concern. However, the cabinet was divided about the idea and he did little to pursue it.

The next day, Buchanan read to the cabinet the first draft of a state paper in which he proposed to ask the South to submit to Lincoln's election. He warned against secession and even hinted at the use of force to prevent disunion. This apparent relapse into his old Federalism touched off a violent debate between the two factions—the Unionists (Cass, Black, Toucey, and Holt) praised the paper while the Southerners (Floyd, Cobb, and Thompson) strongly disagreed.

Cobb and Thompson telegraphed Jefferson Davis, who was in Mississippi, and implored him to hasten to Washington and bring Old Buck back under control.

When the telegram came, Davis was meeting in Jackson, the state capital, with others of the Mississippi congressional delegation and Governor J. J. Pettus. They were debating whether or not Mississippi should secede soon after South Carolina. Davis, while upholding the state's legal right to secede, argued that secession would lead to war. From his firsthand experience as a soldier in the Mexican war, and his four years as secretary of war, the senator had no illusions about a quick and easy victory on the battlefield.

"My associates considered me 'too slow,'" he later said, "and they were probably right."

Poor, old bewildered Buchanan relied heavily upon the friendship and counsel of the strong-minded Southerners who dominated his administration—especially Davis, Slidell, and others in the Democratic Senate. He shared their belief that the Founding Fathers had created a union of friendly states, which could be held together only by fraternal ties, never by force. So Davis, hurrying back to his side, was able to tone down the Federalist cast of the draft message.

Some of Buchanan's friends in Pennsylvania also agreed that the Constitution was a compact of equal states, and the federal government was their agent, not their master. Judge George W. Woodward of the state supreme court wrote to Attorney General Black on November 18 that he could not, in justice, condemn the South for withdrawing from the Union if it no longer protected its rights. He would let the Southern states go in peace and said: "I wish Pennsylvania could go with them."

Even Horace Greeley, the abolitionist editor of the *New York Tribune*, wrote: "If the Cotton States should decide that they can do better out of the Union than in it, we insist on letting them go in peace. ... We shall resist all coercive measures designed to keep it in. We hope never to live in a republic, whereof one section is pinned to the residue by bayonets." Greeley would later change his tune and back Lincoln's policy of using bayonets.

In view of South Carolina's imminent secession, Buchanan worried about the safety of the three federal forts in Charleston harbor: Sumter, Moultrie, and Castle Pinckney. He summoned Secretary of War Floyd and said, according to one version of the interview: "I would rather be at the bottom of the Potomac tomorrow than that those forts would be taken by South Carolina in consequence of our neglect to put them in a defensible position. It will destroy me, sir; and if that thing occurs, it will cover your name—and it is an honorable name, sir—with an infamy that all time can never efface."

"Sir," Floyd replied, "I would risk my life and my honor that South Carolina will not molest the forts." He said Governor Gist had assured him that everything would stay quiet "if no more soldiers or munitions are sent on."

Major Robert Anderson, the commander of the federal forces at Charleston, became alarmed by the swarms of state troops drilling in the city streets and boasting of their intention to attack. He telegraphed Washington for more troops and guns, but Floyd refused them and Buchanan went along, trusting the promises by Governor Gist.

South Carolina's legislature called a secession convention to open on December 17. In quick succession, Alabama, Mississippi, Georgia, and Florida also arranged for similar sessions. "South Carolina will certainly secede," Senator Hammond informed a committee of

Georgians. "She will ... go out, high and dry, forever. If Georgia will back her, there will be little or no trouble."

Fear provided the strongest emotional motive behind the average Southerner's acceptance of secession—fear that the agents of the Lincoln administration would stir up sentiment for abolition, take away the white man's sense of superiority over the Negro, and cause the ultimate nightmare, slave insurrections.

A Tennessee man wrote to a New York newspaper that the true source of the intense agitation among the people "is the mortal dread of negro insurrection." "Should it be temporarily successful, is there a single Northern man or woman who would not shudder at the scenes that would ensue?" he asked. "The murder of innocent women and children and the butchery of men."

In Alabama, a few white men and several blacks were arrested and charged with plotting a slave uprising during the Christmas holidays, and some were executed.

"My wife and children are almost crazy from fright at the hourly prospect of a negro rising, which some of the executed men (negro and white) confirmed would take place about Christmas," a Union man wrote to friends in the North. "Life is worth nothing and I can only compare our situation to the Reign of Terror in the first French Revolution."

A traveler in Kentucky, Tennessee, and Georgia reported in the Northern press: "No citizen not from a slave holding state is safe now in the South. The people are, to a certain extent, mad upon the slavery question and the recent election of the Republican nominee."

The traveler said that, when he encountered a band of Georgians sporting the blue cockade of secession in their hats, "someone pointed at me and asked, 'Who is that?'

"A man answered by telling him my name and place of residence, New York City. One of the other blue cockades thereupon growled out: 'There, what did I tell you? *I knew* he was a *damned* Yankee!'"

"The negroes have already heard of Lincoln's election and they have heard also that he is for giving them their liberty," a South Carolina woman wrote to a relative in New York. Trembling with fear of an insurrection, she went on:

Not a night passes that we do not securely lock our field servants in their quarters. Our most loved and valued house servants, who in ordinary times we would trust to any extent, are watched and guarded against. ...

You have heard that our servants all love their masters' families and would lay down their lives for them—that the colored race in the South prefers slavery to freedom. ... The reality consists in sleeping on our arms at night, in doubly bolting and barring our doors; in maintaining an effective patrol force; in buying watchdogs and in taking turns watching our sleeping children to guard them and ourselves from the vengeance of these same "loving" servants.

The secessionists exploited these fears so successfully that their opponents—mostly Old Line Whigs—despaired of heading off the mass stampede out of the Union. Former Senator Jere Clemens of Alabama lamented in a letter to Senator John J. Crittenden, Kentucky Unionist, November 24:

"There is not a shadow of a doubt that, if the election was held tomorrow, more than two-thirds of the members elected would be for immediate secession. *Time* is everything to us, and if we fail to gain that, we are lost. ... My plan is to urge a consultation of all the Southern states, and I hope in that way not only to prevent immediate secession but that a remedy may be found for the Northern disregard of constitutional obligations, which is disgraceful to them and dangerous to our peace."

Foes of disunion in Georgia, led by Alexander H. Stephens, also stalled for time and called for a convention of the states rather than separate state action. The secessionists shied away from that trap, fearing that it would lead only to endless talk, the Southerners being masters of that.

Those demanding quick action ran into stubborn opposition in the Upper South, where there were fewer slaves and more loyalty to the old Union. In North Carolina, Governor John Ellis personally favored secession but his people held back from jumping off the cliff. Another prominent Democrat, W. W. Holden, appealed to state pride and jealousy when he pleaded to the readers of his Raleigh newspaper, the *Standard*:

"Will you be the tail to the chivalry kite of South Carolina? What allegiance do you owe to a people who rejoiced over Lincoln's election, because it gave them a fancied pretext for consummating their long-cherished schemes of disunion and placed in their hands, as they claim, the power to drag you into the same vortex of ruin into which they are madly rushing?"

While fears of slave uprisings caused the masses in the Deep South to favor secession, the leaders of the oligarchy who controlled the region's politics were impelled by a different motive not shared by the common people: They dreamed of creating a grand "Empire of the Golden Circle," embracing the cotton kingdom and annexing Cuba, several states in Mexico, and Central America. This vision enraptured the men who determined the Democratic Party's foreign policies throughout the 1850s, an age of territorial expansion.

The election of President James K. Polk, a Tennessee politician and native of North Carolina, led directly to U.S. annexation of Texas in 1845. Then Polk carried the nation through the successful war against Mexico and, as a result of the 1848 victory, the United States acquired California and another large slice of Mexico now embracing Arizona and New Mexico. Almost immediately, the discovery of gold in California touched off the great gold rush, and California—much to the disappointment of the Southerners—came in as a free state through the Compromise of 1850.

In the 1850s, there were repeated efforts to take Cuba away from Spain, through filibustering forays and diplomatic pressure on Madrid. Louisiana's two senators, Slidell and Benjamin, were among the most ardent advocates of acquiring the island called "the Pearl of the Antilles." They warned that Spain, backed by Great Britain, might soon create a free Negro colony there—a second "Haiti" off the Florida coast—and spread the abolition fever to the United States.

The crafty Slidell sought a little help from his nephew, August Belmont, Pierce's minister to The Hague. The financier was to persuade the chief holders of Spanish bonds to induce Madrid to sell Cuba to the United States for as much as $120 million and thus increase the value of the bonds.

Then came the Ostend Manifesto, in which the United States proposed to buy Cuba or, if Spain refused, to simply seize it. The bad publicity about the manifesto signaled the end of Slidell's clever maneuvers. Next, he moved in the Senate to get $30 million as a down payment for Cuba and to arm President Buchanan with new powers to carry out the scheme.

The "thirty million dollar men," reported J. S. Pike of the *New York Tribune*, "want to get both sword and purse into their hands. If they would succeed, their filibustering folly might involve the country in a scrape ... a general war."

"Mr. Buchanan is Cuba-crazy," Pike added, "and John Slidell ... is one of the most reckless of men." Their Cuba scheme was blocked in the Senate in 1859.

In another visionary enterprise, Senator Benjamin headed a syndicate of investors proposing to build a railroad across the Isthmus of Tehuantepec in Mexico. Such a line could greatly speed traffic and communications to California, booming in the wake of the gold rush, and give the port of New Orleans access to the Pacific and the beckoning trade of the Orient.

As president, Buchanan aided Benjamin's railroad project but it ran into delays, caused by political upheavals in Mexico. But its promoters refused to give up. Congressman John J. Perry, a Maine Republican, charged in a House speech on May 29, 1860, that Buchanan planned to set up "temporary military posts" in the Mexican states of Sonora and Chihuahua, ostensibly to protect American citizens and their interests. Buchanan also asked Congress to let him use U.S. naval forces to defend "the lives and property of American citizens passing in transit across the Panama, Nicaragua, and Tehuantepec routes against sudden lawless outbreaks and depredations."

"This means war upon Central America," Perry warned. "The old Ostend Chief," he said, also wants more millions for buying Cuba and "his goal is the annexation of Cuba, Mexico and Central America."

"The President has not only been intriguing for Cuba, but his paid emissaries have been plotting with Juarez for Sonora, Chihuahua, and Lower California in Mexico," the Congressman warned. He said any deal with Juarez, the leader of one faction in Mexico's never-ending civil strife, would be denounced by Miramon, who controlled Mexico City, and that could lead to another war.

The men promoting the idea of the great new "Southern Republic," said Perry, would logically follow a scenario like this: "Purchase Cuba, make the Federal government pay for it, go down into Mexico with the filibustering schemes and plots of James Buchanan and his party, under the false pretense of bringing peace to a distracted people; then declare 'war exists by act of Mexico,' go into a fight, seize Chihuahua, Sonora, and some half a dozen other states ... then overrun Mexico and Central America with slavery, until you have Cuba and some half-dozen new slave states."

Congressman Perry talked like a man who had been reading the minds of Senator Slidell and the others scheming for the expansion of the United States into fresh new territory to the South, where the soil would provide fertile fields for cotton, rice, and sugar. Their dreams of acquiring the lands in the "Golden Crescent" provide a key to the Southern Democrats' demand for federal protection of slavery in all the territories. They were not fighting for the right to take slaves into the prairies and the mountains of the West, hardly the places to raise lots of cotton; they intended to acquire more slave states farther south.

If they could have maintained their power in the Union, through something like the Breckinridge platform, most of the Southern leaders would have preferred to keep their states in the Union rather than taking the riskier course of setting up a separate new confederacy. They needed some new slave states, however, to maintain their control of the Senate.

Already, in 1860, the free states had an eighteen to fifteen edge over the slave states. The Southerners still controlled the Senate with the help of sympathetic Democrats from California, Oregon, Indiana, Minnesota, Pennsylvania, and New Jersey. But as the Republicans gained control of more state legislatures, which elected the senators, the antislavery senators were inevitably going to increase. Already marked for departure, after the 1860 elections, were pro-Southern Senators Gwin of California, Lane of Oregon, Fitch of Indiana, and Bigler of Pennsylvania.

The notion of bringing in more Democratic senators from new slave states in Cuba, Mexico, and Central America might seem like a pipe dream to critics of the scheme. But Texas and California had been parts of Mexico only fifteen years before and nobody seriously proposed giving them back to the Mexicans. Then, why not take the remainder of Mexico, along with Cuba and Central America?

The Republicans were frustrating these glorious plans by their negative votes in Congress. But a brand-new Southern confederacy would not have any Republicans. So the wonderful Empire of the Golden Circle seemed, to its sponsors, not so wild a dream.

"The secession movement is founded on reasons purely selfish," the *Louisville Democrat* charged.

> The principal men engaged in it … have cherished their purpose for a long time, and only seize this opportunity to carry it out—an opportunity they have made themselves. …
>
> The politicians think they can be more in a Southern Confederacy than they can in the Union. Others think their seaport towns will be the great marts of trade, which now goes principally to Northern ports. They think slave labor can be had cheaper, whilst the price of their great staple will be enhanced.
>
> They dream of getting Mexico and Cuba and Central America and building up a great southern confederacy. They have dwelt on this prospect until it is quite enchanting. … Charleston is to be the New York of the South and Louisville is to be a little frontier town.

❧ *10* ❧

Lincoln Keeps Cool

All the alarms about secession and civil war, all the marching and shouting of the "Minutemen" in the Southern cities, all the cries of merchants and speculators as the stock market dropped, had not the slightest effect upon the serenity of the President-elect as he received throngs of visitors at his office in Springfield as if he had not a worry in the world.

Newspaper reporters marveled at the way the tall, loose-limbed prairie lawyer mingled informally with the sturdy farmers who flocked to see him in the executive chamber of the State House. "These are men with rough clothes, who put up their muddy boots on the stove, roll up their pants, wear seedy hats, and are bronzed with toil in the open air—hard-fisted, sharp-featured, blunt-spoken men, who say 'Uncle Abe,' before they think of it, and then beg his pardon. ... He tells them to call him what they please," one newsman wrote.

> They find him the same jovial, pleasant, sociable, affable, story-telling companion, while they cannot but admire the remarkable shrewdness, the keen insight into human nature, and the active intellect which a moment's conversation is sure to develop.
>
> He has a pleasant word and smile for all, and his oldest friends say they do not see that he has given way one particle to the natural self-esteem which most men would develop under such circumstances. His facial distortions and animated gesticulations are the same as ever, and, although some may deem them undignified, all admit that they are expressive.

"Mr. Lincoln's faculty of remembering individuals is remarkable," another correspondent reported, in awe. "He is continually receiving visits from those whom he has not seen for years, and seems to recall readily the most unimportant details—the boundaries of farms, the peculiarities of maiden aunts, the hobbies of venerable farmers, all seen to have retained a place in his memory without having crowded out more important matters, and he patiently hears the latest news on these subjects, while he tosses about carelessly the huge ax and wedges which are strewn on his table, and which manufacturers have sent him in case he should ever take to rail-splitting again."

One sharp observer noted that, while Lincoln conversed freely on general topics, told jokes, and swapped tales with the old-timers, his mouth snapped shut whenever anyone brought up a timely topic, such as his policy in regard to secession, or his selection of his cabinet members.

Another correspondent found a clue to Lincoln's hush-mouthed caution in the way he played chess—not boldly but defensively, keeping his next move entirely to himself.

"He has a habit of whistling and singing all the time—his musical ability being limited to one tune. ... ' Dixie's Land,'" the reporter observed. "While playing chess Mr. Lincoln seems to be continually thinking of something else. Those who have played with him say he plays as if it were but a mechanical pastime to occupy his hands while his mind is busy with some other subject. ...

"He plays what chess-players call a 'safe game.' Rarely attacking, he is content to let his opponent attack while he concentrates all his energies in the defense—awaiting the opportunity of dashing in at a weak point or the expenditure of his adversary's strength."

Lincoln played "a safe game," also, in revealing very little about his probable choices for the cabinet. By indirection, he let the reporters surmise that high places would be given to William Henry Seward and Salmon Portland Chase, his most prominent rivals for the Republican presidential nomination that had fallen into his lap.

Lincoln brushed aside all the secession talk as just political "humbug." To one correspondent, he said he had received many assurances from the South that "in no probable event will there be any formidable effort to break up the Union." To another, he said he had no intention of interfering with slavery in the states, and added:

"I should have no objection to make, and repeat the declaration a thousand times, if there were no danger of encouraging bold bad men to believe they are dealing with one who can be scared into anything."

Lincoln seemed obsessed with the idea that he should make no gesture of friendship toward the South, for that would be interpreted as timidity and cowardice, and his enemies would exploit that as a sign of apparent weakness. The more he would give in, the more they would demand, so he would give them nothing.

Still, every day following his election, Lincoln received more written and verbal pleas for him to abandon his silence and issue some conciliatory statement.

General Winfield Scott confided to Senator Crittenden that Lincoln must speak out and give some encouragement to the Southern people who yearned to stay in the Union if assured that they could remain there in safety. "The Union is at the mercy of the President-elect even before he is inaugurated," the old soldier observed. "His silence may be fatal."

Lincoln finally made an indirect response to the many appeals for him to offer an olive branch to the South. Illinois Republicans staged a great celebration on November 20, honoring their election victory. Senator Lyman Trumbull delivered the main address and, since Lincoln sat on the platform as the guest of honor, the speech was advertised as really representing his own views. The *New York Herald* hailed it as the "forthcoming semi-official exposition" of his future policy.

In keeping with his secretive nature, Lincoln privately wrote two paragraphs of the speech, expressing confidence that the Union-loving people would resist the schemes of the secessionists. In a memorandum to Trumbull, Lincoln wrote: "I am rather glad of this military preparation in the South. It will enable the people the more easily to suppress any uprisings there which their misrepresentations of purposes may have encouraged."

David M. Potter, in his authoritative book, *Lincoln and His Party in the Secession Crisis*, deplores these remarks as "consummate folly," showing Lincoln's "complete and tragic failure to understand the temper of the South."

"Thus," says Potter, "the President-elect recorded a delusion to which he clung throughout the crisis. That is, he looked upon the secessionists not as leaders of a force with which he would have to deal, but a losing minority group, faced with repudiation by the Unionist majority, and pushing their policy frantically, just as a speculator plunges most recklessly when he faces bankruptcy."

While his secret paragraphs in Trumbull's speech implied that the Union-lovers in every Southern state would rise up against secession, he offered them no incentives to do that. His mouthpiece, Trumbull, warned that, if South Carolina would try to block the collection of federal revenues, that would be revolution, and if anyone should attack the national authorities, the "traitors" would be punished.

If Lincoln imagined that Trumbull's speech would calm the South, he was keenly disappointed. Did a single newspaper, previously against him, change its view and urge that speech upon its readers "with a purpose to quiet public anxiety?" he asked editor Henry J. Raymond of the *New York Times* on November 28. "No one, so far as I know. On the contrary the *Boston Courier*, and its class, hold me responsible for the speech, and endeavor to inflame the North with the belief that it foreshadows an abandonment of Republican ground by the incoming administration, while the *Washington Constitution*, and its class, hold the same speech up to the South as an open declaration of war against them.

"This is just what I expected, and just what would happen with any declaration I could make. These political fiends are not half sick enough yet. 'Party malice' and not 'public good' possesses them entirely."

"They seek a sign, and no sign shall be given them," he concluded, quoting the words of Jesus Christ rebuking his enemies in the New Testament.

Lincoln sometimes planted anonymous stories in friendly news-papers, and his unseen hand must have been behind a *Chicago Tribune* article of November 21, which quoted an anonymous "gentleman who talked with him on this secession question, only a day or two ago," as saying that the President-elect was "unquestionably firm in his belief that the laws should be upheld."

Lincoln "does not believe that any of the states will ... go off and organize a confederacy in which slaveholding and the slave trade are the bonds of union. ... He cannot conceive how ... the disunionists can work their people up to the point of consummating their threatened treason.

"That he will try all methods of conciliation consistent with his sense of right and his obligations to the country, we have no doubt," the Chicago writer said, also assuring his supporters that he "will not fail ... to use all the means at his command to insure respect for the obligations with which the states have entered."

This is the kind of euphemistic language that governments use in threatening others with war. Clearly, if Lincoln would use "all the means at his command," that would include armed force and, therefore, he would wage war.

Lincoln's blithe assumption that the South would not actually go ahead with secession was challenged by Thurlow Weed, the boss of the New York Republican Party and close associate of Senator Seward. The Albany editor warned:

"We must not deceive ourselves with the idea that the South is not in earnest in its clamor for secession. It *is* in earnest, and the sentiment has taken hold of all classes with such blind vehemence as to 'crush out' the Union sentiment. ... Mad, however, as the South is, there is a Union sentiment there worth cherishing. ... This calls for moderation and forbearance."

Weed's appeal reflected the growing alarm of the responsible business leaders in the North, as they saw the New York stock market plunging, banks contracting credit, business sinking into the doldrums, and merchants fearing that they could never collect millions of dollars owed by customers down South.

Amid all of this turmoil, North and South, Congress came back to Washington on December 3 and the next day President Buchanan sent up his annual message.

Buchanan began by saying the North's "intemperate interference" with slavery has inspired some bondsmen "with vague notions of freedom" and raised fears of "servile insurrection."

In words that could have been written by Jefferson Davis, the President said: "Many a matron throughout the South retires at night in dread of what may befall herself and her children before the morning." No political union can long endure, he warned, if it renders "homes and firesides ... hopelessly insecure."

"If Congress shall break up the present Union by unconstitutionally putting strife and enmity, and armed hostility, between different sections of the country, instead of the 'domestic tranquility' which the Constitution was meant to insure," he asked, "will not all the states be absolved from their federal obligation?"

Yet the old Federalist rejected the idea that any state could withdraw from the Union at will; if it could, he said, then the Union would be a mere "rope of sand."

The government of the United States "was intended to be perpetual," he said. On the other hand, he argued, no power to coerce, or "to make war against a state ... has been delegated to Congress or to any other department of the federal government." Instead, he said, such power was expressly refused by the convention which framed the Constitution in 1787.

"Our Union rests upon public opinion, and can never be cemented by the blood of its citizens shed in civil war," Buchanan continued. "If it cannot live in the affections of the people, it must one day perish."

To avert such a calamity, the President proposed a constitutional amendment. It should recognize the right of property in slaves in the states; it should protect such property in the territories; and it should declare all state laws interfering with the Fugitive Slave Act "null and void."

In essence, Buchanan declared that the states had no right to secede but that he could do nothing to stop them. Sarcastically, Senator Seward commented: "The message shows conclusively that it is the duty of the President to enforce the laws—unless somebody opposes it—and that no state has a right to go out of the Union—unless it wants to."

The *New York Times* could explain the "eccentricities" of his message only on "the supposition that Mr. Buchanan is a candidate for the presidency of the new Southern Confederacy."

"He has earned the place," it said, "but he will not get it. There is nothing so useless or odious as a cast-off tool."

Soon after the message was read in the Senate, North Carolina's Thomas Lanier Clingman declared that most of the Southern states would be moving toward secession "at an early day." In his state, he said, "the absolute submissionists are too small to be called a party; but the mass of the people consist of those who are for immediate action and those who are waiting for a few months to see whether any guarantees will be proposed that are sufficient to save our honor and insure our safety."

Lincoln was elected "because he was known to be a dangerous man," who "declares that it is the purpose of the North to make war upon my section until its social system has been destroyed," Clingman told the Senate. Republican Senator John P. Hale of New Hampshire said the Southerners "must submit" to Lincoln's election or "war will naturally follow."

"Where is this war to come from?" demanded Senator A. G. Brown, Mississippi Democrat. "From South Carolina, Georgia, Alabama, Mississippi, Florida and Texas? Does the senator mean they are going to make war on the North? ... He is most egregiously mistaken. All we ask is that we be allowed to depart in peace. ... But if you choose to make war upon us, let God defend the right."

Senator Alfred Iverson, Georgia Democrat, accepted Hale's challenge of war and asserted that several Southern states would secede to prevent the Black Republicans from using the federal power to "extinguish slavery." Nothing could stop at least five states from going out, he said, and Texas would be right behind them.

"There is a clog in the person" of Governor Sam Houston, who refuses to call the Texas legislature into session, Iverson said, and if he doesn't yield, "some Texas Brutus will arise to rid his country of the hoary-headed incubus that stands between the people and their sovereign will."

Iverson's threat—which amounted to a call for someone to assassinate Sam Houston—drew a reply from Senator Louis Trezevant Wigfall, a notorious duelist from Texas.

"I have no apprehension, sir, that the dagger of a Brutus will relieve us from this 'incubus' on our state," Wigfall said. He forecast that the Texans would soon convene "and again assume their position of separate nationality."

Wigfall, a native of South Carolina, predicted that, if the people concluded that the federal government "intends to keep them in the Union by the power of the sword," they will seize the forts "and blood will then begin to flow."

If blood did flow, it would be on the hands of the Northern President who uses military force to coerce a state, said Senator Joe Lane of Oregon, the vice-presidential nominee on the Breckinridge ticket. "I will say now, sir," he said, "that the man who shall inaugurate civil war ... will be the greatest murderer that ever disgraced the form of man, and will go down to his grave covered with the curses of Heaven from his head to his heels, besides the curses of thousands of widows and orphans."

Iverson not only forecast the certain secession of half a dozen Deep South states; he advised Virginia and Maryland to pull out quickly, too, and made the novel suggestion that Washington, D.C., could then become the capital of the new Confederacy. "If Maryland secedes," he said, "I see no reason why Washington should not be continued the capital of the Southern Confederacy. (Laughter and applause in the galleries.)"

"Some people laugh—I do not know why—at that suggestion," Iverson continued. "It is a very important one to the people who own brick and mortar in this city; for, sir ... obstructed as we may be by the tardy action of Virginia and Maryland in this great movement, we may form our republic and establish our seat of government so permanently that it can never be removed; and then these marble palaces, now teeming with life and luxury, the habitations of beauty and elegance, instead of echoing with the songs of mirth and melody, will become the habitations of the bats and the owls."

Iverson was not joking. The *New York Times* reported in early December that "there is no doubt about the eventual secession of South Carolina, Georgia, Alabama, Mississippi and Florida" and that, if Virginia and Maryland should join them, the new government "will fix its capital at Washington."

Roars of laughter also greeted Senator Wigfall when he made a violent speech warning the Northern senators: "You cannot save this Union by making Fourth of July speeches. Whipped syllabub is not the remedy for the patient." Constitutional amendments protecting slavery must be voted by the Northern states, he said, or the South will not be satisfied.

The Republican senators responded with peals of laughter and Wigfall angrily replied: "Senators laugh in my face. I beg that the Union-savers on this floor will look and see the derision, the contempt, that is expressed in every senator's face on the other side."

To his snickering critics on the Republican side of the aisle, the Texan shouted: "I say that you shall not excite your citizens to make John Brown raids or bring fire and strychnine within the limits of the state to which I owe my allegiance. You shall not publish newspapers and pamphlets to incite our slaves to insurrection. ... We will have peace; and if you do not offer it to us, we will quietly ... withdraw from the Union and establish a government for ourselves. ... And when you laugh at these impotent threats, as you regard them, I tell you that cotton is king! (Loud applause in the galleries.)"

More laughter rippled through the chamber and among the Northern senators at their desks. Pointing to Preston King, whose rotund belly was shaking with mirth, the Texan cried: "The senator from New York may laugh on. Laugh on, laugh on." But, he predicted, within a week, "South Carolina will revoke the ratification of the treaty which made her one of the United States. Then she will send an Envoy Extraordinary to this court."

Amid more laughter, clapping, and foot-stamping in the galleries, Wigfall declared: "Ah, Senators, Nero laughed while Rome was burning. ... South Carolina may become the grave of freemen but never the habitation of slaves!"

11

LINCOLN
REJECTS COMPROMISE

O n Saturday, December 8, President Buchanan reluctantly faced
up to the question of protecting the federal forts at Charleston from being seized by trigger-happy South Carolina troops. He
received four South Carolina congressmen: Laurence M. Keitt, W.
L. Bonham, William Porcher Miles, and John McQueen. They urged
him to promise not to reinforce the forts and assured him that, given
such a pledge, the state would make no attempt to capture them.

Buchanan replied that he did not intend to reinforce the forts or
to change their status, but he declined to make such a promise in
writing; the old intriguer was too cagey for that. Instead, he asked his
visitors to bring back a written statement. They did so two days later,
when they returned along with a fifth congressman, W. W. Boyce. In
their paper, they expressed their "strong convictions" that South Carolina would not molest the forts, provided that no reinforcements would
be sent and the relative military status of the harbor would remain
unchanged.

Buchanan assured them they had a gentleman's agreement on these
terms and, if he should change his policies, he would return their
statement. He thought he had made no commitment; but they were
sure he had. As Keitt had claimed earlier at Columbia, they had Old
Buck pledged to secession and would hold him to it.

In the Senate on December 10, Ohio Democrat George Pugh
said that, if Buchanan should send a federal army to coerce South
Carolina, he would be "arraigned at our bar by an impeachment."
Pugh evoked a scornful reply from New Hampshire Republican John
P. Hale, who said: "Instead of sending an army down to South Carolina,
Mr. Buchanan is on his knees before them, begging them for God's

sake to stave this thing off until the Fourth of March, so that he may get out of the way of the shower before it comes."

Buffeted by the arrogant South Carolinians, the President suffered a blow from another Southern source: Howell Cobb resigned as secretary of the treasury so that he could rush home and help in the effort to pull Georgia out of the Union. It was a painful, personal loss, because the roly-poly little figure of Cobb probably was closer to the President than any other member of the cabinet. During the long intervals when Mrs. Cobb would be in Georgia having a baby, Buchanan would demand that Cobb reside in the White House.

Cobb, in a published address, told the Southern people that, after March 4, the federal government would cease to have the slightest claim on their confidence or loyalty; that the time had come "to announce and maintain your independence out of the Union, for you will never again have equality or justice in it."

Augustus Schell of New York was mentioned as a possible successor to Cobb, who had left the federal treasury almost empty. Hearing this report, one witty official quipped: "There is nothing to *shell*; the corn is gone and the *Cobb*, too."

Even worse for the President's tattered reputation in the North, where his enemies were accusing him of being a "traitor" in cahoots with the disunionists, was his next loss—the resignation of Lewis Cass, the secretary of state. Cass, at seventy-eight, had the aura of an elder statesman, best known as the Democrat who lost the presidency to General Zachary Taylor in 1848. The public could not know that, in cabinet sessions, Cass sometimes dozed beneath his ill-fitting black wig, and his staff carried on most of the work of his office.

Several times in cabinet meetings, the secretary demanded that the Charleston forts must be reinforced. When Buchanan refused and struck his deal with the South Carolinians, Cass angrily resigned.

"Secretary Cass has left the scuttled Ship of State and fled in dismay," commented Congressman Isaac Morris. The Illinois Democrat said the President had knuckled under, bowing to warlike threats from the secessionists.

"The state already had its grasp upon the throat of the general government while the poor, trembling victim, Mr. Buchanan, with protruding tongue, eyes straining from their sockets, with short and painful breath, crooked hinges of the knee and outstretched arms, implored for forbearance and mercy," Morris told the House.

The resignation of Cass sparked another round of Northern press attacks upon Buchanan. The *New York Tribune* spread a rumor that the President had gone crazy. Conceding that the rumor was probably false, Horace Greeley's paper said, that, in view of Buchanan's recent actions, confirmation of the story would not cause astonishment.

In a dispatch headlined "The Latest from Washington," the *New York Times* quoted a "high source" as saying that, "rather than coerce the South, Mr. Buchanan would resign."

"It is stated in Democratic circles that he said as much to a prominent secessionist," the *Times* reported. "His vacillation betrays the weakness of the administration and gives color to the report that he will give up in despair rather than meet the crisis.

"In case he resigns, Vice President Breckinridge will succeed which, his friends believe, would save the Union."

Here was an echo of Senator Douglas's charge that Buchanan had made a deal with the disunionists whereby the President would resign and hand over his office to Breckinridge, who would thus become commander-in-chief of the army and navy and reassure the Southern states that they had no reason to fear federal coercion.

After Buchanan, in his State of the Union message, had denied the right of secession, key Southern leaders turned against him as a faithless friend who no longer deserved their trust. Their mistrust increased when he named his confidant and fellow Pennsylvanian, Jeremiah S. Black, to succeed Cass as secretary of state. To replace Black as attorney general, Buchanan chose Edwin M. Stanton, a wiry, black-bearded Pennsylvania Democrat with a penchant for double-dealing and intrigue. To succeed Cobb at the treasury, Buchanan chose Philip Thomas of Maryland. Thomas served briefly, then was replaced by General John A. Dix of New York, a Breckinridge Democrat who was strongly for the Union.

Congressman S. S. Cox, an Ohio Democrat, charged in his memoirs that Stanton originally was "a secession sympathizer—as Judge Black proved and as the author personally confirms"—but switched sides and became Lincoln's secretary of war.

Cox and other Northern Democrats protested when they were excluded from the "Committee of Thirty-three," created by Speaker

Pennington in an effort to find some peaceful solution to the secession crisis. One member from each state was chosen and those from the North were Republicans, most of whom had little interest in any deal that would weaken the power that their victorious party would achieve on Lincoln's inauguration day.

Representative Dan Sickles, a New York City Democrat, accused the Republicans of "the responsibility, before God and country, of breaking up the Confederacy, rather than tolerate slavery within the Union."

Representative George S. Hawkins, Florida's spokesman on the Committee of Thirty-three, blamed Lincoln for the Republicans' refusal to "yield anything." "Why is it," he asked, "at this moment, when the whole country is agitated, the President-elect has kept a most ominous silence?"

Sickles also called for Lincoln to speak out in the cause of peace. "Let the sealed lips of the Medusa head at Springfield be opened, and send back to their caverns the mad winds which are driving our good ship of state to destruction," the New York Democrat said. "Why may not the President-elect speak to the nation, and especially to his supporters in the aggressive states?"

Lincoln remained incommunicado in Springfield, but he became an unseen but influential presence in Washington. In December, he fired off a series of letters to Republicans in Congress, ordering them to reject any compromise that would extend slavery over a single inch of new land.

Lincoln denounced proposals that would extend the old Missouri Compromise line of 36° 30', guaranteeing that all lands above it should be forever free while slavery would be permitted in all areas south of the line, including territory "hereafter acquired." He saw the two little words, "hereafter acquired," as a loophole opening the way for fili-bustering to take over Cuba, more of Mexico, and Central America, and to create a slave empire around the Gulf of Mexico. With his shrewd insight, Lincoln had caught on to the Southerners' schemes for their glorious "Empire of the Golden Circle."

"Private and confidential," he scribbled on top of several letters, with his familiar passion for secrecy. To Senator Trumbull, he wrote: "Let there be no compromise on the question of *extending* slavery. ...

Have none of it. Stand firm. The tug has to come, & better now, than any time hereafter."

To Representative William Kellogg, Lincoln admonished: "Entertain no proposition in regard to the *extension* of slavery. The instant you do, they have us under again; all our labor is lost, and sooner or later must be done over."

To Representative E. B. Washburne: "Prevent, as far as possible, any of our friends from demoralizing themselves, and our cause, by entertaining propositions for compromise of any sort on 'slavery extension.'" With any such deal, including the extension of the Missouri Compromise line, he warned: "Immediately, filibustering and extending slavery recommences. On that point hold firm, as with a chain of steel."

Thurlow Weed, trying earnestly to prevent a civil war, proposed that the Republican governors combine their power and influence both Lincoln and Congress. Lincoln advised Weed to tell the governors that "you judge from my speeches that I will be inflexible on the territorial question," that either extending "the Missouri line" or Douglas's "popular sovereignty" would "lose us everything we gained by the election; that filibustering for all South of us, and making slave states of it, would follow."

Then Lincoln signaled that he would use an iron hand to suppress secession, advising the Albany editor, Weed: "I believe you can pretend to find but little, if any thing, in my speeches, about secession; but my opinion is that no state can, in any way lawfully, get out of the Union, without the consent of the others; and that it is the duty of the President, and other government functionaries, to run the machine as it is."

Lincoln persisted in his mistaken belief that the secession movement did not represent the real, pro-Union feeling of the masses in the South, but was just an artificial panic stirred up by a small group of "bad men" who were determined to bully him into backing down from the Chicago platform's firm policy against all slavery extension. He viewed the popular Crittenden Compromise as merely the Breckinridge platform dressed up as a "peace" proposal.

Lincoln could not see that the venerable Kentucky Senator, John J. Crittenden, had offered his plan in an unselfish effort to avert the worst of all disasters, a brothers' war. Crittenden, an Old Line Whig, sought to emulate his party's eloquent Kentuckian, Henry Clay, who was credited with saving the Union through the Compromise of 1850. Crittenden proposed to write the Missouri Compromise, and a perpetual guarantee of slavery in the Southern states, into the Constitution.

In early December, Crittenden sent a personal envoy to Springfield. The envoy is named only "B" in Crittenden's papers. He is reported to have been Breckinridge but has not been positively identified.

"B" told Lincoln, in a two-hour interview, that, to save the Union, he must form "a national and representative cabinet, consisting of three Southern Union men of good character, and four moderate Republicans."

Lincoln retorted, "Does any man think that I will take to my bosom an enemy?" This, he qualified by saying, "any man who voted against me."

Lincoln, with his customary caution, said little during the meeting, remaining silent much of the time. So the result of the talk was "indefinite and unsatisfactory." The visitor left with the impression that the President-elect was "rather an Ultra" Republican.

Crittenden, who aspired to be a statesman like the Founding Fathers, was born in Versailles, Kentucky, September 10, 1787, at the very time the Constitution, which he revered, was being drafted in Philadelphia. He entered the Senate at age thirty and his service there extended to 1861, with interruptions for two periods of work as the U.S. attorney general and one term as governor. Crittenden's plan brought him a torrent of letters praising him and pleading for a compromise to avert a civil war.

Horatio Seymour wrote: "I feel perfectly confident that New York would give one hundred and fifty thousand majority for this measure" if Congress would only let the people vote on it. Although Lincoln carried the state by fifty thousand votes in November, the Democratic ex-governor explained, thousands who voted the Republican ticket had no confidence in the party's doctrines.

John Brodhead, president of the Camden and Atlantic Rail Road Company of Philadelphia, told Crittenden: "I am satisfied that three-fourths of the people of Pennsylvania and New Jersey warmly approve of your plan and would hail its adoption with rejoicing."

Major Robert Anderson, the native Kentuckian in command at Fort Sumter, wrote Crittenden: "God save our country from fratricidal strife."

However, the Republicans, following Lincoln's guidance, opposed the Crittenden measure and refused to have a referendum in which the people could vote it up or down—because they felt sure the voters would approve it as a way of avoiding a civil war.

Lincoln's emphatic orders to the Republicans in Congress further hardened their opposition to any compromise that would ease the Southerners' fears that he really did mean to carry out his "House Divided" speech, which called for an eventual end to slavery.

Only a few of the slave-state senators joined Iverson and Wigfall in proclaiming their intention to have their states go out of the Union and never come back. At this stage of the conflict, the Southerners were far from a solid bloc.

Of the thirty senators from the fifteen slave states, all were Democrats except the two Old Line Whigs, Crittenden of Kentucky and Anthony Kennedy of Maryland. South Carolina's senators, James Chesnut, Jr., and James Hammond, had resigned, leaving their desks and chairs standing empty in the Senate chamber as silent symbols of the state's secession, coming later in December.

Senators from the border states—Delaware, Maryland, Kentucky, and Missouri—expressed irritation over the way the cotton states of the Deep South were rushing toward secession. The proud South Carolinians were accused of "going off half-cocked" and forcing other states to consider leaving the Union when they really would rather look for an easy way to wiggle out of the crisis without doing anything.

Only a few senators were noisy "fire-eaters," ranting and raving on the Senate floor: Wigfall of Texas, Iverson and Toombs of Georgia, and Brown of Mississippi were the noisiest. Mason of Virginia, Clay of Alabama, and Clingman of North Carolina were less vocal but no less determined to protect states' rights. Davis of Mississippi, though firm in his belief in the right of secession, held back because, as a former secretary of war, he knew the North had the strength to wage a long war upon the South.

No state possessed a more astute, intelligent, and sophisticated pair of senators than Louisiana, and both of them were exotics, as much at home in Paris as in New Orleans. Neither was a native son of the South: John Slidell had come from New York City, and Judah P. Benjamin from the West Indies. Both were outstanding and wealthy members of the bar.

Slidell would have preferred to continue running the United States government behind the scenes with a puppet president such as his creature, James Buchanan. Having lost that game, Slidell now considered the Union not worth saving, and he looked to a new Confederacy to realize his dream of creating a Caribbean-and-Gulf empire.

Benjamin had hoped to preserve the Union but, since Lincoln's election and the Republicans' firm opposition to any compromise in Congress, he had concluded that "no prospect remains of our being permitted to live in peace and security within the Union." For their own "self-preservation," Benjamin said in a letter published in the New Orleans press in mid-December, all the slave states, by "separate state actions," must promptly sever all connection with the federal government.

One night in early December, some slave-state senators caucused and drafted a manifesto, appealing to the Southern people to take their states out of the Union now. Their message was telegraphed to the home-state newspapers, to have the maximum effect upon the voters. In all, thirty members of Congress signed the manifesto, but they did not make up a clear majority of the House members and senators from the slave states. The senators who signed it were Davis and Brown of Mississippi, Benjamin and Slidell of Louisiana, Hemphill and Wigfall of Texas, and Iverson of Georgia.

"All hope of relief in the Union is extinguished," they declared. "The honor, safety and independence of the Southern people require the organization of a Southern Confederacy—a result to be obtained only by separate state action; that the primary object of each slave-holding state ought to be its speedy and absolute separation from a union with hostile states." The declaration appeared in print December 14.

Revealing the caucus, the *New York Times* said it was agreed that "eight states are certain to secede."

"A large majority considered it too late to save the present confederacy but expressed the belief that a new Union would be speedily formed. ...

"The impression is gaining ground here that Virginia and Maryland will have joined the other Southern states in secession before the Fourth of March. As these states would carry the District of Columbia with them, the question is being asked here: 'Where will Lincoln be inaugurated?'"

The advocates of immediate action were confident of building a bloc of Gulf states which would follow South Carolina to the exit within a few weeks. But they were frustrated by the states of the upper South, which yearned to cling to the old Union and delay any action in hope of some concession by the Republicans, who were refusing to do anything except to seize power on March 4.

The governors of the Deep South states sent commissioners to those of the reluctant states, trying to persuade them to jump aboard the secession bandwagon. In several cases, the governor selected a local man who was a native son of an upper South state, and sent him as an envoy to his kinfolks and friends back home, spreading the gospel of Southern unity. Thus, Interior Secretary Jacob Thompson, who had left North Carolina as a poor youth and made his fortune in Mississippi, was dispatched as a missionary to his native state.

Thompson saw nothing wrong in a member of the cabinet going to a Southern state to counsel members of its legislature about secession. Before leaving for Raleigh, he asked Senator Clingman for advice about the best way of selling secession to the North Carolina lawmakers.

"I didn't know you had resigned," Clingman said.

"Oh, no, I have not resigned," Thompson replied.

"Then I suppose you'll resign in the morning."

"No, I do not intend to resign, for Mr. Buchanan wishes all of us in the cabinet to stay and go out with him on the Fourth of March."

"But does the President know for what purpose you are going to North Carolina?"

"Certainly!"

Surprised, Clingman said the President could not possibly permit a member of his own cabinet to go down to a Southern state and urge its secession. To make sure, Thompson checked again with the President and reported back to the skeptical senator:

"The President told me he wished me to go and hoped I might succeed."

Clingman later commented, in amazement: "Was there ever before any potentate who sent his own cabinet ministers to incite insurrection against his own government?"

Thompson's wife, Kate, a vivacious social butterfly who loved wearing expensive gowns and jewels and going to parties, also had no doubt that Old Buck knew exactly why the secretary would return to his native state on the mission.

"The President approves the visit," she said. "I am going with him. I can't stay here by myself. My head is nearly crazy and my heart goes *pit-a-pat* at every sound I hear."

It was certainly more fun to travel than to stay in Washington, where the secession crisis had spread "gloom and depression" and sharply reduced the number of dinners and brilliant balls.

"Poor Harriet Lane!" Kate Thompson exclaimed. The President's niece evoked much sympathy, for the White House hostess had to keep up appearances although many of her former friends no longer called to see her. "Miss Lane and I keep silence on political questions," Mrs. Thompson said. "I go to see her and the President as often as I can because, I know they feel their old friends are, many of them, deserting them."

The *New York Times* editorially blistered the President for letting Thompson go on his "disunion" mission. "If the President has not become imbecile with age, or been frightened out of his manhood by the clamor of the disunionists," it concluded that he was deliberately encouraging the Southerners to demand "impossible conditions of peace."

Ohio Republican Senator Benjamin F. Wade told the Southerners, in a December 17 speech: "You own the cabinet, you own the Senate, and, I may add, you own the President of the United States as much as you own the servant upon your own plantation." Scorning all compromises, Wade insisted that Lincoln must be inaugurated on the Republicans' platform which affirmed that "we would, if we had the power, prohibit slavery from another inch of free territory."

Two days later, Andrew Johnson of Tennessee broke publicly with his fellow Southerners in the Senate when he made a sensational speech denouncing secession as "treason" and vowing that he would never desert the Union. When he proposed to accept Lincoln's election as no excuse for disunion, he found many House members from the slave states, standing around the Senate chamber as a hostile claque, uttering expressions of contempt for the man whom they considered a traitor to the South.

"A bevy of conspirators gathered in from the other House, and crowded around, with frowns and scowls and expressions of indignation and contempt towards me, because I dared to raise my voice in vindication of the Constitution and the enforcement of the laws of the Union," he later recalled. He bitterly resented "the taunts, the jeers, the derisive remarks, the contemptuous expressions" of the Southern congressmen who branded him an ally of their Northern oppressors.

Johnson's critics could not understand how he could have campaigned and voted for Breckinridge on a Democratic ticket and yet could consent to live under the rule of Lincoln, who ran a million votes behind his three opponents combined. Johnson had this answer:

"I voted against Lincoln, I spoke against him, I spent my money to defeat him, but still I love my country; I love the Constitution; I intend to insist upon its guarantees."

Johnson took great pride in styling himself a humble "man of the people," and he had a lifelong grudge against the rich, slave-owning aristocrats who dominated Southern society. He envied the "snobs" who looked down their noses at him and froze him out of their circle.

Born into poverty at Raleigh, North Carolina, in 1808, Johnson was three when his father died while saving two people from drowning. As a child he was a "bound boy," apprenticed to a tailor; he quit the job and was advertised as a runaway. At eighteen, with his mother and stepfather, he moved to Tennessee and opened a little tailor shop at Greeneville, a mountain town. At nineteen, he married Eliza McCardle, a shoemaker's daughter. She taught him to read and write.

A black-haired, square-faced man with a prominent nose and beetling eyebrows, the tailor plunged into politics as an Andrew Jackson Democrat. He liked to boast that he climbed the ladder of political success all the way from the town council, through the legislature, the U.S. House of Representative, the governorship and, finally, the U.S. Senate.

Along the way, he made many enemies with his sharp tongue and his belligerent way of campaigning. He became accustomed to jeers, catcalls, and hisses from his foes. Once at Nashville, when the hissing was especially loud, he quipped: "Did I hear someone hiss? Well, there are but two things in the world besides man that ever hiss—the serpent in his venom and the goose in his simplicity."

After he had achieved national fame, a Raleigh newspaper published this spiteful description of him:

> Andrew Johnson was born and reared in this city, and some of our inhabitants remember him as a low down blackguard, without character save for viciousness and depravity. His antecedents were also of the vilest and most degrading caste. He never was reputable or trustworthy as a tailor or in any other craft—he always disgraced the trade. He was a vagabond and a thief when a boy, and in manhood he has been a swaggering and profane swearer, and publicly and privately a lying adventurer, mighty in promises which he never performed.

Of all the epithets flung against him, the one that cut the deepest was "prick louse."

"Prick louse," or "prick the louse," was a vulgar slang term meaning "tailor." It was thus painfully appropriate for insulting the pugnacious tailor from Greeneville. His foes ridiculed him as a slovenly commoner, but in fact he was usually attired in a neatly fitted black broadcloth suit, with snowy white linen and black cravat.

Johnson proudly called himself a plebeian who followed Andrew Jackson, the Tennessee hero who had snuffed out South Carolina's nullification attempt with a presidential show of force in 1833. For his outspoken Unionism, he had bitter enemies among the Southerners who dreamed of empire.

It was against such secessionists that Johnson fired his verbal fusillades on December 19, the day before South Carolina formally left the Union.

Coercion, in his opinion, was just a lot of "slang-wanging" and he had no use for it. "Tennessee will not be dragged into any Confederacy," he said. "We are not to be frightened or coerced." He had equally blunt language for the "gentlemen of the North," saying: "We do not intend that you shall drive us out of this house that was reared by the hands of our fathers."

With uncanny foresight, Johnson accurately predicted that "dissolution of the Union will, in the end, overthrow the institution of slavery."

Senator Joe Lane of Oregon arose immediately in reply. He said "the gallant band of Democrats North" would never march with Johnson under Lincoln's "bloody banner" to invade the soil of a Southern state. "The Republican party," he said, "will have war enough at home."

Lane, who had won the stars of a major general for his exploits in the Mexican war, said he had seen the courage of the Tennessee soldiers who fought in his brigade, and they would not follow Johnson, either, into battle against any Southern state.

Breckinridge's running mate said that federal coercion of seceding states would bring about civil war and "drench this country in blood."

Lane, who had spent most of his life in Indiana before becoming the first governor of the Oregon Territory, expressed confidence that the people of Indiana, Illinois, Ohio, and other states of the Old Northwest would maintain friendly ties with the South. "Indeed, sir," he said, "if a dissolution of this Union shall take place, I look to the day when every one of those great Northwestern states shall become a portion of the Southern Confederacy." This was one of the first hints that some Democrats would try to form a Northwest Confederacy and link it to the new Southern republic.

Johnson's speech evoked praise from the North, and curses from the South. When his remarks appeared in his home-state newspapers, they brought forth a torrent of abuse from the secessionists, who called him a "traitor."

In Memphis, Nashville, Knoxville, and elsewhere in Tennessee, Johnson's enemies burned him in effigy. His son, Robert, sent him these reassuring words: "I presume you have heard of the burning of your effigy. As John Tyler once said, they merely give you light for a man to walk by."

Johnson, who had campaigned for Breckinridge and defended him against charges that he was just a handsome young front man for disunionists, found the vice-president drifting toward the secession camp in the wake of Lincoln's victory.

"Sir, your strength has failed to satisfy the country," the Tennessee senator told him when they met in Washington after the Democrats' disaster.

"I am disappointed in my calculations," Breckinridge replied, according to Johnson's version of their interview. "I firmly believed myself capable of carrying the border states."

"Are you willing to disunite the states because of Mr. Lincoln's success and because discontented South Carolina agitates the subject?" Johnson demanded.

"To this," the Tennessee senator remembered, "he replied about 'subjugation' and 'the horrors of a civil conflict,' convincing me he had gone into the arms of disunion."

"It was there that Breckinridge showed the cloven foot," Johnson charged. "South Carolina was basely and adroitly attempting to dissolve the Union. I told him that we had all been caught in a snap; secessionists would break up the Union."

The vice-president opposed using military force against a seceding state. "Would you coerce a state?" he asked.

"It is our duty to save the government," Johnson answered.

"Will you coerce?" Breckinridge demanded.

"We are obliged to sustain the laws," Johnson retorted.

Breckinridge's attitude, Johnson said later, "was like an iceberg in my bosom."

On the afternoon of December 20, President Buchanan attended a wedding reception at the home of a wealthy Washington grocer named Parker. A host of Southern friends gathered there to celebrate the marriage of Parker's daughter to a Louisiana congressman, John Edward Bouligny. The bridegroom's uncle, Charles Joseph Dominique Bouligny, had been a United States senator and the family ranked high in Creole society.

Buchanan gave the couple his wishes for "a great deal of happiness," then settled his weary body into a chair. Washington buzzed with rumors that he was "pale with fear" and dividing his time between "praying and crying." But he insisted that, despite all the turmoil over secession, he "never enjoyed better health or a more tranquil spirit" and had lost not one night's sleep or missed a single meal. He also kept up his spirits with plenty of his favorite Monongahela whiskey.

Mrs. Roger Pryor, a Virginia congressman's wife, stood behind his chair at the reception and looked closely at his silver-haired figure. She believed that he had aged a great deal since the past summer.

From the front hall came the sound of a mighty commotion. Startled, the President said to Mrs. Pryor, "Madam, do you suppose the house is on fire?"

Out in the hall, she found the dark and handsome Congressman Laurence Keitt had burst into the house and was leaping high in the air, waving a piece of paper shouting, "Thank God! Thank God!"

"Mr. Keitt, are you crazy?" she asked. "The President hears you and wants to know what's the matter!"

"Oh, South Carolina has seceded!" Keitt jubilantly cried. "Here's the telegram. I feel like a boy let out of school!"

Running back into the drawing room, Mrs. Pryor whispered the news from Charleston to the President. He slumped in his chair, his wrinkled face as white as a sheet.

"Madam," he whispered, "might I beg you to have my carriage called?"

Moments later, the distraught chief executive was on his way back to the White House.

12

SECEDERS' WILD SCHEMES

South Carolina's official secession sent shock waves over the North, and especially over Washington. Skeptics who had laughed over the silly idea of the little Palmetto state, cutting loose and going off on its own, finally realized that it meant business, and that the loud boasts of the "fire-eaters" were true: Half a dozen other states in the Deep South were preparing to follow.

In New York, the speculators and merchants shuddered, and George Templeton Strong confided to his diary: "That termagant little South Carolina has declared herself out of the Union and resolved to run away and go to the sea. How many of the Southern sisterhood will join the secession jig she thus leads off remains to be seen."

"The Cotton States *are going*," Horace Greeley told Lincoln in a letter December 22, filled with foreboding.

> Nothing that we can offer will stop them. The Union-loving men are cowed and speechless; a Reign of Terror prevails from Cape Fear to the Rio Grande. Every suggestion of reason is drowned in a mad whirl of passion and faction. You will be President over no foot of the cotton States not commanded by Federal Arms.
>
> Even your life is not safe, and it is your simple duty to be very careful of exposing it. I doubt whether you ought to go to Washington via Wheeling and the B&O Railroad unless you go with a very strong force. And it is not yet certain that the Federal District will not be in the hands of a Pro-Slavery rebel army before the 4th of March.

To Lincoln's law partner, William H. Herndon, the panicky editor of the *New York Tribune* sent more bad news: "The Secessionists are now doing their utmost to coerce Gov. Hicks of Maryland into calling the Legislature (Democratic) which is to call a State convention. If they fail, I think the Legislature will be called irregularly—that is, will get together in something which will be made to pass for authority. If they can get Maryland into their clutches, *every Slave State but Delaware and perhaps Missouri will have seceded before the 4th of March, and Mr. Lincoln must fight for the possession of Washington City.* Of course, the plot may miscarry; but Yancey, Wise & Co. are pushing it with all their might, and the virtual dissolution of the Government gives them every facility. I tell you I think it today an even chance that Mr. Lincoln will *not* be inaugurated at Washington on the 4th of March."

John Minor Botts, a former Whig Congressman from Virginia and a ferocious foe of secession and Democrats, was certain that the Southerners planned "to possess themselves of Washington, seize upon the archives of the nation, and control of the army, navy and treasury, and spread Democracy and slavery all over the United States."

The secessionists first planned only "to set up a Southern Confederacy and add Cuba and much of Mexico to it," Botts believed. But, when they found the Southerners in the cabinet helping them and Buchanan doing nothing to stop them, they became bolder and decided to strike for nothing less than control of the capital city.

Young Southern hotheads, many sporting the blue cockade of secession, boasted in the barrooms about their plans for taking over Washington. Their gasconade was often fueled by copious drafts of whiskey. One of their favorite pastimes was to gather in front of the saloons and jostle women and "white-livered Black Republicans" off the sidewalks.

"The city is overrun with Southerners," Republican Senator Solomon Foot of Vermont complained. "A few of them are gentlemen, but the large majority are roughs and adventurers, who profess great contempt for what they call the cowardice of Northern men. They are all armed. They believe that Northern men will run rather than fight, that they can be insulted with impunity. Street fights would be common if these fellows were not ruled with an iron hand by their leaders, who do not want any fighting until they are prepared."

Joseph Medill of the *Chicago Tribune* sent Lincoln further frightening details of the secessionists' drive to take Maryland out of the

Union. From Washington he wrote that a secret organization of several hundred men planned to block the presidential inauguration and to take over Baltimore. He charged: "It is the intention of the dis-unionists, if they get Baltimore on their side, to prevent you reaching the city by force, and with the aid of the lodges here and in Virginia and south to 'clear out' the Republicans here, take possession of the Capitol and proclaim the Southern confederacy. It is whispered that they intend to proclaim Breckinridge President and Bell Vice President or H. C. Johnson. At all events they will call a Southern convention here to 'reconstruct' the Constitution, as they term it."

Urging that Illinois and other Western states mobilize their militia units, the Chicago editor cautioned: "The secession epidemic is spreading with fearful rapidity and violence thro' the Slave States, and if Maryland gives way your friends will have to fight their way with the sword from the Pa. line to the Capitol. ... If the Capitol should fall into the hands of the insurgents the world will regard them as victorious, and their government will be recognized as among the powers of the earth."

Leonard Swett, another Illinois friend who had helped to win the presidency for Lincoln, sent him the essence of two interviews with Senator Seward, who shared the alarm over the secessionists' plots.

> He thinks the Southern plan now is, to draw Maryland and Virginia into the revolution before the 4th of March so as to get possession of the RR from Baltimore to this place, and the telegraph wires. With these advantages and these two states swept by the same ma-nia, that is now sweeping the South, they hope to prevent your in-auguration.
>
> This revolution has startled the North, but it has frightened the whole South, to utter desperation. They consider secession & a collision inevitable, so instincts of self-preservation stimulate them to save the Capital and get the prestige and power this would give them. As visionary as this seems, all men here have serious fears about it. The most sagacious & calm talk little but are in great doubt and alarm.

Southern men "have taken exclusive possession" of the President, Swett told Lincoln. "They constantly walk about the grounds of the mansion and, although they despise Mr. Buchanan, they seem to have him completely in their power."

"The White House is abandoned to the Seceders," Senator Seward told his wife. "They eat, drink and sleep" with Buchanan, he charged. To Thurlow Weed, Seward wrote: "The plot is forming to seize the capital and usurp the government, and it has abettors near the President." Seward insisted that he was not merely peddling idle gossip but had certain knowledge of the scheme. He maintained friendly personal relations with several Southern senators and their California ally, Senator Gwin, hence he had excellent sources of information within the secession camp.

The Southern senators, led by Slidell and Davis as the masterminds, did maintain their grip over the President. They advised him to make concessions to keep civil war from breaking out over the status of the forts at Charleston. Their game was to play for time until the seceding states could form a strong confederacy and deal, as equals, with the government in Washington.

South Carolina's new governor, Francis W. Pickens, sent Buchanan a message, asking permission to dispatch an officer and not more than twenty-five men to guard the Charleston forts and thus ease the concerns of the people in the city.

Two South Carolinians, Assistant Secretary of State W. H. Trescot and former U.S. marshal D. H. Hamilton, brought the governor's letter. When Buchanan read it and snapped that he would answer it next day, Trescot quickly sensed that the President resented it as an affront to his presidential authority. The diplomat consulted Slidell and Davis and they agreed that, to press Pickens's offer could make the President renege on the gentleman's agreement against changing the status of the forts. A warning telegram to the governor brought the desired response: He withdrew the offending letter.

Buchanan had good reason to feel that he had done enough to keep the peace at Charleston. He had removed Anderson's predecessor, Colonel John L. Gardner, for trying to move some ammunition from the arsenal to Fort Moultrie. Later, Captain J. G. Foster at Moultrie drew forty muskets from the arsenal, touching off an uproar among the citizens. Under orders from Washington, he sent the muskets back.

General Winfield Scott had long favored sending more troops to Fort Sumter, but he was checkmated by Buchanan's deal with the South Carolinians to maintain the status quo peacefully in Charleston harbor. Francis Preston Blair, Sr., the Maryland "gray eminence" who aspired to be a confidential advisor to the new president, sent a private account of the general's views to Lincoln, who replied on December 21:

"Yours giving an account of an interview with Gen. Scott is received, and for which I thank you. According to my present view, if the forts shall be given up before the inauguration, the General must re-take them afterward."

With his customary caution, Lincoln labeled his letter "Confidential."

Buchanan hoped to keep the truce at Charleston while he pressed for a convention to propose some constitutional amendments that might pacify the South. He saw some faint prospect of congressional action since the House had set up its Committee of Thirty-three and Vice President Breckinridge had named a committee of thirteen senators to seek a compromise.

William H. Seward stood foremost among the Senate committee's five Republicans, having the added prestige of his selection as Lincoln's secretary of state, and presumably the "premier" of the incoming administration. The four other Republicans were Ben Wade of Ohio, James W. Grimes of Iowa, Jacob Collamer of Vermont, and James Doolittle of Wisconsin, all committed to their party's anti-slavery platform.

Spokesmen for the Northern Democrats were Stephen A. Douglas, Henry M. Rice of Minnesota, and William Bigler of Pennsylvania. There were four Democrats from the slave states: Jefferson Davis, Robert Toombs, R.M.T. Hunter of Virginia, and Lazarus Powell of Kentucky. The lone Whig was Senator Crittenden.

At their first meeting, December 22, Davis moved that no measures be reported to the Senate without the backing of a majority of both parties. There was no point, he said, in the Democrats approving some plan that the Republicans refused to carry out. His rule was adopted.

In the Senate Committee of Thirteen, Douglas, Crittenden, and Bigler strongly backed the Kentuckian's constitutional amendment; Powell and Rice would go along; and even Davis, Toombs, and Hunter said they would accept it—if the Republicans would provide three of their five votes for it.

But Wade, Doolittle, Grimes, and Collamer voted against it, and Seward was absent. Therefore, Davis and Toombs also voted "No" and the result was a 6-6 tie. On Christmas Eve, Seward arrived and also cast a "No" vote.

It was a crushing blow to Crittenden—and quite an unnecessary defeat. Toombs seized upon the vote as the death of the South's last hope for safety inside the Union. He telegraphed his friends in Georgia that they should let their votes thunder for secession in their crucial election on January 2.

Congressman S. S. Cox said the defeat of the Crittenden Compromise in the Committee of Thirteen tipped the balance in Georgia in favor of secession. The Ohio Democrat quoted Senator Bigler as saying: "When the struggle was at its height in Georgia between Robert Toombs for secession and Alexander Stephens against it," if the Republicans had given three votes for the Crittenden plan it would have passed. "Stephens would have defeated Toombs and secession would have been prostrated," Cox said.

"I heard Mr. Toombs say to Mr. Douglas that the result in Georgia was staked on the action of the Committee of Thirteen," Cox recalled. "If it accepted the Crittenden proposition, Stephens would defeat him; if not, he would carry the state by 40,000 majority. The three votes from the Republican side would have carried it any time; but union and peace in the balance against the Chicago platform were sure to be found wanting."

If Georgia had followed Stephens and voted against immediate secession, South Carolina would have found itself isolated from its neighbors, so a strong new Southern republic could not have prevailed.

Seward kept trying to pull Lincoln over to the idea of soothing the slave states with reassurances, so that secession could be stopped from spreading all across the South. His political ally, Thurlow Weed, advocated extending the Missouri Compromise line to the Pacific and tried to sell the President-elect on this during a conference at Springfield. But Lincoln had already told the Republicans in Congress to stand like "a chain of steel" against slavery extension, and he refused to budge from that stand.

Lincoln sent the Albany editor back with three little resolutions for Seward to sponsor. The first said the Fugitive Slave Law must be enforced; the second called for the repeal of any state laws in conflict with it; the third said "the Federal Union must be preserved." That was all.

President Buchanan sent a personal envoy to Springfield to seek Lincoln's cooperation in bipartisan measures to keep the Union intact. His emissary was Duff Green, who had edited a newspaper, the *United States Telegraph*, in Washington in Andrew Jackson's day.

Buchanan, backed by Senators Davis and Toombs, instructed Green to invite Lincoln to come to Washington at once. He would be received "with all the respect due to the President-elect" and Buchanan would cordially join with him "in the measures necessary to preserve the Union."

Green requested a letter from Lincoln agreeing that Congress should refer "the measures for the preservation of the Union to the action of the people of the several states." Green thought Lincoln promised to give him such a letter; but he went back to Washington empty-handed. Lincoln had written a letter but sent it, instead, to Senator Lyman Trumbull with instructions that it should be given to Green only if "our discreet friends" should agree that it would do no harm.

The letter, which was never given to Green, said: "I do not desire any amendment of the Constitution." However, since the question of amending the Constitution belonged to the people, he added, "I should not feel justified nor inclined to withhold from them, if I could, a fair opportunity of expressing their will thereon through either of the modes expressed in that instrument."

"The maintenance inviolate of the rights of the states, and especially the right of each state to order and control its own domestic institutions according to its own judgment exclusively, is essential to that balance of powers on which the perfection and endurance of our political fabric depend," Lincoln added. This was a roundabout, legalistic way of saying the states could maintain slavery if they wished.

With his customary caution against being caught in a trap, the shrewd Illinois lawyer would allow his letter to be published only upon one condition—that six of the twelve United States senators from Georgia, Alabama, Mississippi, Louisiana, Florida, and Texas would sign a postscript written beneath his own signature, "and allow the whole to be published together."

Lincoln required that the Southern senators sign this statement: "We recommend to the people of the states we represent respectively, to suspend all action for dismemberment of the Union, at least until some act deemed violative of our rights shall be done by the incoming administration."

Lincoln knew full well that the senators would thus be trapped into stopping the secession movement in its tracks and, of course, they would never sign any such thing.

As Lincoln and the Republicans stood rock-solid against any real concessions, the Southerners in Congress felt driven towards secession as the only way to guarantee the safety of their people and their social system. The secessionists were no longer sure that their pliant tool, James Buchanan, would do their bidding much longer, either—especially since he denied the right of secession. They saw him slipping under the malign influence of the strong Union men in his cabinet: Black, Holt, and Stanton. Something drastic must be done soon, some thought, to restore their waning power in the White House.

Texas's arrogant Senator Louis T. Wigfall shouted the most loudly for action. Being a native of South Carolina, he felt keenly concerned about her future, now that she had proclaimed herself an independent commonwealth. The English newspaper correspondent, William Russell, painted the most vivid pen-portrait of this strange man:

"His face was not one to be forgotten—a straight broad brow from which the hair rose up like vegetation on a river bank; beetling black brows—a mouth coarse and grim yet full of power, a square jaw—a thick argumentative nose—a new growth of scrubbly beard and mustache—these were relieved by eyes of wonderful depth and light, such as I never saw before but in the head of a wild beast ... the eyes of a Bengal tiger."

A New York society matron, shuddering at the sight of Wigfall in the Senate, said: "His speech was half crazy, full of foul language. His manners were such as would exile him from any drawing room and any other place except a barroom. He chewed and spat and sat with his heels on his desk and was so disgusting altogether that I should have liked to have hurled something at him."

"He has a profusion of hair on his face, and he tugs and fondles his mustache and whiskers all the time he is seated," a *Philadelphia Bulletin* reporter wrote.

> When he rises to speak, he puts his hand in his pockets, thus spreading apart his frock coat and exhibiting a black satin waistcoat, such as Southern congressmen especially affect.
>
> Wigfall has a good, clear voice that fills the Senate chamber, and when not confused or excited by too frequent refreshment, he speaks deliberately. ... He can bring in a Latin line at times but there is nothing classical about Wigfall except his book of quotations. ...
>
> After each climax or anti-climax in the oratorical passages of Wigfall, he lifts the tumbler from his desk to take a fresh sip of his inspiring fluid. He then resumes his remarks with new vigor.

Born into the Low Country aristocracy of South Carolina in 1816, a descendant of French Huguenots, Wigfall became notorious in his youth as a rash, impulsive, and ruthless fighting man. One acquaintance said: "He was ready to fight a rattlesnake and give him first bite."

In five months when he was twenty-four, Wigfall was involved in two duels, three near-duels, and one shooting scrape that left one man dead and two men wounded. Wigfall and Preston Brooks wounded each other in a duel, Brooks being shot through the hip and Wigfall through both thighs. This was the same "Bully" Brooks, the Congressman who, in 1856, beat up Charles Sumner at his Senate desk, severely injuring the Massachusetts abolitionist about the head and shoulders with a rain of blows from his cane.

The Wigfall family liked to repeat an amusing incident involving General Wade Hampton, who met a slave near his own plantation. When asked, "Whom do you belong to?" the black man proudly replied: "Colonel Wigfall, sah, de best shot in Souf Calina, sah!"

After a series of financial reverses, Wigfall left his native state a bankrupt. He moved to Texas to make a new start in life. He rose swiftly in the political turmoil of the frontier and emerged as the most radical and violent "fire-eater," shouting for disunion and daring the Yankees to wage war on the South.

The anonymous author of "The Diary of a Public Man," the oft-quoted source of much writing about the Secession Winter, quoted a friend identified only as "B" as vouching for this story about Wigfall's solution to the Buchanan problem: The Texas senator called together "a few choice spirits" and proposed that the President be kidnapped!

His idea was to have Buchanan carried out of Washington to a secure place, which had been indicated to him by some persons in his confidence, and so his administration would be over.

Assuming that Vice President Breckinridge would become the acting president, Wigfall believed that the entire South would feel secure against "being trapped into a war." Breckinridge was not an Ultra secessionist, and most of the people in his home state, Kentucky, would like to cling to the Union. But he strongly opposed a military attack upon any seceding state, sharing the widespread belief that using force to "coerce" a state would violate the Constitution. So, as commander-in-chief, Breckinridge would pose no threat to his fellow Southerners.

"Wigfall fully prepared his plans," the "Public Man" recorded. "All he needed was to be sure of certain details as to the opportunity of getting safely out of Washington with his prisoner, and for this he needed the cooperation of Floyd." Whether the senator wanted Secretary of War Floyd to provide some soldiers to guard the kidnapped President, or a "safe house" for his confinement, the writer did not say.

"On Christmas night," he wrote, "Wigfall went to Floyd's house with one companion to make this strange proposal and there in the basement room, Floyd's usual cozy corner, set it forth and contended for it earnestly, quite losing his temper at last when Floyd positively refused to connive in any way at the performance."

"B," the source of the story, vouched emphatically for the truth of it. Many people who knew Wigfall and his wild, reckless character, would have said, in the Southern vernacular, "I wouldn't put it past him."

"B" could have been any one of several men in Washington, but the diarist dropped a hint indicating that it was William Browne, editor of Buchanan's official newspaper, the *Constitution*, and an ardent secessionist who would have been compatible with Wigfall. A few pages earlier in his diary, "B" was identified as "the editor of the official paper." Within a few weeks, "Constitution" Browne would wind up in Montgomery, Alabama, in the employ of the new Confederacy.

There is no evidence that Senators Slidell, Davis, or other prominent Southern leaders, were even aware of Wigfall's scheme. The terrible Texan merely decided that it should be done and, by God, he would do it. Those Yankee senators had laughed at him just once too often; he would give them something they wouldn't laugh about!

His plot fizzled because the sickly, timid secretary of war was in no position to be involving himself in any harebrained scheme to kidnap the President. Floyd had to worry about how long he could hang onto his own cabinet post in the midst of a thunderstorm of financial scandal that was breaking about his head.

Throughout nearly four years in the cabinet, Floyd had been playing fast and loose with certain contractors, catering to favorites on profitable deals but apparently not profiting personally. When Congress delayed passage of the appropriations bill for the army, speculating contractors who had supplied the troops in the Far West came to Floyd demanding payment. Floyd, ever accommodating, would endorse their bills and certain banks would lend them cash on the basis of this collateral. The chief beneficiaries of this largess were identified in the press as William Russell of the Great Overland Pony Express; army transportation contractors Russell and Waddell; and Suter, Lea & Co., Washington, D.C., bankers.

Buchanan had ordered Floyd to stop this loose practice, but the secretary went right on until the acceptances reached about $5 million. Eventually the banks stopped discounting them and Russell, desperate to redeem his credit, appealed for help.

Lea, the banker, was formerly a clerk in the Indian Bureau of the Interior Department and knew all about the Indian Trust Fund, which consisted of about $3 million worth of negotiable bonds locked in a safe and in the charge of a young clerk. The clerk was a gambler named Godard Bailey, a relative of Mrs. Floyd, and thus described by the *Chicago Tribune*:

"This Bailey is a South Carolinian, although hailing from Alabama, a married man about thirty years of age, a disunion brawler strutting about with a palmetto cockade. He has been a fast liver and a frequent visitor of faro banks." Bailey, said the *Tribune*, was typical of the employees of the Interior Department, which was "stuffed with disunionists, from Secretary Thompson down to the porters ... nearly all fast young men."

Russell implored Bailey to lend him stacks of the Indian Trust bonds in return for Floyd's acceptances, assuring him that, when Congress voted the army's money, they would all be paid. Russell promised to redeem the bonds within a few weeks, but the stock market panic, touched off by the secession scare, made it impossible to raise the necessary cash.

In late December, Bailey faced a terrible dilemma: On January 1, he must present the coupons on the missing bonds so that the payments due to the Indian tribes could be made. Since the bonds were gone, there was no way he could hide the mess any longer.

Bailey had to confess that bonds worth $870,000 were missing from his safe, with nothing but Floyd's acceptances in their place. He sent a written statement to Secretary Thompson and a copy to Secretary Floyd, who was sick in bed. The bad news hit Thompson in the face when he returned from his mission to the North Carolina legislature. According to press reports, the key to the safe could not be found, so Thompson had a blacksmith break open the safe with a sledge hammer.

Thompson spent three sleepless nights trying to find Russell, and Marshall Rynders finally arrested the contractor in New York City on Christmas Eve and sent him to jail in Washington.

Republican newspapers naturally made the most political capital out of the smelly revelations. The *Chicago Tribune* roared: "Had Lincoln been defeated, this monster defalcation would have been concealed. Some other fund would have been used to pay the annuities. But this is believed to be only the first installment of a long catalogue of robberies and peculations on the public treasury that will come to light ere long. The pro-slavery administration is rotten in every department, its finances and its patriotism on par with each other. The government seems to be administered by men who unite the double characters of thief and traitor."

For Secretary Floyd, for Secretary Thompson, and their poor, befuddled president, worse news was soon to come.

❧ *13* ❧

CONFUSION
IN BUCHANAN'S CABINET

Early on the morning of December 27, Jefferson Davis called at the White House, clearly agitated by a telegram from South Carolina. He announced to Buchanan that Major Robert Anderson, "last night, under cover of darkness, spiked the guns at Fort Moultrie and moved his full force to Fort Sumter!"

Governor Pickens had sent the wire to three commissioners whom he had sent to Washington to negotiate with the federal government about the terms of a peaceful settlement. W. H. Trescot, the former assistant secretary of state, had resigned and now served openly as their agent, setting up a meeting with the President for the twenty-seventh.

Davis, accompanied by Trescot and Senator Hunter of Virginia, informed Buchanan: "Now, Mr. President, you are surrounded with blood and dishonor on all sides."

"My God!" cried Buchanan, who was standing by the mantelpiece, crushing a cigar in his hands. "Are calamities never to come singly? I call God to witness, *you* gentlemen, better than anybody, *know* that this is not only without but against my orders; it is against my policy."

Soon, several more Democratic senators—Bigler of Pennsylvania, Lane of Oregon, David Yulee and Stephen Mallory of Florida, and Slidell of Louisiana—came in. They implored the President to order Anderson to move his men back to Moultrie at once. He must do this, they said, to honor his gentleman's agreement that the status quo at Charleston would be preserved. Nervous and distraught, the President refused to act before consulting his cabinet.

When the cabinet met, Secretary Floyd, although still weak from illness, staged a great display of outrage, "emotions of rage and panic," according to Joe Holt, who later said, "His fury seemed like that of a baffled fiend."

Secretary Black disputed Floyd's charge that the major had disobeyed his orders. Black flourished a copy of the December 11 orders, endorsed by Floyd, which told the commander:

"The smallness of your force will not permit you, perhaps, to occupy more than one of these three forts, but an attack or an attempt to take possession of any of them will be regarded as an act of hostility, and you may then put your command into either of them when you may deem most proper, to increase its power of resistance."

Anderson also was "authorized to take similar steps when you have tangible evidence of a design to proceed to a hostile act."

But did Anderson have any such "tangible evidence"? No, he did not, Floyd declared. "Anderson left the guns at Moultrie spiked and burnt the carriages," the secretary said. "Such warlike tactics utterly violate the solemn pledge given by this government."

"When was any such pledge given?" demanded feisty, bearded Attorney General Stanton. "Does it exist in writing?"

No, it did not, for Buchanan was too cagey to sign any piece of paper; but he knew perfectly well that he had made the verbal pact with the South Carolina congressmen and they, with their strict code of honor, had carried out their end of the bargain; their people had refrained from any move against the forts.

Black, Holt, and Stanton defended the major; Thomas and Thompson assailed him, and the argument waxed hot. Floyd demanded the right to issue an order withdrawing all the federal troops from Charleston Harbor. Stanton shouted that any president who approved such an order would be "guilty of treason!"

"Oh, no!" Buchanan protested. "Not so bad as that, my friend. Not so bad as that!"

The cabinet wrangled on into the night until the weary President said he would delay a decision until he could receive official word from Anderson himself. If convinced that the major had violated his instructions by fleeing from Moultrie on a false alarm, "he might then think seriously of restoring for the present the former status quo of the forts."

The three South Carolina commissioners, after cooling their heels for a day, were brought to the White House on December 28. They

were a trio of veteran politicians: former U.S. Senator Robert
Barnwell, former Governor James H. Adams, and former U.S. House
Speaker James L. Orr. Buchanan received them, not as official agents,
but as "private gentlemen of the highest character."

Buchanan said he had just learned that state troops, under orders
from Governor Pickens, had seized Fort Moultrie and Castle Pinckney,
the customs house and the post office. So how, he asked, could he
order Major Anderson to go back to Moultrie?

Senator Barnwell said that South Carolina had had the power to
seize all three federal forts in Charleston at any time in the past sixty
days but, to avert bloodshed, had "determined to trust to your honor."
Now he demanded that Buchanan maintain his honor by ordering
the immediate withdrawal of all the federal troops, to avoid war.

"Mr. Barnwell, you are pressing me too importunately," the President protested. "You don't give me time to consider. You don't give
me time to say my prayers. I always say my prayers when required to
act upon any great state affair." Frustrated, the commissioners yielded
to the President's desire for divine guidance and left in a huff.

When the cabinet reassembled that evening, the Southern members pressed their demand for the removal of all the troops from
Charleston. Poor, sickly Secretary Floyd lay on a sofa between the
windows. Secretary Thompson pleaded for the withdrawal as a peace
gesture to show that the great and powerful United States meant no
harm to little South Carolina.

But Attorney General Stanton said this administration did not
dare to retreat like that. It had already lost the people's confidence, he
said, and now they were further shocked by the revelation that almost
a million dollars' worth of bonds had been stolen from a vault in
Thompson's office and Floyd's notes substituted for them.

"No administration, much less this one," Stanton said, "can
afford to lose a million of money and a fort in the same week."

The *Chicago Tribune*'s Washington correspondent provided a lively
account of the President's interview with the three South Carolinians, whom it mocked as the envoys of the "Palmetto Empire." Then
the *Tribune* recounted the ensuing meeting of the cabinet:

"It was a stormy session. The members were equally divided with
one—Toucey—in the attitude of the donkey between two bales of

hay. Black, Holt and Stanton approved of Anderson's conduct and insisted that he should be sustained. Floyd, Thompson and Thomas denounced him and demanded that he should not only be censured, but removed from his command and the garrison be returned to Fort Moultrie."

Reporting on the cabinet's row the following day, the Republican paper said:

> The President, like a pusillanimous coward, refused to take sides, but said he would do whatever a majority of his cabinet directed. Toucey finally screwed his courage up to the sticking point and voted to sustain Anderson.
>
> Thereupon Floyd announced that he would resign. High words passed, and a personal collision between the fire-eaters and doughfaces almost ensued. The Old Pub Func., shaking like an aspen leaf, entreated them not to quarrel, and offered them some old whiskey—his unfailing remedy. The old man has become little better than a sot. He keeps saturated with Monongahela whiskey. He drinks to drown remorse and stultify his brain as he staggers along with the treasonable gang who have possession of him.

The miserable secretary of war realized that, because of the scandal over his "acceptances," substituted for the missing bonds, the jig was up. He had to resign. But he need not creep out in disgrace over the financial scandal. Instead, he could walk out proudly in a blaze of righteous indignation over Buchanan's refusal to withdraw the troops from Charleston. He had to give up his post, he said in a letter of resignation, "because I can no longer hold it, under my convictions of patriotism, nor with honor, subject as I am to the violation of solemn pledges and plighted faith."

The *Chicago Tribune* added this verbal kick to Floyd's departing posterior: "The decent people of the city were wild with delight when the news was made public that the arch traitor and 'head devil' among the disunionists had actually tendered his resignation and that it had been accepted by the President."

On Saturday evening, December 29, the President gave the cabinet the formal letter from the South Carolina commissioners and a draft of his own reply. Again, Black, Holt, and Stanton furiously opposed it as too weak. The President must not appear to be negotiating with these self-styled "ambassadors," Stanton insisted. "They are lawbreakers, traitors; they should be arrested."

Once more, the cabinet broke up in disarray.

On Sunday morning, the secretary of the navy, Isaac Toucey, went to the White House and told the President that Black was seriously thinking about resigning. Buchanan summoned Black, who soon arrived and confirmed his intention to quit unless the weak reply to South Carolina's commissioners could be greatly strengthened.

Aghast at the prospect of losing his oldest friend, and probably Holt and Stanton to boot, the President pleaded with Black not to desert him at this darkest hour. He thrust his draft paper into Black's hands and told him to rewrite it to suit himself.

Black and Stanton quickly stiffened it up in several ways. They cut out the soothing phrases which indicated that he would like to negotiate some arrangement about the forts; they tried to explain his belief that he really had made no binding pledge to keep the status quo of the forts. They also left out any reference to his idea that the federal government could not coerce a state. In the end, the statement did not sound like Buchanan at all.

In his final, revised version, the President said that, when he found out about the transfer of the troops from Moultrie to Sumter, he first thought of ordering them back; but then the South Carolinians had taken over Moultrie, Castle Pinckney, and other federal property. Now he was being asked to withdraw all the federal forces from Charleston.

"This I cannot do; this I will not do," he declared, in iron words that did not sound as if they had come from the pen of the vacillating "Old Public Functionary." Indeed, they had actually been written by Black and Stanton.

Major Anderson's forces would remain at Sumter, the President said, and the fort would be defended "against hostile attacks from whatever quarter they may come."

Thus, under the intense pressure by Black, Holt, and Stanton, Buchanan moved away from the grip of the Southerners who had been instrumental in placing him in the White House. Senator Clingman of North Carolina observed that Senators Davis and Slidell "were especially urgent" in ordering him to keep his word about maintaining the status quo as a point of honor. "Though he admitted the obligation," said Clingman, "he was afraid to comply."

He was afraid because of threats against his home in Pennsylvania, said South Carolina Congressman Laurence Keitt. Whenever we tell him he must move out the troops, Keitt told Clingman, "the old fellow cries and says, if he does, they will burn his house at Wheatland."

After Buchanan's clash with the South Carolina commissioners, Jefferson Davis wrote to Mississippi Governor J. J. Pettus:

> President Buchanan has forfeited any claim which he may have had on our forbearance and support. I regard his treatment of South Carolina as perfidious, and place no reliance upon him for the protection of our rights or abstinence from hostility to us. In this do not understand me as alleging a wicked purpose—his evil deeds rather spring from irresolution and an increasing dread of Northern excitement. He is said to fear that his house at Wheatland may be burned & it is reported that he apprehends impeachment when the withdrawal of Southern Senators shall give the requisite majority in the Senate to convict him.

The *Chicago Tribune* said that Buchanan, "alternately praying and cursing," switched from Southern to Northern counselors "upon threats made to his face" by men of both parties, who warned him that, if he did not take a firmer pro-Union stand, he would face a "trial for treason."

The Southerners who, for so long, had considered Buchanan as their friend, realized now that he had slipped away from them and would no longer dance to their tune. Slidell and Davis were especially bitter over his transfer of allegiance and felt that they could no longer trust him to act like a gentleman. They steeled themselves to go forward with the secession programme as their only hope for future power.

All hope of compromise is gone, Senator Judah P. Benjamin said, sadly, in a speech on Monday, December 31, which attracted a capacity crowd of spectators jamming the Senate galleries and spilling over into the Capitol corridors. "Our committee has reported this morning that no possible scheme of adjustment can be devised," he said, referring to the failure of the Committee of Thirteen.

South Carolina has declared her independence and "We, the representatives of these remaining states, must permit her peaceful secession or put her down by force of arms. That is the sole issue. No artifice can conceal it." Within a few weeks, he said, seven more states would go out and trying to coerce them must lead to civil war.

The crowd in the galleries cheered as Benjamin defended the South in his musical voice, which was once described as similar to the chiming of silvery bells.

His short, stout figure was clad in a beautifully tailored black broadcloth suit, and he played with a gold watch chain as he calmly recited an array of legal authorities justifying secession. His broad forehead, thick fleshy nose and lips, curly black hair, and silken chin whiskers completed the picture of an extremely intellectual Hebrew scholar, highly acclaimed as a brilliant lawyer but still rather lonely in a hostile Gentile world. His lips curled up at the ends to produce a smile that never seemed to vanish, even when his mood could not match it. Friends believed that his smile meant he was forever in a good mood, calm, serene, sincere. His enemies accused him of being sly, crafty, secretive, and insincere.

Born in the West Indies, he had arrived in New Orleans as a penniless, friendless boy. By sheer hard work and study he had advanced to the front rank of the exotic city's legal profession. Forty-nine in 1860, Benjamin teamed with Louisiana's senior senator, John Slidell, to make the most powerful pair in the Senate's exclusive club of gentlemen.

Benjamin accused the Republicans of vilifying the Southerners as "thieves, robbers, murderers, villains of the blackest dye, because we continue to own property we owned at the time we all signed the compact"—the Constitution. He cried:

"You do not propose to enter into our states, you say ... to kill or destroy our institutions by force. Oh, no ... you propose simply to close us in an embrace that will suffocate us ... and when we say, 'Let us go in peace,' we are answered by your leading spokesmen, 'Oh, no, you cannot do that; ... your people will be hanged for treason.'"

Pleading with the North to avoid "invading our states or shedding the blood of our people," Benjamin declared:

"The fortunes of war may be averse to our arms; you may carry desolation into our peaceful land, and with torch and fire you may set our cities in flames; you may, under the protection of your advancing armies, give shelter to the furious fanatics who desire ... nothing more than to add all the horrors of a servile insurrection to the calamities of civil war ... but you can never subjugate us ... Never! Never!"

His closing cry, "Never! Never!" was greeted by the crowded galleries with screams and uproarious applause, the *New York Times* said the next day. "All over the galleries there were shouts and cheers and waving of handkerchiefs and hurrahs, and the greatest confusion and excitement prevailed all over the house."

As the presiding officer pounded his gavel and shouted for order, and the galleries were cleared and the people filed out, the *Times* correspondent heard many expressions like these:

"That's the talk!"

"Now we'll have war!"

"Damn the abolitionists!"

"Abe Lincoln will never come here!"

❧ 14 ❧

"THE MEANEST TRICK
IN THE WORLD"

The three commissioners from South Carolina were astounded when they read the iron language in the message sent to them by the President, declaring his intention to keep all the federal troops in Charleston. They fired back a blistering reply that virtually called him a liar, guilty of deceit and dishonor. Buchanan considered it so insolent that he sent it back to them after endorsing it with these words:

"This paper, just presented to the President, is of such a character that he declines to receive it."

The full text of the South Carolinians' indictment is missing from practically every book about this dispute. Senator Preston King, New York Republican, tried to keep it from being printed in the *Congressional Globe* but, by a roll call vote, the Senate published it with a speech by Jefferson Davis.

The text clearly shows why Buchanan would have preferred that it never see the light of day. For the South Carolinians insisted that he had broken a gentleman's agreement with their state's congressmen to maintain the status quo of the federal troops at Charleston if the state would refrain from any attack on the forts.

The commissioners recalled that, on the day after Washington learned that Major Anderson had moved his men from Fort Moultrie to Fort Sumter, "we saw you, and we called upon you then to redeem your pledge. You did not deny it. ... You do not deny it now, but you seek to escape from its obligation."

Then the South Carolinians noted Buchanan's ringing declaration, refusing to withdraw the troops: "This I cannot do; this I will not do. Such an idea was never thought of by me in any possible contingency.

No allusion to it had ever been made in any communication between myself and any human being."

How could that possibly be the truth? the visitors wondered. "Your conversation with us left upon our minds the distinct impression that you did seriously contemplate the withdrawal of the troops from Charleston harbor."

"You ought to know, better than any other man," they told Buchanan, that the people of Charleston could have taken Fort Sumter at any time "without blood," but they were restrained after receiving "many and reiterated assurances on your behalf, which we cannot believe unauthorized.

"In good faith, they sent their commissioners to negotiate with you. ... Scarcely had these commissioners left than Major Anderson waged war. ... He abandoned his position, spiked his guns, burnt his gun carriages, made preparation for the destruction of his post, and withdrew under cover of the night to a safer position. ... By your course, you have probably rendered civil war inevitable."

The South Carolinians "packed up their duds and left for Charleston yesterday," the *Chicago Tribune* reported January 4. "They go away with a big bug buzzing in their ears. ... Negotiations broke off abruptly and the three knaves in buckram bought through tickets to Charleston and checked their baggage to the kingdom of South Carolina."

The angry and frustrated South Carolinians had good reasons for suspecting that Buchanan was preparing to send more troops to Charleston. They picked up a tip from some source in New York that "the President has ordered reinforcements to be sent to Sumter and they are convinced, accordingly, that he has been trifling with them simply to gain time for perfecting what they call a policy of aggression," the "Public Man" recorded in his diary.

The tip was correct. On Sunday, December 30, General Winfield Scott had sent a note to the White House, saying: "Will the President permit Genl. S., without reference to the War department & otherwise as secretly as possible, to send two hundred & fifty recruits, from New York Harbor, to reinforce Fort Sumter, together with some extra muskets or rifles, ammunition, & subsistence stores? It is hoped that a sloop of war & cutter may be ordered for the same purpose as early as tomorrow."

Realizing that Scott's idea would touch off another fight in his cabinet, the President moved stealthily. He transferred the tough pro-Unionist, Postmaster General Joseph Holt, to the War Department, to replace the departed and unlamented Secretary Floyd, and Holt went to work very quietly to find a suitable ship for the mission to Charleston.

Holt selected the light-draft steamer *Star of the West*, because it could sail over the sunken vessels blocking the Charleston harbor. Loaded with about 250 troops and their weapons, the ship slipped secretly out of New York City on January 5, bound for Charleston. Interior Secretary Jacob Thompson learned about the relief ship the night before it was due to arrive, and he telegraphed a warning to the South Carolina authorities to give her a warm reception.

They did. The guns of Fort Moultrie, now in the state troops' hands, poured forth shot and shell barrages that forced the *Star of the West* to turn about and sail ingloriously for the open sea.

Thompson indignantly resigned, charging that Buchanan and Holt had "played the meanest trick in the world on me." He said the President had promised that no reinforcements would be sent until after the cabinet approved them. Buchanan asserted that, after dismissing the South Carolina commissioners, he had told the cabinet: "It is all over and reinforcements must be sent." Thompson should have heard him, he said; other cabinet members apparently did.

Thompson correctly surmised that General Scott had cooked up the idea of sending the shallow-draft relief ship. "He convinced Holt that she could steal into Sumter without fear of discovery or collision," the irate Mississippian recounted in a letter to Howell Cobb, the former treasury secretary now drumming up support for secession in Georgia.

"To do this, it was necessary to keep the movement in secret," the secretary explained, "and, as they all knew that I would resign for such an order and thus blow the order, it was necessary to keep me in ignorance of it."

Thompson realized that Buchanan was no longer the Southerners' puppet; he was the Northerners' puppet now. "Old Buck, at heart, is right with us," Thompson told Cobb, "but after Stanton came in, I have seen him gradually giving way. ... He has not the nerve or the backbone to adopt our views."

"I am now very anxious to see a new confederacy formed," Thompson went on. "The Black Republicans do not intend to give back one inch. It is now naked submission or secession. I consider every Southern state disgraced who will quietly surrender her rights without a struggle, and, by Jove, the work goes bravely on. Va. will be out in time. The feeling is getting up in Ten. and Ky. and I think Maryland. I hope Georgia will make quick work of it."

Thompson's vivacious wife, Kate, turned against Buchanan in this letter to a friend: "Now you can guess what I think of the President's heart—as black as the man of war Brooklyn. ... Judge Black is the meanest man living. ... Stanton ... a mean, low-life Pen. Scamp. I wish I was Military Dictator. I would take his head off to the tune of Yankee Doodle."

Republican newspapers hailed the departure of Thompson with delight. Typical was this blast from the *Chicago Tribune:* "Another traitor has left the cabinet!"

"Thus," the Chicago paper commented, "the traitorous triumvirate—Cobb, Floyd and Thompson—are gone from the cabinet and their places filled by Union men. These three bad men have been the cause of the decline and fall of the President. ... He was plastic clay in the hands of three treasonable plotters ... assisted by Gwin, Slidell and Davis."

Soon thereafter, the relentless *Tribune* gave a farewell boot to Treasury Secretary Philip Thomas. He "was supposed to be a Union man, but turned out to be a snake in the grass," the partisan paper said. "It was by his orders that all the disunion members were paid their full salaries, while the Union members were told there was no money in the Treasury."

Buchanan decreed a day of prayer and fasting for the troubled nation, on January 4, 1861. In obedience to the proclamation, Lincoln attended church in Springfield that day. "It is to be presumed," wrote one irreverent newspaper reporter, "that in his prayers, Mr. Buchanan's backbone was not forgotten."

Buchanan had tried, however timorously, to prevent civil war by pressing the idea of a constitutional convention in which the delegates could work out amendments that would reassure the worried Southern people. But Lincoln refused to endorse the plan, and his fellow

Republicans in Congress insisted that there were no grievances to discuss; it was necessary only for the laws to be enforced throughout the land.

Lincoln's refusal to favor a convention or a compromise drew fire from his defeated rival, Stephen A. Douglas. To the Republicans' claim that the people had endorsed their Chicago platform by electing Lincoln—although 61 percent of the voters had favored other candidates—Douglas replied: "Better that all platforms be scattered to the winds, better that every public man and politician in America be consigned to political martyrdom, better that all political organization be broken up, than that the Union be destroyed and the country plunged into civil war."

Douglas, who had consistently urged the Southerners to stay in the Union rather than flee from the prospect of Lincoln's presidency, told the Senate on January 3 that he still opposed secession but it was, nevertheless, a fact that must be faced.

Only three courses were open, he said, for dealing with South Carolina's secession: Reunion through compromise, peaceful separation, or war. "Are we prepared *in our hearts* for war with our own brethren and kindred?" he asked.

"Why cannot you Republicans accede to the re-establishment and extension of the Missouri Compromise line?" Douglas asked. They certainly had dumped countless curses on his head for repealing it with the passage of his Kansas-Nebraska Act. He had accepted the Crittenden plan a few days before in the Senate Committee of Thirteen, and even Senators Davis and Toombs would have approved it as a final settlement if the Republican members had only given three votes for it. But the Republicans refused, so they bore "the sole responsibility" for its failure, the Little Giant said. They were following the orders of Lincoln, who told them to spurn all plans that might open new lands to slavery. Lincoln and the Republicans were totally consistent: To all such compromise ideas, they always answered: "No."

Douglas said:

> A war upon a political issue, waged by the people of eighteen states against the people and domestic institutions of fifteen sister states, is a fearful and revolting thought.

The South will be a unit, and desperate, under the belief that your object in waging war is their destruction and not the preservation of the Union; that you meditate servile insurrection, and the abolition of slavery in the Southern states, by fire and sword, in the name and under pretext of enforcing the laws and vindicating the authority of the government. You know that such is the prevailing, and, I may say, unanimous opinion at the South, and that ten million people are preparing for the terrible conflict under that conviction.

Douglas's speech stung the Republicans, and they struck back furiously. Illinois Congressman E. B. Washburne told Lincoln in a January 4 letter: "Douglas' speech yesterday was infamous and damnable—the crowning atrocity of his life." Douglas was determined to make all possible efforts for peace, even at the cost of compromising with some politicians who had doomed his own dreams of the presidency. Exhausted by his hopeless campaign and unsure about his health, he may have known, instinctively, that this could be his last fight. He could have no greater cause than the prevention of a disastrous civil war.

❦ 15 ❦

WASHINGTON —
CONFEDERATE CAPITAL?

On the night of January 5, 1861, United States senators from seven states of the Deep South met privately at the National Hotel in Washington and determined to step up the pressure on the other slave states to secede without delay.

Their own states were on the verge of leaving the Union and joining South Carolina in the drive for independence. But their leaders knew that a new confederacy embracing only about half of the slave states would hardly be large or strong enough to maintain its existence if challenged by the industrial and commercial might of the states remaining in the Union. More states in the upper South must be enlisted in the secession crusade so that the Confederacy could become a powerful government, not a mere collection of cotton-growing states that would be no match for the federal government.

Senators from Mississippi, Alabama, Georgia, Florida, Louisiana, Arkansas, and Texas approved a four-point manifesto to be circulated throughout the South as a spur to united action in support of little South Carolina.

- First, the senators "resolved, that, in our opinion, each of the Southern states should, as soon as may be, secede from the Union."
- Second, they called for a Confederacy of the seceding states to be formed at a convention at Montgomery, Alabama, no later than February 15.
- Third, they asked for instructions as to whether the Southern members of Congress should remain in their seats until March 4 to defeat hostile legislation.
- Fourth, they appointed a committee consisting of Jefferson Davis of Mississippi, John Slidell of Louisiana, and Stephen Mallory of Florida "to carry out the objects of this meeting."

Lucius E. Chittenden, a treasury official, recorded that Davis was to be the "head and general" manager of the intensified drive to build a strong confederacy. "The border states could not be voted out of the Union in time," Chittenden said, "but they were nearest Washington and could provide the men to seize the government on the 4th of March."

Davis himself, on January 8, wrote to a friend:

> We are advancing rapidly to the end of "the Union." The cotton states may now be regarded as having decided for secession. South Carolina is in a quasi war, and the probabilities are that events will hasten her and associates into general conflict with the forces of the federal government. The Black Republicans, exultant over their recent successes, are not disposed to concede anything, and the stern necessity of resistance is forcing itself upon the judgment of all the slaveholding states. The Va. legislature met yesterday and took promptly and boldly the Southern ground.

Although not ready yet for secession, the Virginians vowed to defend any Southern state against federal coercion. They arranged for a state convention in February to decide the next move for the Old Dominion. The drive for "immediate secession" was fast gaining strength in this state, a Virginian wrote to Senator Crittenden. "Thousands of Bell men have joined the seceders, and nearly all the Douglas men besides, and unless we can bring about a speedy reaction, I fear all will be lost."

The Washington correspondent of the *Cincinnati Gazette* reported in early January that he had "ascertained ... in a manner that leaves no room whatever for doubt, that it is the purpose of the South to seize the Capital at some time prior to, or on, the 4th of March. ... A secret society exists throughout the South for this purpose. ... Southern members of Congress have been sending home their wives and daughters and few now remain. There are not over one hundred lady boarders at the three principal hotels."

High on the Southerners' list of states essential to their success were Virginia and Maryland. Maryland was important because it had supplied the land on the north side of the Potomac River, making up the District of Columbia. Virginia had provided the land on the south side for the rest of the ten-mile-square Federal District, but had taken it back, without much of a fuss, in 1846.

Secessionist lawyers claimed that, upon leaving the Union, Maryland could legally reclaim all of its former land, plus the federal buildings erected on it—including the Capitol and the White House. Then, they reasoned, where would Abe Lincoln be inaugurated, and where would he reside, when Washington became the capital of the new Confederacy?

Maryland's Governor Thomas H. Hicks, an Old Line Whig who opposed secession, warned the people of his state in early January: "The secession leaders in Washington have resolved that the border states, and especially Maryland, shall be precipitated into secession with the cotton states before the Fourth of March.

"They have resolved to seize the federal Capitol and the public archives, so that they may be in a position to be acknowledged by foreign governments as 'the United States,' and the assent of Maryland is necessary, as the District of Columbia would revert to her in the case of a dissolution of the Union."

Hicks adamantly refused to call the legislature into session, as demanded by many of his citizens who sympathized with the South, because he knew full well that the Democrats' majority would pressure it into secession. "The men shouting most loudly for the legislature to meet have their own agenda," secession, he said.

A majority of the Maryland state senators, mostly Democrats, demanded that the governor call the legislature. So did a mass meeting of citizens in Baltimore. A delegation from that rally called upon Hicks and threatened him with bodily harm if he persisted in his stubborn refusal, he told a congressional investigating committee.

"Taunts were used, my personal safety was threatened, and I was warned about the hazard I would run if I persisted in declining to convene the legislature," he said. "Reference was made to shedding blood and refusing to allow Lincoln to be inaugurated. I remarked to them that I could not see the necessity for shedding blood; they knew I was a Southern man and a slaveholder."

Commissioners sent from Mississippi, Alabama, and Georgia urged the governor to let Maryland secede, but every time, he refused.

"I know what they desired," Hicks said later, in Washington. "They wanted this Capitol. They wanted this District. They had no other very particular reason for desiring Maryland to go with the Southern states, except that the territory on which this Capitol and the other government buildings had been erected was ceded to the General government by the State of Maryland, and they said that, if Maryland went out of the Union, it would revert to her."

When one of the Southern commissioners told him that Maryland would regain all of its District land, plus the federal buildings, Hicks asked: "If we had the power to do it, would it be right?"

"Well," said the commissioner, "we will settle one thing at a time; let us decide that Maryland shall go with the South, and then we will arrange other things."

"Sir, what is to become of Maryland if she should decide to go with the South?" the governor asked.

"Oh," the visitor replied, "Maryland will become the greatest state in the Confederacy, and Baltimore will be the London of the Southern Confederacy."

"That will do to tell to boys," Hicks answered scornfully, "but it will not be credited by men of mature age."

Hicks also said the ambassadors from the Cotton States told him, "You may just as well yield, for, despite of all that can be done, King Cotton will control this government."

"But, sir," Hicks said, "I acknowledge no other king than a sovereign people."

J.L.M. Curry, a former congressman, came from Alabama as a commissioner empowered to treat with Maryland with a view of forming a "mutual league" for the protection of Southern rights. But he failed to sell that bill of goods to the stubborn governor.

Judge A. H. Handy, a Maryland native, came from Mississippi as its envoy seeking to pull Maryland out of the Union. "Mr. Lincoln and Mr. Hamlin will never be inaugurated," Handy said. "We want Mississippi to go out, say, today, Maryland tomorrow and so on, until all the states south of Mason's and Dixon's line are out, and then we will form a Southern Union."

"Maryland and the other slave states must go out before the Fourth of March," Handy said. Hicks asked, "Why?"

"We never intend that Abraham Lincoln shall have dominion over us," the judge replied.

Hicks became convinced that "there was a positive design, and numbers of armed men in Baltimore and Washington were engaged in it."

Judge Handy revealed more details of the secession scheme at a public meeting at the Maryland Institute. This was the plan:

"All the Gulf States are sure to secede. Then the rest of the fifteen slave states must quickly follow before March 4, form a confederacy, reconstruct the existing government on a Southern basis, re-adopt the old constitution, take possession of the federal capital and invite Northern states to come in.

"Then, instead of Mr. Lincoln and Republicans, with the North in power, we would have Mr. Breckinridge and Democracy, with the South dictating the terms."

Lord Lyons, the British ambassador, informed his government: "The plans of the Secessionists are settled. They intend to have a Confederacy fully established ... before the 3rd of March. They declare that they shall then be prepared to negotiate on equal terms with the United States for a Union of the two Confederacies.

"Such a union they say they should be prepared to form, provided the constitutional arrangements were such as would prevent the vastly larger population of the Northern Confederacy having power to overwhelm by the number of their votes the influence of the South in the general Government."

Senator R.M.T. Hunter of Virginia unveiled the Southern plan for reconstructing the Union in a speech on January 11, evidently as the chosen spokesman for the region. The *Chicago Tribune* said Hunter "made a deep impression" as he declared that the old Union was gone and "nothing was left but to reconstruct it on a Southern basis."

As Hunter explained it, the newspaper went on, "the slave states must make a new constitution incorporating guarantees for slavery that would protect it beyond the power of Northern opinion. Then the North would be invited to annex themselves to the Southern Confederacy, and live thereafter under the new pro-slavery Constitution, which would make slaves property and prevent the majority from ruling. It was no more a question of union but of reunion."

As if on cue, a Virginian arose in the House of Representatives and offered a similar "reconstruction" plan to avert the horrors of a brothers' war. Representative Muscoe Russell Hunter Garnett warned the North that at least seven states would form the new confederacy and as many as eight others would join if armed force should be used against the South. "I invite you to negotiate," he said. "First secure a truce; and then seek for terms of adjustment."

Senator Judah P. Benjamin, after Louisiana's secession on January 26, assured a Northern friend that the "reconstruction" could work. "We shall all be back here in two months and you will join us," he said. "New York and several other states will come in. We don't care for most of the Eastern ones; they may stay out if they please; New York will certainly come."

Benjamin's friend, Judge Charles Patrick Daly, a New York City Democrat, disputed the prediction in the incident, which the jurist's wife recorded in her diary. Maria Daly also noted that the wife of Senator John Slidell, on the eve of her departure for Louisiana, said she would not remove her furniture or most of her wardrobe because "we will be back in Washington in March or April."

Mrs. Daly also said General Winfield Scott knew about the secessionists' plans because the Southerners assumed—incorrectly—that, as a native Virginian, he would cooperate with them. She said Judge Edwards Pierrepont of New York, a friend of the Dalys, interviewed the old commander and learned this:

> The original plan was told him [Scott] and he was asked, he said, to keep quiet and take no part on either side. The first plan was that Buchanan was to be allowed either to die or resign. Breckinridge was vice president. He was to be inaugurated by Ex-President Tyler. Maryland, Virginia, Kentucky and Missouri were to secede from the Union, thus enclosing Washington, which was to be in their hands, with the Congress, archives and foreign ministers, and everything would go on under the new state of things, as before. ... It was supposed that all the other states would come into the new arrangement except New England, which was not to be permitted to do so.

General Scott was quoted as saying that his knowledge of the plans for making Washington the capital of the new Confederacy troubled him so much that he could not sleep. So he arose from his bed one night and wrote out all the details and sent the document to the government, which made no use of it and never returned it to him. Mrs. Daly did not say which official received the general's warning and ignored it.

The *New York Times* also reported that the secessionists "had no doubt that their Southern Confederacy would speedily absorb and attach to it all the free states except 'the fanatical states of New England.'" The *New York Tribune* editor, Horace Greeley, claimed that former Governor Horatio Seymour favored this idea "in private conversation" and Governor Rodman Price of New Jersey openly urged his state to join the Confederacy.

Senator Benjamin, a lawyer of international reputation, continued his close contacts with rich and influential Democratic friends in New York, notably the financier August Belmont and the attorney and railroad promoter S.L.M. Barlow. They encouraged him to believe that sensible Northern businessmen also favored some way of reorganizing the Union, with the South welcomed in and the New England fanatics frozen out and left to cling, all alone, to the Canadian border.

Horatio King, who became postmaster general when Joseph Holt left that job and took over the War Department, said in his memoirs that the Southern leaders met secretly at night at their Washington headquarters and "here their plans were concocted which were to carry all the slave states out of the Union and give them the city of Washington as their seat of government." Washington could be taken peacefully, however, "only when both Virginia and Maryland should be fairly out of the Union." Hence the intensified efforts to pull both states into the Confederacy before March 4.

Governor Hicks, resisting terrific pressure for him to call the Maryland legislature into session, appealed to his fellow Whig, Senator Crittenden, to keep on trying to have Congress enact his compromise. "Great God! Can it be that this once great and beautiful country, this government, the admiration of the world, will be broken into fragments?" Hicks asked. "No! It cannot be. Then, sir, what is to be done in our extremity? Patriots, peace men must stand up and beat back the powers of darkness. They must, by prudence and perseverance, head off these fiends now engaged in the effort to overthrow our government."

On January 9, Hicks urged Crittenden to press forward with his measure allowing the people to vote on his proposed compromise. This, he said, would gain time and check "the mad secessionists and corrupt politicians."

The Northern men in Congress could cover themselves with glory by acting to restore the peace, the governor wrote. "Otherwise, let them go to Hell and take the country with them."

Hicks's near-hysteria could be explained by the intensifying pressures upon him to let Maryland secede.

"The disunionists have despaired of being able to dragoon Governor Hicks into convoking the legislature," the *Chicago Tribune* reported. "They are now at work getting up an internal revolution. One scheme proposes that the speakers of the Senate and House shall call the legislature together."

The legislature could assume to act like a sovereign body in the present crisis, "and pass an act annulling the cession of the District of Columbia and claiming possession of the federal capital as part of Maryland," the *Tribune* said. "The next step in the programme is to deed it to the Southern Confederacy. This would give the disunionists the color of title and afford them a sort of legal pretext for attempting to seize upon this city with its public property."

"Maryland is to be forced into the disunion lines," Congressman Isaac Morris told the House on January 16. "Then the District will be claimed as belonging to the South, and a Southern army will be encamped here before the Fourth of March. ... The enemy is battering at the very doors of the Capitol, and meditates a seizure of our national records, plus the army and navy. ... This capitol is to be seized and, if necessary, forcible resistance made to the inauguration of Mr. Lincoln."

"We are sleeping on the verge of a volcano," the Illinois Democrat cried, "which is sending forth is lurid lights and casting up its red-hot lava. The fires of civil discord are ready to burst forth in one wild destructive flame!"

❧ 16 ❧

"THERE WILL BE NO REVOLUTION"

Through January 1861, the march of the Deep South states from the Union proceeded with relentless speed, as the state conventions called up their measures of secession as requested by the Southern senators after their caucus in Washington. Mississippi went out on the ninth; Florida on the tenth; Alabama on the eleventh.

In these three states, the majorities were decisive, but among the advocates of the old Union, who were knocked down and run over by the mass stampede for the exit, were many who mourned the decision as a grave mistake. Former U.S. Senator Jeremiah Clemens, a member of the Alabama convention, who had stalled desperately for time, thus bemoaned its vote in favor of secession:

"We are out; we have bid adieu to the Stars and Stripes and abandoned the high privilege of calling ourselves 'American citizens.' I am not ashamed to confess that I could not restrain my tears when the old banner, which I have followed through so many dangers, was torn down and the flag of Alabama was raised in its place. I cannot restrain them now, but the deed is done."

Clemens, who had fought for Texas in its war for independence and in the war against Mexico, said in his letter to Senator Crittenden that civil war would come soon.

On January 12, Senator Seward delivered a speech that was heralded as a reflection of concessions that Lincoln might make to halt the march of secession. Masses of spectators jammed the Senate galleries, lobbies, and cloakrooms to hear the senator, hailed as the "premier" of the new administration, for Lincoln had offered to make him secretary of state.

Short, stoop-shouldered, with a large beaklike nose, protruding ears, and silvery white, wiry hair, Seward did not loom as a towering figure; but he still commanded respect for his intellect and his long leadership of the Republican Party. In truth, however, he would no longer dominate the party, although he would wage a silent struggle with the new president over its policy toward the South.

Bowing to the dictates of Lincoln, Seward offered the South, in his speech, only the few concessions which the President-elect allowed him to give: He would enforce the fugitive-slave law and ask the states to repeal any personal liberty laws in conflict with it. He would back a constitutional amendment protecting slavery in the states—but he would never safeguard it in any territories. He would admit Kansas as a free state and divide the remaining territories into two states; and he would build two Pacific railroads, one with a terminus in the North and the other with a terminus in the South.

Seward's conciliatory tone, and his fervent pleas for the Union, brought praise from moderate Americans, but radical Republicans complained that he sounded too soft toward the "treason" of the disunionists, while the Southerners scorned his peace offerings as too little, too late.

Senator James Mason telegraphed the pro-secession forces in the Virginia legislature: "Let none be deceived by reports of Seward's speech yesterday. It was fraudulent and tricky under cloak of seeming mildness, and no offer of concession worth consideration."

North Carolina's Senator Thomas Bragg telegraphed a political ally in Raleigh that Seward had "conceded more than ever before but not enough. War the result of secession."

Senator Robert Toombs of Georgia, who would have accepted the Crittenden Compromise if the Republicans had not opposed it, said 90 percent of the people in his state would prefer to stay in the Union but only with their rights fully respected, and that was impossible under the rule of Lincoln, who "accepts every cardinal principle of the abolitionists."

"Yes, Mr. Lincoln says it is a fundamental principle that all men are entitled to equality in government everywhere," Toombs roared. He told the Republicans: "You not only want to upturn our social system; your people not only steal our slaves and make them freemen to vote against us; but you seek to bring an inferior race in a condition of equality, socially, and politically, with our own people."

A *Chicago Tribune* correspondent painted this word-portrait of the Georgia "fire-eater" at the height of his harangue, which clearly was intended to whip up pro-secession votes in the Georgia state convention opening on January 16:

> Imagine a big, obese, swarthy-looking, savage—a perfect specimen of a plantation overseer, who rolls about with a whip in hand, with a hoarse, gruff voice, ordering the hands like so many dogs. ... Now listen to his roar in harsh, cracked, thick, guttural cadences—pitching his voice in the middle of every sentence so loud that he could be heard all over a plantation a league in extent; dropping it at the end of each sentence to a conversational tone, and rattling and jumbling his words together so fast, and thick, as to defy the swiftest phonographer to keep up, and most practiced ear to understand all he is saying.

Toombs was well aware that there was a furious struggle, back home in Georgia, between the politicians, like himself, who demanded immediate secession and those who favored "cooperation" with other slave states in an effort to win guarantees of their rights. There were strong men on both sides: For immediate action there were Governor Joseph E. Brown, U.S. Senators Toombs and Iverson, T.R.R. Cobb, and his brother, Howell; advocates of delay included Alexander H. Stephens, Benjamin H. Hill, and former Governor Herschel V. Johnson, the vice-presidential nominee on the Douglas ticket.

One Atlanta newspaper charged that thousands had been induced to vote for the immediate secession ticket, in choosing the convention delegates, because they were "dragooned and bullied by threats, jeers and sneers" by the Minutemen. "Sensational dispatches and inflammatory rumors manufactured in Washington City—that cess-pool"—had aided the drive for secession, the paper said. "There never has been as much lying and bullying practiced since those of Sodom and Gomorrah."

On January 16, the opening day of the Georgia convention, the Senate called up the Crittenden Compromise for a crucial vote. The opponents of immediate secession hoped they could win in Georgia if the Crittenden plan could be passed, including its most important provision—that slavery would be protected in the South and in the territories below the 36° 30' line "now held or hereafter to be acquired."

The Republicans were determined to kill the Crittenden plan, which Lincoln adamantly opposed. They did not care whether Georgia voted for secession or not. So, on January 16, they set aside the Kentuckian's measure and substituted one of their own, sponsored by Senator David Clark of New Hampshire. It said the Constitution was already "ample for the preservation of the Union" and "it needs to be obeyed, rather than amended." Attempts at reconstruction of the Union, it added, were "dangerous, illusory and destructive."

Clark's amendment carried by 25 to 23, with six Southern senators in their seats but refusing to vote. They were Benjamin and Slidell of Louisiana, Wigfall and Hemphill of Texas, Iverson of Georgia, and Johnson of Arkansas. Tennessee's pro-Union senator, Andrew Johnson, sat directly behind Benjamin and demanded: "Why do you not vote? Why not save this proposition and see if we can bring the country to it?" Benjamin snapped that if he wanted Andy Johnson's advice, he would ask for it.

"Vote and show yourself an honest man," the Tennessee senator insisted, but the six Southerners refused.

"So, who defeated the Crittenden Compromise?" Johnson asked later. "Southern traitors, they did it. They wanted no compromise."

But it was really the Republicans, following Lincoln's orders, who torpedoed all compromises acceptable to the secessionists, as the total voting record showed. Ohio Congressman S. S. Cox asserted in his memoirs that the responsibility for the defeat of the Crittenden amendment "belongs to the Republicans" and its author had confirmed this to him in several conversations.

"Could not this Union have been made permanent by timely settlement, instead of being cemented by fraternal blood and military rule?" the Democratic Congressman asked.

> By an equitable adjustment of territory this was possible. This proposition the radicals denounced.
>
> Notwithstanding the President-elect was then in a minority of a million popular votes, they were determined to use the power while they had it, and prevent a settlement.
>
> The people favored the compromise. Petitions signed by thousands of citizens were showered upon Congress, for passage of the compromise. There was nothing but sneers and skepticism from

the Republicans at any settlement. Their policy was the destruction of slavery at the peril of war and disunion.

The Senate's vote against Crittenden played into the hands of the secessionists. It enabled the Georgians in Washington to send a telegram to their convention: "Does this not satisfy men of every shade of opinion that Georgia must rely upon herself? Will she not act promptly, and as a unit?"

She did. On January 18, the decisive vote was cast at the Milledgeville convention on a substitute proposing some constitutional amendments and delaying final action until the North could have time to reply. The secessionists won, with 164 votes to 133 for the substitute, a very close victory. Then, the next day, the ordinance of secession sailed through, 208 to 89. The secessionists were jubilant. But Herschel V. Johnson "never felt so sad before."

Louisiana followed suit January 26 by a convention vote of 103 to 17. Texas went out February 1, by 166 to 8.

So the original bloc of seven seceding states formed a solid phalanx of territory, stretching from the Atlantic coast of South Carolina to the Rio Grande.

On Monday, January 21, five Southern senators, whose states were seceding, arose, one by one, in the crowded Senate chamber and made farewell speeches that stirred the emotions of the people packing the galleries. The wife of Alabama Senator Clement C. Clay, Jr., noted: "Women grew hysterical and waved their handkerchiefs. Men wept and embraced each other mournfully. Scarcely a member of the Senate but was pale with the terrible significance of the hour. There was everywhere a feeling of suspense as if, visibly, the pillars of the temple were being withdrawn and the great government structure was tottering."

First, Senator David Yulee formally announced that Florida had seceded, so he must withdraw. His colleague, Stephen Mallory, "wept as he spoke, drawing tears from many eyes," a newspaperman wrote. "Clay of Alabama next arose and delivered his valedictory, which was bitter and criminative, vituperative and false," the reporter added, "the hiss of the secession snake. His colleague, Benjamin Fitzpatrick, concurred in the foul slanders on the free states."

Senator Clay was racked by illness, a chronic asthma that left him extremely emaciated, yet his voice rang steady and clear and, his wife recorded, "it seemed as if the blood within me congealed."

Finally, Jefferson Davis arose and stood stiffly, with the erect bearing of a soldier who had distinguished himself in the Mexican war, although he was haggard and gaunt because of excruciating migraine headaches and he felt hardly able to speak. His wife, Varina Howell Davis, looking down from the gallery, thought he gazed about him "with the reluctant look the dying cast on those upon whom they gaze for the last time."

The Mississippi aristocrat had striven desperately to bring about some compromise to save the old Union of fraternal states but all his efforts had meet with cold rebuffs. "We have piped and they would not dance, and now the devil may care," he had written in a note to Senator Clay. Now he reminded his fellow senators that "I have for many years advocated, as an essential attribute of state sovereignty, the right of a state to secede from the Union." Mississippi was carrying out that right and he would be faithful to his allegiance.

Davis still held out a faint hope that the North would allow the Southern states to leave in peace; but, if it chose war, he said, "then Mississippi's gallant sons will stand like a wall of fire around their state; and I go hence, not in hostility to you, but in love and allegiance to her, to take my place among her sons, be it for good or for evil. ... I bid you a final farewell."

Amid a storm of applause, the proud soldier resumed his seat at his desk and covered his face with his hands. Some spectators in the galleries thought they saw him weeping.

Two days later, the *New York Times* reported: "Jefferson Davis has gone South. There is no doubt that he has been offered command of the Southern army; and it is equally well understood that he is in a state of mind bordering on despair.

"He does not disguise his gloomy apprehensions from his friends, and his only remaining hope is that war may be prevented and the Union reconstructed."

The departure of the Deep South senators weakened the secession movement in Washington "very much," Illinois Congressman E. B. Washburne assured Lincoln in a letter that also reported progress in the efforts to quell the widely rumored plot for the secessionists to seize control of Washington. "The thread of the conspiracy to seize this city will be broken" by the senators' retirement, Washburne said, and by General Scott's vigorous preparations for regular troops to defend the capital.

In a warning to Lincoln earlier in January, Washburne had said: "It appears to be well understood that there now exists a formidable conspiracy to seize the Capitol."

"To find out the thread of the conspiracy," Washburne, Senator Seward, Senator Grimes of Iowa, and Congressman Mason W. Tappan of New Hampshire hired two New York City detectives "who are now pursuing the trail," Washburne told Lincoln. "Certain it is, there are traitors everywhere."

In a "strictly confidential" follow-up letter, Washburne gave the President-elect a firsthand report of a detective's trip to Baltimore: "Things look more threatening to-day than ever. I believe Va. and Maryland are both rotten to the core. We have had one of our friends from N.Y. (the kind I wrote about) in Baltimore, sounding matters there, and he gives most unfavorable reports. Great danger is to be apprehended from that quarter."

By this time, Lincoln had become accustomed to tales about plots to assassinate him. He received many hateful letters from the South, and Henry Villard reported on January 20 that someone in South Carolina had sent a "scandalous painting." "It depicted Mr. Lincoln with a rope around his neck, his feet chained, and his body adorned with tar and feathers."

Former U.S. Senator Thomas Ewing of Ohio was among the first to warn General Scott about the danger that some secessionists might try to seize Washington and make it the capital of their new Confederacy. Visiting the capital during the Secession Winter, Ewing went to the Winder Building, west of the White House, and called upon the army's venerable commander. He found the old warrior, suffering from the effects of his wounds and ill health, reclining on a sofa in his office. With a mighty effort, the general raised himself and stood erect, all of his six feet, four and a half inches, arrayed in his gorgeous blue uniform, gleaming with gold braid, medals, and epaulets.

At seventy-four, the general savored the pleasures of the palate, among the few left to him at his age, when his weight and his wounds made it difficult even to walk up a flight of stairs, much less to mount a spirited steed as he had done in his days of glory, climaxed by his triumph over the Mexicans in 1848.

Despite his ailments, the ancient warrior seemed to be still mentally alert and he displayed his customary air of command as he welcomed his guest, who was almost as old (seventy-one) and almost as tall and massively built.

Ewing went straight to the point. He expressed grave fears that "a band of desperadoes" would attack Washington and the public offices would be "at once surrendered." When Ewing asked what the general planned to do about it, Scott declared: "Sir, they must first march over my dead body."

"What military force do you have at your command to repel an attack?" Ewing asked.

"Sir," Scott replied, "I have thirty-five marines and that is all except for my own military family and the city militia."

Ewing urged the general to go at once to President Buchanan, demand a sufficient force of regular troops, and throw the responsibility on him.

The next day, Scott advised Ewing that a thousand regulars would be called from bases around the country and assigned to protect Washington.

Although proud of his Virginia heritage, the general placed the nation first in his heart with these words: "My country extends from Maine to the Rio Grande, from the Atlantic to the Pacific; the Union is my country, and I will spill the last drop of my blood in maintaining it intact."

Later in January, General Scott hauled his massive body, bedecked in his gorgeous uniform with his glittering array of medals, up to Capitol Hill. He squeezed his bulk into a witness chair before a House committee investigating the reports of plots to seize the city.

He revealed that he had received many warning letters which convinced him that some sort of conspiracy existed. A New York businessman had written: "The Southern leaders say that secession is dead unless they can seize Washington City by the Fourth of March."

A man in Nashville, Tennessee, had written: "A secret society exists through all the Southern states, bound together by solemn oaths, to prevent—even to the extent of assassination—Mr. Lincoln from taking the oath of office. ... Several are members of Congress. Treason is all around you."

Senator Foot of Vermont was sure that "the plot to seize the Capital and prevent the inauguration of Lincoln is already formed." He said Lincoln's foes "will prevent the counting of votes, if they dare."

Lincoln himself realized that he could not be officially elected to the presidency until February 13, when the two houses of Congress would meet in joint session and count the electoral votes sent in by the states, and then announce the winner. When Seward warned him of the dangers ahead, Lincoln replied:

"Our adversaries have us now clearly at disadvantage. On the second Wednesday of February, when the votes should be officially counted, if the two Houses refuse to meet at all, or meet without a quorum of each, where shall we be? I do not think that this counting is constitutionally essential to the election; but how are we to proceed in the absence of it?"

Jacob Thompson, the former interior secretary who was now an open secessionist, told the House investigating committee that plans for preventing Lincoln's inauguration had been actually discussed in his presence.

Without revealing the identity of these men, he said: "Some proposed that it should be done through the agency of Congress, by refusing to count the votes; or by the refusal of the Senate to meet the House of Representatives to count the votes for President and Vice President."

His testimony proved that there really had been a solid basis of truth behind the lurid rumors of plots to seize the capital, and Lincoln's fears that he might be cheated out of his victory if Congress did not count the electoral votes. Because of the Southern secession, however, Thompson said, all modes of blocking the inauguration, by violence or otherwise, were no longer being actively considered.

The House committee concluded that different ways of keeping Lincoln out of the White House had, indeed, been discussed by "disaffected persons of high and low position." But any plan for taking over Washington "seems to have been rendered contingent upon the secession of either Maryland or Virginia or both, and the sanction of one of those states."

So far, all the efforts to pull Virginia and Maryland out of the Union had failed, but they would go forward in the coming weeks, for the secessionists in both states refused to give up.

In response to an urgent appeal by General Scott, Vice President Breckinridge promised to preside fairly and firmly over the joint session of Congress on February 13, to announce the official election of Lincoln and Hamlin, and to allow no appeal to force.

Furthermore, said the battle-scarred veteran, "I have said that any man who attempted by force or parliamentary disorder to obstruct or interfere with the lawful count of the electoral vote should be lashed to the muzzle of a twelve-pounder and fired out of a window of the Capitol. I would manure the hills of Arlington with fragments of his body, were he a senator or chief magistrate of my native state!"

By such threats, and by summoning regular troops to guard the capital, Scott destroyed the hotheads' plots. "I do not believe there is any immediate danger of revolution," he said in February. "That there has been, I know. But the leaders of secession are doubtful of the result. They are satisfied that somebody would get hurt."

"A few drunken rowdies may risk and lose their lives," he said. "While I command the army there will be no revolution in the city of Washington."

❧ *17* ❧

"TRUST TO US,
THE UNION MEN OF THE SOUTH"

While the immediate threat of an attack on Washington sub-
sided, the secessionists intensified their drive to bring the
upper South into the Confederacy of the seven states that had pulled
out and prepared to form their own government. Throughout the
region, most of the people felt allied emotionally with their fellow
Southerners, and there were strong ties of family and friendship to
promote unity; but the conservatives also loved the old Union and
dreaded leaving it unless convinced that they must go in self-defense.

In Maryland, the people were frustrated by Governor Hicks's
refusal to call the legislature into session, even to talk about a state convention, and his enemies denounced him as a tyrant who deserved rough
treatment, even death. "Going through the city of Baltimore, I have
heard men say that I should be hung in less than two hours as a damned
old rascal, and another would say, 'I have a mind to blow a bullet
through you,'" the governor said. "Some carried ropes in their pockets
to hang me with, and revolvers in their pockets to shoot me with."

Pro-secessionists drilled in Baltimore and wore red ribbons in
their coats in a defiant show of zeal for their cause. A witness before
the House investigating committee said: "If you send your sergeant-
at-arms over there, I expect you could get a thousand of them almost
any time."

Hicks remained equally defiant. When the governor of Mississippi telegraphed that his state had seceded, Hicks wrote on the
accompanying envelope: "Mississippi has seceded and gone to the
devil." Georgia's secession "struck a melancholy blow to the hopes of
Maryland," an observer reported. "Now we are at the mercy of Virginia. If she secedes and no speedy compromise is made in Congress,

similar to Crittenden's resolution, I have positive knowledge that the people of Maryland are preparing, independent of the governor, to elect and convene a sovereign convention which will certainly withdraw Maryland from the Union. ... Marylanders pray for peace but will not part from Virginia."

Two thousand people attended a mass meeting at the Maryland Institute in Baltimore on February 1 and nearly all the speakers denounced the governor for blocking a convention. One orator called for Hicks to be hanged.

In Congress, conservative members made fervent pleas to the Republicans to give the Southern people some assurances to calm their fears so that a majority would vote "pro-Union" in several state elections. North Carolina scheduled its vote for January 28 on whether or not to call a convention. Virginia set a similar vote for February 4 and Tennessee followed on February 9.

The House debated a report by its Committee of Thirty-three, which proposed a few minor concessions, including a constitutional amendment barring interference with slavery in the states. Chairman Thomas Corwin, Ohio Republican, made a conciliatory speech. Representative John S. Millson, a Virginia Democrat, pleaded with the Republicans to give up their platform plank opposing slavery in the territories and approve some simple language stipulating the slaveholders' rights as decreed by the Supreme Court.

Using force against the seceding states would drive out other states, such as Virginia, which earnestly wanted to stay in the Union, the Norfolk representative warned. He called for all the states to assemble in a convention and, "if they cannot live peaceably together, let them determine peaceably to separate."

"I look upon the waging of war now," he said, "not merely as a violation of the Constitution but as a crime against humanity."

The next day, Representative Sherrod Clemens of Wheeling, a city in Virginia's northern "Panhandle," a thin finger of land between Ohio and Pennsylvania, arose in the crowded House chamber. He stood with painful difficulty, because his thighbone of one leg had been shattered by a bullet in a duel and, he said, "I am at this instant laboring under physical infirmity—suffering from a reeking wound not yet healed" after two years of agony. The wound had been inflicted in a "personal encounter" with O. Jennings Wise, son of Virginia's fiery ex-governor Henry A. Wise.

Boldly defying the secessionists, Clemens said: "It remains to be seen ... whether treason can be carried out with the same facility it can be plotted and arranged. ... Sir, before this political conspiracy, I may stand alone with my colleague from the Norfolk district, but here I take my stand!"

"At this moment, when a sudden frenzy has struck blind the Southern people," the crippled duelist said, "I may be scoffed and hooted at with that perversity in ill which masses of men sometimes display who are intent upon their own inevitable destruction."

As if he could foresee the devastation to be wrought by war in the next four years, Clemens vividly portrayed the ruin that would ensue if secession should lead to a bloody civil war. His pro-Union speech "completely overwhelmed and stunned the secessionists," the *Chicago Tribune* exulted. "When he attacked secession and showed his own section the disasters to them, and the loss contingent on dissolution and the formation of two confederacies, there was intense excitement on the Democratic side."

When his allotted time expired, and a motion was made to extend it, several Southerners hotly opposed it; and "a boisterous scene occurred, which at one time threatened a row." A Virginia secessionist, Elbert Martin, shouted: "Let him go on with his treason; we will teach the traitor when he goes to Virginia!"

Clemens refused to let Martin's insults provoke him into another duel. He had no desire to be "standing on one leg, with a cane in one hand, and a pistol in the other," for such an encounter. If any man wants to gain "cheap notoriety" by personal attacks on him, he said, "they are welcome to it."

Thousands of copies of the speeches by the pro-Union Virginia congressmen were mailed all over the Old Dominion, in an effort to persuade the voters to send a majority of anti-secessionists to the coming state convention.

Anti-secessionist congressmen from North Carolina and Tennessee joined in the fervent pleas for the Republicans to grant some concessions to reassure their people and keep them in the Union. They said that "if the North will do anything now to give them any basis on which to stand at home, the Border states can't be dragged out of the Union and will undertake themselves to crush out secession and rebellion all over the South," the *New York Times* reported.

Representative John A. Gilmer of North Carolina, an Old Line Whig whom Lincoln was seriously considering for a place in his cabinet, said "a desperate struggle" was going on to keep secession from spreading from the seven original Confederate states to the eight other slave states. Gilmer, the Whig candidate for governor in 1856, spoke for the many conservatives who resisted being stampeded into secession.

Representative Emerson Etheridge, a Tennessee Whig, urged the Republicans to give up their platform plank barring slavery from the territories. They adopted it, he said, for the same reason the Democrats, for years, had made "the negro issue paramount—*to carry an election.*" "At last our Southern friends have found to their sorrow," he quipped, "that this Sambo game is one that two can play at."

Pleading for Northerners' help to save the Union, Etheridge said:

> The true Union men of the South are standing today, struggling with all their power, to preserve this government. They are surrounded by a tempestuous despotism—everywhere confronting a panic which is made to feed itself. ... Wherever this disunion sentiment predominates, it is simply a reign of terror.
>
> What is the state of affairs now in all the villages and cities of the Gulf states? Bold men, educated men, ambitious men, men of chivalry and daring, are heading the military forces. Men, women and children are excited, just as the pomp and circumstance of war will excite everybody. Thousands believe honestly that Lincoln and his cohorts are coming down to apply the torch and the knife to the dwellings and the people of the South.
>
> Go to Charleston, to Tallahassee, to Montgomery, to Jackson—to any place where these conventions were assembled—and you see the military in full control of everything. These conventions deliberated three or four hours only over the fate of an empire.

A Virginia congressman, Shelton F. Leake, demanded to know whether Etheridge was "speaking on the side of the North or South?"

"I am speaking on the side of my country," Etheridge replied, touching off a storm of applause from the galleries.

Horace Maynard, congressman from Tennessee's Knoxville district, pleaded for passage of the Crittenden amendment as a peace measure favored by huge numbers of people, North and South. "Go to your Clerk's desk, and read the thousands and tens of thousands of petitions praying us to adopt it," he told the Republicans. "Trust to us, the Union men of the South. Give us pledges, assurances, guarantees, with which we can go before our people and satisfy them that their rights shall not be invaded, that their equality in the Union shall be maintained inviolate ... and I pledge you that we will return your forts and arsenals, your ships and navy yards, your mints and bullion. We will do it without the firing of a gun; without the shedding of a drop of blood."

Maynard, a Massachusetts native, "a tall man with long, dark straight hair, of Indian features and sallow complexion," implored the Northerners to abandon the idea of waging war against the seceding states. "Believe me," he warned, "the moment you wage war, you array the entire South, as one man, in behalf of the portion that is attacked."

"Appeals from the Union men in the Border states for something of concession or compromise are very painful," Senator Seward told Lincoln in a letter January 27, "since they say that without it those states must all go with the tide, and your administration must begin with the free states, meeting all the Southern states in a hostile confederacy." Seward continued:

> Chance might render the separation perpetual. ... It is almost in vain that I tell them to wait, let us have a truce on slavery, put our issue on Disunion and seek remedies for ultimate griefs in a constitutional question. ...
>
> In any case, you are to meet a hostile armed Confederacy when you commence. You must reduce it by force or conciliation. The resort to force would very soon be denounced by the North, although so many are anxious for a fray. The North will not consent to a long Civil War. ...
>
> For my own part I think that we must collect the revenues— regain the ports on the gulf and, if need be, maintain ourselves here. But that every thought we think ought to be conciliatory, forbearing, and patient, and so open the way for the rising of a Union Party in the seceding states which will bring them back into the Union.

It will be very important that your Inaugural Address be wise and winning.

The temper of your administration, whether generous and hopeful of Union, or taut and reckless, will probably determine the fate of our country.

May God give you wisdom for the great trial & responsibility.

The next day, precisely the opposite plea went to Lincoln from Salmon P. Chase, who would be his secretary of the treasury. Chase perceived a great danger, "the disruption of the Republican party, through congressional attempts at compromises."

He begged Lincoln to pass the word to some trusted member of Congress that "you desire the adoption of no compromise measure before the Republicans become charged with the responsibility of administration through your inauguration. Inauguration first—adjustment afterward."

Seward presented to the Senate a monster petition, 1,206 feet long and signed by 38,000 of his New York constituents, begging Congress to enact some measure like the Crittenden Compromise to avoid a terrible civil war. Protests against the Republicans' plans to "coerce" the South and to wage civil war were loudly voiced by a crowd of workingmen in New York City, mostly Irish Democrats. The *New York Times* published this account:

Sympathy for Secession
Workingmen of New York City opposed to the Republican party met last night at Brookes Hall. The group was composed almost entirely of rough-spun sons of the Celtic Isle. Sentiments such as these were heard:
"Hang the Republicans!"
"Kill Lincoln!"
"I will be one to kill him!"
"A nigger isn't as good as I am!"
"Oh, Lincoln will never be inaugurated!"
D. W. Groot, chairman, said: "We have met tonight to protest against civil war and to denounce coercion." (A voice: "Hang old Lincoln!")
Groot said: "Our factories are closed, stout men willing to work can find nothing to do. Starvation stares us in the face. Why?

Because an administration coming into power is hostile to the civil and domestic institutions of the Southern states." (Three groans for Lincoln.)

"Now, to cap the climax of their infatuated madness, they propose to use the power of the federal government to coerce those states which have rightfully seceded.

"We are losing from this city twenty million dollars a month in Southern orders. This trade has been drawn from this city by the election of Lincoln and ten thousand workingmen thrown out of employment.

"And what is the next proposition of this party? It is civil war, which shall entirely ruin us. These wicked politicians will 'touch' sufficient gold to save themselves and their families from ruin, but what is to become of the working class?"

The workers adopted strong resolutions condemning the "negro equality" policy of the Republicans and "unalterably opposed" any attempt to coerce the Southern states.

New York Democrats, at a large state convention in Albany, January 31, also attended by many former Whigs, deplored the Republicans' drift toward civil war and called for "conciliation, concession and compromise." Horatio Seymour, who might have been the President-elect if the Democrats had united behind him in a race against Lincoln, declared:

"Already six states have withdrawn from this confederacy. Revolution has actually begun. ... All virtue, patriotism, and intelligence seem to have fled from our national capital; it has been well likened to the conflagration of an asylum for madmen—some look on with idiotic imbecility; some in sullen silence; and some scatter the firebrands which consume the fabric above them and bring upon all a common destruction."

The former governor pleaded with the Republicans to accept some compromise that would reassure the pro-Union forces in the Border States and thus save them from following the Cotton States into the new Confederacy.

The venerable chancellor, Reuben H. Walworth, said: "It would be as brutal to send men to butcher our own brothers of the Southern states as it would be to massacre them in the Northern states. We are told, however, that we must enforce the laws. But why? And what laws are to be enforced?"

Not only the Democrats, but many Whigs and Republicans in New York, earnestly favored the Crittenden Compromise. Seymour predicted that it would carry New York State by 150,000 votes if the people were given a chance to vote on it.

Lincoln's old Whig friend, Orville Browning, spent an hour with him at Springfield on February 9, and found him "firmer than I had expected." "He agreed with me that no concession by the free states short of a surrender of everything worth preserving and contending for, would satisfy the South, and that Crittenden's proposed amendment to the Constitution, in the form proposed, ought not to be made," the future senator recorded in his diary.

Lincoln thought concessions to hold the upper South were unnecessary because of apparent Union victories in three states. North Carolina voters chose a majority of anti-secession delegates to the proposed state convention and, by a margin of about six hundred votes, decided against having a convention at all. Tennessee voters also rejected a convention, by a margin of twelve thousand, and the Union delegates won even greater triumphs, especially in the mountain counties of the east, Andy Johnson's stamping ground.

Virginia's convention, to open February 13, would contain about a three-fourths majority of men who opposed immediate secession. In all three states, the citizens were saying by their votes that they were not ready to plunge into secession—not yet. They hoped the "Peace Convention" could devise some formula to patch up the Union and they wished to wait and see the outcome. But they would not be "submissionists"—a dirty word in the South, meaning those who would submit to anything Lincoln might do. They certainly would not "coerce" another Southern state, or send soldiers to fight against their neighbors. That was unthinkable.

Lincoln failed to understand the Southerners' emotions. He misinterpreted the election returns as indicating a strong "Union forever" sentiment against the secessionists, whom he considered merely a little band of troublemakers. His blindness to the masses' instinctive aversion to any federal "coercion" caused him to follow a totally mistaken policy of firmly opposing compromise.

He should have heeded the warning in a Richmond news dispatch which said: "While a large proportion of those elected are called Union men, *there are very few submissionists.* ... They intend to exhaust every honorable effort to preserve the Union; but *unless the rights of the South are fully guaranteed* they will go for secession."

Rebuffing Seward's plea for conciliation to hold the upper South in the Union, the President-elect told him, in a February 1 letter, that, in opposing any compromise that might extend slavery into new land, "I am inflexible."

The dimming prospects for congressional action in the secession crisis depressed Representative Tom Corwin, the Ohio Republican who headed the House Committee of Thirty-three. Corwin hated war. He had opposed his own country's war against Mexico and said the Mexicans should tell the Yankee invaders: "We will welcome you with bloody hands to hospitable graves!" After weeks of wrangling in his committee the gloomy chairman told Lincoln in a confidential letter:

> If the states are no more harmonious in their feelings and opinions than these thirty-three Representative men, then appalling as the idea is, we must dissolve, and a long and bloody civil war must follow. I cannot comprehend the madness of the times. Southern men are theoretically crazy. Extreme Northern men are practical fools. The latter are quite as mad as the former.
>
> Treason is in the air around us everywhere. It goes by the name of patriotism. Men in Congress boldly avow it & the public offices are full of acknowledged secessionists. God alone, I fear, can help us. ... I think, if you live, you may take the oath.

William Kellogg, the Illinois member on Corwin's committee, went to Springfield and implored his friend, Lincoln, to come to Washington and assist in drawing up an acceptable compromise. Lincoln refused.

The *New York Herald*, on January 28, quoted Lincoln as having told a recent visitor—probably Kellogg:

> I will suffer death before I will consent or will advise my friends to consent to any concession or compromise which looks like buying the privilege of taking possession of this government to which we

have a constitutional right; because, whatever I might think of the merit of the various propositions before Congress, I should regard any concession in the face of menace the destruction of the government itself, and a consent on all hands that our system shall be brought down to a level with the existing disorganized state of affairs in Mexico.

But this thing will hereafter be, as it is now, in the hands of the people; and if they desire to call a convention to remove any grievances complained of, or to give new guaranties for the permanence of vested rights, it is not mine to oppose.

The available evidence is that Kellogg handed the Lincoln statement to the *Herald*, and it was later featured by the *New York Tribune* and the *Chicago Tribune*, both of which occasionally served as mouthpieces for official Republican doctrine.

Despite Lincoln's policy, Kellogg introduced a bill to amend the Constitution so that "North of 36° 30' north latitude slavery shall not exist, and that south of it neither Congress nor the territorial legislature shall prevent or prohibit the emigration of settlers from the Southern states with persons held to service or labor."

Under the Supreme Court's Dred Scott decree, slavery was legal in all the territories, Kellogg said on February 8, so his amendment would restore freedom to those north of the Missouri Compromise line.

Then, dramatically gesturing to an Illinois Democrat, Representative John A. McClernand, a friend of Senator Douglas, the Republican said: "And you, Sir, and I will march hand in hand to consummate the glorious triumph of the reunion of the states in the spirit in which they were first formed."

McClernand advanced and seized Kellogg's hand in a display of bipartisan friendship, amid thunderous applause on the floor and in the galleries.

Hailed as a hero in Washington, Kellogg quickly found himself branded a "traitor" by Republican newspapers back home. The *Illinois State Journal*, which often reflected Lincoln's views, charged that the maverick "has sold himself to the Slave Power." The *Chicago Tribune* read him out of the Republican Party.

Kellogg had previously warned the *Tribune* to stop editorially assailing him. Enraged by the continuing fusillades, he confronted the editor, Joseph Medill, one February night in the National Hotel in Washington. The husky Congressman struck the smaller, and sickly, editor, "with all his might, full in the face," knocked him down, grabbed him by the hair and "beat his head two or three times against the marble floor" before several bystanders rushed in and separated the two men.

The *New York Tribune* condemned the Congressman as "a ruffian and a bully" for beating up the journalist, who was "so crippled by rheumatism in the spine as to be a mere child in his hands."

Nearly two hundred Republicans of Kellogg's Fourth District met at Peoria and adopted resolutions denouncing him and his proposal to amend the Constitution.

His plan went down to defeat, as the Republicans closed ranks around Lincoln and his decree: "No compromise."

Senator Charles Sumner, the radical abolitionist from Massachusetts, praised the President-elect for steadfastly rejecting all forms of compromise, even those proposed to avert a terrible civil war. "Mr. Lincoln is perfectly firm," Sumner assured a constituent. "He says the Republican party shall not with his assent become 'a mere sucked egg—all shell and no meat—the principle all sucked out.'"

❧ *18* ❧

THE CONFEDERACY BEGINS

On February 4, 1861, delegates from six seceding states met at Montgomery, Alabama, to form a new republic, the Confederate States of America. On the same day, in Washington, representatives of twenty-one states assembled, at the urgent invitation of Virginia, in a "Peace Convention" for a last desperate effort to hold the Union together.

In general, the men at the Peace Convention were elderly gentlemen who talked at length about the past glories of America and pleaded for the North and the South to come together again and avert the worst of calamities, a civil war. The men at Montgomery were younger, more assertive, and determined upon fast action to create their own government, which they viewed as necessary to protect their region from social disruption.

Breckinridge Democrats dominated the scene at the Alabama capital. While a few were "fire-eaters" who dreamed of creating a slave empire around the Gulf of Mexico, most were more conservative politicians who hoped to induce the reluctant states of the upper South to join them, and even to welcome free states—outside of New England—which might adopt the new Confederate Constitution, a reformed version of the original, and thus "reconstruct" the Union.

Montgomery, a little city on the Alabama river, with only eight thousand residents, was inadequate to serve as the capital of an empire. Its streets were quagmires of mud. The Exchange Hotel could not cope with the influx of visitors; some complained that they could not find a decent meal in any restaurant in town.

The Alabama people were proud of their new capitol, a white Grecian temple standing high on a hill above the city. It was here, in an octagonal chamber, that the Southern statesmen created their Confederacy.

Howell Cobb was elected president of the convention by acclamation. "The separation is perfect, complete and perpetual," the former treasury secretary said, in an apparent shaft at those faint-hearted men who yearned to "reconstruct" the old Union if only the Yankees would compromise.

Georgia, being the largest state in the new republic, had reason to expect that it would furnish the president. But it had too many candidates. Thomas R. R. Cobb lobbied hard for his elder brother, Howell; Senator Bob Toombs seemed a strong contender until he showed up "high on wine" in public, on too many nights. Alexander H. Stephens was respected for his intellect, but he had campaigned for Douglas and had fought to the bitter end against Georgia's secession. Clearly his heart was not in a permanent, independent confederacy.

South Carolina's fiery secessionist editor, R. Barnwell Rhett, and Alabama's eloquent orator, W. L. Yancey, who had been agitating for a Southern republic for years, now had the joy of seeing their dream become a reality; but they were both disappointed in their hopes of becoming its president. The time for revolutionary oratory was past. Someone with a solid conservative record as a statesman of national stature must be chosen for that role in order to bring in the reluctant states of the upper South.

Virginia's Senators Hunter and Mason had warned that the Old Dominion, so proud of its heritage from the great Washington, Jefferson, and Madison, could not be lured into the Confederacy if some radical such as Yancey or Rhett should become its president. Hunter and Mason proposed, as the safe and sound choice, Jefferson Davis.

Davis, with his long record of service as a soldier in the Mexican war, as secretary of war, and as a senator from Mississippi, filled the bill. He was accustomed to command but he did not seek the presidency. He had been chosen already to lead Mississippi's troops and he aspired to become the chief of the whole Confederate army. His advocates lined up enough states for him in the convention; Cobb withdrew and backed Davis; Toombs went along, and as a consolation prize to Georgia, "Little Aleck" Stephens was made vice-president.

"No stronger pair of men could have been selected," one noted historian has written, praising the Davis-Stephens team. Perhaps so.

Both were intellectually superior, it is true; but both were also physical wrecks. Both were racked by dyspepsia and painful neuralgia. Davis was sometimes bedridden with "sick headaches" that made him tense, edgy, and difficult to please; proud, cold, inflexible in his opinions, he never learned how to handle other men skillfully, as Lincoln did. Stephens, an emaciated figure, was physically unable to provide strong leadership and, eventually, became a political enemy of Davis. So the Confederacy began its life with a pair of sick men at its helm.

Bob Toombs, despite his crude bombast and drinking sprees, would have been a stronger president—more vigorous, more aggressive, more likely to win the hearts and minds of the Southern people and carry them through the terrible times of civil war. He might even have led them to independence.

The most vivid pen-portrait of Jefferson Davis, who looked like a sick old man at fifty-two, was painted by Murat Halstead, in his *Caucuses of 1860.*

"Why, that is the face of a corpse, the form of a skeleton. Look at the haggard, sunken, weary eye, the thin, white, wrinkled lips clasped close upon the teeth in anguish. That is the mouth of a brave but impatient sufferer. See the ghastly, white, hollow, bitterly puckered cheek, the high sharp cheek bones, the pale brow full of fine wrinkles, the grizzly hair, prematurely gray; and see the thin, bloodless, bony nervous hands! ... It was painfully evident that he was ill."

Thomas R. R. Cobb's letters to his wife, from inside the Montgomery assembly, provide one of the few glimpses of the debates and decisions usually made behind closed doors. Naturally, he was bitterly disappointed because his brother had been passed over for the presidency, and the selection of "Little Aleck" Stephens for second place was "a bitter pill" to swallow: "Mr. Stephens is most arrogant ... a poor, selfish demagogue."

With keen insight, young Cobb appraised the new president as being "as obstinate as a mule. ... He is not *great* in any sense of the word. The power of will has made him all that he is."

On the evening of February 16, Davis arrived in Montgomery by train, delighted by a series of ovations that had greeted him all the way from his home in Mississippi. To the throng at the railroad station he declared: "Our separation from the old Union is complete."

If necessary, he said, the South must make all opponents "smell Southern powder and feel Southern steel."

That evening, at the Exchange Hotel, Yancey introduced him to the cheering crowd by saying: "The man and the hour have met."

Two days later, with bright sunshine and balmy breezes bringing hints of spring, the stiff-backed, gaunt-faced president solemnly took the oath of office on the portico of the Alabama capitol. "We have entered upon the career of independence and it must be inflexibly pursued," he said. He wished to avoid war but, he said, if "the lust of dominion should cloud the judgment or inflame the ambition of the Northern states," then the Southerners must maintain, by the sword, "the position which we have assumed among the nations of the earth."

To his wife, at their Brierfield plantation, Davis wrote: "The audience was large and brilliant. Upon my weary heart were showered smiles, plaudits and flowers, but beyond them I saw troubles and thorns innumerable. ... We are without machinery, without means and threatened by a powerful opposition, but I do not despond, and will not shrink from the task imposed upon me."

Davis knew that Lincoln, although a cautious, conservative man, was heading for Washington to lead a government that would insist upon ruling all the states of the old Union and refusing to recognize those claiming their independence. Lawyer Lincoln believed that no state could legally leave the Union and he would try to enforce the laws in the seceded states. So, while calling for peace, both presidents had to prepare for conflict.

Davis faced divisions at home among the delegates who were drafting the permanent constitution for the Confederacy. In an attempt to head off any moves towards "reconstructing" the Union by inviting in any free states, Rhett proposed that only slave states be allowed in the Confederacy. This idea tentatively passed but later was scrapped because Davis opposed any limits on the area of the new republic.

A Union, rebuilt on lines of the Breckinridge platform, could also provide a basis for reuniting the fractured old Democratic Party and enabling it, perhaps, to drive the Republicans out of power in Washington four years hence. That was a dream cherished by Democrats who liked to think that secession was only a temporary phenomenon. There was a lobbyist in Montgomery, dabbling as usual in backroom politics: It was Steve Douglas's bearded, burly wire-puller, George Nicholas Sanders.

"I found out yesterday why George Sanders was here," Thomas R. R. Cobb wrote to his wife. "He is an agent from Douglas and is working to keep out of the constitution any clause which will exclude 'Free States.' The game, now, is to reconstruct under our Constitution.

"There will be a hard fight on that question. ... Stephens & Toombs are both for leaving the door open. ... Confidentially and to be kept secret from the public, Mr. Davis is opposed to us on this point also and wants to keep the door open."

Davis prevailed in the behind-the-scenes struggle and, when the permanent constitution was adopted by the delegates, acting as a provisional congress, on March 11, the door was kept open for other states to join the new republic. The Confederates made determined efforts to pull out the states of the upper South, and sympathetic Democrats in the Old Northwest— Indiana, Illinois, Ohio— also talked of forming a "Northwest Confederacy" and allying it with the South. Senator Joe Lane of Oregon, formerly of Indiana, openly advocated this idea on the Senate floor.

The Confederates took the original U.S. Constitution as their model and made various changes that they considered reforms.

To stress that the new document was prepared by the individual states, they left out the "We, the people" line in the old preamble. They scrapped the "general welfare" clause; barred protective tariffs; restricted business subsidies, internal improvements, and other raids on the treasury. They ordered that the post office be deficit-free, that river and harbor projects must be financed by fees levied on those benefiting the most from the work. They required a two-thirds vote in the Confederate congress to pass money bills, and they gave the president power to veto specific items in appropriations measures through a "line item veto," which the present United States Congress finally passed in 1996.

The president was allowed a single, six-year term and could not run for reelection. As in the old Constitution, the states could not coin money, make alliances, or enter into compacts with other states.

Instead of the circumlocutions of the original document, the Confederates frankly called "slavery" by name. They specified that the federal government could never impair the right to hold property in slaves—and they barred reopening the African slave trade. So, men who had hoped an independent Southern republic would enable them to import black workers from Africa for about a hundred dollars a head would still have to pay ten times as much for slaves brought in from Virginia.

The actual creation of the Southern Confederacy finally opened the eyes of those in the North who had clung to the naive belief that the Southerners were merely bluffing, and playing a political game of "brag" to extort concessions as the price of their continued presence in the old Union. The *New York Times* discovered that "we at the North have been the quiet and unsuspecting dupes of the disunionists' plot for a slave empire." In an editorial entitled "The Great Conspiracy" the newspaper charged:

> The first step of the conspirators was to seize upon *our own* government. ... The election of the feeble and compliant Pierce was the stepping-stone to their entrance to power, which was fully secured to them by the appointment of Jefferson Davis as Secretary of War. This gentleman was the master spirit of the administration as he is of the present secessionist movement.
>
> The election of Mr. Buchanan followed and we now know that his nomination was effected upon the express assurance of cooperation and sympathy with the extreme Southern sentiment.

After Lincoln's election victory, the *Times* observed, the Southern states had seized all the important forts in their region except Fortress Monroe in Virginia, Fort Sumter at Charleston, and Fort Pickens and Key West-Tortugas in Florida.

"As soon as the Southern army now forming is relieved from the fear of coercion from the North, it is to be launched against Mexico," the editorial went on. "It is well known that a number of retired officers and military men in New York stand ready to join the expedition at the first tap of the drum."

Thus, another editorial claimed, "the Seceders are seeking to realize their grand design, the construction of a great slaveholding empire, to embrace the whole territory fronting upon and lying within the Gulf of Mexico." The Southerners, it said, were counting upon their production of cotton, which involved millions of workers and hundreds of millions of dollars in the textile industries of the North and of Europe, to assure their commercial power. ...

"After the formation of their Confederacy, a demand is to be made on Cuba, another on Central America. Cuba they regard as necessary to control the great field for the culture of sugar as they now do of cotton. With these two, they expect to 'lead the world by the nose.'"

Senator John Slidell, who had masterminded the unsuccessful effort to buy Cuba from Spain in the days when he dominated President Buchanan's administration, now looked to the new Confederacy to realize his dreams of empire. The Louisiana Democrat had made his final break with his puppet, Buchanan, when his own brother-in-law, Pierre G. T. Beauregard, was removed as superintendent of the military academy at West Point—a move engineered by Secretary of War Joseph Holt and approved by the President.

In bidding farewell to the Senate, the white-haired, hatchet-faced senator asked the Northerners how long they expected the great powers of Europe to let a blockade "impede their free intercourse with their best customers for their various fabrics and to stop the supplies of the great staple which is the most important basis of their manufacturing industry." In brief, Slidell believed "cotton is king."

His colleague, Judah P. Benjamin, the man with the perpetual smile and the voice like silvery bells, paid his respects to Buchanan in these words: "A senile executive, under the sinister influence of insane counsels, is proposing 'to secure the better execution of the laws' by blockading ports and turning upon the people of the states the artillery which they provided at their own expense for their own defense."

Benjamin paid a moving tribute to those "noble and generous friends" of the North who have "made a willing sacrifice of life's most glittering prizes in your devotion to constitutional liberty."

"When, in after days, the story of the present shall be written, when history shall have passed her stern sentence on the erring men who have driven their unoffending brethren from the shelter of their common home, your names will derive fresh luster from the contrast," Benjamin said. His eloquence in his farewell address moved many senators to tears.

But at least one senator remained aloof and unaffected by sentiment: Andrew Johnson, the Tennessee Democrat who had found himself hanged and burned in effigy at home for his speeches denouncing secession. To Republican Congressman Charles Francis Adams, Johnson said: "There's another Jew—that miserable Benjamin! He looks on a country and a government as he would a suit of old clothes. He sold out the old one, and he would sell out the new if he could, in so doing, make two or three millions."

Senator William M. Gwin, a California Democrat who sympathized with the South, commented as the Confederacy began: "The cotton states are out forever. The border states will follow; it is only a question of time. If no collision takes place reconstruction is barely possible. The chances are there will be two republics, North and South, with amicable relations. Time will probably turn it into three."

Gwin's reference to "three" possible republics could be interpreted as a sign that Gwin seriously considered the talk about forming a new, independent California republic. Other Californians were saying that the Pacific Coast could break away unless a transcontinental railway would soon be built to provide the West with quick access to the East.

When the two houses of Congress met in joint session February 13, to count the electoral votes sent in from the states, General Scott had his armed forces on the alert to block any attempt to disrupt the proceedings and thus keep Lincoln from being officially elected.

Even blowing up the Capitol was regarded as not impossible, so, every night for three weeks before the ballot count, the Capitol police made a through search of the building, inspecting its maze of cellars and vaults to make sure that no explosives were hidden there.

General Scott stationed about twelve hundred armed men in the Capitol and vicinity, including six companies of flying artillery, handling twenty-four guns; six companies of sappers and miners, and sharpshooters, and a squadron of dragoons, plus two companies of marines.

Thousands of people jammed the Capitol to see the official ballot count by the joint session of Congress in the House chamber. They found themselves surrounded by policemen in uniform and plainclothesmen, heavily armed.

When the senators had filed over from their side of the Capitol and joined the House members in their chamber, the packets of electoral votes from each of the states were formally opened and counted. Vice President Breckinridge, as he had promised General Scott, presided with strict and impartial demeanor. His handsome face showed no trace of emotion as he declared himself defeated, along with Douglas and Bell, and Lincoln elected.

Soon after the joint session ended, the House reconvened and the pent-up emotions of the frustrated Southerners burst forth in shouts against Lincoln and General Scott. One spectator reported:

"There were jeers for the 'rail splitter,' cheers for Jeff Davis and South Carolina. Curses for 'old Scott' broke out everywhere on the floor and in the galleries"—

"Super-annuated old dotard!"

"Traitor to the state of his birth!"

"Coward!"

"Free State pimp!"

"Pennsylvania Avenue, near the Treasury, was choked with a howling, angry mob, which had possession of the avenue far into the night," one witness said. "Southerners drank bad whiskey and cheered for Jeff Davis."

Seizing Washington by a coup de main "was certainly on the conspirators' programme, but Scott's preparations to receive them and the unexpected attitude assumed by the Border states have brought that project to naught," George Templeton Strong recorded in New York. "This was the critical day for the peace of the capital. A foray of Virginia gents, with Governor Wise at their head and Governor Floyd at their tail, could have done infinite mischief by destroying the legal evidence of Lincoln's election (after they had killed and beaten General Scott and his flying Artillery, that is)."

🌸 *19* 🌸

LINCOLN SLIPS SAFELY
INTO WASHINGTON

On the cold, gray, drizzly morning of February 11, Lincoln boarded a special train at the little brick Great Western Railroad station in Springfield to begin his journey to Washington. Several hundred people assembled there to bid him farewell. The atmosphere seemed somber when the President-elect and his party climbed aboard the single passenger car. The three Lincoln sons were there, but their mother was doing some last-minute shopping in St. Louis and would join them in Indianapolis.

Lincoln paused on the rear platform and, one witness said, "he turned to bid adieu amid an imposed silence, many persons seeming deeply affected and he himself scarcely able to check the emotions of the hour."

"My friends," he began, in his high, piercing voice, "no one, not in my situation, can appreciate my feeling of sadness at this parting. To this place, and the kindness of these people, I owe everything. Here I have lived a quarter of a century, and have passed from a young to an old man. Here my children have been born and one is buried. I now leave, not knowing when, or whether ever, I may return, with a task before me greater than that which rested upon Washington. Without the assistance of that Divine Being, who ever attended him, I cannot succeed. With that assistance, I cannot fail.

"Trusting in Him who can go with me, and remain with you and be everywhere for good, let us confidently hope that all will yet be well. To His care commending you, as I hope in your prayers you will commend me, I bid you an affectionate farewell."

In response, he heard some of his listeners call out, "We will pray for you."

"At Decatur, in Mason county, where Mr. Lincoln had resided in 1838, an immense crowd had gathered," one correspondent reported. "Long lines of saddle horses fastened about the station told that the farmers had ridden far over the prairies to bid good-bye to Honest Old Abe." Similar scenes were enacted at every stop as the train chugged nearly two thousand miles in the ensuing twelve days and there were huge crowds at the principal cities on the route—Indianapolis, Cincinnati, Columbus, Pittsburgh, Cleveland, Buffalo, Albany, New York City, Philadelphia, and Harrisburg.

At Indianapolis, Lincoln finally ended his long public silence abut his future policies and challenged those who opposed "coercion" and "invasion" of the seceded states. Marching an army into South Carolina would be "invasion," he said, "but if the United States should merely hold and retake its own forts and other property, and collect the duties on foreign importations, or even withhold the mails from places where they were habitually violated, would any or all of these things be 'invasion' or 'coercion'?"

"In what consists the special sacredness of a state?" he asked. "If a state and a county, in a given case, should be equal in extent of territory and equal in number of inhabitants, in what, as a matter of principle, is the state better than a county?"

In these remarks, Lincoln revealed himself to be, not a disciple of Thomas Jefferson, the father of the "states' rights" principle so dear to the Democrats, but a true follower of Federalist Alexander Hamilton, who wanted to wipe out the state lines as a hindrance to supreme federal power. Lincoln implied that a state was no better than a county, and certainly not sovereign.

His Indianapolis speech was the first clue to Mr. Lincoln's mystic, almost religious belief that the Union, which he revered, was somehow older than the states that created it—and too sacred ever to be broken.

On his fifty-second birthday, Lincoln crossed into Ohio and was hailed by an enormous crowd at Cincinnati. Addressing the state legislature at Columbus, he made some impromptu remarks that touched off much criticism in the press.

Although the Southern Confederacy had been officially formed and a possible civil war loomed, he said: "There is nothing going wrong. ... When we look out there is nothing that really hurts anybody.

We entertain different views on political questions, but nobody is suffering anything."

Jeering at Lincoln, the *Baltimore Sun* snickered: "We heard this Columbus speech read yesterday amidst irresistible bursts of laughter." The *New York Herald* scorned "the twaddling puerilities" of the President-elect's remarks.

At Pittsburgh, Lincoln said "our friends over the river" in the South had no cause for the course they were pursuing. "There is no crisis," he said, "excepting such a one as may be gotten up at any time by turbulent men aided by designing politicians."

Lincoln, a master politician himself, used his long journey as an opportunity to let the people see their new president, the first one born west of the Appalachians. He charmed the crowds by modestly saying that he had been chosen by mere accident, that he was the humblest of all the men ever called to the presidency, a man with "no name."

At Westfield, New York, he summoned Grace Bedell, the little girl who had advised him to grow a beard, and gave her a kiss. "You see," he said, "I let these whiskers grow for you, Grace."

At Buffalo, Rochester, Syracuse, and Albany, the President-elect encountered large, friendly crowds. He enjoyed a fairly polite reception in New York City, although he had polled a minority of the votes in that stronghold of "the Democracy" in the November election. At City Hall, he had a chilly encounter with Mayor Fernando Wood, who sided with the South and promoted a scheme for New York City to secede and set itself up as a free city.

Noting that the city's business was "paralyzed" by the current crisis, the mayor told the President-elect: "To you, we look for a restoration of friendly relations between the states, only to be accomplished by peaceful and conciliatory means, aided by the wisdom of Almighty God."

Before the New Jersey State Assembly at Trenton, Lincoln promised to do everything in his power "to promote a peaceful settlement of all our difficulties." But, he added, "it may be necessary to put the foot down firmly. And if I do my duty, and do right, you will sustain me, will you not?" In response, there were loud cheers and cries of "Yes," "Yes," "We will." Lincoln said he needed their help in piloting the ship of state through its perilous voyage ahead, for "if it should suffer wreck now, there will be no pilot ever needed for another voyage."

On Thursday night, February 21, after the President-elect had arrived in Philadelphia, two men called upon Norman Judd, a member of his traveling party from Illinois. They were S. M. Felton, president of the Philadelphia, Wilmington and Baltimore Railroad, and Allan Pinkerton, chief of a national detective agency. They said Pinkerton, hired by Felton to protect trains and bridges from sabotage, had infiltrated gangs of Baltimore toughs and learned about a plot to murder Lincoln when he changed trains in Baltimore.

When his train would arrive at the Calvert Street station, Lincoln would have to cross town to the Camden Street station and board the Baltimore and Ohio train which would carry him the rest of the way to Washington. It was during this transfer, when his sleeping car would be pulled by horses from one station to the other, that the police were to be diverted by a fight, and the assassins would surround Lincoln and kill him with knives or pistols, Pinkerton claimed. He said his spies had penetrated to the inner circle of the plotters by hanging around Baltimore saloons and posing as red-hot secessionists.

Pinkerton even said he had a personal conversation with the ringleader, a murderous Italian barber named Cypriano Ferrandini. The barber called himself "Orsini" and aspired to emulate Orsini, a revolutionary who gave his life for Italy.

Lincoln was reluctant to believe that his life was threatened by a "half-crazed foreigner," but Pinkerton insisted that his agents had ample proof of the plot, and Judd and Felton advised that it must be taken seriously. The three proposed that Lincoln foil the plot by going to Washington immediately. But he refused. He had promised to raise a flag over Independence Hall the next morning and address the state legislature at Harrisburg in the afternoon, and he would keep his word.

Upon returning to his hotel room, Lincoln found young Frederick Seward, the senator's son, who had hurried up from Washington with urgent letters from his father and General Scott, confirming the danger of assassination in Baltimore.

"My dear Sir," the senator wrote, "My son goes express to you—He will show you a report made by our detective to General Scott—and by him communicated to me this morning. I deem it so important as to dispatch my son to meet you wherever he may find you—I concur with Gen. Scott in thinking it best for you to reconsider your arrangements. No one here but Gen. Scott, myself & the bearer is aware of this communication.

"I should have gone with it myself but for the peculiar sensitiveness about my attendance in the Senate at this crisis."

General Scott wrote: "A New York detective officer who has been on duty in Baltimore for three weeks past reports this morning that there is serious danger of violence to and the assassination of Mr. Lincoln in his passage through the city should the time of that passage be known—He states that there are banded rowdies holding secret meetings, and that he has heard threats of mobbing and violence, and has himself heard men declare that if Mr. Lincoln was to be assassinated they would like to be the men."

More corroborating details of the murder plot were relayed to Illinois Congressman Elihu B. Washburne, a trusted friend of Lincoln, by Lucius E. Chittenden, a Vermont delegate to the Peace Convention. Chittenden recalls in his memoirs that he and a few other trusted Republicans met in Baltimore with several prominent citizens, who warned them: "We want you to help us save Baltimore from disgrace and President Lincoln from assassination."

The Baltimore men said a gang of "plug uglies" planned to rush into a narrow vestibule of Lincoln's railroad car and each man had taken a blood oath to stab him with a dagger—just as Julius Caesar had been slain in the Senate in Rome. When this gory tale met a skeptical response from Chittenden and his friends, they were brought face to face with a man purported to be one of the gang, who had turned against the others.

"He looked like an Italian bandit," Chittenden remembered. "His square, bull-dog jaw, ferret-like eyes furtively looking out from under a low brow ... a coarse mat of black hair, a dark face ... advertised him as a low, cowardly villain." According to Chittenden, this man said:

"A bad president is coming in the cars to free the negroes and drive all the foreigners out of the country. The good Americans want him killed."

The same Italian barber named by Pinkerton as the chief of the assassins turned up in this version of the plot as well. The Baltimore

Republicans added this detail—that certain "leading secessionists" in their city had agreed to pay the killers, in the belief that "Lincoln's murder would prevent greater bloodshed and war."

After conversing with young Seward, Lincoln promised to consider the warnings carefully and make a decision the following day. He knew he was unpopular in Maryland, where he had run a poor fourth in the election, polling fewer than two thousand votes, while Breckinridge carried the state. Furthermore, the fiercely pro-Southern city, where the gangs of "plug uglies" were notorious, had given him no official invitation and no sign that he would be welcomed there.

When he raised the flag over Independence Hall the next morning, George Washington's birthday, Lincoln told the crowd that the men who wrote the Declaration of Independence there were inspired by its great principle, "which gave liberty not alone to the people of this country, but, I hope, to the world for all future time." The declaration promised that, "in due time, the weights would be lifted from the shoulders of all men," he said. "But if this country cannot be saved without giving up that principle, I was about to say I would rather be assassinated on this spot than surrender it."

After his speech to the legislature and a conference with Governor Curtin and other political leaders at Harrisburg, Lincoln reluctantly decided to slip through Baltimore in the dead of night. Wearing an overcoat and a soft felt hat instead of his usual "stovepipe," he boarded a special one-car train, accompanied only by his faithful bodyguard, Ward Hill Lamon, who was armed with two pistols, two derringers, and two large knives. At Philadelphia, with only Lamon and Pinkerton, he quietly entered the last sleeping car of the night train to Baltimore and occupied a berth reserved for an "invalid passenger."

At 3:30 in the morning, the sleeping car was pulled through Baltimore without incident and waited at the Camden Street station for an hour to join the Baltimore and Ohio train steaming in from the west. Pinkerton later said he spent the time chatting with Lincoln while a drunk on the platform sang "Dixie."

At 6 A.M., Lincoln left the train at the Washington station, safe and sound. One man, recognizing him in spite of his overcoat and soft felt hat, came up and said, "Abe, you can't play that on me."

Lamon raised his big fist to strike him, but Lincoln restrained him. The man was Congressman Washburne, who had been tipped off to the change in plans and had come to escort his friend to the Willard Hotel for breakfast with Senator Seward.

Over the telegraph wires, which had been cut at Harrisburg the night before as a safety precaution, but were restored now, flashed the coded message that Pinkerton had devised to report Lincoln's safe arrival at Washington: "PLUMS DELIVERED NUTS SAFELY."

Willard's hotel, like a parasitic plant, had gradually grown around the block at Pennsylvania Avenue and Fourteenth Street and taken in an old church, renamed Willard Hall. Here the Peace Convention delegates reconvened on that Saturday morning, February 23. Delegate Chittenden sat between James Seddon, a Virginian destined to become the Confederate secretary of war, and Waldo Johnson of Missouri, later a Confederate general.

"Seddon's body servant handed him a scrap of paper," Chittenden recalled. "Seddon glanced at it and passed it before me to Johnson, so near to my face I could not avoid reading it. The message: 'Lincoln is in the hotel!'

"'How the devil did he get through Baltimore?' Johnson exclaimed."

This incident gave Chittenden the distinct impression that the plot to kill Lincoln in Baltimore was known to some men who were neither Italian assassins nor Baltimore "plug-uglies."

Lincoln's wife and three sons, and others in the traveling party he had left behind in Harrisburg, came through Baltimore early Saturday afternoon. Some accounts have said they met with no disturbance, but eyewitnesses say otherwise.

No less than ten thousand people were there, L. K. Bowen wrote to Howell Cobb, "and the moment the train arrived, supposing Lincoln was aboard, the most terrific cheers ever heard were sent up, three for the Southern Confederacy, three for 'gallant Jeff Davis,' and three groans for the 'Rail-Splitter.'"

A woman traveling with Mrs. Lincoln said that, upon their arrival at Baltimore, a vast crowd surrounded the railroad cars, shouting:

"Trot him out!"

"Let's have him!"

"Come out, Old Abe!"

"We'll give you hell!"

"Bloody Black Republican!"

After a half-hour ordeal Mrs. Lincoln and her sons were taken in a carriage to the home of the railroad president. Others of her party escaped the mob by boarding an omnibus that took them to the Eutaw House. Following a luncheon and rest, Mrs. Lincoln and her party boarded the Washington-bound train and proceeded to the capital.

Newspapers across the land printed sensational stories about Lincoln's secret ride to Washington to avoid assassins. Unfortunately for him, the *New York Times* published a dispatch saying he wore "a Scotch plaid cap and a very long military cloak." This erroneous report touched off waves of ridicule in the press; cartoonists depicted him disguised in a tam and kilts.

"Mr. Lincoln soon learned to regret the midnight ride, to which he had yielded under protest," Lamon later wrote. "He ... frequently upbraided me for having aided him to degrade himself at the very moment in all his life when he should have exhibited the utmost dignity and composure." All the same, his defenders believed the ruse was justified by the evidence of the plot. He would indeed have "exhibited the utmost dignity and composure" if laid out in a casket for a funeral. He had a host of enemies, some of whom would have rejoiced over his death, and, after four years of the Civil War's slaughter, one finally did succeed in taking the President's life.

On his first day in Washington, Lincoln paid a surprise visit to President Buchanan and his cabinet at the White House. That evening, the delegates to the Peace Convention formally called upon him at Willard's hotel. They were mostly unfriendly, because partisan Republicans were boycotting the conference. But the critics had to respect the tall, stooping figure whose clothes hung loosely upon him. In the grasp of his huge hands and the cheery tones of his high-pitched voice, some delegates realized why this awkward countryman had won the love of so many people. "His kindly eyes looked out from under a cavernous, projecting brow," one wrote, "with a curiously mingled expression of sadness and humor."

Lincoln said he had been represented as an evil spirit, a goblin, the implacable enemy of Southern men and women. He did not set

THE NATIONAL GAME. THREE "OUTS" AND ONE "RUN".

This 1860 cartoon, one of the first to feature a baseball theme, shows the victorious Lincoln telling his three opponents, "You must have 'a good bat' and strike a 'fair ball' to make a 'clean score' and a 'home run.'" From left to right, the defeated rivals complain about their fate: John Bell, of the Union Club, holds a "fusion" bat, symbolizing the attempt at a "fusion" ticket of electors to combine the trio's votes. Bell says: "It appears to me very singular that we three should strike 'foul' and be 'put out' while old Abe made such a 'good lick.'" "That's because he had that confounded rail to strike with. I thought our fusion would be a 'short stop' to his career," says Stephen Douglas, the Little Giant. Lincoln's rail is marked "Equal Rights and Free Territory," while Douglas's bat is marked "Non-intervention." Vice President John C. Breckinridge, whose belt denotes the "Disunion Club," holds his nose and says, "I guess I'd better leave for Kentucky, for I smell something strong around here and begin to think that we are completely 'skunk'd.'" From the collections of the Library of Congress.

up for a beauty, he added, but they would not find him so ugly or so black as painted.

"It is not of your *professions* we complain," said the spectral Virginian, James A. Seddon, whose gray face, sunken eyes, and thin body indicated the last stages of consumption. "It is of your sins of omission, your failure to enforce the laws, to suppress your John Browns and Garrisons, who preach insurrection and make war upon our property."

"I believe John Brown was hung and Mr. Garrison imprisoned," Lincoln replied.

William E. Dodge, a millionaire merchant from New York City, who had given up his luxurious suite at the hotel to Lincoln and his family, told him: "It is for you, sir, to say whether the whole nation shall be plunged into bankruptcy, whether the grass shall grow in the streets of our commercial cities."

"If it depends on me, the grass will not grow anywhere but in the fields and the meadows," Lincoln answered.

"Then you will *yield* to the just demands of the South," said Dodge. "You will leave her to control her own institutions. ... You will not go to war on account of slavery."

A sad but stern expression swept over Lincoln's face. Under his oath, he said, he must faithfully execute the office of President and "preserve, protect and defend the Constitution" in every part of the United States. "It must be respected, obeyed, enforced and defended, let the grass grow where it may."

A New Jersey delegate suggested that the North should make further concessions to avoid civil war.

"In a choice of evils," Lincoln replied, "war may not be the worst."

Lincoln's clear intimation that he would choose war, rather than compromise, confirmed the worst fears of the conservatives.

One night, soon after Lincoln's meeting with the men of the Peace Convention, several delegates returned to his hotel suite along with some other men from the Border States. Their leader was Charles S. Morehead, former governor of Kentucky, who had served with Lincoln when they were Whig congressmen in 1847–1849. In the group were another Kentuckian, former Treasury Secretary Guthrie, Colonel A. W. Doniphan of Missouri, and two eminent Virginians, former Senator William Cabell Rives and Judge George W. Summers.

Earlier, Morehead had made a plea for peace to Senator Seward, who replied: "Let me once hold the reins of power firmly in my hands, and if I don't settle this matter to the entire satisfaction of the South in sixty days, I will give you my head for a football."

This is Morehead's account of the parley with Lincoln:

Lincoln began by saying that he had never uttered a sentence that could be misinterpreted as feeling enmity toward the South. Morehead replied that the Southern people did not consider Lincoln a personal enemy but feared his party, and the new president must give them guarantees of their security to assure peace.

"You hold in the hollow of your hand," Morehead said, "the destiny of thirty millions of people."

Lincoln said he would not interfere with slavery in the states where it already existed, nor in the District of Columbia and federal forts and arsenals, but he positively would not let it be extended into the territories. By consenting to that, he said, he would betray the party that had elected him on a platform barring slavery from any new lands. He had made his position clear in his letters to Republicans in Congress, emphatically ordering them to oppose any such measure.

Morehead, who had opposed Lincoln's election, said "you are now my President" but "some little deference is due to the opinions of those who constitute the majority."

Lincoln did not like this reminder that 61 percent of the voters had favored other candidates for the presidency, and he had run almost a million votes behind his three opponents combined, although achieving a majority of the electoral votes. "If I am a minority president, I am not the first," he snapped. "At all events, I obtained more votes than you could muster for any other man."

With great emotion, Morehead said he prayed to God that Lincoln would not try to force the seceded states into obedience. If he did, the history of his administration would be written in blood "and all the waters of the Atlantic Ocean could not wash it from his hands."

"What would you do?" Lincoln demanded. "Do you mean by 'coercion' the collecting of the revenue and the taking back of the forts which belong to the United States?"

Lincoln recalled an incident that had occurred during his early days as a lawyer: He had brought a lawsuit for an old man but, as the evidence was placed before the jurors, it clearly appeared so weak that the plaintiff whispered in Lincoln's ear, "Guv it up."

"Now, Governor," Lincoln said, "wouldn't this be 'guvin' it up?"

Maybe so, Morehead retorted, "but hadn't you better 'guv it up' without bloodshed than drench this land with blood?"

Lincoln said he must take an oath swearing that he would faithfully execute the laws, so how could he fail to carry it out?

As commander-in-chief, Lincoln could withdraw the troops from the forts and thus prevent a "deadly and ruinous war," Morehead said.

Lincoln recalled Aesop's fable of the lion who fell in love with a beautiful lady and asked permission to marry her. Her parents required that his claws be cut off and his teeth drawn, lest they injure the bride. The lion consented; he lost all his claws and his teeth, and her parents then "took clubs and knocked him on the head."

Morehead, in no mood for funny stories, retorted that this was the most serious issue he had ever faced in his career. "I look to the injury that a fratricidal war is to do, not only to my section that is to be desolated and drenched in blood, but to the cause of humanity itself," he said. "I appeal to you, apart from these jests, to lend us your aid and countenance in averting a calamity."

Former Senator Rives chimed in and said he agreed with every word that Morehead had said. If Lincoln did coerce the seceding states, Virginia would leave the Union, Rives cried. "Old as I am, and dearly as I have loved the Union, in that event I go with all my heart."

Lincoln arose from his chair, advanced toward the elderly Virginian, and said: "Mr. Rives, Mr. Rives, if Virginia will stay in, I will withdraw the troops from Fort Sumter!"

"Mr. President, I have no authority to speak for Virginia," Rives replied. "But if you do that, it will be one of the wisest things you have ever done. Give us guarantees and I can only promise you that whatever influence I possess shall be exerted to restore the Union to what it was."

According to the account that he sent to Senator Crittenden, Morehead begged Lincoln to evacuate Fort Sumter and said this act would save the eight slave states still in the Union, while the seven states already out would be drawn back in by "the force of gravitation."

Rudolf M. Schleiden, minister from the Hanseatic Republic and the Free City of Bremen, Germany, found out about the Border State men's appeal to Lincoln to give up Fort Sumter. The envoy told his government that Lincoln answered: "Why not? If you will guarantee for me the state of Virginia, I shall remove the troops. A state for a fort is no bad business."

One evening, the President-elect, General Scott, and other officials dined with Dr. Schleiden, and Scott told Lincoln: "I did not vote for you; I haven't voted in 54 years."

"But I have voted for *you*, General," Lincoln fired back, "and you will have to make up for it in *war*."

Lincoln's repeated references to war, and his view that it was "not the worst" evil facing the country, gave no help whatever to the conservative men who were striving in the Peace Convention to bring out some panacea that could prevent such a terrible calamity. The most eloquent pleas against a "brothers' war" came from elderly men of the Whig Party, to which Lincoln himself had formerly belonged.

Francis Granger of New York State, whose mane of silvery hair gave his Whig faction the nickname of the "Silver Grays," spoke out most forcefully against those who treated war as a lark. Some men blithely talked to him about "re-taking the forts," now held by the seceded states, he said, "as they would about sending a vessel for a cargo of oranges from Havana."

"War! What a fearful alternative!" Granger exclaimed. "It cannot come to this country without a fearful expenditure of blood and treasure ... an awful legacy of widows' tears, of the blighted hopes of orphans, with a catalogue of suffering, misery and woe too painful to contemplate. For God's sake! Let such a fate be averted at all cost!"

But most Republicans, including Lincoln, were unwilling to pay the price demanded for peace: a retreat from the antislavery plank of their Chicago platform. They viewed the Peace Conference as a futile assembly of "fossils," men of a bygone day. Granger, for example, had lost the vice-presidency to Democrat Richard Mentor Johnson of Kentucky in 1837, and had been postmaster general in the brief administration of President William Henry Harrison in 1841. Now Harrison's successor, John Tyler of Virginia, had been brought out of retirement at seventy to preside over the peace parley.

The *Chicago Tribune* said Tyler was the perfect choice for his new role because, as president, he had been a traitor to the Whigs, and was "a rank disunionist at heart." The *Tribune's* man denounced the peace-lovers who would swallow the compromise like "a bottle of gin, as mothers supply screaming brats with sugar."

After three weeks of debate behind closed doors, the delegates adjourned on February 27 without reaching a formula that Congress would adopt to prevent a civil war. Their seven-point proposal was similar to the Crittenden measure that the House of Representatives rejected, 113 to 80. The Republicans in Congress kept their perfect record: Just as Lincoln ordered, they never cast a single vote for the Crittenden Compromise.

Virginia Clay, the wife of Alabama's Senator Clement C. Clay, Jr., recalled: "Senator Clay was exceedingly depressed by the failure of the Peace Convention, for he foresaw that the impending conflict would be bloody and ruinous. Just after its close, Ex-President Tyler came to our home. He was an old man now and very attenuated. He was completely undone at the failure of the peace men, and tears trickled down his cheeks as he said to Senator Clay with indescribable sadness: 'Clay, the end has come.'"

Indirectly, the Peace Convention did play a role in keeping Virginia and Maryland from leaving the Union before Lincoln's inauguration day March 4. Virginia, which had invited the other states to participate, could not secede as long as there was a flicker of hope for a compromise; and although most Maryland people sympathized with the South, they would not secede except in concert with Virginia; for, obviously, Maryland could not survive as a lonely Confederate state with pro-Union Pennsylvania on its northern border and pro-Union Virginia forming its border on the Potomac.

Governor Hicks continued to resist all efforts to pull Maryland out. A. R. Wright, the commissioner sent by Georgia to talk Hicks into secession, glumly reported his own failure. When he finally obtained an interview on February 25, the governor scolded Georgia for going out. "He thought our action hasty, ill-advised, and not justified ... that we were attempting to coerce Maryland to follow our example," Wright reported.

If the Union should dissolve, Hicks said, he would urge Maryland to join the middle states in a central confederacy. He was already in contact with the governors of New York, Pennsylvania, New Jersey, Ohio, and others about such an alliance.

Hicks shocked his Georgia visitor even more by saying that "in the event of the federal government's attempting to coerce the seceding states, he would interpose no objection to the marching or transporting of troops through his state and their embarkation at Baltimore." This was heresy, indeed, to Confederate ears!

The Maryland governor's firm pro-Union stand seemed much stronger than in the earlier weeks of the Secession Winter, when some hotheads among his people were threatening him with injury, or even death, if he did not knuckle under to their demands that the Free State join the Confederacy. Maria Lydig Daly, the New York diarist, wrote that Hicks "wavered" at that time and came to General Scott for help. She continued: "The General told him to stand firm and arrest this great atrocious rebellion." By keeping Hicks firm in opposition, she said, the general prevented the success of the scheme to pull Maryland out and make Washington, D.C., the capital of the Confederacy.

The Southerners branded Hicks a coward and a traitor to their cause and charged that "to his cowardice, therefore, all this bloodshed is to be attributed," Mrs. Daly wrote in the second year of the Civil War, "for they intended by this *coup de main* to make the North feel that opposition was useless."

Former Virginia Congressman John Minor Botts asserted that his state's delay in joining the secessionists torpedoed their plans for taking over Washington and making it the capital of their new government. Botts quoted the *Richmond Sentinel* as saying: "Indeed, a formidable organization existed all the winter in Baltimore and the counties adjacent to Washington, having for its object the capture of that city, the seizure of the government offices and the inauguration of a provisional government. ... Such a step would have given the South the command of the U.S. Army and Navy ... but it was too rash to be hazarded until the support of Virginia could be secured, and for that there was no chance."

So, despite all the plots and schemes and alarms, Maryland and Virginia both remained in the Union on March 4, so Lincoln could be inaugurated in Washington and not in some city of the North. It was a victory for Lincoln and for the Unionists in both of the important Border States.

❧ 20 ❧

"To Hold,
Occupy, and Possess"

For ten days after his arrival in Washington, Lincoln's suite in the Willard Hotel became the new center of national power, eclipsing the Buchanan White House and the last gasps of the expiring Congress on Capitol Hill. Already weary from his long, roundabout journey from Springfield, the President-elect had to cope with endless streams of callers, countless requests for federal jobs, and tense negotiations with spokesmen for the various factions that made up his Republican Party.

Lincoln felt whip-sawed between the radicals—who demanded that he enforce the Chicago platform in toto, declare secession illegal and even treasonous, and use force to regain the forts and other federal property seized by the seceding states—and the moderates, who implored him to forget about the platform and partisanship, stress conciliation and compromise so that he could hold onto the eight slave states still clinging to the Union, and above all, to avoid a bloody civil war.

Lincoln engaged in an intellectual tug of war with William Henry Seward, who expected to run the administration as its "premier" in his role as secretary of state. Seward felt bitter and hurt because the presidential nomination, which he believed to be rightfully his, had been handed over to this ignorant prairie lawyer from Illinois, who had served only one term in Congress, had never been a governor or a senator, and had no executive experience whatever. Being a realist, though, the New York senator resolved to make the best of the situation and to become the power behind the throne.

From the first hour after Lincoln had breakfast with him at the Willard Hotel, Seward filled various roles as his guide, mentor, social secretary, and political counselor, hosting dinners for him and even accompanying him to church. With his own place apparently assured, Seward repeatedly urged Lincoln to fill his cabinet with moderate men who would conciliate the Union-loving leaders in the South who were holding out against secession; thus he could limit the Confederacy to its original seven states, which probably were not strong enough to survive very long as a nation.

Seward's political partner, Thurlow Weed, strongly urged the conciliation course in an editorial in his *Albany Evening Journal*, calling for the North to restore the old Missouri Compromise line, which could leave slavery alone in the South. This editorial was intended to hold the border slave states in the Union, Weed said, "so that the boundaries and strength of the rebellion might be narrowed and weakened."

For this peaceful gesture, Weed found himself fiercely assailed by the "ironback" Republicans, who suspected that the editor was sending up a signal for a great compromise to be advanced by Seward. Republican senators, at a caucus, chastised Seward, who insisted that he did not dictate the policies of editors. Senator Preston King of New York told Weed, in a sharp note: "You and Seward should be among the foremost to brandish the lance and shout for war."

Lincoln read the editorial just as Weed arrived at Springfield, at his invitation, to discuss the new administration's policies and to advise him about "cabinet-making."

Weed urged the President-elect to reserve at least two places in his cabinet for conservative Union men from the slave states. Lincoln replied that he did not like Southern speakers and newspapers telling him that he must not engage in any "coercion" of the states, and he asked if any Southern men could be trusted.

Yes, Weed replied, "there are Union men in Maryland, Virginia, North Carolina and Tennessee, for whose loyalty ... I would vouch."

"Well," said Lincoln, "let us have the names of your white crows, such ones as you think fit for the cabinet."

Quickly, the Albany editor reeled off the names of Henry Winter Davis of Maryland, John Minor Botts of Virginia, John A. Gilmer of North Carolina, and Balie Peyton of Tennessee. All four had distinguished records as members of the House of Representatives, and all opposed secession.

With a laugh, Lincoln commented that his close friend, Judge David Davis, who had moved from Maryland to Illinois in his youth, was promoting his cousin, Henry Winter Davis, for a place in the cabinet. Nevertheless, Lincoln ruled him out and chose Montgomery Blair of Maryland to be postmaster general. Weed warned him that Blair "represents nobody, he has no following, and ... his appointment would be obnoxious to the Union men of Maryland." As far as Weed could find out, Blair was being backed only by his father, the old Jacksonian Democrat Francis Preston Blair, Sr.

The President-elect seriously sounded out James Guthrie, Kentucky railroad executive, former treasury secretary, and a rival of Douglas for the Democratic presidential nomination, as a potential cabinet officer. But Guthrie, a prominent member of the Peace Convention, declined further public service on the grounds of age and infirmity.

Lincoln made a direct appeal to Gilmer, a Whig congressman who was struggling, against heavy odds, to keep North Carolina from leaving the Union. In a letter that Weed personally delivered to Gilmer, Lincoln tried to show that he wanted to be fair to the South. "I have no thought of recommending the abolition of slavery in the District of Columbia, nor the slave trade among the Slave States," he wrote.

"As to the use of patronage in the Slave States where there are few or no Republicans, I do not expect to inquire for the politics of the appointee or whether he does or does not own slaves ... I never have been, am not now, and probably never shall be in a mood of harassing the people either North or South."

But Lincoln declared that he was inflexible in his opposition to the extension of slavery into new territories, and he would not budge from that stand. Nor would he make any new public declaration that could be twisted by his enemies to indicate that he was in retreat. "It would make me appear," he said, "as if I repented of the crime of having been elected, and was anxious to apologize and beg forgiveness."

With his terms thus clearly laid out, Lincoln could hardly expect a conservative Southerner to feel at home in his cabinet. So Gilmer, after conferring with his colleagues, stayed out of it.

From the outset of the struggle over his cabinet, Lincoln had hoped to include the rivals whom he had defeated at Chicago— Seward, Salmon P. Chase of Ohio, Edward Bates of Missouri, and Simon Cameron of Pennsylvania. Bates was an early choice for attorney general, without opposition. But Seward and the moderates tried earnestly to keep out Chase, former senator and governor of Ohio, whom they viewed as a radical abolitionist, while the antislavery "ironbacks," such as Massachusetts Senator Charles Sumner, sought desperately to force out Seward, whom they viewed as an appeaser of the South. They also objected to Cameron, accusing him of being a corrupt machine politician whose appointment would disgrace the Republican Party.

A tremendous intraparty row erupted over a cabinet post for wily Senator Cameron, who had thrown his crucial bloc of Pennsylvania delegates to Lincoln at Chicago. Judge David Davis, Lincoln's manager there, had positively pledged that, as a reward, Cameron would be named secretary of the treasury, the senator said. At Lincoln's invitation, Cameron visited him in Springfield in late December, explained the political facts of life, and came home with a letter, signed by Lincoln, promising to name him secretary of the treasury or secretary of war.

Cameron made the mistake of showing the letter to some friends, who began boasting that he was sure of a cabinet post; whereupon they stirred up a hornet's nest of protests. A. K. McClure, an influential Pennsylvania editor allied with Governor Andrew Curtin in his long-running feud against Cameron, hastened to Springfield and warned Lincoln that naming Cameron would be a disaster.

Wilting under the heat, Lincoln sent Cameron another letter January 3, saying: "Since seeing you things have developed which make it impossible for me to take you into the cabinet. You will say this comes of an interview with McClure; and this is partly, but not wholly, true. The more potent matter is wholly outside of Pennsylvania, and yet I am not at liberty to specify it."

Lincoln asked Cameron to send him a letter declining the appointment. He added a P.S.: "Telegraph me instantly on receipt of this, saying, 'All right.' A.L." Cameron refused to send any such telegram. Instead, he inspired a flood of letters from his friends, vouching for his integrity and insisting that Pennsylvania Republicans would be furious if he were barred from the cabinet after all he had done to make Lincoln president. In other words, a deal was a deal, and Lincoln must keep his end of the bargain.

The "most potent matter wholly outside of Pennsylvania," cited by Lincoln's letter, apparently was the radicals' demand that Chase positively must be the next secretary of the treasury. Lincoln solved the dilemma by giving Chase the treasury post and making Cameron secretary of war. In another reward for delegates delivered at Chicago, Caleb Smith of Indiana became the secretary of the interior. Gideon Welles, a Connecticut newspaper editor and former Democrat, was chosen as secretary of the navy. Bates and Blair completed the cabinet.

Seward was dismayed by the prospect of a "compound cabinet"; he especially opposed Chase, as well as Blair and Welles. Seward issued an ultimatum: If Chase went into the cabinet, Seward would stay out. "There are differences between myself and Chase," he said, "which make it impossible for us to act in harmony."

Shrewdly, Lincoln indicated to some of Seward's New York friends that it might be necessary to part with their hero and hand the State Department over to William L. Dayton of New Jersey, Fremont's running mate in 1856. Seward might be sent, instead, on the mission to London. Lincoln thereby showed his determination to be master of his own house. "I can't afford to let Seward take the first trick," he told his secretary, John G. Nicolay.

Seward got the message. He gave in, on Inaugural Day, and explained to his wife: "I did not dare to go home, or to England, and leave the country to chance."

Seward had more success with his efforts to modify the inaugural address. On their way home from church on February 24, Lincoln gave him a copy of it and asked for his suggestions. The first draft had been written and set in type at Springfield. At Indianapolis, Lincoln had shown it to Orville H. Browning, who persuaded him to make one major change: Lincoln intended to say that he would "reclaim" all the forts and other federal property seized by the seceding states; on Browning's advice, he struck that word out.

Seward advised removing two paragraphs pledging to carry out the Republicans' Chicago platform; he thought they smacked of partisanship. Lincoln agreed. At first, Lincoln had opposed new constitutional amendments. At Seward's suggestion, he changed his mind and said he would "favor, rather than oppose, a fair opportunity being afforded the people to act upon it."

As Lincoln put the finishing touches on his inaugural address, the members of Congress spent their closing hours in partisan wrangling over his future policies. Representative Muscoe R. H. Garnett of Virginia cited the President-elect's speeches and recent conversations as proof that Lincoln favored coercing the seceding states, not compromise. Lincoln, he said, was manly and frank and did not try to hide "the claws of a tiger underneath the velvet fur." Lincoln, he said, "intends to make war on the South."

"Lincoln and his party declare that they will make no concessions to traitors and rebels, as they characterize the seceding states," North Carolina Senator Thomas Lanier Clingman told a constituent. If North Carolina joined Lincoln in the war against the seceding Southern states, Clingman warned, she must expect to have slavery "abolished by force of arms and to see the South reduced to the condition of Jamaica or St. Domingo ... to a condition of free negro equality."

Senator Joe Lane of Oregon ended his career with a bitter attack upon the victorious Republicans, who had wrecked the hopes of the Breckinridge-Lane ticket. Lane, who had earlier championed the South by asserting that he would never "follow Lincoln's bloody banner" in a civil war, drew a verbal assault by a fellow Democrat, Andrew Johnson, who denounced the secessionists as traitors.

Johnson, despised by the Southern aristocracy as a mere tailor or "prick louse," vowed that his state of Tennessee would remain in the Union and keep faith with its great hero, Andrew Jackson.

Zach Chandler, the hard-drinking Michigan Republican, assailed the Buchanan administration and the Democrats generally as a pack of thieves and scoundrels. His tirade caused Senator Lane to call it "a whiskey insurrection." Chandler did not shrink from a civil war. "Without a little blood-letting," in his view, "the Union will not, in my estimation, be worth a rush."

If the right of secession were ever conceded to any state, he said, he would resign his Senate seat and leave the country. "Sir," he shouted, "I would rather join the Comanches."

"God forbid! I hope not," cried Louis T. Wigfall, the "Texas Terror," in an equally alcoholic reply. The poor Indians, he said, "have already suffered much from their contact with the whites."

Wigfall, who often tossed off a glass of whiskey several times during a speech, evoked laughter by ridiculing Lincoln. Sneering at Lincoln as "an ex-rail splitter, an ex-grocery keeper, an ex-flatboat captain, and ex-abolition lecturer," the bearded Texan with the eyes of a Bengal tiger challenged one of Lincoln's favorite ideas—that the Declaration of Independence affirmed that all men were "created equal." The authors of that declaration "were speaking of the white men" who created "republican forms of government in the thirteen sovereign, separate, and independent colonies," he said. "Yet the Declaration is constantly quoted to prove negro equality. It proves no such thing."

So the Senate debate raged on until, on the dawn of Lincoln's inaugural day, the Corwin amendment affirming the legality of slavery in the Southern states passed by the bare minimum two-thirds margin, 24 to 12. Then the Peace Convention's proposals were defeated, 28 to 7, and the Crittenden measure was finally placed in its grave, 20 to 19.

Senator Wigfall's teenage son, Halsey, reveling in the notorious duelist's tirades on the Senate floor, wrote to his sister, Louise: "Tomorrow is the day, par excellence, for on that day is to be inaugurated, with all the pride, pomp and circumstance of glorious war, with spirit-stirring drum and ear-piercing fife and trumpet ... a long, gaunt and bony rail splitter. Shades of Washington, how are the mighty fallen!"

After all the alarming reports of plots to disrupt Lincoln's inauguration and even to kill him, the ceremonies on March 4 proved a great success—largely because General Scott had overawed the potential mischief makers with his threats and his fierce display of military might. He had hundreds of soldiers and militiamen marching with the presidential carriage from the Willard Hotel to Capitol Hill, an honor guard of soldiers and marines screening the carriage; cavalry on guard on the side streets; riflemen hidden on the roofs of houses along the avenue; and sharpshooters peering out the windows of the Capitol.

A throng estimated at twenty-five thousand filled the area at the east front of the Capitol as Lincoln, accompanied by members of Congress, diplomats, and Supreme Court justices, reached the flag-decked platform. Lincoln looked around for some place to park his new stovepipe hat. The *Cincinnati Commercial*, on the authority of an Ohio congressman, first reported the symbolic gesture that followed.

The *Commercial* said that Lincoln kept moving the hat awkwardly from one place to another and finally, in despair, started to put it on the stage under his seat, when Senator Douglas, who had been looking on "apparently with some apprehension of a catastrophe to the hat," said, "Permit me, sir," and gallantly held the hat throughout Lincoln's speech. Although several witnesses have mentioned the incident in their memoirs, some historians have doubted its authenticity, claiming there was no contemporary evidence of it. The evidence can be found in the *Cincinnati Commercial* and reprinted in the *New York Times* of March 15, 1861.

In his inaugural address, the new president uttered many conciliatory remarks intended to soothe the Southerners and to reassure them that he had no intention of ending slavery in their states, or of sending "obnoxious strangers" among them as federal officials. But there was an iron hand inside his velvet glove.

Denying that any state had the right of secession, he asserted that the Union was perpetual and "much older than the Constitution." The secession ordinances, he said, are "legally void," and any acts of violence against the federal authority are "insurrectionary or revolutionary."

He, therefore, vowed to do his duty and take care that the laws be faithfully executed in all the states—and he included those that claimed to have seceded. "I trust this will not be regarded as a menace," he said, "but only as the declared purpose of the Union that it will constitutionally defend and maintain itself.

"In doing this there needs to be no bloodshed or violence and there shall be none, unless it be forced upon the national authority."

Then Lincoln made the iron-clad declaration that Senator Seward had tried, but failed, to modify:

"The power confided to me will be used to hold, occupy and possess the property and places belonging to the government, and to collect the duties and imposts; but beyond what may be necessary for these objects, there will be no invasion—no using of force against or among the people anywhere."

Then Lincoln astutely maneuvered to place on the Southerners the blame for any war that might result from his policy: "In your hands, my dissatisfied fellow countrymen, and not in mine, is the momentous issue of civil war. The government will not assail you. You can have no conflict without yourselves being the aggressors. You have no oath registered in Heaven to destroy the government, while I shall have the most solemn one to 'preserve, protect and defend' it."

In his original draft, Lincoln had planned to throw down this gauntlet and leave it there, but Seward had begged him to close with an appeal to patriotic sentiment in hopes of persuading the Border States to stay in the old Union, and so he concluded with these words, first written by Seward but transformed by Lincoln with poetic phrases that have made it immortal:

"I am loth to close. We are not enemies, but friends. We must not be enemies. Though passion may have strained, it must not break, our bonds of affection. The mystic chords of memory, stretching from every battlefield and patriot grave, to every living heart and hearthstone, all over this broad land, will yet swell the chorus of the Union, when again touched, as surely they will be, by the better angels of our nature."

After his address, Lincoln took the oath of office, administered by the octogenarian Chief Justice Taney, a bent and wrinkled wraith in black robes.

During Lincoln's speech, a reporter heard Senator Douglas uttering, "sotto voco," several remarks of approval: "Good! That's so! No coercion! Good!" Afterwards, Douglas told the press: "He does not mean coercion. He says nothing about *retaking* the federal property. He's all right." That evening, the Little Giant escorted the First Lady into the inaugural ball.

When President and Mrs. Lincoln hosted their first levee, a few nights later, for a mob of three thousand people, "little Douglas, who is playing the deepest game for the Union ticket of 1864, was there in all his glory," a *New York Times* correspondent reported.

Here one minute, there the next—now congratulating the President, then complimenting Mrs. Lincoln; bowing and scraping and
shaking hands, smiling, laughing, yarning, and saluting the people
who know him, he was a pleasant sight to behold.

He deserves credit for doing a great deal of good for the administration by setting a good example to his followers and, as he is
unable to hoodwink Old Abe or honeyfugle Madam L., we, as good,
sound Union men, should be thankful that Douglas is inclined, as
he says, "to play the part of the patriot."

Of the real star of the show, the reporter said:

In the Blue Room, near the door, stood the President, his tall form
towering above the crowd, his head bowing constantly, his arm
working uninterruptedly, and a happy general smile playing about
his mouth. He was dressed in a plain black suit—frock coat, vest
and trousers—a wide turn-over collar and white gloves. ...

Mr. Lincoln looked good. His face was slightly flushed, his demeanor dignified and calm. ... Mrs. L. stood near her husband with
dignity and ease. ... She wore a very rich and becoming crimson
watered silk, with pearl ornaments, a very elegant point lace cape, a
head dress of natural camellias interspersed with pearls.

Many in the throng were office seekers and lobbyists, and some
had come from New York, Philadelphia, and Baltimore to share in
the excitement of the Lincolns' first levee. They pushed and shoved
through the line in their eagerness to obtain a Lincoln handshake—
"pushed, tumbled, foot-trodden, hat-smashed, jostled and squeezed,"
but happy to be there anyway.

The general tone of Lincoln's inaugural address left the impression that he sought peace, although he firmly declared his intention
to hold the forts and other federal property and that policy, of course,
would require force. Republican newspapers sang hosannas of praise,
but the *New York Herald* said the speech "abounds with traits of craft
and cunning" while the *New York Daily News* said the casual reader
could be deceived by the "honeyed phrases." But the Southerners
weren't fooled. The Richmond newspapers called it a virtual declaration
of war. The *Baltimore Sun* said Lincoln would use despotic powers for
"war and bloodshed."

"The Southern secession papers and their Northern allies have resolved to construe the President's inaugural to mean 'coercion,' and they cry out with one voice that 'we are on the eve of disastrous, bloody and desolating war,'" said the *Chicago Tribune*. "The wish is father to the thought. The fire-eaters desire a collision with the Federal forces, believing that it would unite the slave states against the government."

Senator Wigfall, who arrogantly held onto his Senate seat although Texas had seceded, expressed his keen disappointment over the events of March 4. He was disgusted with his Southern friends. They had sworn that Lincoln should be killed, and now he was peaceably inaugurated, after all. Wigfall was tempted to say he would have nothing more to do with such a "damned set of humbugs."

He sent a telegram to the Confederate secretary of war: "Inaugural means war. There is strong ground for belief that reinforcements will be speedily sent. Be vigilant."

21

CABINET FAVORS GIVING UP FORT SUMTER

On his first day in office, President Lincoln received a shock: A letter from Major Robert Anderson, saying that all of his officers agreed with him that it would be unwise to attempt reinforcing Fort Sumter "with a force of less than twenty thousand good and disciplined men." Anderson's food and other supplies were running low; the people of Charleston, who had treated him politely until now, were refusing to sell him provisions. The South Carolinians had spent the winter ringing the fort with their batteries, so they could batter it to pieces at will. Clearly, he must give up the fort within weeks.

This was most distressing news to greet a very green chief executive, totally inexperienced in managing the myriad problems of his new position, and besieged by mobs of job seekers who consumed most of his waking hours with their selfish demands for offices as the spoils of the Republican victory. For three decades, except for eight years of Whig regimes, the Democrats had held all the offices, ranging from postmasters to marshals, revenue collectors, and department clerks; now, under the practice of "rotation in office," their jobs must all be given to loyal Republicans for the first time.

Lincoln felt compelled to fritter away so much time and energy refereeing disputes over patronage, that he could hardly concentrate on the far more important issues arising from the secession crisis. On the question of "War or peace?" he received the advice of General Scott, who had sent it in a letter to Secretary Seward. Scott spelled out four possible courses of action:

"First, throw off the *old* and assume a *new* designation—the Union party; adopt the conciliatory measures proposed by Mr. Crittenden or the Peace Convention, and, my life on it, we shall have no new case of secession but, on the contrary, an early return of many, if not of all, of the states which have already broken off from the Union. Without some equally benign measure, the remaining slaveholding states will probably join the Montgomery Confederacy in less than sixty days."

If Maryland should secede, Scott warned, "this city, being included in a foreign confederacy, would require a permanent garrison of at least thirty-five thousand troops to protect the government within it."

Second, Scott suggested that Lincoln "collect the duties on foreign goods outside the ports of which this government has lost command, or close such ports by an act of Congress and blockade them."

Third, the general estimated that invading armies might conquer the seceded states in two or three years, with "a young and able general" and three hundred thousand disciplined soldiers, "estimating a third for garrisons and the loss of a yet greater number by skirmishes, sieges, battles and Southern fevers."

"The destruction of life and property by the other side," he said, "would be frightful, however perfect the moral discipline of the invaders."

"The conquest completed, at that enormous waste of human life in the North and the Northwest, with at least $250,000,000 in federal debt," Scott added, what would be the result? "Cui bono?" he asked. "Fifteen devastated provinces!"

Finally, Scott mentioned one policy that Lincoln would surely reject, although it would save all those lives and all that destruction: "Say to the seceded states—'Wayward sisters, depart in peace.'"

When Major Anderson had thrown his men into Fort Sumter at Christmas time, it would have been easy to reinforce them, Scott said, but, in the past two months, the difficulty had increased ten or fifteenfold because the secessionists had strengthened Fort Moultrie and built a series of batteries in the harbor. The officers in the fort, he said, "now see no alternative but a surrender, in some weeks ... if, indeed, the worn-out garrison be not assaulted and carried in the present week."

Like Seward and Scott, Stephen A. Douglas sought to push Lincoln into a policy of peace rather than an unnecessary war. So, while

Southerners were branding the inaugural address a war message, Lincoln's defeated foe told the Senate that he viewed it as actually one of peace. He noted that the new president had promised to refrain from any violence or invasion, and to use only defensive forces to hold and possess the federal property; and he had agreed to let the Constitution be amended.

The "Public Man" wrote in his diary: "Mr. Douglas says that the President sent for him after his speech of Wednesday [March 6] to assure him that he sincerely agreed with all its views, and sympathized with its spirit. All the President desired was to get the points of present irritation removed, so that the people might grow cool, and reflect on the general position all over the country, when he felt confident there would be a general demand for a National Convention at which all the existing differences could be radically treated."

On March 7, Douglas informed the Senate that he expected no effort to reinforce Fort Sumter, because that would be "impossible." His lines of information to sources inside the administration obviously were quite good. Reflecting the views of General Scott, Douglas said that, to subjugate the South, the Lincoln administration would need to raise "an army of a quarter of a million men" and spend $250 million to support it for a single year, and that the choice lay between that and a policy of peace.

So, he concluded, "we are to have no war, no bloody collision, and that the peace policy is going to prevail."

Unfortunately, events were destined to prove that Douglas's prophecy was totally wrong. Although Lincoln deplored war, and yearned for peace, he followed a policy of enforcing the laws in all the states, including those that had seceded. Partisan Republicans insisted upon holding him to this policy, which necessarily involved using military force.

Senator Mason of Virginia, disputing Douglas's cheery optimism about Lincoln's love of peace, said there was only one real "peace policy"—to admit that the seven Deep South states had seceded, and to withdraw the federal troops from them. But that policy, "so far from being contained in this inaugural, is repelled and repudiated by its whole tenor and purpose," Mason said.

Although the Virginians differed about secession, the senator warned, if the federal government used any force on the plea of "enforcing the laws," "Virginia will become, by the unanimous consent of her people, a party to that war when the first gun is fired."

Hard-line Republicans resented the attempt by the Democratic senator from Illinois to interpret the policies of the new Republican administration and guide it toward peace. Bitterly, the *Chicago Tribune* said that, since his defeat by Lincoln, "Mr. Douglas has passed out of politics. His interviews with Seward, to devise ways and means of amending the Constitution, serve to keep him alive in public recollection; but his influence in the Senate, and with the country, is gone."

In an attempt to show the world that it yearned for peace, not war, the Confederate government sent three commissioners to Washington, hoping to obtain recognition and to draft treaties of friendship with the United States. Chosen by President Davis for the mission were a Douglas Democrat, John Forsyth, Mobile newspaper editor and former minister to Mexico; a Breckinridge Democrat, Martin J. Crawford, until recently a Georgia congressman; and A. B. Roman, a former governor of Louisiana who had voted for Bell.

Crawford arrived first, and on the evening of Lincoln's inaugural day, met with Senator Wigfall and three Virginia congressmen, Daniel DeJarnette, Roger Pryor, and Muscoe R. M. Garnett. "We all agreed that it was Lincoln's purpose at once to attempt the collection of the revenue, to reinforce and hold Forts Sumter and Pickens, and to retake other places," they reported to the Montgomery government. "He is a man of will and firmness. His cabinet will yield to him with alacrity."

To Robert Toombs, the Confederate secretary of state, Crawford wrote that John Bell had warned Lincoln that "any attempt to reinforce the forts, collect the revenue, or in any way whatever to interfere with your government would be the signal for every border state to secede from the Union and join the Southern Confederacy."

Bell, he added, "advises an *indefinite* truce, the withdrawal of the troops from the forts (except a sergeant with a nominal force); the flag of the U.S. to be kept floating on the fortifications to satisfy the war party North; in the meantime the Confederate States are to be left alone, to do as they may choose, prepare for war, strengthen defenses, in short to do whatever may seem good to them. The advantages to the U.S. being, that the more we may do, looking to independence and safety, the greater will be the amount of taxation upon the people and the sooner will a current of dissatisfaction and discontent set in, resulting at last in a reconstruction upon the most permanent and durable basis."

However, Crawford realized that the "war party North" was pressuring Lincoln to show his courage by a stiff policy toward the seceded states; and that "whatever the Republican Party can do without driving out Virginia it will do and such coercive measures as the new Administration may *with safety* adopt it will most certainly."

Commissioner Forsyth, in a letter to Toombs, quoted Seward as bragging: "I have built up the Republican party, I have brought it to triumph, but its advent to power is accompanied by great difficulties and perils. I must save the party, and save the government in its hands. To do this, war must be averted, the negro question must be dropped, and irrepressible conflict ignored, and a Union party to embrace the border slave states inaugurated." Then Seward predicted, "The people of the cotton states, unwillingly led into secession, will rebel."

Armed with General Scott's assertion that it was a military necessity to evacuate Fort Sumter, Seward sent reassuring messages to that effect to the Confederate leaders in Montgomery—not directly but through intermediaries. One of his go-betweens was Dr. William Gwin, a pro-Southern Democrat whose service as a senator from California had expired March 4. Seward and Gwin had worked closely together in efforts to have Congress finance construction of a transcontinental railroad to California, hoping that it could help to bind the states together. Dr. Gwin's dream of a Pacific railway, subsidized by generous land grants and funds from Congress, had almost become an obsession. But his efforts were frustrated by disputes over which cities should have the eastern connection. Chicago, St. Louis, and New Orleans were three of the rival cities; each had lobbyists in Washington.

Dr. Gwin, a Tennessee native and former Mississippi congressman with large land investments in Texas, had carved out a profitable career in California during the gold rush days. He had close ties with the Gulf State senators now running the Confederacy, notably President Davis and Attorney General Judah P. Benjamin. In March, the Vicksburg, Mississippi, *Whig* quoted a letter from Dr. Gwin to "a gentleman of Jackson" as saying "there will be no war." "He says Mr.

Seward, if permitted, and President Davis can settle the matter in thirty days," the newspaper said. "Mr. Seward is the Premier of the new administration and his policy is peace."

Another of Seward's confidential agents, providing him with accurate information from the Confederate chieftains, was Sam Ward, a Washington lobbyist and bon vivant who acted as the agent for some wealthy New York investors. One of his clients was the Manhattan lawyer and railroad promoter S.L.M. Barlow, an influential Democrat who had played a hand in elevating Buchanan to the presidency. Barlow continued corresponding with his friend, Attorney General Benjamin, although the former Louisiana senator was technically an official of a foreign government.

In a chatty letter to Seward on inaugural night, Ward reported a visit to Dr. Gwin at his home in Washington. "Whilst we were discussing the probable action of Virginia, which Dr. G. maintained *would not go out*, Constitution Browne came in from the p.m. train, fresh from Montgomery." "Constitution" Browne was an Englishman who had edited Buchanan's official capital newspaper, the *Constitution*, and had recently obtained a sinecure in the Confederate government.

These were Browne's news bulletins:

"1. Mr. Davis has shown Browne a letter received from Dr. G. some days since, foreshadowing peaceful policy on the part of the incoming administration. ...

"2. There is perfect unanimity in the Southern Congress—no jar. Tom Cobb, a cleverer man than his brother, is the leader of debate.

"3. Toombs is the master spirit of the new government."

Ward warned Seward that he must not refuse to deal with the three Confederate commissioners. If they are spurned, the lobbyist said, "President Davis cannot hold back the people from attacking the forts."

Ward also said Barlow, in New York, had word directly from Benjamin that the officials in Montgomery were becoming impatient and would not merely "await events."

Seward knew that he could not possibly bring the Confederate envoys in to see Lincoln, who flatly refused to admit that the seven states, calling themselves a "nation," had even left the Union and, therefore, he insisted that he was their president. An outright rejection, however, could send the commissioners rushing angrily back to Montgomery and could even touch off an attack on Fort Sumter. So Seward stalled for time. He asked the commissioners—through their agent, Senator Hunter of Virginia   to wait a while and all would be well.

The *New York Herald* said on March 13 that, through Seward and Dr. Gwin, it had been arranged that Commissioners Crawford and Forsyth "would have an interview with the President" but, "fearing the howl that would ascend from the Republican grog shops of the country at the startling change in the anticipated policy of the government"—that is, the pending decision to give up Fort Sumter— "Mr. Seward sent a note to the commissioners stating that it would be impossible to carry out his programme, and that Mr. Lincoln would not receive them."

Lincoln made a mistake in rebuffing the commissioners, the *Herald* said. "If they be the legitimate representatives of five millions of citizens of the Union, he should listen to them patiently. If they are simply ambassadors from a foreign power, it is equally incumbent upon him to find out officially, what they want." A conversation need not be construed as recognizing the Confederacy, the *Herald* argued. It could have laid the basis for "a future reconstruction of the Union" and peace, the newspaper said, but the opportunity had been "malignantly and stupidly thrown away."

The commissioners, on March 12, drafted a formal request for an interview with Lincoln. Seward wrote a memorandum stating his refusal to comply and "filed" it in the State Department. It was not delivered to the three Confederates until three weeks later.

The secretary sent oral messages next through two more go-betweens, Supreme Court Justices Samuel Nelson of New York and John Campbell of Alabama. On March 15, Justice Nelson called on Seward, Treasury Secretary Chase, and Attorney General Bates, and tried to dissuade them from any acts of coercion. His recent studies, the jurist said, had convinced him that the President could not carry out coercion without seriously violating the Constitution and the federal statutes.

Seward replied that the Confederates' request for a meeting with the President had caused much embarrassment, and an immediate refusal would lead to much "irritation" in both the North and the

South. The two justices had another parley with Seward, urging him to tell the three commissioners that Lincoln desired a friendly adjustment.

Seward became upset and cried: "If Jefferson Davis had known the state of things here, he would not have sent those commissioners; the evacuation of Sumter is as much as the Administration can bear!"

Seward assured Justice Campbell on March 15 that Sumter would be evacuated within five days and there would be no change in the status of Fort Pickens. The judge said he would see the commissioners and write to President Davis. When he asked what he should tell Davis, Seward replied: "Before that letter could reach him, he would learn by telegraph that the order for the evacuation of Sumter had been made."

Commissioner Forsyth told Senator Douglas that "Seward had, several times, assured him most positively, in the presence of Judge Nelson of the Supreme Court, that the cabinet had determined to evacuate Sumter."

Senator Wigfall telegraphed General P.G.T. Beauregard, commander of the federal troops at Charleston, March 11, that the cabinet had informally agreed to evacuate Fort Sumter and the order would go out within five days.

Wigfall wired Davis that the cabinet had made this "informal conclusion" Saturday night, March 9.

Attorney General Bates wrote in his diary about that cabinet meeting: "I was astonished to be informed that Fort Sumter in Charleston harbor *must* be evacuated and that Gen. Scott, Gen. Totten, and Major Anderson concur in opinion that, as the place has but 28 days provisions, it must be relieved, if at all, in that time; and that it will take a force of 20,000 men, at least, and a bloody battle, to relieve it!"

Although naval officers contended that "with light rapid vessels, they can cross the bar at high tide of a dark night, run the enemy's forts (Moultrie and Cummings Point) and reach Sumter with little risk," Bates added, "yet, as the doing of it would be almost certain to *begin the war*, I am willing to yield to the military counsels and evacuate Fort Sumter, at the same time strengthening the forts in the Gulf."

After a long talk with Douglas, the "Public Man" wrote in his diary March 11: "Mr. Lincoln has assured Mr. Douglas positively, he tells me, that he means the fort shall be evacuated as soon as possible and that all his cabinet whom he has consulted are of the same mind excepting Mr. Blair."

This indicates that, on March 11, Lincoln intended, "positively," that Fort Sumter must soon be given up. Seward arranged for the reassuring news to be relayed at once to the Virginia convention and the Confederate commissioners.

Seward apparently felt confident that he had a majority of the cabinet with him in opposing any attempt to reinforce Fort Sumter. The effort, he warned, "would lead to war, by our own act, without an adequate object, after which reunion would be hopeless." Even the radical Chase cautioned against a resupply effort if it would lead to civil war. Only Blair, at this time, insisted that the North must maintain the fort to show that the secessionists were wrong in thinking that Northern men lacked enough courage to defend the government.

Why did Seward feel so supremely confident that Fort Sumter would be given up, although Lincoln detested the idea? One reason is that General Scott had already drawn up an order to be sent to the gallant Major Anderson. Dated March 11, it said:

> Sir:
>
> The time having been allowed to pass when it was practicable to fit out an expedition adequate to the succor of your garrison, before the exhaustion of its means of subsistence—you will, after communicating your purpose to His Excellency, the Governor of So. Carolina—engage suitable water transportation & peacefully evacuate Fort Sumter, so long gallantly held—& with your entire command embark for New York; your officers and men taking with them their small arms, accoutrements & private effects.
>
> Very respectfully yrs.
> WINFIELD SCOTT

The original of this order remained in Lincoln's papers, because he could not bring himself to send it. Determined to avoid the humiliation of such a surrender, and the political abuse and ridicule that he would suffer for it, the harried president cast about for some way of either supplying the little garrison in the Charleston fort or blaming the Confederates for starting the civil war that would result, inevitably, from an attempt to relieve it. The influence of General Scott and Seward was so great, in the early days of the administration, that Lincoln could see no way out of dispatching the evacuation order, which he dreaded.

Major newspapers began featuring authoritative stories predicting that Fort Sumter would be given up soon. On March 11, the same day that Scott drafted his proposed order to Major Anderson, the *Cincinnati Commercial* disclosed that Lincoln's cabinet "fully understood that, at no distant day, the troops will be withdrawn from Fort Sumter." The *Cincinnati Gazette* said Scott had convinced "a great many Republican senators that there was no alternative left but the withdrawal of the garrison."

On March 12, the *Chicago Tribune*'s Washington correspondent reported that certain "gentlemen in prominent positions confidently assert that Fort Sumter will be abandoned in consequence of the peremptory opinion of General Scott." Also on March 12, the *Charleston Mercury* proclaimed that Sumter soon would be in Confederate hands.

If Seward were acting true to form, he played a part in privately spreading the word that Sumter must be given up. Republican editors, dismayed by the bad news, joined in efforts to make it look good by saying it might promote peace. (In the press agents' lingo of the modern day, that would be called putting the right "spin" on it.)

It is "humiliating," said the loyal *Chicago Tribune*, but it "will strike one of the most effective blows at secession. Southern commercial men welcome the movement; ... it will tend to revive business ... as it destroys all excuse for the hotspurs of the South to keep up a war excitement." The usually belligerent *Tribune* evidently had been briefed by someone, probably Seward.

Also seeing a ray of sunshine in the dark clouds, a Cincinnati corespondent wrote, "The fort has no strategic importance," while the *New York Post* surmised that it would take away an excuse for Virginia to join the "Cotton Confederacy."

Another Republican propaganda line affirmed that giving up the fort was not the fault of the new Republican administration; the blame belonged to the Democrats of the timid Buchanan regime, who had failed to reinforce the fort when it could have been done.

Edwin M. Stanton, Buchanan's attorney general, who remained in Washington as a critic of the new regime, wrote to the former president on March 14: "There is no doubt of Sumter being evacuated." Stanton privately ridiculed Lincoln as "a low, cunning clown."

A dispatch from Charleston on March 15 said: "The proposed evacuation of Fort Sumter is almost the exclusive topic of conversation. No one really doubts it now. The authenticated report affords inexpressible relief to hundreds of families in Charleston and elsewhere that had husbands and brothers in the rebel ranks ... although there are some who prefer a fight."

The "authenticated report," of course, came from Seward to the Confederate commissioners. They "have received such assurances, from high sources, of the pacific intentions of the administration, in reference to the Southern forts, that they will make no official demand at present and, pending movements at Sumter, will remain quiet." Later they would bitterly regret having been such naive and trusting souls, to rely upon the word of the slippery Secretary Seward.

"I confidently believe Sumter will be evacuated," Commissioner Forsyth told General Beauregard on March 14. With boyish optimism, Forsyth informed his government, "There is a terrific fight in the cabinet. Our policy is to encourage the peace element in the fight, and at least blow up the cabinet on the question. The outside pressure in favor of peace grows stronger every hour. Lincoln inclines to peace, and I have now no doubt that General Scott is Seward's anxious and laborious coadjutor in the same direction.

"If Seward were not a coward, and could have had an unofficial conference with us, we could have strengthened his hands."

"The great danger," Forsyth added, "is that from ignorance of the true state of things in the South they may blunder us into a war when they really do not mean it. I think the great problem with the Administration is how to get out of a fight without blowing up the Republican party. They believe, and we encourage the pleasant thought, that in case of war their precious persons would not be safe in Washington. With prudence, wisdom, and firmness we have the rascals 'on the hip.'"

Forsyth was right on one point: There was, indeed, "a terrific fight in the cabinet" now. Montgomery Blair, standing alone at first in opposition to giving up Sumter, began a furious fight to keep Lincoln from approving Scott's evacuation order.

The postmaster general called to Washington his brother-in-law, Gustavus Vasa Fox, a former naval officer, who had a plan for bringing more troops and supplies into the fort aboard several small boats, backed by some U.S. warships. Fox had first prepared his proposal in February but Buchanan had rejected it. This time, Blair took Fox to lay it all out before Lincoln, who was delighted to find someone suggesting a relief expedition that might save him from the embarrassment of having to yield the Charleston fort.

On March 15, Lincoln requested each cabinet member to give him a written reply to this question: "Assuming it to be possible to now provision Fort Sumter, under all the circumstances is it wise to attempt it?"

Seward said "No." Trying to send in supplies would be just as unsuccessful as moving in reinforcements, and would surely touch off war. "Suppose the expedition is successful," he argued, "we have a garrison in Fort Sumter that can defy assault for six months. What is it to do then? Is it to make war by opening its batteries and attempt to demolish the defenses of the Carolinians? ... I would not initiate war to regain a useless and unnecessary position on the soil of the seceded states."

Salmon P. Chase, the treasury secretary, wrote: "If the attempt will so inflame civil war as to involve an immediate necessity for the enlistment of armies and the expenditure of millions, I could not advise it in the existing circumstances of the country and in the present condition of the nation's finances." Besides, Chase privately believed "it would be better to allow the seven states to try the experiment of a separate existence rather than incur the evils of a bloody war."

Navy Secretary Gideon Welles wrote: "By sending, or attempting to send, provisions into Sumter, will not war be precipitated? ... I am not prepared to advise a course that would provoke hostilities."

Secretary of War Cameron advised that reinforcement of the fort "cannot be done without the sacrifice of life and treasure not at all commensurate with the object to be obtained; and, as the abandonment of the fort in a few weeks ... appears to be an inevitable necessity, it seems to me that the sooner it's done, the better."

Attorney General Bates opposed any act that would seem like "beginning a civil war, the terrible consequences of that would ... form no parallel in modern times." To avoid the "horrors" of a war which would soon become a "social war" and even a "servile war," the Missouri Whig "would make great sacrifices, and Fort Sumter is one."

Only Blair, of all the cabinet, welcomed war; or, to say the least, did not turn away in horror from the prospect of Americans killing each other over a fort. Most of the cabinet members agreed with Seward and General Scott that the risk of war, and the likely losses from combat, were too great to justify trying to hold the Charleston fort, which had comparatively little strategic value. But Blair insisted that giving up the fort would greatly strengthen the Confederacy's claim to be an independent power. The relief of Fort Sumter, Blair argued, "would completely demoralize the rebellion."

Blair's father, the venerable but still peppery Francis Preston Blair, Sr., came to see Lincoln and implored him to take bold action to hold Fort Sumter, just as his own hero, Andrew Jackson, had done when he had brought the rebellious South Carolinians to heel in the nullification crisis. Surrendering Fort Sumter would be virtually a surrender of the Union and "compounding with treason was treason to the government," the former Democrat declared.

"His earnestness and indignation aroused and electrified the President," Secretary Welles recorded in his diary, "and when, in his zeal, Blair warned the President that the abandonment of Sumter would justly be considered by the people, by the world, by history, as treason to the country, he touched a chord that responded to his invocation." Welles believed that the old editor's eloquent appeal caused Lincoln to decide in favor of sending supplies to Sumter.

"Frank P. Blair talked some backbone into Old Abe one day this week, after his outspoken, unsparing fashion," the *New York Herald* revealed. "He told him plainly that peaceable secession or separation was an impossibility, that the success of the Republican administration depended on the fulfillment of the assurances held out in the inaugural." Lincoln had promised "to hold, occupy and possess" the federal property, so he had to do it, regardless of the cost.

In their fervor for a fight, both of the Blairs brushed aside the warnings that reinforcing Sumter would surely touch off a bloody war. Senator Douglas made this bitter comment about the Blairs:

"What they really want is a civil war. They are determined, first, on seeing slavery abolished by force, and then on expelling the entire negro race from the continent. This was old Blair's doctrine, sir, long ago, and it is Montgomery's doctrine, sir. If they can get and keep their grip on Lincoln, this country will never see peace or prosperity again, sir, in your time or mine or in our children's time."

In mid-March, Douglas touched off a Senate debate aimed at finding out if Lincoln's apparently peaceful intentions were really to be carried out by his administration. He introduced a resolution of inquiry to determine whether the Republicans would ask for a military force large enough to hold their present forts or a much larger army to recapture those lost to the seceding states and to subdue the Southern people.

"I should like to know whether or not, in the opinion of the highest military authority in America, it would require 35,000 men to protect the capital and 250,000 more for field operations to reduce those states to obedience to our laws and our authority," he said. Douglas must have known that General Scott had cited comparable figures in his message to Lincoln and Seward.

"Is it your purpose," Douglas asked the Republicans, "to rush this country blindly into war at a cost of $300 million per annum, to levy $200 million in direct taxes upon the people? ... Are we prepared for civil war, with all its horrors and calamities? I proclaim boldly, the policy of those with whom I act: We are for peace!"

"The President of the United States holds the destiny of this country in his hands," the Illinois senator went on.

> I believe he means peace, and war will be averted, unless he is over-ruled by the disunion faction of his party. ... We all know the irre-pressible conflict is going on in his camp; even debating whether Fort Sumter shall be surrendered when it is impossible to hold it; whether Major Anderson shall not be kept there until he starves to death, or applies the torch with his own hand to the match that blows him and his little garrison into eternity, for fear that some-body in the Republican party might say you had backed down.

What man in all America, who knows the facts connected with Fort Sumter, can hesitate in saying that duty, honor, patriotism and humanity require that Anderson and his gallant band should be instantly withdrawn? Sir, I am not afraid to say so, I would scorn to take party advantage or manufacture partisan capital out of an act of patriotism.

Then, throw aside this petty squabble about how you are going to get along with your pledges before the election; ... peace is the only policy that can save the country and save your party.

Several Republican senators, whom Douglas tagged as the leaders of their party's "war wing," assailed him in reply. Senator Henry Wilson of Massachusetts, accusing Douglas of making "a mischievous, wicked, unpatriotic speech," asked if the Democratic senator wished "to create a political party out of the ruins of the defeated factions of Hunkerism."

Douglas retorted that he would not let the "war wing" Republicans prevail. "I know their scheme," he said. "I do not mean that they shall plunge this country into war."

Senator Thomas Lanier Clingman said Lincoln would not call the members of Congress into special session at that time because, if he would ask them to go to war against the Confederate states, "I do not believe they would agree to do it."

With unerring prophecy, the North Carolina Democrat said the Republicans "intend ... as soon as they can collect the force to have a war, to begin; and then call Congress suddenly together and say, 'The honor of the country is concerned; the flag is insulted. You must come up and vote men and money.'"

Montgomery Blair ardently promoted the proposal by his brother-in-law, Captain Fox, for supplying aid to the Fort Sumter garrison by sea. Fox outlined it in these words: "I propose three tugs, convoyed by light draft men-of-war. These tugs are sea-boats, six-foot draft, speed fourteen knots. The men would be below, protected from Confederate grape shot; provisions would be on deck. The first tug is to head in empty, to open their fire, the other two to follow."

Fox thus signaled that he expected the tugs would quickly draw fire from the rebel guns in Charleston harbor; then the escorting

U.S. warships could steam in and help Fort Sumter's gunners in firing back, and the war would be on.

"Finding that there was great opposition to any attempt at relieving Fort Sumter," Fox later reported, "I judged that my arguments in favor of sending in supplies would be strengthened by a visit to ... the fort."

So, Fox persuaded Lincoln to send him as a confidential agent to Charleston to obtain the latest facts about the fort's garrison, which was running low on provisions. With the escort of a Confederate captain, formerly in the U.S. Navy, Fox won permission from Governor Pickens to visit Sumter on March 21. Pickens gave this courtesy upon a pledge that Fox was there only for "pacific purposes." Fox conferred with Major Anderson without revealing the true aim of his mission. The major was expecting to receive orders, any day now, to give up the fort.

The *Cincinnati Gazette* on March 23 quoted the *Charleston Courier* as saying: "Major Anderson stated he is in daily expectation of receiving by mail the orders for the evacuation of Fort Sumter and hoped to get them that day. His supply of fuel and provisions is nearly exhausted, so much that, if he is not speedily relieved, the garrison would be compelled to burn some of the gun carriages for fuel. ... He stated that the fort would be given up to the South Carolina authorities after an examination by the authorized officer and a receipt taken for the property."

A few days later, Ward Hill Lamon came to Charleston as another "confidential agent" of the President. The huge Illinois lawyer, who had guarded Lincoln from potential assassins in Baltimore on his train ride into Washington, now found his own life in danger. Some hostile Carolina Minutemen, suspicious of Lincoln-loving Yankees, threatened to tie a rope around his neck. Fortunately, ex-congressman Laurence Keitt dashed to his rescue and invited him in for a drink.

Soon, the burly bodyguard had an interview with the governor, saying he had come to arrange for the removal of the garrison from Fort Sumter. When Lamon asked if a warship could be brought in to carry out the troops, Pickens replied that "no war vessel could be allowed to enter the harbor at any time" but an ordinary steamer would be permitted. Lamon also spoke to Major Anderson at the fort, leaving the distinct impression that evacuation was only a matter of time. Then he spoke to the governor again and said he hoped to come back in a few days and make the arrangements for it.

He never returned.

Lamon delivered this message to Lincoln from the governor: "Let your President attempt to reinforce Sumter, and the tocsin of war will be sounded from every hilltop and valley in the South." Both Lamon and Fox reported that the Sumter garrison would run out of food by April 15, so a decision about its fate must be made very soon.

Another Northern visitor to Charleston at this time, along with Lamon, was Stephen Hurlbut, a Charleston native who had moved to Illinois and practiced law there, becoming acquainted with Lincoln. Hurlbut visited his sister in his old hometown and conferred with James L. Petigru, his law teacher who was respected by the natives for his wit and erudition although considered rather eccentric— he opposed secession. Petigru was Charleston's "only citizen loyal to the nation," Hurlbut reported to Lincoln. When South Carolina seceded, Petigru won fame for his witty remark: "South Carolina is too small for a republic and too large for an insane asylum."

From his conversation with Petigru and various friends and kinfolk, Hurlbut concluded that "there is no attachment to the Union," and the seven states in the Confederacy form a de facto nation. "They exercise today every prerogative of sovereignty and within their limits are readily and cheerfully obeyed," he wrote. "They are seeking to make treaties abroad. They are seeking to annex territory to the West and north of Texas, they are soliciting a separation of Northern Mexico. They have an army, they are endeavoring to construct a navy."

The power in South Carolina and the Confederacy, he added, was in the hands of "the conservatives, of men who desire no war, seek no armed collision, but hope and expect peaceable separation, and believe that, after separation, the two nations will be more friendly than now."

> But it is equally true that there exists a large minority indefatigably active and reckless, who desire to precipitate collision and inaugurate war and unite the Southern Confederacy by that means. ... These are the men who demand an immediate attack on the forts.

I have no doubt that a ship known to contain only provisions for Sumter would be stopped and refused admittance. Even the moderate men, who desire not to open fire, believe in the safer policy of time and starvation. ...

If Sumter is abandoned, it is to a certain extent a concession of jurisdiction, which cannot fail to have its effect at home and abroad. Undoubtedly, this will be followed by a demand for Pickens and the keys of the Gulf. To surrender them, if Pickens has been or can be reinforced, tarnishes the national honor and the U. States cease to be a respectable nation.

Any attempt to enforce the federal laws and authority in the Confederate States—which Lincoln had proclaimed his intention of doing—"will be war in fact," Hurlbut warned the President. He advised Lincoln to "be prepared for the worst."

❧ 22 ❧

"You Have Got to Fight …
or Resign"

Behind the scenes at the White House, a furious war of words raged between two factions, each seeking to sway the mind of the indecisive President. Lifting the veil on this conflict, the *Chicago Tribune* said that on one side were Secretary of State Seward and the conservatives who favored his peace policy toward the South, while against them were the earnest advocates of a tough policy even though it could lead to war.

"The advocates of … administration weakness and cowardice were mostly representatives of heavy national interests, Wall Street magnates, dry goods millionaires, and other high priests of the altar of the imperial dollar. … 'fat, sleek-headed men that sleep nights,'—whose gospel is the stock list and whose highest ambition is to sell so many hundred thousand dollars' worth of shares per annum," the *Tribune* raged.

Striking at Seward, who was preaching "peace" to the President, the hard-liners hammered hard at Lincoln to be brave and do his duty, hold the forts and uphold federal authority. Foremost among these—all heroes on the *Tribune's* list—were Senators Fessenden, Sumner, Wade, Chandler, Trumbull, Harlan, Doolittle, Howe, and Wilkinson, and Congressmen Frank P. Blair, Jr., Gurley, Lovejoy, Kelly, and the Washburne brothers.

The Confederate commissioners, writing to Secretary Toombs on March 22, said the Senate Republican caucus members were "violently and bitterly opposed" to giving up Fort Sumter and were using their influence and power to prevent it. Three western members of Congress, one of them a senator from Wisconsin, called at the White House one evening in March and found the President studying maps of the gulf coast. They told him that the Republicans in their home states were worried about "the demoralizing and humiliating effect" of a passive attitude toward the secessionists. While accepting the "inexorable necessity" of evacuating Fort Sumter, they insisted that all other federal property must be protected.

In reply, the President told the visitors that "the evacuation of Fort Sumter was not by any means a settled fact; that it was certainly his anxious desire to retain possession of the fort," and he would hold the other forts to the last.

The news about the cabinet's tentative decision to give up Sumter had sent a shock wave of "indignant surprise throughout the Republican North," the *New York Herald* reported. "Yet the dose of mortification, compounded for them by Mr. Lincoln's predecessor, had to be swallowed, large and bitter," and the humiliated Republicans had to endure the Democrats' "taunts, jeers and ridicule."

The Republicans could not understand why the Charleston fort, which had not been surrendered by the pitifully weak Democrat, President Buchanan, should be given up now by the strong new Republican, President Lincoln. The distressing news brought a torrent of letters to Lincoln from angry partisans who felt betrayed.

"I voted for you, thinking that in you the country would find a defender of its rights and honor," wrote "a Republican" from New York. "I am terribly disappointed. You are as destitute of policy, as weak, and as vacillating as your predecessor. ... Do you imagine your course is meeting the favor of Republicans—even in New York? No, sir, Democrats rejoice over it, knowing it will demoralize and overthrow the party."

"Give up Sumpter [*sic*], sir, and you are as dead politically as John Brown is physically. You have got to fight. ... Either *act, immediately, and decisively*, or resign and go home."

"You have not only run upon the rocks and quick sands ... but you are abandoning the old ship and leaving the crew to take care of themselves," complained D. H. Whitney of Belvedere, Illinois. "I pray God that the man for whose political advancement I have toiled, *unremittingly*, for a quarter of a century, may not be ... unwittingly the instrument of the downfall of the Republic."

"Are you the commander-in-chief of the U.S. Army and Navy?" demanded Joseph Blanchard of Elmira, Illinois. "Then, in God's name, and in the name of humanity and liberty, put them forth, and trust to Providence for the result and all is well. ... Don't subject our country to ... disgrace and shame ... by evacuating any of the forts and defenses without an effort to save them from that lawless rattlesnake crew."

"The reinforcement of Fort Sumpter [*sic*]," wrote W. H. West of Bellefontaine, Ohio, a delegate to the Chicago convention, "would secure to you an immortality of fame, which Washington might envy. The surrender of Fort Pickens, under any circumstances, will consign your name, and fame, to an ignominy in comparison with which that of your immediate predecessor will be ... illustrious.

"I but reflect the universal sentiment when I say the loyal people of the Northwest would tolerate any stretch of power on your part, and prefer to see you 'wade through slaughter to a throne' rather than have our country humiliated and its glorious flag dishonored, by a voluntary surrender."

"If it be possible (no matter what the cost of money or life) Fort Sumpter [*sic*] should be supplied with provisions," wrote J. H. Jordan of Cincinnati. "But it would be better, a thousand times, that the fort be attacked, *captured*, and Anderson and his men made prisoners of war, or all killed—than that it be evacuated!"

A peace policy is a "fatal infatuation," Jordan warned. The secessionists, he said, "want to get the administration and the Republican party committed to a 'peaceable secession,' and at that moment the question will be sprung upon us: 'Reconstruction' on the basis of the Southern Constitution, or Disunion; and we will be placed on the side of disunion—and *beaten to death!* ...

"For God's sake! *Give not an inch*—and *don't* be afraid of *war!*"

These, and many similar letters, added to the burdens of the new president, who was striving to adopt a policy that would carry out his inaugural promises of strength without driving the Border States into the Confederacy. Sherrod Clemens, a pro-Union congressman battling to keep Virginia from yielding to the secession fever, protested that the administration's practice of removing federal officeholders throughout Virginia was having a "fatal effect" upon the Union Party.

"Forces are here ready for revolution," he wrote. "Bankruptcy and delinquents with no property to lose, they are ready for anarchy. Funds are supplied from the extreme South. ... Arms are at hand, and if the Union men are to be crushed, you will find an army marching on Washington City, and a civil war inaugurated in Maryland and Virginia.

"I know these facts. The troops in the seceding states can be transferred here in a few days and we will then have the horrors of the French Revolution upon us."

General Scott also repeatedly warned that his native state, Virginia, torn between its sympathies for the South and its pride as the "mother of Presidents," was teetering between the old Union and the new Confederacy, and any conflict at Charleston could tip Virginia into the Confederacy.

After his first state dinner on March 28, Lincoln met with his cabinet and read a letter from Scott, urging that both Forts Sumter and Pickens be evacuated to reassure the eight slaveholding states still clinging to the Union. This action would "instantly soothe" those states and "render their cordial adherence to the Union perpetual," the old chieftain advised.

Montgomery Blair blew up at the very idea of yielding Fort Pickens, where the federal troops occupied a strong position, backed by the navy. Suspecting that Seward was influencing the general, Blair declared: "Mr. President, you can now see that General Scott, in advising the surrender of Fort Sumter, is playing the part of a politician, not a general." Blair was so angry that he threatened to resign unless his plan for provisioning the Charleston fort by sea was carried out.

Lincoln spent a sleepless night. He agonized over the conflicting advice from army and navy officers and cabinet members, and the anguished cries from the Republicans who feared that their party would be ruined unless he made a brave stand for keeping the forts. He was also sick and tired of the horde of office seekers plaguing him constantly for jobs.

The next morning, the exhausted President was "in the dumps," as he expressed it, from worry over the possibility of war. He had a bad "sick headache" and "keeled over," his wife told a friend.

North Carolina's Senator Thomas Lanier Clingman observed the vacillation of the emotionally tortured president. "Though perhaps not averse to a small war, to be finished by blockading a few ports," Lincoln hesitated to become involved in a major war against the majority of the Southern states. General Scott had earlier warned him that such a conflict could last three years and cost many thousands of lives.

In late March, Clingman encountered Confederate Commissioner Crawford and asked him about the prospects for peace. "Very bad," Crawford answered. "It now looks as if we were to have war." Crawford said that, since the Virginia convention had voted, by a large margin, against secession now, the Lincoln administration believed that only the Cotton States would fight and they could easily be beaten.

When the cabinet met again March 29, Seward found a change in its attitude toward Fort Sumter. Two weeks before, nearly all the members had stood with him in advising that the fort must be abandoned, and he had happily passed the word to friendly editors and the three Confederate commissioners. Now he was caught in a trap. The protests by angry Republican senators and voters had swung several cabinet members over to the Blair-Fox scheme for sending provisions to the beleaguered garrison by sea.

In a memorandum to the President, Seward stood his ground. "The dispatch of an expedition to supply or reinforce Sumter would provoke an attack and so involve *war at that point*," he warned. He also said: "I would instruct Maj. Anderson to retire from Sumter, forthwith."

Then he proposed a new idea—to call in Captain M. C. Meigs of the army engineers, who was directing the expansion of the Capitol building. "Aided by his counsel," Seward said, "I would at once and at every cost prepare for a war at Pensacola and Texas, to be taken, however, only as a consequence of maintaining the possession and authority of the United States."

Montgomery Blair, who had stood alone in early March in demanding a sea-borne relief effort to save Fort Sumter, had the satisfaction of seeing some of the cabinet swing over to his side. Lincoln came around, also, and decided that he could try sending food to the hungry garrison and he could label it a peaceful mission, not an aggressive act or an "invasion." If the supply ships should be attacked by the artillery ringing Charleston harbor, it would not be his fault; the Confederates must take the blame for firing the first shot. Lincoln thus seized upon Captain Fox's plan and told him to draw up a brief order listing the ships, ammunition, weapons, and supplies needed for the mission.

Fox wrote: "Steamers Pocahontas at Norfolk, Pawnee at Washington, Harriet Lane at New York to be under sailing orders for sea, with stores, etc., for one month.

PROF. LINCOLN IN HIS GREAT FEAT OF BALANCING.

This Vanity Fair *cartoon shows President Lincoln as a circus juggler, trying to hold "Fort Sumter" and "peace" through the same tricky balancing act, in the spring of 1861. From the collections of the Library of Congress.*

"Three hundred men to be kept ready for departure from on board the receiving ships at New York.

"Two hundred men to be ready to leave Governor's Island in New York.

"Supplies for twelve months for one hundred men to be put in portable shape, ready for instant shipping. A large steamer and three tugs conditionally engaged."

Lincoln accepted Fox's memorandum and wrote on the bottom an order to Secretary of War Cameron: "Sir: I desire that an expedition, to move by sea, be got ready to sail as early as the 6th of April, next, the whole according to memorandum attached, and that you cooperate with the Secretary of the Navy for that object." A similar order went to Secretary Welles, and Fox hustled up to New York to prepare for the mission.

On March 30, the three Confederate commissioners received a telegram from Governor Pickens, asking why the garrison remained at Fort Sumter, long after Ward Hill Lamon had positively assured him it would leave. This date was also fifteen days after Seward had given his pledge that the fort would be quickly abandoned. Justice Campbell, also concerned about the long delay and possibly beginning to smell a rat, took the telegram to Seward, who relayed it to Lincoln.

The next day Seward told the judge that the President disavowed anything Lamon may have said at Charleston—that "Lamon had no agency from him, nor title to speak" or make promises for him. It was difficult for Justice Campbell to believe that Lamon had gone to Charleston entirely on his own and that such an agent, supposedly very close to the President, had lied in talking to Governor Pickens about the best ship to be used in moving the Fort Sumter garrison out of Charleston. Somebody was playing a double game, and the Southerners were being fooled. Now the Confederates had reason to believe that they were being tricked like the victim of a shell game at the county fair, the "thimble-rigger" being the secretary of state.

Justice Campbell went back to Seward and demanded to know what he should tell the Confederate commissioners about Fort Sumter now. Seward no longer could assure him, absolutely, that it would be given up. After conferring with Lincoln, the secretary gave Campbell a note to be relayed to the Confederates: "The President may desire to supply Fort Sumter, but will not undertake to do so without first giving notice to Governor Pickens."

Startled by this sudden change in policy, the Justice asked: "Does the President design to attempt to supply Sumter?"

"No, I think not," Seward answered. "It is a very irksome thing to him to evacuate it. His ears are open to everyone, and they fill his head with schemes for its supply. I do not think that he will adopt any of them. There is no design to reinforce it."

How could Seward say such things when he knew that Lincoln had approved the resupply mission and had sent Captain Fox to New York to carry it out? The only answer must be that he didn't tell the truth. In his defense, it might be argued that Seward still hoped that the expedition to Charleston could be halted at the last moment.

Advised of Lincoln's new position—that he would give advance notice to Governor Pickens about any move to resupply Sumter—Commissioner Crawford informed his government: "My opinion is that the President has not the courage to execute the order agreed upon in cabinet for the evacuation of the fort." Crawford did not know that the cabinet, under the intense Republican pressure for action, had reversed itself and that Lincoln was going along with the Blair-Fox expedition, as a way out of a political box.

The commissioners could have learned about the switch from Seward's "peace policy" to the hard line by reading the *New York Tribune*. Its Washington correspondent, in a March 31 dispatch, revealed that the fort would be reinforced, and that the Lincoln administration had yielded to extreme pressure from Northwestern Republicans in Congress for a strong policy of holding the forts at all hazards. Horace Greeley's man must have had sources in high places, who made sure the inside information came out—as long as they weren't quoted.

"The war wing presses on the President; he vibrates to that side," Commissioners Crawford and Roman told Secretary Toombs. "Their form of advice to us may be that of the coward, who gives it when he strikes. Watch at all points."

Lincoln showed great ambivalence about his next move, as he was tugged this way and that by the "war wing," which had captured him, and the "peace wing," led by the conservative merchants and financiers of the Eastern cities.

Furthermore, Lincoln's health was declining toward the breaking point as he wrestled with the secession issue and yet had to waste hour after hour every day, dealing with factional squabbles over the distribution of the federal jobs.

"The President ... is working early and late," one newsman reported. "His time is taken up mostly with the ceaseless tide of office-seekers constantly pouring in upon him. ... His family see him only at dinner, he being compelled from fatigue to retire to his room as soon as he leaves the office."

Worried about his old friend's health, Orville Browning asked: "Why don't you disperse the selfish, mercenary crowds? You should not permit your time to be consumed and your energies exhausted by personal applications for office. Let it be understood that you will have your nights and your Sabbaths for rest." If the work load were not lightened soon, Browning warned, "even your constitution may sink under it, and the country cannot afford to lose you now."

The patient, long-suffering president's nerves finally snapped on March 31, when a delegation of Californians brought him a strong protest against Senator Edward Baker's influence in parceling out the federal jobs in their state although he represented Oregon. Baker, a native-born Englishman, was an old and dear personal friend of Lincoln from Illinois days and had introduced Lincoln at the inaugural ceremony. Lincoln's son, "little Eddie," who died in childhood, was named for Baker.

So, it was with rising emotions that the President listened to the Californians' complaints that they had been "left out in the cold" when Baker distributed the plums. One of their leaders, J. W. Simonton, read a written speech and presented the resolutions drafted by his friends. When Simonton finished his tirade, he gave the President the written text as well as the formal protest.

"This paper," Lincoln said, referring to the delegation's letter, "being somewhat respectful in tone, I think I will keep. But this one," he said, shaking the abusive anti-Baker speech aloft—"I will show you what I will do with it!" Stepping over to the fireplace, he tossed the paper into the flames and soon it was reduced to ashes. In a withering voice, the President told the dumb-struck Californians: "I have known Col. Baker longer and better than any of you here, and these attacks upon him I know to be outrageous. I will hear no more of them!"

The visitors trooped out, crestfallen, like a band of schoolboys tongue-lashed by their teacher.

On April Fool's Day came another headache for the nerve-racked chief executive; Seward gave him a memorandum captioned: "Some Thoughts for the President's Consideration." After a month in power, he began, the administration still had "no policy, domestic or foreign." The domestic question must be changed from slavery to "Union or Disunion." Since the fate of Fort Sumter was generally viewed as a slavery or party issue, he would "terminate" it by giving up the fort. But he would defend Fort Pickens and all the other forts in the Gulf of Mexico, recall the navy from foreign stations, prepare for a blockade, and clamp Key West under martial law.

Only days before, Spain had annexed Santo Domingo and, through a deal with France, was about to grab Haiti, the other half of the island. Seward would view these moves as European powers meddling in American waters. He would demand explanations from France and Spain and, if the answers were unsatisfactory, declare war on both of them.

This was a startling idea, coming from a man who was desperately pleading for Lincoln to follow a peace policy at home. But, to Seward, it made more sense to rally Americans, North and South, to fight side by side against a foreign enemy than to be killing each other in a senseless war over slavery. So he advised the President to follow an aggressive foreign policy and "send agents into Canada, Mexico and Central America, to rouse a vigorous continental spirit of independence on this continent against European intervention."

Seward knew that the Democrats, in their zeal for Manifest Destiny, had long advocated acquiring Cuba. They proposed it again in their 1860 platform. Southern politicians especially wanted to annex Cuba, to make one or more slave states, and Buchanan, who had favored it in the Ostend Manifesto, still had his eye on the prize.

Since Seward's handwriting was almost illegible, his son, Frederick, copied the "Thoughts for the President's Consideration" and "dispatched it by private hand" to keep it confidential. Frederick Seward, in his memoirs, said the President agreed with several points in the paper and the proposals were carried out. "On the very next day," Spain was called upon to account for her acts in Santo Domingo. The secret expedition for the relief of Fort Pickens went forward; and on succeeding days, said the secretary's son, "The 'explanations' from France, Great Britain, Russia and Spain were called for with more or less satisfactory results."

Seward's memorandum has been considered a power play by the secretary to make himself the de facto president, as he considered himself far better equipped than Lincoln to run the country. "Whatever policy we adopt, there must be an energetic prosecution of it," he wrote. "Either the President must do it himself ... or devolve it on some member of the cabinet. ... It is not in my especial province. But I neither seek to evade nor assume responsibility."

In his reply, the President said he did, indeed, have a domestic policy, outlined in his inaugural address, which Seward himself had approved—"to hold, occupy and possess the property and places belonging to the government and to collect the duties and imposts." This, he said, is "the exact domestic policy you now urge, with the single exception, that it does not propose to abandon Fort Sumpter [*sic*]." As for Seward's offer to direct the policy, Lincoln said simply, "If this must be done, I must do it."

The existence of Seward's remarkable document remained a secret for three decades, until Lincoln's secretaries published it in their biography. But James Gordon Bennett apparently had a tip about it on April 4, when he published this Washington item in his *New York Herald*: "It is argued in high official circles here that the best policy for the administration is to inaugurate a war with Spain or Mexico, or both, as the best means of averting internal strife."

Seward's memorandum has been ridiculed by various historians as naive, impractical, egotistical, stupid, or even criminal. But the Republican administration of President William McKinley waged a "splendid little war" against Spain in 1898, collected Cuba, Puerto Rico, and the Philippines as the loot of empire, and magnanimously awarded the Cubans their freedom. U.S. military bases still bristle at Guantanamo Bay, Cuba, and Puerto Rico, and others were transferred to the Philippines' government only in recent years.

So it would seem that Seward was not so dumb, after all, just thirty-seven years ahead of his time.

❧ 23 ❧

LINCOLN'S "FATAL MISTAKE"

Refusing to give up his frantic efforts to head off a clash at Fort Sumter, Secretary Seward moved, swiftly and secretly, to provoke a showdown with the Confederates, instead, at Fort Pickens. He urged Lincoln to send an expedition to the fortress near Pensacola, Florida. If that should result in a fight, it would stir up the Northern people to a patriotic fervor, at the same time assuaging their anger over the evacuation of Fort Sumter.

When he became president, Lincoln had inherited a touchy situation at Pickens. The federal garrison at Pensacola had moved from Fort Barrancas on the mainland to Fort Pickens on Santa Rosa Island when Florida seceded. Confederate troops had taken over Barrancas and the navy yard.

On January 24, the warship *Brooklyn* went to Pickens with soldiers, guns, ammunition, and provisions. But Stephen Mallory, then senator, made a truce with President Buchanan, whereby the government promised not to disembark any troops from the *Brooklyn* and the Confederate commander agreed not to attack the fort.

On Lincoln's instructions, General Scott issued an order in March to transfer the troops from the *Brooklyn* into the fort. The order was delayed and did not reach the commander of the federal naval forces, Captain Henry Adams, until March 31. Captain Adams refused to break the truce until he received further orders from his superiors, not from the army. On April 1, he dispatched a messenger to Washington with a letter of protest and a reminder that "he was operating under an armistice which both are faithfully observing." He dreaded "the fearful responsibility of an act which seems to render civil war inevitable."

Lincoln determined to disavow the armistice without notifying the Confederates, whom he refused to recognize. Secretary Welles drafted a new order directing Captain Adams to place the soldiers inside the fort without further delay. The fifty soldiers then in the garrison were facing about a thousand Confederates in the Pensacola region, under the command of General Braxton Bragg.

It was at this point, in early April, that Seward stepped in and persuaded Lincoln to send an expedition to Florida. It was headed by Captain Montgomery C. Meigs of the army engineers, assisted by Lieutenant Colonel Erasmus D. Keyes and Navy Lieutenant David Dixon Porter. The three youthful officers received confidential orders from the President to carry out their mission. It was kept a secret from Navy Secretary Welles and Secretary of War Cameron. The secretive President thus followed a policy of holding all the reins in his own hands.

Captain Fox, who was in New York assembling his relief expedition for Fort Sumter, expected the eleven-gun *Powhatan* to be his flagship. Secretary Welles instructed Captain Samuel Mercer to command the *Powhatan* for the Sumter mission. But Lieutenant Porter, upon arriving in New York, delivered this order to Captain Andrew H. Foote, commandant of the Brooklyn Navy Yard:

"Sir: You will fit out the Powhatan without delay. Lieutenant Porter will relieve Captain Mercer in command of her. She is bound to secret service, and you will under no circumstances communicate to the Navy Department the fact that she is fitting out. ABRAHAM LINCOLN."

Obviously, the *Powhatan* could not take part in two different expeditions at the same time. Meigs telegraphed Seward to clarify the dispute. Seward and Welles went together to the White House about midnight and discussed the mix-up with the President. Embarrassed, Lincoln confessed that, by mistake, he had signed orders giving the ship to both commands. He ordered Seward to send a telegram to New York restoring Captain Mercer as the skipper, but Seward stalled for time. The *Powhatan* sailed April 6 with Captain Mercer on the bridge and Lieutenant Porter in a stateroom below. When the ship reached Staten Island, Porter came out, Mercer presented him to the executive officer as the new skipper, and Mercer went ashore.

Seward's belated telegram arrived at the navy yard at last. A fast launch caught up with the ship at the Narrows and Porter read the wire: "Give the *Powhatan* up to Captain Mercer. SEWARD."

Porter sent back this response: "I received my orders from the President and shall proceed and exercise them." He reasoned that the new command, signed only "Seward," could not countermand the orders signed by Lincoln. Thereupon Porter steamed away to Florida on a mission that would turn out to be unnecessary. Captain Fox did not learn about the loss of his precious flagship until he reached the waters off Charleston. Forever after, he blamed Seward for it.

Secretary Welles, who also accused Seward of trickery, complained in his diary that the whole plan for relieving Sumter was thereby defeated. "At the moment of sailing, the expedition was deprived of its commander and flagship without the knowledge of the Secretary of the Navy. ... The Powhatan, with boats, supplies, and men destined for Sumter, had been sent...without naval orders or record, under a secret and useless mission to Pensacola, by the Secretary of State."

It was a "useless mission" because of Lincoln's order to Navy Captain Adams to move the artillery company from the *Brooklyn* into Fort Pickens. Lieutenant John L. Worden went to Pensacola, got an interview with Confederate General Bragg and won his permission to take "a verbal message of a pacific nature" to Captain Adams.

General Bragg was fooled. The next morning, Lieutenant Worden made a copy of the memorized order and delivered it. That afternoon, he boarded a railroad train at Pensacola and hastened northward before the Confederates could discover his trick. That night the artillery company from the *Brooklyn* was sneaked into the fort.

While keeping his Fort Pickens project a deep, dark secret, the secretary of state casually talked about Fort Sumter to a journalist from South Carolina—James Harvey, his candidate for the post of U.S. minister to Portugal. A friend of Harvey's in Charleston, Judge A. G. Magrath, thereupon received a telegram April 6, saying: "Positively determined not to withdraw Anderson. Supplies go immediately, supported by naval force ... if their landing be resisted." The message was signed, "A friend." Magrath quickly relayed it to the Confederate secretary of war, adding: "The person is high in the confidence of the government in Washington."

The next day, Justice Campbell sent a letter to Seward asking if his previous assurances about the early evacuation of Fort Sumter were still true. Seward answered: "Faith as to Sumter fully kept. Wait and see." This was a week after Lincoln had ordered Fox's expedition to resupply the fort, and the ships were ready to sail for Charleston— and Seward knew it.

On April 7, the *New York Herald*'s Washington correspondent, evidently reflecting White House officials' views, disowned Seward's manipulations, in these words: "Southern men have been flattered by the public and private declarations of Mr. Seward, that there would be a peaceful settlement of our internal difficulties.

"It is said that the Confederate States commissioners now here assert that they have had assurances from Mr. Seward that it was not the intention of the administration to reinforce Fort Pickens, but on the contrary to evacuate Pickens and Sumter."

The *Herald* writer said, "I am authorized"—by whom? Lincoln? a Lincoln spokesman?—"to say that if Mr. Seward had any communication with the Confederate State Commissioners whatever, that he had done so on his own individual authority, and that it was never the intention of this administration to abandon any post in the United States unless it became a military necessity to do so."

Lincoln's administration, it said, was determined "to pursue a vigorous policy; to find out whether we have a government worth preserving. While doing this, it is not to pursue an aggressive policy."

The *Herald* story repeated Lincoln's claim that it would not be an "aggressive" act to send supplies to a beleaguered fort; and that he would not "make war on any state or community" unless it struck first, and then he would "act promptly on the defensive."

While Captain Fox prepared his Sumter relief expedition to sail from New York to Charleston, Seward played one last card in his attempts to call it off. He persuaded Lincoln to invite a leader of the Union men then controlling the Virginia convention and offer some deal that might keep the Old Dominion from joining the secession parade.

The first choice for the go-between's role was George W. Summers, the former Whig congressman who had witnessed Lincoln's appeal to several of the Peace Convention delegates. To former Senator Rives, participants said, Lincoln had cried, "Mr. Rives, Mr. Rives, if Virginia will stay in, I will withdraw the troops from Fort Sumter!"

Summers declined to leave the Richmond convention. He sent John B. Baldwin, a Staunton lawyer and a "most thorough-going Union man" among the sharply divided delegates.

Baldwin later testified that the President led him into a White House bedroom and locked the door. It was the morning of April 4, shortly before the ships were to sail for Charleston.

"Mr. Baldwin, I am afraid you have come too late," the President began.

"Too late for what?" Baldwin asked, protesting that he had come immediately after receiving the President's summons the previous day.

"Why do you all not adjourn the Virginia convention?" the President demanded. "It is a standing menace to me, which embarrasses me very much."

Surprised, Baldwin said the Union men had a majority in the convention and could control it, "but only if you will uphold our hands by a conservative policy." He urged Lincoln to withdraw the troops from both Forts Sumter and Pickens.

The President said the supply ships for Sumter were only on a peaceful mission to bring food to the hungry garrison there. But Baldwin warned that sending those vessels, backed by warships, would surely lead to war.

"Sir," he said, "if there is a gun fired at Fort Sumter, as surely as there is a God in heaven, the thing is gone. Virginia herself, as strong as the Union majority in the convention is now, will be out in forty-eight hours."

"Oh," said Lincoln, "that is impossible."

With his fixed idea about the Union majority in the convention, Lincoln could not bring himself to face the truth—that, as he had been repeatedly warned, any clash or attempt at coercion would drive Virginia out of the Union. Baldwin later denied reports that Lincoln had offered him a deal—that, if the Virginia convention would adjourn at once, he would withdraw the troops from Sumter. Baldwin said Lincoln "made no suggestion" of that and gave him no letter or memorandum. There is no record of such a document in the Lincoln Papers.

Several members of the Virginia legislature met with Lincoln the next day and begged him to continue "the present military status of the South" but they failed to get "any satisfactory assurances," the *Cincinnati Commercial* reported. It quoted one member, named Segar, as declaring that "they could do nothing with the Executive and that the country was on the verge of civil war."

The *Commercial* also said the Virginia politicians "were assured that the President contemplated no hostile movements." Yet, at that moment, Captain Fox's ships were preparing to sail and a New York dispatch said: "The impression at the navy yard is that Sumter and Pickens are both to be reinforced." Whatever game Lincoln was playing, he was keeping all his cards close to his vest.

On the same day of Baldwin's White House visit, the *Cincinnati Gazette* reported that several Northern governors had a long interview with Lincoln, and these Republican partisans all favored "holding the fortifications." Baldwin also said he met the governors that day. If they had come, as Old Man Blair had come earlier, to stiffen Lincoln's "backbone," they succeeded.

The next day, the *Cincinnati Commercial*'s correspondent reported from Washington that an Ohio Congressman, "who has spoken to the President within the last twenty-four hours, told me today that blood would be spilled in less than ten days," in a collision "between the federal government and the Southern rebels"—evidently at Charleston.

Both the President and the cabinet were now resolved to carry out Lincoln's inaugural pledge to hold the federal forts, the newsman reported. "Letters from the West say that the demoralization arising from ... continued unpunished defiance of the federal authorities, contributed largely to the defeat of the Republicans in their late municipal elections. Their remonstrances doubtless did a good deal towards spurring the Executive to the present exhibition of greater vigor."

On the same April 5, the *Cincinnati Gazette* reported that Washington was "experiencing a great deal of excitement over the rumors of war, which seem to be fully credited in all quarters." According to these dispatches, Lincoln and his cabinet knew on April 5 that their decision to send the ships to Charleston would surely lead to a "collision" and civil war.

Later, the *Chicago Tribune* revealed that the Northern governors and Lincoln had "agreed upon a plan of concerted action to aid the national government in the execution of the laws." Governor Andrew G. Curtin of Pennsylvania led the way by calling upon his legislature to raise troops and money for defense. Clearly, Lincoln expected that the dispatch of the fleet to Charleston would touch off civil war and he wanted the Northern states to be ready for it.

In contrast to Baldwin's account of his talk with the President on April 4, another Virginian told a somewhat different story. John Minor Botts, who had served in Congress with his fellow Whig from Illinois, reported having a four-hour conference with Lincoln on the rainy Sunday night of April 7. Botts's version, in his 1866 book, *The Great Rebellion*, follows:

Lincoln said he had informed Baldwin about the fleet preparing to sail from New York, including "a vessel loaded with bread" to feed the hungry men at Fort Sumter. If that vessel is fired at, he said, the fleet will go in to protect her.

According to Botts, Lincoln quoted himself as having said to Baldwin:

"This afternoon, a fleet is to sail from the harbor of New York for Charleston; your convention has been in session for nearly two months, and you have done nothing but hold and shake the rod over my head. You have just taken a vote, by which it appears you have a majority of two to one against secession.

"Now, so great is my desire to preserve the peace of the country and to save the Border States of the Union, that if you gentlemen of the Union party will adjourn without passing an ordinance of secession, I will telegraph at once to New York, arrest the sailing of the fleet, and take the responsibility of evacuating Fort Sumter."

Botts said he asked how Baldwin replied to the proposition, and Lincoln threw his hands in the air and exclaimed: "Oh! he wouldn't listen to it at all; scarcely treated me with civility; asked me what I meant by adjournment. Was it an adjournment sine die?"

"Of course," Lincoln said he told Baldwin, "I don't want you to adjourn and, after I have evacuated the fort, meet again to adopt an ordinance of secession."

Botts said he offered to rush back to Richmond and take the same offer to the Union men in the convention, and promised that they would quickly approve it. But, he said, Lincoln refused, saying: "Oh, it's too late. The fleet has sailed and I have no means of communicating with it."

On April 6, the day before Botts's White House visit, Lincoln had already ordered Robert S. Chew, a State Department clerk, to go directly to Charleston, seek an interview with Governor Pickens, and read him this statement: "I am directed by the President of the United States to notify you to expect an attempt will be made to supply Fort Sumter with provisions only, and that, if such an attempt be not resisted, no effort to throw in men, arms, or ammunition will be made without further notice, or in case of an attack upon the fort."

So Lincoln was already committed to Fox's expedition, which was to run supplies into the fort in small boats, if possible, with warships standing by to come in and fire on any Confederate attackers. The die was cast.

Botts said the President mentioned to him his message to Governor Pickens. Botts also added something that obviously was not true: He said Lincoln's message informed the governor that, if he would supply food for the troops "or let Major Anderson procure his marketing in Charleston, I would stop the vessel."

The truth, however, is that not a word in Lincoln's message to Pickens said anything about "stopping the vessel" if the governor would allow food for the fort. This clear error casts doubt upon the accuracy of the former congressman's recollection of the exact words of his chat with Lincoln.

Some other quotations sound like vintage Lincoln: "Botts, I have always been an Old Line Henry Clay Whig and if you Southern people will let me alone, I will administer the government as nearly upon the principles that he would have administered it as it is possible for one man to follow in the path of another. ...

"What do I want with war? I am not a war man. I want peace more than any man in this country, and will make greater sacrifices to preserve it than any other man in the nation."

These words resemble the kind of appeal that Lincoln would make to a fellow Whig in hopes of reassuring the South. But he did not say the same thing to the Northern Republican governors who were browbeating him in the White House and demanding that he hold the forts, even at the cost of war.

To the Southerners, Lincoln portrayed himself as a man of peace; to the Northerners, he looked like a man preparing for war. If the contrast makes Lincoln resemble a man with two faces, the record must speak for itself.

Botts wrote that he "often wondered" why Lincoln had not told the country the same story about his offer to give up Fort Sumter if the Virginia convention would go home without passing an ordinance of secession. "I suppose," Botts surmised, "it was because he felt that he had assumed a heavy responsibility in thus proposing to surrender a fort of the United States, and he did not want it known in the North."

The news of the frenzied preparations of the naval ships in New York reached Richmond the same weekend and spread panic among the people. A resolution was introduced in the state convention, protesting against all such warlike measures and declaring that the federal government had no lawful power to subjugate a Southern state.

Then a delegate named Jackson, of Wood County in western Virginia, arose and declared that, if the convention intended to take Virginia out of the Union on the pretext of coercion, he was "ready to raise the banner of revolt and secede with his people from the state of Virginia!" Had a bombshell exploded in the hall, it could not have created more consternation, one newsman reported. Jackson's move would prove to be the first step in a drive that would end in the creation of the new, pro-Union, state of West Virginia.

At the moment, the secessionists hailed it as signaling a split in the majority and the Unionists' loss of the control of the convention. "The secessionists are in ecstasies," the *New York Times* lamented. "One blow struck in the South, no matter on what side, will give them Virginia and all the slave states."

Roger A. Pryor, an ardent secessionist, who had given up his seat as a Virginia congressman, hastened to Charleston to make sure that someone soon would strike that "one blow." He stood on a Charleston hotel piazza on the night of April 10, his long black hair tossing in the breeze, and shouted to a cheering crowd that his proud, but slow, Old Dominion would soon secede. According to the *Charleston Mercury*'s account, he cried: "And I will tell you, gentlemen, what will put her in the Southern Confederation in an hour by Shrewsbury clock: STRIKE A BLOW!"

A Charleston lady, who had heard previous orators calling for bloodshed, commented: "Oh, they all say the same thing, but he made a great play with that long hair of his, which he is always tossing aside."

At Fort Sumter, Major Anderson fumed over the delay in the delivery of the order, which he had been expecting daily, telling him to leave his post. He had no way of knowing that the order, drafted by General Scott on March 11, had been held up while Lincoln changed course and decided upon the attempt to send him "bread" by sea, at the risk of touching off a war.

"The truth is that the sooner we are out of this harbor the better," the major told the War Department. "Our flag runs an hourly risk of being insulted, and my hands are tied by my orders, and, if that was not the case, I have not the power to protect it. God grant that neither I, nor any other officer in our army, may be again placed in a position of such mortification and humiliation."

Kentucky-born, Anderson sympathized with the feeling of his wife, a Georgia native, and dreaded the calamity of a totally unnecessary civil war, waged over a political issue that should be settled peacefully by civilians, not by shedding the blood of the men in uniform. He did not intend to end his long and honorable career in the army by killing fellow Americans.

Anderson was shocked when informed of Confederate Commissioner Crawford's bulletin to Governor Pickens, which stated: "I am authorized to say that this government will not undertake to supply Fort Sumter without notice to you." Appealing to Washington for some clear orders, the major said: "After thirty-odd years of service, I do not wish it to be said that I have treasonably abandoned a post. ... Unless we receive supplies, I shall be compelled to stay here without food, or to abandon this post very early next week."

On Monday evening, April 8, Robert S. Chew of the State Department arrived at Charleston by train. He was accompanied by Captain Theodore Talbot of Fort Sumter, who had reported to his superiors at Washington. Finding Fort Sumter neither surrendered nor under attack, they met with Governor Pickens and General Beauregard at the Charleston Hotel.

Carrying out his orders from the President, Chew read the notice that "an attempt will be made to supply Fort Sumter with provisions only; and that, if such an attempt be not resisted, no effort to throw in men, arms or ammunition will be made without further notice, or in case of an attack upon the fort." Chew gave the governor a copy of the message and declined to receive an answer. Since a crowd of excited citizens swarmed around outside the hotel, Chew and Captain Talbot were escorted by South Carolina soldiers on their way to the railroad station. They left Charleston on the next northbound train.

The next morning, former Governor John Manning, a handsome and charming man, came to see Mary Boykin Chesnut, bowed low in mock heroic style, and announced:

"Madame, your country is invaded."

"There are six men-of-war outside of the bar," he said. "Talbot and Chew have come to say that hostilities are to begin. Governor Pickens and Beauregard are holding a council of war."

Mary's husband, former Senator Chesnut, came in and confirmed the story. Then in walked Senator Wigfall, rejoicing in the prospect of a fight. Mrs. Chesnut crept silently to her room and wept.

At long last, Major Anderson had received his instructions, officially informing him of the Fox relief expedition. Lincoln's orders, relayed over the signature of Secretary Cameron, followed:

> Hoping that you will be able to sustain yourself till the 11th or 12th instant, the expedition will go forward; and, finding your flag flying, will attempt to provision you, and, in case the effort is resisted, will endeavor also to reinforce you.
>
> You will, therefore, hold out, if possible, till the arrival of the expedition.
>
> It is not, however, the intention of the President to subject your command to any danger or hardship beyond what, in your judgment, would be usual in military life, and he has entire confidence that you will act as becomes a patriot and soldier, under all circumstances.
>
> Whenever, if at all, in your judgment, to save yourself and command, a capitulation becomes a necessity, you are authorized to make it.

Major Anderson's reply reflected his dismay over having been deceived about the prospect that he could soon leave Fort Sumter without a fight. He had been kept in the dark, all along, about his superiors' plans for his future. Ward Hill Lamon, when he had visited the fort as Lincoln's confidential agent and had talked to Governor Pickens about taking the garrison home by steamship, had given no inkling of any warships coming down and carrying out Captain Fox's scheme.

"I ought to have been informed that this expedition was to come," the veteran officer protested. "Colonel Lamon's remark convinced me that the idea, merely hinted at to me by Captain Fox, would not be carried out.

"We shall strive to do our duty, though I frankly say that my heart is not in the war which I see is to be thus commenced. That God will still avert it, and cause us to resort to pacific measures to maintain our rights, is my ardent prayer."

Thus Major Anderson, in the view of one historian, "placed the blame for starting the war squarely on the Lincoln administration."

The major's letter never reached Washington. Governor Pickens, on April 9, seized the mail from Fort Sumter and confiscated all the letters except purely private ones. He did so "in return for the treachery of Mr. Fox," who had been permitted to visit the fort after he had promised the governor that his mission was strictly "pacific." Lincoln might claim that the ships bringing "bread" to the soldiers in the fort were on a "pacific" mission, but the accompanying warships certainly did not look that way.

On April 10, Jefferson Davis, at Montgomery, received an imperative telegram from ex-senator Wigfall at Charleston: "No one now doubts that Lincoln intends war. The delay on his part is only to complete his preparations. All here is ready on our side. Our delay therefore is to his advantage and our disadvantage. Let us take Fort Sumter before we have to fight the fleet and the fort."

The Confederate commissioners' last dispatch from Washington, addressed to General Beauregard at Charleston, said on April 11: "The 'Tribune' of today declares the main object of the expedition to be the relief of Sumter, and that a force will be landed which will overcome all opposition."

Now, the commissioners finally learned the true value of Secretary Seward's word and his assurance: "Faith as to Sumter fully kept."

They decided to "wait and see" no longer. They picked up the memorandum that he had written, with Lincoln's approval, weeks before, and squirreled away in his files.

Lincoln and Seward refused all direct contact with the Confederates, on the theory that the seven states, which the Southerners called an independent nation, did not exist, except as part of the old Union.

In view of Lincoln's inaugural address proclaiming the Union as unbroken, Seward said, he could not admit that the seven seceding states "constitute a foreign nation, with whom diplomatic relations ought to be established."

Now, the commissioners told Seward in reply, they must go home and tell their countrymen that their "earnest and ceaseless efforts in behalf of peace had been futile, and that the government of the United States meant to subjugate them by force of arms."

"Impartial history will record the innocence" of the Confederacy and blame the federal government for "the blood and mourning" that would result from war, they said. The "military demonstrations against the people of the seceded states," they said, were inconsistent with Seward's own theory that "these states are still component parts of the late American Union, as the undersigned are not aware of any constitutional power in the president of the United States to levy war, without the consent of Congress, against a foreign people, much less upon any portion of the people of the United States."

The commissioners "conclude they have been abused and overreached," Justice Campbell told Seward in a stiffly worded letter. He expressed his "profound conviction" that the leaders of the Montgomery government believe that "there has been systematic duplicity practiced on them through me." The jurist twice asked Seward for an explanation. He never received a reply.

"The crooked paths of diplomacy can scarcely furnish an example so wanting in courtesy, in candor and directness, as was the course of the United States Government toward our commissioners in Washington," President Davis told the Confederate Congress. He accused the Lincoln administration of following "a protracted course of fraud and prevarication. ... Every pledge made was broken, and every assurance of good faith was followed by an act of perfidy."

The *New York Herald* said on April 10 that Lincoln had made "a fatal mistake" in sending the fleet to Charleston and thus provoking civil war. As a result, it predicted, Virginia and other Border States would secede, Maryland would go out and "undoubtedly claim that the District of Columbia reverts to her possession under the supreme right of revolution," so the Confederates could even claim title to the Capitol and the White House.

Why would the administration wage this war? asked James Gordon Bennett's newspaper. "To 'show that we have a government'—to show that the seceded states are still in our Union, and are still subject to its laws and authorities. This is the fatal mistake of Mr. Lincoln and his cabinet and his party. The simple truth—patent to all the world—is that the seceded states ARE out of the Union, and are organized under an independent government of their own." They could be brought back, not by a ruinous war, the *Herald* said, but only "by conciliation and compromise."

"Our only hope now against civil war of an indefinite duration," said the *Herald,* "seems to lie in the overthrow of the demoralizing, disorganizing and destructive sectional party of which 'Honest Abe Lincoln' is the pliant instrument."

The news of Lincoln's real intentions—to supply Fort Sumter by sea—cut the ground out from under the pro-Union delegates to the Virginia convention. A private dispatch that a steamer had been seen off the mouth of Charleston, and that Sumter would be reinforced at all hazards, produced "a decided sensation."

The impulsive ex-governor Wise offered a resolution: "That the people of Virginia consent to the recognition and independence of the seceded states and they be treated as an independent power." It sailed through to passage by a vote of 128 to 20.

War fever raged in Washington, where thousands of people crowded the streets, all anxious to know, "Are we going to have war in Washington?" President Lincoln began calling upon the Northern governors to mobilize their militia to defend the capital against an attack—even before his fleet had arrived in Charleston. Governor Curtin of Pennsylvania was closeted with him for an hour and they had long conversations with General Scott and Secretary Cameron. A Harrisburg dispatch said Lincoln had warned Curtin of "a design to attack the city of Washington." Curtin sent a special message to his legislature, calling for arms and men to defend the capital.

General Scott mobilized about a thousand men from the district militia and stationed them around the Capitol, the White House, and department buildings. Several militiamen refused to take the oath of allegiance, fearing it would force them to fight against Maryland and Virginia. Those recruits were marched back to the armories amid the hisses of spectators, then disarmed and stricken from the rolls.

Despite the war alarms, an Ohio newspaperman reported, "the prospect of civil war has rendered the onslaught of office-seekers upon the Executive nonetheless fierce. There is an increase rather than a decrease of the crowds that daily while away the weary hours in patient expectation in the ante-rooms of the White House."

Under the caption, "Abraham Perpetrates Another Joke," the *Cincinnati Commercial* said: "The President is said to have humorously remarked that he would henceforth require all applicants to demonstrate their patriotism by serving three months at Sumter and Pickens."

After enduring the armies of office seekers many hours a day for more than a month, the President realized that his health was breaking down under the strain. At a time when he should have been concentrating on the critical issues involving war and peace, he had wasted time and energies in talks with petty politicians greedy for offices.

Finally, Lincoln reduced his reception hours, resolving henceforth to see the importunate job hunters only from 10 A.M. to 1 P.M. daily. "This week, for the first time since his inauguration, he was permitted to leave the Executive mansion for an hour or two daily for recreation," the *Chicago Tribune* said April 10, while the fate of Fort Sumter hung in the balance. "In the afternoon yesterday, he, with his lady and a few friends, rode out to Oak Hill Cemetery and passed an hour or so in the beautiful city of the dead."

Lincoln's thoughts, as he mused among the tombstones in the graveyard, can only be imagined. But it would have been totally in keeping with his melancholy temperament if he had meditated upon the many fresh graves that would surely follow the commencement of a civil war.

Knowing his fleet was approaching the guns in Charleston harbor, the President told an inquiring visitor: "The country will see whether they dare to fire upon an unarmed vessel carrying relief to our starving soldiers."

"He expressed little hope for peace and intimated a determination to relieve Major Anderson and hold other Southern forts at all hazards," a newspaper reported.

❧ *24* ❦

FORT SUMTER FALLS

In Montgomery, President Davis and his cabinet pondered the official word that President Lincoln was sending several ships with "provisions only," to feed the soldiers inside Fort Sumter. They could see how cleverly the master politician in the White House had framed the issue: In his view, he was not "invading," he was not "attacking," he was not committing "aggression." He was merely upholding his promise to hold the federal property and making a peaceful effort to deliver some "bread" to the hungry men. If the Confederates should attack, then *they* would be aggressors; *they* would be blamed for starting the war.

Davis could see how astute his secretive, stubborn foe could be. But he considered Lincoln's argument a sophistry, designed to disguise the truth that Lincoln was sending, not only food, but ships loaded with troops to reinforce the fort, and warships to fight their way into Charleston harbor after the shooting began. Davis believed that the Lincoln regime had followed a "protracted course of fraud and prevarication"; it had promised to evacuate the fort but had broken its word. So Davis placed no confidence in any pledge it might make now.

The federal warships might try to come into the harbor immediately and even attack the city, for all he knew. He viewed the advancing federals as an enemy aiming a loaded gun at a man's heart. The man would be foolish, he thought, to delay any defensive action until the gun was actually fired; he must act in self-defense.

While the Confederate president and his aides were in the office of Secretary of War Leroy Pope Walker, debating their response to Lincoln's move, former U.S. Senator Jere Clemens came in. The Alabama

Unionist said he heard a legislator named Gilchrist exclaim to Davis: "Sir, unless you sprinkle blood in the faces of the people of Alabama, they will be back in the old Union in less than ten days!"

Robert Toombs, the usually belligerent secretary of state, sang a different tune. He warned that the bombardment of Fort Sumter would be "suicide, murder, and will lose us every friend in the North. The firing upon that fort will inaugurate a civil war greater than any the world has yet seen."

Secretary Walker, under Davis's orders, telegraphed General Beauregard on April 10: "If you have no doubt of the authorized character of the agent who communicated to you the intention of the Washington government, to supply Fort Sumter by force, you will at once demand its evacuation, and if this is refused proceed, in such manner as you may determine, to reduce it."

The next day, a small boat flying a white flag arrived at the fort from Charleston, and former U.S. Senator Chesnut stepped out, along with Captain Stephen D. Lee and Lieutenant Colonel A. R. Chisholm, all representing General Beauregard. They handed Major Anderson a dispatch from the general, stating that the Confederacy could not wait any longer to take over a fort commanding the entrance to one of its harbors. It added:

"I am ordered by the government of the Confederate States to demand the evacuation of Fort Sumter. ... All proper facilities will be afforded for the removal of yourself and command, together with company arms and property, and all private property, to any post in the United States which you may select. The flag which you have upheld so long and with so much fortitude, under the most trying circumstances, may be saluted by you on taking it down."

Major Anderson and his officers conferred privately in another room and unanimously agreed that they could not give up their trust. Anderson wrote this answer:

> General:
>   I have the honor to acknowledge the receipt of your communi-
> cation demanding the evacuation of this fort, and to say, in reply
> thereto, that it is a demand with which I regret that my sense of
> honor, and of my obligations to my government, prevent my

compliance. Thanking you for the fair, manly, and courteous terms proposed, and for the high compliment paid me,

I am, General, very respectfully, your obedient servant,

ROBERT ANDERSON,

Major, Field Artillery, commanding.

As the Confederate military aides prepared to leave, Anderson said: "I shall await the first shot, and if you do not batter the fort to pieces about us, we shall be starved out in a few days."

Anderson's remark and his written reply were transmitted to Beauregard, who was reluctant to shell his old West Point artillery instructor, if the Confederates could take possession of the fort without firing a shot. He telegraphed Anderson's comment to Walker and asked for instructions. Walker replied:

"Do not desire needlessly to bombard Fort Sumter. If Major Anderson will state the time at which, as indicated by him, he will evacuate, and agree that in the meantime he will not use his guns against us, unless ours should be deployed against Fort Sumter, you are authorized thus to avoid the effusion of blood. If this, or its equivalent, be refused, reduce the fort as your judgment decides to be most practicable."

The same three aides rowed back out to the fort after midnight, accompanied by ex-congressman Roger Pryor. They delivered Walker's statement to Anderson. He and his officers debated the proposal for two hours. According to Captain Lee, Anderson "made every possible effort to retain the aides till daylight, making one excuse and then another for not replying." Finally, at 3:15 A.M., he gave his reply. He would evacuate the fort by noon April 15, "should I not receive prior to that time controlling instructions from my government or additional supplies."

Of course, Anderson and his men knew that the federal fleet was then approaching, carrying "additional supplies," and the warships would be at liberty to fight if the Confederates fired first. Within those three days, then, the Confederates could be facing fire from the fleet as well as from the fort, so they could not possibly accept Anderson's terms. As President Davis later explained: "Inasmuch as any attempt to introduce the supplies would compel the opening of fire upon the vessel bearing them under the flag of the United States—thereby releasing Major Anderson from his pledge—it is evident that his conditions could not be accepted."

So, at 3:20 A.M., Anderson received this final word, written in one of the casemates of the fort: "Sir: By authority of Brigadier General Beauregard, commanding the provisional forces of the Confederate States, we have the honor to notify you that he will open the fire of his batteries on Fort Sumter in one hour from this time."

Deeply saddened by the prospect of a civil war that he considered a needless tragedy, the major accompanied his visitors to their boat at the wharf, cordially pressed their hands in farewell, and said: "If we never meet in this world again, God grant that we may meet in the next."

At Fort Johnson on James Island, the men in the boat met Captain George S. James, commanding the battery at that point. He was ordered to fire the signal gun that would alert the crews of the forty-seven other guns encircling Sumter to commence firing. Captain James offered Pryor the honor of firing the first shot. But the orator with long, black, flowing locks—who had told a cheering Charleston crowd, "Strike a blow!"—shied away when invited to strike that blow himself. One possible reason for his refusal was that Virginia had not yet seceded; so, in a husky voice, much agitated, he said, "I could not fire the first gun of the war."

At 4:30 A.M. on Friday, April 12, 1861, Captain James fired a ten-inch mortar with "a flash as of distant lightning." "The shell mounted among the stars, and then descended with ever-increasing velocity, until it landed inside the fort and burst." On Cummings Point, the Palmetto Guards saw the signal and summoned their guest of honor to action. White-haired old Edmund Ruffin, a fanatical Virginia secessionist, pulled the lanyard of a Columbiad and sent off a shell that struck Sumter's parapet. Then the Confederate batteries opened on all sides, "and shot and shell went screaming over Sumter as if an army of devils were swooping around it," Sergeant James Chester of the First Artillery, U.S.A., recorded.

The tremendous noise awakened all of Charleston, and by daylight thousands of men and women were crowding rooftops, porches, church steeples, and other vantage points to see the most exciting show ever staged in their city. Not until nearly seven o'clock in the morning did the guns of Fort Sumter start firing back. Major Anderson had given strict orders that his men must not expose their lives by manning the guns on the ramparts, and those they fired from below lacked the power to inflict much damage on Fort Moultrie, Cummings Point, the floating battery, or others that kept on raining shot and shell on the fortress.

When the news of the attack on the fort reached Washington by telegraph, Edwin M. Stanton commented in an April 12 letter to ex-President Buchanan at Lancaster:

"The impression here is held by many—

"1. That the efforts to reinforce will be a failure.

"2. That in less than 24 hours from now Anderson will have surrendered.

"3. That in less than thirty days Davis will be in possession of Washington."

The Democratic former attorney general, who disliked Lincoln, managed to restrain his grief over the crisis faced by the Republican administration.

Meanwhile, in Charleston, in mid-afternoon Friday, the embattled defenders caught their first glimpse of the U.S. vessels off the bar and eagerly waited for them to come, under cover of darkness, to evade the Confederate guns and bring in the long-awaited food, provisions, and additional troops promised by Washington. With the help of the fleet, the weary men inside the fort would have a chance to fire all of their forty-eight big guns and make it an even battle.

"Major Anderson's only hope now is to hold out for aid from the ships," a *New York Herald* reporter telegraphed from Charleston. "Four vessels, two of them large steamers, are in sight over the bar." But, he added, "the ships appear to lie quietly at anchor. They have not fired a shot."

Captain Gustavus Vasa Fox, the mastermind of the relief expedition, fumed in frustration aboard the *Baltic*. The steamer had arrived in the early morning and joined the paddle-wheeler *Harriet Lane*, waiting for the men-of-war *Pawnee*, *Pocahontas*, and *Powhatan* to reach the rendezvous. Too late, he found that the frigate *Powhatan*, which he had been counting on as his flagship, had been taken away for

Seward's Fort Pickens mission, and was on its way to Florida. Without the *Powhatan*, with its big guns and three hundred sailors, the "fighting portion" of his fleet was gone.

More disasters disrupted Captain Fox's plans: A terrific storm in the Atlantic Ocean delayed the *Pocahontas* and the *Pawnee*, and scattered all three of his tugs that were supposed to go in first to bring in provisions—one, driven by the gale, found refuge in Wilmington, North Carolina; one sought safe haven in Savannah, Georgia; and the third never got out of New York.

When the *Pawnee* arrived, Captain Fox went aboard and asked Commander Stephen C. Rowan to enter the harbor, but the skipper refused to go without orders from a superior, saying: "I am not going in there to begin civil war."

"Vessels cannot get in as a storm is raging and the sea rough, making it impossible to effect reinforcement tonight," the *Herald*'s man reported Friday night. The storm reached a climax with a downpour of rain, which ended about eight o'clock Saturday morning, and the firing on both sides began again.

Now, some Charlestonians thought the warships might try to come in and bombard the city. Major Anderson and his exhausted, bedraggled men hoped to see the vessels move at last, but nothing happened. Confederate soldiers jeered at the federal ships, which remained safely tossing about on the water beyond the reef.

"There is a furious fire on us from Sumter," Governor Pickens telegraphed Governor Letcher of Virginia, who passed his message on to the men in the state convention at Richmond. "We will take the fort and sink the fleet if they attempt to land elsewhere. We can whip them. We have 7,000 of the best troops in the world and a reserve of 10,000.

"We will triumph or perish. Let me know what Virginia will do."

In New York City, newsboys ran through the streets, crying, "Extra! Extra!" and hawking copies of their newspapers' special editions breaking the tremendous story of civil war. Excited citizens read in the Herald: "Civil war has at last begun. A terrible fight is at this moment going on between Fort Sumter and the fortifications with which it is surrounded. ...

Breaches are being made in the several sides exposed to the fire. Portions of the parapet have been destroyed and several of the guns there mounted have been shot away. ...

The excitement in the community is indescribable. With the very first boom of the gun, thousands rushed from their beds to the harbor front, and all day every available place has been thronged by ladies and gentlemen, viewing the solemn spectacle through their glasses.

Most of them have relatives in the several fortifications, and many a tearful eye attested to the anxious affection of the mother, wife, and sister, but not a murmur came from a single individual. ...

Business is entirely suspended. Only those stores are open which are necessary to supply articles required by the army. ... Within an area of fifty miles, where the thunder of the artillery can be heard, the scene is significantly tense.

Early Saturday afternoon, Fort Sumter's flagstaff was shot away and the banner fluttered down. The scene stirred the blood of Louis T. Wigfall, the black-bearded Texas senator, who was standing on Cummings Point as a colonel on General Beauregard's staff. Wigfall immediately embarked on the craziest mission of his career. He leaped into a boat and had two men row him over to the fort, where he intended to demand surrender.

With a white flag tied to his sword, Wigfall stepped from the boat and walked to an open embrasure in the badly battered fortress, heedless of the cannon balls and chunks of masonry falling all about. When the commander came over, the senator said: "Major Anderson, I am Colonel Wigfall. You have defended your flag nobly, sir. It's madness to persevere in useless resistance. General Beauregard wishes to stop this, and to ask upon what terms you will evacuate this work."

"I have already stated the terms to General Beauregard," Anderson replied. "Instead of noon on the fifteenth, I will go now."

Shortly after Wigfall had left, an official delegation rowed out to the fort under a white flag. The *New York Tribune* said the men were Captain Lee, ex-senator Chesnut, former South Carolina Congressman William Porcher Miles, and Roger Pryor. It called Pryor "the embodiment of Southern chivalry, bristling with bowie knives and revolvers like a walking arsenal."

They assured Anderson that they had come directly from Beauregard, and Wigfall had no authority from him to act. The major, who had lowered his flag, ordered it raised again. He proposed to resume firing, but the visitors persuaded him to give up on the same honorable terms as before.

The terms were these: Anderson would evacuate the fort, his men would keep their arms, with personal and company property, and march out with the honors of war, saluting the Stars and Stripes. Realizing his hopeless position, and dreading useless bloodshed, the major gave the order to surrender, and a white bed sheet replaced the U.S. flag. When ex-senator Chesnut conferred with the major, "the fort was like an oven and he could hardly breathe," the *New York Herald* reported.

When asked how many men had been killed, Anderson replied: "None. How many on your side?"

"None."

"Thank God!" the major exclaimed. "There has been a Higher Power over us."

The surgeon general of the South Carolina troops came and offered his personal services to aid the federal wounded. Major Anderson accepted a gift of brandy, saying it was "very acceptable, as the men were completely exhausted."

"Had the surrender not taken place, Fort Sumter would have been stormed tonight," a Charleston dispatch said April 13, noting that the South Carolina men were "crazy for a fight." It added:

"The bells have been chiming all day, guns firing, ladies waving handkerchiefs, people cheering. ... It is regarded as the greatest day in the history of South Carolina."

In Montgomery, Secretary of War Walker shouted to a crowd serenading himself and President Davis: "I will prophecy that the flag which now flaunts the breeze here will float over the dome of the Old Capitol at Washington before the first of May."

Senator Wigfall's wife wrote from Charleston to their teenage son, Halsey:

I hope, my dear boy, that your uneasiness has been relieved before now, and that you have heard the glorious news. ... Your father's conduct is the constant theme of praise. If I had known to what danger he was exposed, how miserable I should have been! Thank heaven it is over, and his daring feat was rewarded. He said he felt very sorry for Anderson and his men. ...

I don't doubt Anderson rejoiced at the opportunity given him to surrender, but had it not been for that opportunity, his obstinacy would very likely have induced him to hold out until night, when it would have been impossible for the cowardly fleet to have refused ... their aid and then the bloody conflict between our men and theirs should have begun! ...

God bless you, my son and may you inherit your dear father's noble courage and heroic daring!

Another reckless voyager traveled through the bombardment at its height, daring the shot and shell, a newspaper dispatch recorded in these words:

"An old slave passed through the hottest fire, with a sloop load of wood, on Friday evening, and came safely to the city.

"Somebody told him he would be killed in the attempt.

"'Can't help dat,' said he, 'mus' go to de town tonight. If anybody hurt dis child or dis boat, Massa see him about it.'

"His sloop received four shots."

On Sunday, a glorious sunny day for the jubilant throngs of Charlestonians who watched the Yankees giving up Fort Sumter, the defenders stood stiffly at attention as their flag was slowly lowered from the ramparts amid a farewell salute. Tragically, a cartridge in one of the guns exploded. It killed Private Daniel Hough instantly, and several other cartridges piled nearby also exploded, wounding five more men. One of these, Private Edward Galloway, later died in a Charleston hospital. They were the first soldiers, out of hundreds of thousands, who would die in a war that Major Anderson deplored as wicked and useless.

On Monday morning, the major and his troops sailed away on the Charleston steamer *Isabel*. As they passed Morris Island, the South Carolina soldiers on Cummings Point lined the beach, silent and bareheaded, in a gesture of respect from the Chivalry. Then the federals boarded the *Baltic*, of Captain Fox's fleet that had signally failed to help them, and headed for New York.

Aboard the *Baltic*, Major Anderson prepared this brief report to Secretary of War Cameron:

> Sir: Having defended Fort Sumter for thirty-four hours, until the quarters were entirely burned, the main gates destroyed by fire, the gorge-wall seriously injured, the magazine surrounded by flames, and the door closed from the effects of the heat, four barrels and three cartridges of powder only being available and no provisions remaining but pork, I accepted terms of evacuation offered by General Beauregard (being the same offered by him on the 11th instant prior to the commencement of hostilities) and marched out of the fort on Sunday afternoon, the 14th instant, with colors flying and drums beating, bringing away company and private property, and saluting my flag with fifty guns.
>
> ROBERT ANDERSON
> Major First Artillery.

❧ 25 ❧

"I Knew They Would Do It"

The news of the surrender of Fort Sumter struck Washington like an earthquake. The mighty fortress, with all its guns, had run up the white flag after thirty-four hours of bombardment by the arrogant South Carolinians! How could this disaster have happened, with United States warships off the Charleston bar, never daring to make a single attempt to help the embattled little garrison?

"You cannot imagine the indescribable fury consequent upon the news of the surrender of Fort Sumter," the Washington correspondent of the *Chicago Tribune* telegraphed. "The Union men were everywhere crying out with wrath and shame, clenching their fists and swearing fearful vengeance.

"The first impression everywhere prevailed that Anderson had turned traitor. The President says, however, that he was instructed to surrender if thoroughly convinced of the impossibility of relief before his scanty stock of provisions was exhausted. The government is utterly at a loss to understand the failure of the fleet to act."

The President, whose craggy face rarely showed his emotions, received the grim news with more coolness than anyone else in the White House when the cabinet gathered Saturday to assess the damage and to wonder what to do next. He was not surprised, he said.

Lincoln knew that, for months, the South Carolinians had been itching to take possession of Fort Sumter, and the trigger-happy youths among them were spoiling for a fight. When told that the Confederates had actually opened fire on the fortress, Lincoln coolly remarked, "I knew they would do it."

That is the remark later relayed to the House of Representatives by a Democrat, Alexander Long of Ohio, who opposed the war. Long insinuated that, after Lincoln had met with the belligerent Northern

Republican governors in early April, the scheme of sending provisions to the garrison by sea had been carried out for the express purpose of provoking the "rebels" to fire the first shot. Outraged, the Republicans tried to kick Long out of the House for advocating that the Southern states be allowed to depart in peace. But the motion for his ouster fell short of the two-thirds majority required.

Defending Major Anderson's decision to give up after the bombardment, Lincoln said: "The supply vessels could not reach him, and he did right." Anderson had wanted to leave without firing a shot, if he could have done so without a stain on his honor. But Lincoln calculated that it would be damaging, politically, for him to give up the fort meekly. It was far better to have the gallant major forced out by the arrogant rebels while his own government was peacefully trying to feed his little band of hungry heroes.

Lincoln's aim, all along, had been to paint the secessionists as "the aggressors" and present himself as the apostle of peace. He started that effort publicly with his inaugural address, when he said: "In your hands, my dissatisfied fellow countrymen, and not in mine, is the momentous issue of civil war. The government will not assail you. You can have no conflict without being yourselves the aggressors."

Then he carefully laid out the scenario for the ships to carry the food on a mission of mercy to the soldiers at Fort Sumter and he had reason to believe that this would entice the proud South Carolinians into firing the first shot. Lamon had told him that Governor Pickens had vowed to let no Yankee warships into Charleston harbor. Furthermore, the *Star of the West* had been chased out in January. Lincoln also knew that those unarmed supply vessels, which he had sent to Charleston, were escorted by warships under orders to fire in case of attack.

Before the fleet could do anything—if it had not been handicapped by stormy weather—the Confederates opened fire on the fort and Lincoln could say that Jefferson Davis had ordered the first shot. Davis could protest, all he pleased, that the man who fires the first shot isn't always the one who makes the first move for war. He said Lincoln became the aggressor, in the first place, by sending the fleet to Charleston to resupply Sumter. But, in the eyes of the multitudes in the North, the innocent-looking rustic, "Old Abe" from the prairie, had outwitted the haughty martinet from Mississippi.

Lincoln expected a war to result from his scenario, and it did. "The plan succeeded," he told his old Illinois friend, Orville Browning. "They attacked Sumter—it fell, and thus did more service than it otherwise could." Consoling Captain Fox, who was disgusted and fit to be tied over the failure of his relief mission, the President wrote: "You and I both anticipated that the cause of the country would be advanced by making the attempt to provision Fort Sumter, even if it should fail; and it is no small consolation now to feel that our anticipation is justified by the result."

On the day of Sumter's surrender, but before the final word had been telegraphed to Washington, the President received three commissioners sent by the Virginia convention to find out precisely what policy he intended to pursue in regard to the Confederate States. The three were William Ballard Preston, Alexander H. H. Stuart, and George V. Randolph.

The convention had called upon Lincoln to recognize the independence of the seven states making up the Confederacy, but he had no intention of ever admitting that they had really seceded and formed their government. In his written reply, he referred to "the states which claim to have seceded." Now that "an unprovoked assault has been made on Fort Sumter," he said, he would try to repossess it and all the others seized by the secessionists, and "to repel force with force."

He considered all the military posts and other federal property in the seven states to be still "belonging to the United States as much as they did before the supposed secession"; and he repeated his vow "to hold, occupy and possess" them. He said he might land a force to relieve a fort but he would not call that "an invasion."

The Virginians heard enough to realize that, in fact, a war was already going on. No matter how much they loved the old Union, they must choose to fight for the North or for the South. Lincoln had hoped to hold the Old Dominion in the Union; but his own war policy made that no longer possible. The Virginians who favored the Union had, until now, a clear majority in the Richmond convention; Lincoln threw it away.

On Sunday, April 14, Lincoln met with his cabinet and drafted a proclamation, to be telegraphed to the nation the next day. He could not declare war—under the Constitution, only Congress could do that—but, in effect, he announced that a war was going on because the federal laws were being obstructed in the seven seceded states by "combinations too powerful to be suppressed" by the courts and the marshals. Therefore, he called for the governors to provide seventy-five thousand militia "to suppress said combinations and to cause the laws to be duly executed."

As the slim legal basis for his policy, Lincoln relied upon a 1795 law he interpreted as giving him this authority, which amounted to summoning a "posse comitatus" of record size—seventy-five thousand men—to enforce the federal laws. He also called upon "the persons composing the combinations aforesaid to disperse and retire peaceably to their respective abodes within twenty days." He pledged that "the utmost care will be observed ... to avoid any devastation, any destruction of, or interference with, property, or any disturbance of peaceful citizens of any part of the country." Those assurances were to prove grimly ironic as the ensuing civil war brought ruin upon the South and the loss of its "peculiar" property, the slaves that had an estimated value of $4 billion, all reduced to zero.

Lincoln also called Congress into special session, but delayed the opening date until the Fourth of July. Why did he not summon the lawmakers to come at once and help him cope with the great crisis? Carl Schurz, the brilliant young German devoted to the Republican cause, provided the answer in a letter to Lincoln in early April: "Some time ago, you told me you did not want to call an extra session of Congress for fear of reopening the compromise agitation." Schurz suggested that, after a show of force to defend the forts, Lincoln should call Congress back and then "the enthusiasm of the masses will be great and overwhelming," and "Congress will be obliged to give you any legislation you may ask for." On the other hand, Schurz darkly prophesied, if Lincoln seemed indecisive, "we shall be beaten in most of the Northern states in the fall elections and your administration will be at the mercy of Democratic demagogues."

Lincoln heeded Schurz's political advice; he also proved the accuracy of Senator Clingman, who had predicted in March that, after the war had begun, the Republicans would call Congress back and say: "The flag is insulted. You must come up and vote men and money."

Realizing that he had a real shooting war on his hands, Lincoln reached out to the Democrats for bipartisan support. He and his long-time foe, Stephen A. Douglas, had patched up their friendship briefly when the senator praised the inaugural speech as presaging a "peace" policy; lately, though, the Little Giant had angered the Republicans by charging that their flurry of military and naval activity, which they cloaked in secrecy, was really aimed at starting a war.

Comparing Douglas to Benedict Arnold, the fiercely partisan *Chicago Tribune* said that Douglas, who had seemed so "enamored of Old Abe" in early March, had thrown off the mask of friendship, "drawn the dagger and declared war" against him. So, when former Congressman George Ashmun of Massachusetts went to Douglas's Washington home on the Sunday after the fall of Fort Sumter and invited him to the White House to help the President, Douglas at first demurred, saying: "I don't know as he wants my advice or aid."

Ashmun assured him that the President really did need his help in unifying the nation in the war crisis. With the aid of the senator's beautiful wife, Adele, the congressman finally persuaded Douglas to ride with him to the White House, where Lincoln gave them a cordial welcome. After seeing an advance copy of the President's proclamation, Douglas declared: "I concur in every word of that document, except that, instead of a call for seventy-five thousand men, I would make it two hundred thousand." Douglas, who could never forget how the Southerners had blasted his dream of the presidency, said: "You do not know the dishonest purposes of those men as well as I do." He pointed out on a map the principal strategic points that he thought must be strengthened at once—Washington, Harper's Ferry, Fortress Monroe, and Cairo, in the pro-secessionist southern tip of Illinois, called "Egypt," for its location at the confluence of the Ohio and the Mississippi Rivers.

Douglas wrote, and gave to the Associated Press, a statement to be telegraphed the next morning along with the President's proclamation. While remaining a political rival of Lincoln, Douglas told the nation "he was prepared to sustain the President in the exercise of all his constitutional functions" to preserve the union and government and defend the capital.

Nowhere in his own proclamation did the President say that troops were being called to protect Washington from a Confederate attack. Yet the fear of such a raid loomed large in the concerns of Lincoln and the men who met with him on Monday morning. Among them were two Pennsylvanians, Governor Curtin and editor A. K. McClure, chairman of the state senate military committee. McClure asked General Winfield Scott how many men he had on hand to guard Washington.

"Fifteen hundred, sir, and two batteries," the commander replied.

How many men did General Beauregard have at Charleston, who could be brought to Washington within a week? the editor inquired.

The old chieftain's head dropped and he said, in tremulous tones: "General Beauregard commands more men in Charleston than I command on the continent east of the frontier."

Then, McClure pressed on, "Is not Washington in great danger?"

"No sir," the general retorted, sitting up straight in his chair. "The capital can't be taken, sir."

The President, whirling his spectacles around in his fingers, said to Scott: "It does seem to me, General, that, if I were Beauregard, I would take Washington."

Scott's inspector general, Charles P. Stone, had previously stated that he considered it not "improbable ... that those who now rule the Southern state intend to secure to themselves the prestige of possessing this capital, and forcing a revolution here and in the middle states." Stone quoted an unnamed "lady recently arrived from Montgomery" as saying that when she had made a farewell call on Mrs. Jefferson Davis there and asked what she should say to her friends in Washington, the Confederate First Lady replied: "Tell them I shall be happy to see them in the White House in Washington in June."

The Charleston correspondent of the *New York Times*, who was locked up in the calaboose as a dangerous Yankee during the attack on Fort Sumter, reported that the "leading spirits of the Confederacy" had boasted to him of their plans for taking over Washington. The reporter, using the pen name "Jasper," said the Confederates hoped to pull Virginia out of the Union, then march on Washington, "force Mr. Lincoln and his entire cabinet into an ignominious flight," then raise their flag in the national capital "and bid defiance to all the free states."

A *New York Tribune* reporter, safely back in Manhattan after traveling for seven dangerous days in darkest Dixie, said the people everywhere were wild with excitement, especially in Eastern North Carolina, where "six 26-pounders from Charleston for Fort Macon had reached Wilmington." Governor John Ellis had seized Fort Macon and intended to lead the Tar Heels, previously pro-Union, into the Confederacy on the wave of enthusiasm stimulated by the fall of Sumter and Lincoln's call for seventy-five thousand troops.

Like a match lighting a powder train, Lincoln's call for the troops touched off an explosion of patriotic fervor all across the North. In every city and town, the war fever blazed like a prairie fire. Crowds waved flags and cheered speakers who called for all-out war against the dirty "rebels" who had dared to fire on Old Glory. The people echoed the orators' demand that the federal armies must crush the damned rebellion and win a great victory in only a few weeks. Governors in state after state telegraphed Lincoln that they would fill their quotas of volunteers and far exceed them.

The hysteria unleashed not only waves of genuine patriotism but also a surge of hatred against the South and persecution of Northerners suspected of being friendly toward the secessionists. In Philadelphia a mob of about two hundred superpatriots converged on the homes of accused "pro-Secesh" and forced them to display the Stars and Stripes. The crowd raided the offices of the *Southern Monitor*, destroyed its printing equipment, and forced it out of business. Its editor, John Beauchamp Jones, narrowly escaped with his life and fled to Richmond.

In their patriotic fervor, Northern newspapers demanded an immediate offensive to achieve a speedy triumph. "We can make the war a short war," the *New York Times* boasted April 20, "and dictate terms at Richmond in sixty days." In the Northern cities, businessmen who had been pleading for compromise to woo back the Southerners, and revive the commerce that had been stagnated by the fear of war, now switched sides and joined in the chorus of demands for a quick victory over the "rebels." In New York City a monster crowd— easily the largest ever assembled there—cheered speakers who denounced the South and praised the President. The enthusiasm carried Lincoln to a peak of popularity that he would never again enjoy, through the next four years of bloodshed. Even Mayor Wood, notoriously pro-Southern, who had suggested that New York should secede and declare itself a "free city," changed his tune in the face of the public's roar for war, and said he favored victory, too.

Only a few hardy souls were brave enough—or foolhardy enough—to stand up against the raging tide and oppose the war. One was Ohio Congressman Clement L. Vallandigham, a Democrat who was appalled at the prospect of Americans killing each other over a political issue that could have been settled without war. "My position in regard to this civil war, which the Lincoln administration has inaugurated," he said, "will be adhered to to the end. ... I know that I am right and that, in a little while, 'the sober second thought of the people' will dissipate the present sudden and fleeting public madness, and will demand to know why thirty millions of people are butchering each other in civil war, and will arrest it speedily."

In a later speech, Vallandigham said that for six weeks after Lincoln's inaugural address, with its apparently pacific tone, a "policy of peace prevailed" and the progress of secession, after winning seven states, was stopped cold. "By overwhelming majorities, Virginia, Kentucky, North Carolina, Tennessee, and Missouri all declared for the old Union, and every heart beat high with the hope that in due course of time and through faith and patience and peace, and by ultimate and adequate compromise, every state would be restored to it," he said. Except for Republican partisans, he said, the great body of the people were resolved that "there should be no civil war upon any pretext."

But Lincoln's peace policy changed, Vallandigham said, when the politicians discovered that it was "crushing out the Republican party ... it was melting away like snow before the sun." After the Republicans suffered losses in the Rhode Island, Connecticut, and New York municipal elections, he said, "the long and agonizing howl of defeated and disappointed politicians came up before the administration.

"The newspaper press teemed with appeals and threats to the President. The mails groaned under the weight of letters demanding a change of policy; while a secret conclave of the governors of Massachusetts, New York, Ohio, and other states, assembled here, promised men and money to support the President in the irrepressible conflict which they now invoked."

Much of the "outburst and uprising in the North," which followed Lincoln's proclamation after the fall of Fort Sumter, arose from the notion that the "insurrection" might be crushed out within a few weeks by an overwhelming force, Vallandigham said. The administration imagined that a show of force, plus its "exceedingly happy and original conceit" of commanding the insurgent states to "disperse in twenty days," would not precipitate a crisis but "would satisfy its own violent partisans and thus revive and restore the failing fortunes of the Republican party."

"I can hardly conceive, sir," he said, "that the President and his advisers could be guilty of the exceeding folly of expecting to carry on a general civil war by a mere posse comitatus of three-months militia."

One other voice outside the Deep South was raised in protest against an administration policy certain to lead to all-out civil war. John C. Breckinridge, who had taken John J. Crittenden's seat in the U.S. Senate on March 4, said the people of Kentucky expressed "abhorrence" at Lincoln's proclamation. The former vice-president said the fifteen slave states should unite and present a solid phalanx of opposition to Lincoln at the extra session of Congress. "This alone," he said, "can prevent general civil war."

❧ 26 ❧

"You Have Chosen to Inaugurate Civil War"

While Lincoln's proclamation stirred the Northern people into a wild display of patriotic fervor, it ruined his hopes of holding most of the upper South states in the Union. His call for those states to send their militia for the warlike purpose of suppressing "combinations" obstructing federal law enforcement in the Confederacy drew a trumpet blast of angry refusals from their governors.

Too late, the President realized that he had wrecked his own efforts to keep Virginia from joining the secession parade. Governor John Letcher, who had never been a red-hot secessionist, indignantly told him: "The militia of Virginia will not be furnished to the powers at Washington for any such use or purpose as they have in view. Your object is to subjugate the Southern states; and a requisition made on me for such an object—an object, in my judgment, not within the purview of the Constitution or the Act of 1795—will not be complied with. You have chosen to inaugurate civil war. ... We will meet you in a spirit as determined as the Administration has exhibited toward the South."

Governor Beriah Magoffin of Kentucky, whose constituents were striving hard to stay in the Union, telegraphed: "Kentucky will furnish no troops for the wicked purpose of subduing her sister Southern states."

Governor Isham G. Harris, who personally favored secession although most of his Tennessee people were pro-Union, telegraphed: "Tennessee will not furnish a single man for coercion, but fifty thousand, if necessary, for the defense of our rights and those of our Southern brethren."

North Carolina's Governor John W. Ellis replied that the call for troops was so "extraordinary" that he first doubted that it could be genuine. "I regard the levy of troops by the Administration for the purpose of subjugating the states of the South as in violation of the Constitution and a usurpation of power," Ellis wired. "I can be no party to this wicked violation of the laws of the country, and to this war upon the liberties of a free people. You can get no troops from North Carolina." To Jefferson Davis, Governor Ellis telegraphed: "We are ready to join you to a man. Strike the blow quickly and Washington will be ours."

Governor H. M. Rector said Arkansas would provide no troops and its people would "defend to the last their honor, lives and property against Northern mendacity and usurpation."

From Missouri, Governor Claiborne Jackson telegraphed that Lincoln's call for troops was "illegal, unconstitutional, revolutionary in object, inhuman and diabolical, and cannot be complied with." Missouri, he said, would not send one man "to carry on so unholy a crusade."

Governor Thomas Hicks of Maryland, under secessionists' fire for stubbornly refusing to call a convention that might take his state out of the Union, said: "No troops will be sent from Maryland, unless it may be for the defense of the national capital." General Scott, who had earlier stiffened Hicks's backbone in the face of the disunionists' threats, assured him of enough federal troops to keep Maryland from following Virginia into the Confederacy.

From Montgomery came a dispatch reporting the Confederate chieftains' reaction to Lincoln's call for the seventy-five thousand troops: "The cabinet were in session this forenoon. Mr. Lincoln's proclamation was read amid bursts of laughter."

On Tuesday, April 16, a "Spontaneous People's Convention" assembled at Metropolitan Hall in Richmond for the purpose of high-pressuring the regular state convention into passing an ordinance of secession. On hand was John Beauchamp Jones, editor of the newly deceased *Southern Monitor* in Philadelphia. He had narrowly escaped from the City of Brotherly Love ahead of the mob that wrecked the printing office of his pro-secessionist paper. The gang brought along a rope to be tied around his neck.

Jones, who would achieve a niche in history as the author of *A Rebel War Clerk's Diary*, recorded the colorful scene in Richmond:

"The door-keeper stood with a drawn sword in his hand. ... The assembly was full, nearly every county represented, and the members were the representatives of the most ancient and respectable families in the state. ... Never, never did I hear more exalted and effective bursts of oratory. ... Messages were constantly received from the other convention. ... It was evident that the Unionists were shaking in their shoes, and they certainly begged one—just one—day's delay, which was accorded them."

The next day, the memorable April 17, came the long-awaited news: The regular convention, in secret session, had approved the ordinance of secession. The vote was 88 to 55, most of the "no" votes coming from the western counties.

Until recently, the pro-Union men had held a clear majority of about two to one, and Lincoln had imagined it would hold fast despite the excitement over Fort Sumter. But his own proclamation, calling for the seventy-five thousand troops, and interpreted as meaning war against the South, pulled the rug out from beneath the Unionists' feet. Bitterly, they blamed him for kicking Virginia out of the Union. Thomas H. Gilmer, who had fought courageously to save the Old Dominion from secession and civil war, poured out his anger and frustration in a letter to Senator Douglas:

"The period of words is past. The time of war is on hand. And may the God of battles *crush to the earth and consign to eternal perdition*, Mr. Lincoln, his cabinet, and 'aiders and abettors,' in this cruel, needless, *corrupt betrayal* of the conservative men of the South. We would have saved the country, but for the fatuity and cowardice of this infernal administration."

By the next evening, April 18, about a thousand Virginia troops arrived near Harper's Ferry, on the Potomac River, where the federal arsenal contained thousands of guns and machinery capable of producing twenty-five thousand more per year. The tiny federal garrison of forty-two men, clearly unable to save the place from capture, set fire to it at night and skedaddled across the bridge into Maryland, heading for safety in Pennsylvania. The next morning, the Virginians found the arsenal and the armory destroyed, but they salvaged several thousand muskets and rifles; and the machinery, almost intact, was later shipped southward to make weapons for the Confederacy.

Another band of Virginians marched to Norfolk to seize the big U.S. navy yard at Gosport. Instead of making at least some resistance, the federals scuttled nearly all of the warships there and tried to leave the yard a smoking, useless ruin, before sailing away Saturday night, April 20. The attempt to blow up the drydock, worth millions of dollars, failed. The *Merrimac*, a powerful steam frigate of 2,600 tons, new and fully equipped, was only partially destroyed. The Confederates saved this mighty vessel and transformed it into the ironclad *Virginia*, which would later wreak havoc with federal ships in Hampton Roads and battle the incomparable *Monitor*.

Congressman Vallandigham pointed out the supreme irony of the federals' attempted destruction of their own property at Harpers Ferry and Norfolk, in contrast to Lincoln's vow that he would hold, occupy, and possess all such installations. "As for Harper's Ferry and the Norfolk navy yard," Vallandigham told the House, "they rather needed protection from the administration, by whose orders millions of property were wantonly destroyed, which was not in the slightest danger from any quarter, at the time of the proclamation."

South Carolina's Governor Pickens told former Governor Floyd of Virginia: "I would have put three thousand men into the navy yard at Gosport before it was burnt if your Governor would have allowed me. ... I wrote to your Governor and urged him, the day after he got the cannon at Gosport, to plank them, with hot-shot batteries, immediately on the Potomac and fire into all transport vessels, and to blow up the Long Bridge and plant batteries there and on Arlington Heights, all of which could have been done without the slightest difficulty, and it would have saved 'Old Virginia' much blood and insult."

In losing Virginia, President Lincoln also lost the preeminent military officer whom General Scott had recommended to head the large army being raised in the North. Colonel Robert E. Lee had been offered the command—the golden opportunity of a soldier's lifetime ambition—by Lincoln's agent, Francis P. Blair, Sr.

Lee loved the army, but he loved Virginia much more. He could never wage war against his native state and against his own people. In his own account of the private interview at the Blair home opposite the White House, Lee said: "I declined the offer he made me to take command of the army that was to be brought into the field, stating as candidly and courteously as I could, that though opposed to secession and deprecating war, I could take no part in an invasion of the Southern States."

After informing his old friend and mentor, General Scott, of his difficult decision, Colonel Lee resigned from the United States Army. On April 23 he accepted the command of the military and naval forces of Virginia, with the rank of major general. While at Richmond, he conferred with Vice President Alexander H. Stephens, commissioner from the government at Montgomery. They agreed that Virginia should quickly enter into an alliance with the Confederacy. Virginia's secession would not become official until formally ratified by the voters on May 23, but that election would be a mere technicality.

Benjamin Brown French, a veteran civil servant at Washington, lamented in his diary, "Awful times! Civil war all around us; secession tramping on. Proud Old Virginia tailing off after crazy South Carolina and the other cotton States." French, who had been the chief marshal of Lincoln's inaugural parade, and admired him very much, nevertheless accused him of driving Virginia and other upper South states out of the Union: "I think the whole thing has been damnably managed by the President and his advisers. When it was seen that secession was determined upon by the seven states where it halted, it would have been better to let them go, than by fighting to hold them, driving out six or seven more. ... Let them go, in God's name, and peace go with them if they can maintain it."

Lincoln had ample warning, from the Union-loving congressmen of the slave states outside the Deep South, that he must hold them in the Union by a policy of peace. One of those House members, Zebulon B. Vance, a North Carolina Whig and later governor, said they told Lincoln, shortly before his inauguration, that the seven Cotton States alone could not make their Confederacy a success without the aid of "the great border states of Missouri, Kentucky, Virginia, Maryland, North Carolina and Tennessee."

"They expressed to him the opinion that the secession movement could be checked and finally broken down if those great states could be kept out of it," Vance recalled. The congressmen said their people were devoted to the Union, but they could not maintain their stand against the intense campaign for secession in case of any federal "coercion." "Lincoln," he said, "promised that, if possible, he would avoid the attempt at coercion."

Armed with Lincoln's promise, and the apparently pacific tone of his inaugural address, the Union congressmen went home and spoke at pro-Union rallies. "I was canvassing for the Union with all my strength," said Vance, who represented a district in the western North Carolina mountains. "I was addressing a large and excited crowd, large numbers of whom were armed, and literally had my arm extended upward in pleading for peace and the Union of our Fathers, when the telegraphic news was announced of the firing on Sumter and the President's call for seventy-five thousand volunteers." When his hand came down, he said, "it fell slowly and sadly by the side of a Secessionist."

"The Union men had every prop knocked from under them and ... were plunged into the secession movement," Vance said. "I charge no bad faith on Mr. Lincoln for this entrapment; doubtless his intentions were as sincere as those of Union men."

Jonathan Worth, also a future governor, and many other North Carolinians who had fought furiously against secession, felt betrayed. Worth, a firm Unionist from a Quaker family, and a Whig leader in the state senate, had played a major role in the vote that blocked the Democrats' scheme for a state convention. It would be a "secession" convention, he warned the voters, and they turned it down. They believed that Lincoln favored peace and conciliation.

Worth called Lincoln "a fool" who had "followed a policy that made it impossible for the Unionists to cast any influence in preventing war," his biographer, Richard L. Zuber, stated. "He felt that the President had undermined the Unionists of the South by employing a policy of coercion," Zuber wrote. "He argued that Lincoln should never have tried to use force, because 'it would result in a bloody civil war.'"

Since Congress in early 1861 had refused to pass a "force bill" authorizing the use of military power to retain or regain federal property, Worth believed that Lincoln had violated the will of Congress.

In one bitter letter, the future governor declared: "The hotspurs of the South, aided by a silly administration in Washington, have at length precipitated the nation into universal ruin."

Pro-Union newspapers in North Carolina echoed the lamentations of Vance and Worth. The *Carolina Watchman*, the voice of the Piedmont area Whigs at Salisbury, denounced "President Lincoln's proclamation and call for volunteers to coerce the seceding states," saying: "If he had spent a whole year in devising a method to unite the Southern people he could not have brought out anything more successful." The *Fayetteville Observer* blamed "the stupid, treacherous administration and malcontent fire-eaters for the guilt and folly of destroying the best government on earth."

Governor Ellis, a Democrat who had pressed hard for secession, was so elated over his victory that he called for the capture of Washington. A Philadelphia news dispatch of April 29 said: "A gentleman just arrived here from Wilmington, N.C., stated that the people of North Carolina were all up in arms and were preparing to come North with several thousand troops for the purpose, as Gov. Ellis informed him, of making an attack on Washington."

In Raleigh, where "the streets were alive with soldiers and officers," the *Standard* said, "North Carolina could send her full quota of troops to unite in the attack on Washington. ... Washington will be too hot to hold Abraham Lincoln and his government."

"The first fruits of Virginia secession will be the removal of Lincoln and his cabinet, and whatever he can carry away to the safer neighborhood of Harrisburg or Cincinnati—perhaps to Buffalo or Cleveland," the *New Orleans Picayune* gloated.

"With independent Virginia on one side and the secessionists in Maryland (who are doubtless in the majority) on the other," said the Eufala, Alabama, *Express,* "our policy at this time should be to seize the Old Federal capital and take Lincoln and his cabinet prisoners of war ... and then perhaps avoid a long and bloody conflict."

The *Richmond Examiner,* the voice of the "fire-eaters," proclaimed: "From the mountain-tops and valleys to the shores of the sea, there is one wild shout of fierce resolve to capture Washington City, at all and every human hazard. That filthy cage of unclean birds must and will assuredly be purified by fire. ...

"Our people can take it—they *will* take it—and Scott, the arch-traitor, and Lincoln, the Beast, combined, cannot prevent it. The indignation of an outraged and deeply injured people will teach the Illinois Ape to repeat his race and retrace his journey across the borders of the free negro states still more rapidly than he came."

In Tennessee, where Senator Andrew Johnson had aroused strong pro-Union emotions by his blistering speeches against disunion, Lincoln's call for troops brought about a stunning reversal of opinion like the quick switch in North Carolina. Governor Harris entered into a military league with the Confederacy even before the people had another chance to vote on secession. In effect, the state was out of the Union when the voters approved the action by a margin of about two to one. But the mountain counties of east Tennessee, Johnson's stronghold, remained defiantly loyal to the Stars and Stripes.

Arkansas's constitutional convention reassembled and adopted an ordinance of secession with only a single dissenting vote.

Virginia's secession opened the way for the secessionists in Maryland to make a new attempt to pull their state into the Confederacy, too, despite Governor Hicks's adamant refusal to call the legislature or to allow a state convention. Lincoln's call for seventy-five thousand troops caused Northern soldiers to start moving southward to the defense of Washington; and thus the troop movements through Baltimore by rail provided the spark for an explosion—a pitched battle between Northern soldiers and a mob of rock-throwing civilians, a melee that caused far more deaths than the bombardment of Fort Sumter.

❧ 27 ❧

BLOODSHED IN BALTIMORE

"Civil war has commenced!" the *Chicago Tribune* exclaimed in a bulletin reporting the bloody clash in Baltimore on April 19 between Northern troops and the local civilian mob.

Hurling bricks and paving stones, the mob assailed about two thousand soldiers from Massachusetts and Pennsylvania, who had arrived in thirty railroad cars. From the President Street Station of the Philadelphia, Wilmington, and Baltimore Railroad, the militiamen tried to go, in horse-drawn cars, about a mile and a half to the Camden Street Station on the west side of the city and board a train for the last leg of their journey to Washington.

The first nine cars went through without much trouble, except for jeers and curses and cries of "Hurrah for Jeff Davis and the Southern Confederacy!" Then, to prevent any more cars from passing, the mob tore up the track for fifty yards and threw paving stones in large piles in the center, along with several immense anchors lying on a nearby wharf.

Six carloads of soldiers descended from the train, intending to march to the Camden Street Station. Amid hoots, hisses, and curses, they formed in ranks, four abreast, and, with the help of the police, started forcing their way through the crowd. About two hundred Baltimore boys walked in front of them, waving a torn Confederate flag and thus forcing the Massachusetts volunteers to march behind the banner they despised.

An enterprising editor named Thomas W. Hall, Jr., launched a brand new Baltimore newspaper, *The South*, with a vivid account of the fatal conflict on the city's streets. Under the caption, "The Fight," the Baltimore newspaper reported the pitched battle between the troops and the civilians:

About a hundred yards from the depot the first attack upon the troops was made by paving stones and other missiles, and one of the Massachusetts troops ... was knocked down and his gun taken from him. The troops now commenced to run, under the pressure of the crowd, and several more of them were knocked down and their arms seized. ...

At the corner of Pratt and Commerce Streets an immense mob was assembled. ... Almost every man provided himself with a large paving stone, and as the troops advanced a shower of the stones was poured into them. ...

Finding themselves hemmed in ... the commanding officer commanded them to "fire," and the order was no sooner given than several of the men foremost in the ranks took deliberate aim, and at the first fire a young man named Francis X. Ward, a member of the City Guard Battalion, fell to the earth, pierced by a Minié ball in the left side of the groin. The remainder of the troops fired in rapid succession upon the crowd in front, shooting several persons. When the young man Ward was shot, he was standing, with others of his acquaintance, upon the pavement, one of whom witnessed the proceeding, and, marking the man who fired the shot, he drew his revolver, took deadly aim, and fired. The soldier fell to the earth and would have been torn to pieces had the police not interfered. ...

A resident of this city was forced by the crush of the crowd into close proximity to one of the soldiers, who raised his gun and, taking deliberate aim, pulled the trigger. The cap exploded and the gun failed to go off. The citizen rushed forward and, seizing the musket, plunged the bayonet almost entirely through his body. ...

The soldier thanked his God that, although he was dying himself, his gun had not exploded, that he never desired this service and was pressed into it under threats of death, that the people of Baltimore did right, and that the rest of the troops deserved his fate. ...

The troops now proceeded in a rapid run up Pratt street, but at the corner of Charles were again assaulted and one of their number, named [Andrew] Robbins, from Stonehaven, Mass., was shot in the neck and carried into the drug store of Mr. Hunt, where he received medical attention. [He recovered.]

At the corner of Howard and Pratt, the flying troops fired a volley without any provocation, and killed the horse of a drayman.

Upon arriving at the station, they hurried into the cars with the greatest speed and immediately opened an indiscriminate fire upon the people from the car windows.

THE TROOPS LEAVE THE CITY

Thirteen cars were then drawn out, which were entirely occupied by troops, and being attached to a locomotive, about a quarter before one o'clock, moved out of the depot, amid the hisses and groans of the multitude.

Marshal Kane ascended the steps of the [Baltimore and Ohio] railroad company amid deafening cheers for "Marshal Kane," and the assurances of those present that they would do whatever he directed. He then exhorted them to obey the laws and wait till they heard the verdict of the true men of Baltimore. The assemblage then dispersed. ...

MURDER OF MR. ROBERT W. DAVIS

After the cars containing the troops had left the Camden station, and as they were approaching the city limits, a group of five gentlemen, one of whom was Mr. Robert W. Davis, of the firm of Paynter, Davis & Co., were standing by the roadside to witness the passing of the train.

As the cars passed, in reply to some menacing gestures from the soldiers, and in utter ignorance of what had taken place in the city, the blood that had been spilt and of the consequent feeling that had been aroused, they raised a hurrah for President Davis and the Southern Confederacy, and without other or further provocation, half a dozen muskets were thrust out of the windows of the cars—a volley was fired—and Mr. Davis fell, pierced with a Minié bullet through the left shoulder, penetrating the lung and severing some of the larger vessels of the heart. Mr. Davis expired almost as soon as he fell—his only words being in reply to the question of a friend who stood beside him—"I am killed."

Dean Sprague, in his book *Freedom Under Lincoln*, records that a Massachusetts soldier, Samuel Needham, was hit by a brick and later died of a fractured skull. James Myers, a rioter, was shot in the back by a Minié ball that killed him. A boy named William Reed, working on an oyster sloop docked at Pratt Street, was shot in the abdomen by a Minié ball and died in the boat that evening. Reed was eighteen. Another eighteen-year-old, John McCann, and two younger boys, Philip S. Miles and Patrick Griffith, were also killed by bullets from Yankee guns, according to *The South*.

The paper published a list of eleven citizens and three soldiers killed, and nine soldiers and three citizens wounded. Before the riot, Baltimore citizens had been about evenly divided over the secession question, but the shock of seeing their own people killed and wounded by Northern soldiers enraged the multitude and turned the city into a secessionist stronghold. Thousands of citizens massed in Monument Square at four o'clock in the afternoon of the melee and cheered a series of speakers who made belligerent orations. Dr. A. C. Robinson began by saying: "The blood which has this day been spilt in our streets has sealed the hearts of all Marylanders. We now stand as a unit."

Amid loud and prolonged cheering, Mayor Brown announced that he and Governor Hicks had sent a telegram to President Lincoln, demanding that no more troops be sent through the city. "A collision between the citizens and the Northern troops has taken place in Baltimore, and the excitement is fearful," they told the President. "Send no troops through here. We will endeavor to prevent all bloodshed." The executives of several railroads, Brown said, had agreed that no more soldiers would pass over their tracks without the approval of the governor and the city authorities.

S. Teackle Wallis, an eloquent Baltimore lawyer, strongly pro-Southern, said:

> If the blood of your fellow citizens, shed this day in your own streets, does not cry out to you, all other voices had as well be silent.
>
> The Governor of the state has left to the Police Board of Baltimore the control of the whole civil and military power of this community, which the law authorizes them to exercise for its protection, and devoted as I am to the cause of the South against its invaders, I for one have perfect confidence that they will use that power in accordance with their duties and our rights.
>
> Fellow citizens, we have been divided heretofore among many opinions. I trust that we are *now* separated no longer. Let us stand together hereafter under the old flag of Maryland, forgetting all parties and distinctions, and may the blood which has been spilt this day among us be the seal of the covenant of our union in the holy cause of the South.

When another speaker, Robert McLane, said he had found the governor in the mayor's office that day, someone in the crowd cried: "Why didn't you choke him?"

"Because," McLane replied amid laughter, "he gave me reason to respect him." This time, he said, the governor "really meant to place the state in an official attitude of honor to herself and her sister states of the South." That came as news to the secessionists, who hated Hicks for having stubbornly refused to allow the legislature or a convention to carry Maryland out of the Union. Could the people's demand for secession finally bring Hicks around to the side of the South?

A committee was immediately sent to invite the governor to face the howling mob and declare where he really did stand. It was an offer he couldn't refuse. Thanking the crowd for "the high compliment conveyed in your cordial cheers," Hicks said he had ever been devotedly attached to the Union and, though it was apparently broken now, he trusted that its reconstruction might yet be achieved.

That remark evoked vehement shouts of "Never," "Never," along with groans and hisses. Sensing the mood of the crowd, he quickly added: "But, if otherwise, I bow in submission to the mandate of the people." "I am a Marylander!" the governor cried. "I love my state, and I love the Union; but I will suffer my right arm to be torn from my body before I will raise it to strike a sister state!"

"Baltimore was a secession volcano in full eruption," Horace Greeley wrote in *The American Conflict*. He had no doubt that, in those hours of passion, an ordinance of secession could have swept Maryland out of the Union. In effect, he said, Maryland was "practically a member of the Southern Confederacy."

The night after the riot, the telegraph wires connecting Baltimore with the free states were cut. Members of the militia destroyed the railroad bridges on the lines leading northward to Harrisburg and Philadelphia, to prevent any more Northern troops from coming in. This destruction was carried out because railway officials had sent word that many more Yankee soldiers were on their way.

Written commissions were made out by the mayor, "by the authority of the governor of Maryland" and himself, ordering Marshall Kane and Colonel Isaac Trimble to direct the work of burning the bridges. Governor Hicks, after recovering from the emotional upheaval of his confrontation with the mob in Monument Square, later denied that he had authorized the bridge burning, but the Baltimore officials insisted that he had.

After a hectic night in Baltimore, the governor went back to Annapolis, the state capital, early Saturday morning. "He pleaded sickness and fatigue," said *The South*, "and was perfectly satisfied to leave the conduct of affairs in the hands of Mayor Brown."

Bridges on the railroad tracks leading southward toward Washington and Virginia were kept intact, the paper explained, because "it was deemed desirable to preserve both the main stem and the Washington branch of the Baltimore and Ohio railroad for the transportation of the troops that may soon be expected from Virginia and the South."

Marshal Kane telegraphed Bradley T. Johnson, militia chieftain at Frederick, soon to join the Confederate army: "Streets red with Maryland blood. Send expresses over the mountains and valleys of Maryland and Virginia without delay. Further hordes will be down on us tomorrow. We will fight them and whip them or die."

On Saturday morning, the city council unanimously voted to raise half a million dollars to defend Baltimore. The directors of the various banks quickly met and offered to lend that amount of money to the city. More than two thousand volunteers enlisted in the militia that day and were armed with guns collected from a variety of places: an auctioneer's home, the office of the Mounted Carbineers, a warehouse on the wharf, and a high school where the pupils had been drilling.

As the news of the battle between the federal troops and the Baltimore citizens spread excitement across Maryland, reinforcements poured in from all over the state. Bradley T. Johnson brought seventy men, marching from Frederick. The Baltimore County Horse Guards brought "a stalwart company, well mounted and armed and well drilled." The Patapsco Light Dragoons galloped in on horseback from Anne Arundel County. Their buglemen struck up "Dixie's Land" and the crowd cheered.

The next day, the chartered steamer *Pioneer* arrived from Easton, bringing sixty men who vowed that the people of the Eastern Shore stood "as a unit in defense of the South." Later came thirty-five Dragoons from Howard County, "thoroughly equipped" for a fight.

"Parties of men are roaming the streets, armed with shotguns, pistols and muskets," the *Chicago Tribune* reported. "The stores are closed, business is suspended, and a general state of dread prevails."

"Popular excitement" continued to rage in Baltimore through Saturday, *The South* reported, and a crowd of men broke into the Turner Hall on Pratt Street, the rendezvous of the German Turners organization, and completely demolished the interior. The wreckers sought revenge because the Germans "a few nights since, gathered together about two hundred stands of arms, which had been provided a year or two since by the state of Maryland for their use, and left for the city of Washington to tender their services to the Federal Government."

"The office of *The Wecker*, a German abolition paper on Frederick Street, was visited shortly afterwards by a large crowd of infuriated people, who demanded that the Confederate flag should be displayed." A small Southern flag soon was hung out from a window, but the mob came back, smashed the windows with bricks and stones, and the occupants fled to take refuge with their neighbors.

"A respectably attired man from New York," *The South* reported, "was set upon by the people, who thought him a New York reporter, and but for the police would undoubtedly have been lynched. He finally declared himself a good Southern man and, after being cheered, was allowed to depart quietly."

Thus did superpatriots wreak havoc in Baltimore as in Philadelphia.

Frankly asserting its desire for Maryland to join the Confederacy at once, *The South* proclaimed:

> It is to Maryland, after all, not to South Carolina, not to Florida—
> that belongs the glory of having fought the first battle in the new
> War of Independence. In Baltimore—not at Charleston nor at
> Pensacola—the first blood has been spilt on both sides in the con-
> flict, compared with which the bombardment of Fort Sumter was
> but child's play—a conflict between the unarmed populace and the
> armed troops of the Government—the victory remaining with the
> people. On the 19th of April, 1861, the anniversary of the Battle of
> Lexington—the first real battle of another Revolution took place.

When the news of the Battle of Baltimore reached James Ryder Randall, twenty-two, a Maryland man teaching English at a college in Louisiana, he became so thrilled that he quickly wrote the nine stanzas of "Maryland, My Maryland." It was a spirited appeal for the Old Line state to "spurn the Northern scum" and rush to rescue the Southern states from "the tyrant's chain."

Here are two of the stanzas:

> The despot's heel is on thy shore, Maryland!
> His torch is at thy temple door, Maryland!
> Avenge the patriotic gore
> That flecked the streets of Baltimore
> And be the battle queen of yore,
> Maryland, my Maryland!

> I hear the distant thunder-hum, Maryland!
> The Old Line bugle, fife and drum, Maryland!
> She is not dead, nor deaf, nor dumb—
> Huzza! She spurns the Northern scum!
> She breathes! She burns! She'll come!
> She'll come!
> Maryland, my Maryland!

Quickly, the appeal provided the lyrics for various tunes, the most popular being "Tannenbaum" or "Christmas Tree." Eventually, it became Maryland's official song. Thomas W. Hall, Jr., published the poem in his paper, *The South*, on May 31, 1861. Federal authorities, controlling Baltimore then, arrested him on a charge of sedition.

❧ 28 ❧

"My God, Sir,
What Am I to Do?"

President Lincoln found himself in a desperate situation in mid-
April, totally cut off from communication with the Northern
states. The telegraph lines were cut, the railroad bridges above Baltimore burned, and panic had gripped Washington.

Possible famine threatened the capital because no trains could
bring in food from the North and suppliers in Maryland and Virginia
refused to bring any in. "Women and children were sent away in great
numbers; provisions advanced to famine prices," Edwin M. Stanton
informed ex-president Buchanan, who was delighted to be back home
at his Wheatland estate in Pennsylvania, away from the chaos in
Washington.

The former attorney general gloated over the discomfiture of the
new Republican administration and its president. "No description
could convey to you the panic that prevailed here for several days
after the Baltimore riots," Stanton told Buchanan. "This was increased
by reports of the trepidation of Lincoln that were circulating through
the streets." Later, Stanton added that no one could "imagine the
deplorable condition of this city, and the hazard of the government,
who did not witness the weakness and panic of the administration
and the imbecility of Lincoln."

Lincoln had good reason for his panic. He kept hearing reports
of Confederate troops preparing to bombard the White House from
batteries on the Virginia side of the Potomac, and "fire-eaters'" boasts
of plans to invade Washington, take him prisoner, or even kill him.
Of the seventy-five thousand troops he had called, only a few thousand had reached Washington, chiefly from Pennsylvania and Massachusetts, and those who survived the Baltimore mob were beaten

up. Lincoln had to act with speed and vigor to break up the impasse in Maryland.

The first of a series of envoys from Baltimore—Hugh L. Bond, John C. Brune, and George W. Dobbin—visited the President and General Scott on Saturday, April 20. They telegraphed Mayor Brown that they were coming home with a letter from Lincoln "declaring that no more troops shall be brought through Baltimore, if, in a military point of view and without interruption or opposition, they can be marched around Baltimore."

Next, U.S. Senator Anthony Kennedy of Maryland and J. Morrison Harris went to Washington by a special train on Saturday and met with the President. Under the caption, "President Lincoln Scared," *The South* newspaper published this account of the conversation at the White House:

Harris began by saying the purpose of the visit was "to prevent further bloodshed" and to obtain an order canceling further movement of federal troops through Maryland.

Referring to the offer he had just made to Dobbin, Brune, and Bond, Lincoln exclaimed: "My God, Mr. Harris, I don't know what to make of you people. You have sent me one committee already, and they seemed to be perfectly satisfied with what I said to them."

Harris replied that he knew nothing about that; he had come as a citizen to state facts as they actually existed, and to say that an attempt to send any more troops through Maryland would lead to "a very sanguinary battle."

"My God, sir, what am I to do?" the anxious President cried. "I had better go out and hang myself on the first tree I come to, than to give up the power of the Federal Government in this way. I don't want to go through your town, or near it, if I can help it; but we must have the troops here to relieve ourselves, or we shall die like rats in a trap!"

Secretary Seward drew Harris over to a window and, pointing to the bluffs of Arlington in Virginia, said: "On top of that hill is a battery commanded by General Robert E. Lee, of Virginia, and we do not know at what moment a shell might burst into this very room."

"It might be necessary," General Scott said, "for the troops to cut their way through Maryland for the defense of the Federal capital."

On that same Saturday, two Baltimore women called upon Mrs. Lincoln and found her so terrified that she was talking about Lincoln "abdicating" and going home to Illinois. Under the caption, "Mrs. Lincoln Alarmed," *The South* newspaper printed this story:

"On Saturday last, two ladies of this city called upon 'the short of the presidency,' as her husband calls Mrs. Lincoln, and were anxiously questioned by her as to whether our citizens would allow them to pass safely and quietly through here if they abdicated.

"She says she would prefer returning to Springfield as beggars, to living in Washington under such a complete reign of terror."

On Saturday, also, Confederate Secretary of War Walker received a telegram from a railroad superintendent named H. D. Bird, at Petersburg, Virginia, saying:

> Colonel Owen, president of the Virginia and Tennessee railroad, has just reached here from Baltimore by way of Norfolk. He witnessed the butchery of Baltimore citizens by the Massachusetts regiment yesterday. He states the city is in arms and all are Southern men now. ...
>
> Lincoln is in a trap.
>
> He has not more than twelve hundred regulars in Washington and not more than three thousand volunteers. We have three thousand in Harper's Ferry. Our boys, numbering four hundred, went down today to Norfolk, to join the companies there and your forces coming from Charleston. You know how many we want. As leader, we want Davis.
>
> An hour now is worth years of common fighting. One dash and Lincoln is taken, the country saved, and the leader who does it will be immortalized.

At three o'clock Sunday morning, April 21, Mayor Brown received an urgent dispatch from Lincoln, asking him and Governor Hicks to meet with the President at once. Hicks did not go, but the mayor hurried to Washington by special train, taking along three other Baltimore men: Brune, Dobbin, and S. Teackle Wallis, an open secessionist.

Brown had already told the President, "It is not possible for more soldiers to pass through Baltimore unless they fight their way at every step." According to the *Chicago Tribune*, the governors of New York, Pennsylvania, Massachusetts, and Ohio, all Republicans, had telegraphed Brown that they intended to send ten thousand troops through Maryland for the protection of Washington, and, if obstructed, "they will reduce the city of Baltimore to ashes."

Mayor Brown informed the President that the people of Baltimore considered his call for the seventy-five thousand troops was a declaration of war, so it was not surprising that they resisted the passage of the Northern soldiers through their city. These words, according to Brown, caused Lincoln to leap from his chair, stride back and forth and declare, with deep emotion, "Mr. Brown, I am not a learned man! I am not a learned man!"

Lincoln said his proclamation had been misunderstood, that he had no intention of bringing on war, but merely to defend the capital, which was in danger of being bombarded from the Virginia heights. He said the line of communications to the North via Baltimore absolutely must be reopened within a few days and kept open—for, without it, "this city can never be safe."

With great earnestness, Lincoln said none of the troops brought through Maryland would be used for any purposes hostile to the state or aggressive against the Southern states. Being unable to bring the soldiers up the Potomac in security, he said, the government must either bring them in through Maryland or abandon the capital.

The long discussions that Sunday, involving the President, General Scott, Secretary Cameron, and the men from Baltimore resulted in an agreement that the soldiers' route through Baltimore would be given up. Henceforth, they would travel by train from Philadelphia, to Perryville, at the mouth of the Susquehanna River, then go by boat to Annapolis, and cover the final forty miles from the state capital to Washington by rail. They would still defile the sacred soil of Maryland, but they would stay away from Baltimore.

The mayor and his men accepted this deal and started to board a train for home, but received a telegram from John W. Garrett, president of the Baltimore and Ohio Railroad, stating that more Yankee soldiers were at Cockeysville, about a dozen miles above Baltimore. "Three thousand Northern troops are reported to be at Cockeysville," he wired. "Intense excitement prevails. Churches have been dismissed and the people are arming in mass. To prevent terrific bloodshed, the results of your interview and arrangements are awaited."

Startled, the Baltimore men rushed back to the White House and showed Garrett's telegram to the President. Lincoln said he had no idea that the troops were there. "Lest there be the slightest suspicion of bad faith on his part in summoning the mayor to Washington and allowing troops to march on the city during his absence," the mayor said later, "he desired that the troops, if it were practicable, be sent back at once to York or Harrisburg." On Monday morning, the soldiers at Cockeysville climbed aboard a train and went home to Pennsylvania.

A New York news dispatch of April 21 reported that Mayor Alberter of Buffalo "arrived here today, with several other gentlemen, having chartered a canal boat" that enabled them to flee Baltimore. "They report the condition of the city is fearful," it said. "Streets are barricaded, shutters of houses loop-holed for musketry, and every gun store emptied. ... A Northerner's life is not worth an hour's purchase when the next gun in the war is fired ... the Union men are fleeing for their lives."

Lincoln received still another delegation from Baltimore on April 22, this time from the Young Men's Christian Association, on a mission of peace. The visitors pleaded with him to avert a bloody conflict between the Northern and Southern people. Their leader, Dr. Fuller of the Baptist Church, said Lincoln held the responsibility of choosing war or peace.

"But," asked the President, "what am I to do?"

"Why, sir," the minister replied, "let the country know that you are predisposed to recognize the independence of the Southern states ... and peace will instantly take the place of anxiety and war may be averted."

Maryland, "who had shed her blood freely in the War for Independence" from Britain, has given up her attachment to the Union, now that "the blood of her citizens has been shed by strangers on their way to a conflict with her sisters of the South," the pastor said. He begged that no more troops be sent through Maryland.

"I must have troops and they must come through Maryland," the President insisted. "They can't crawl under the earth, and they can't fly over it, so mathematically, they must come across it."

PUNCH, OR THE LONDON CHARIVARI—August 23, 1862.

LINCOLN'S TWO DIFFICULTIES.

Lin. "WHAT? NO MONEY! NO MEN!"

This cartoon from Punch, *or the* London Charivari, *depicts Lincoln in a dilemma early in the Civil War, having to raise a large army and heavy taxes to pay for it. From the collections of the Library of Congress.*

Fearing a Confederate attack on Washington, Lincoln told the Marylanders that the only effect of their prayers for peace "would be the destruction of the government as well as his own death or captivity."

"Why, sir," he said, "those Carolinians are crossing Virginia to come here and hang me and what can I do?"

Once again, Lincoln showed his obsession with the idea that his enemies must never consider him a coward or a weakling, and they would do so if he did not fight to hold the Union together. If he should let the seceding states go in peace, he said, "there would be no Washington in that, no Jackson in that, no spunk in that." Fuller retorted that the President should not allow "spunk" to override patriotism.

As the delegates were about to leave, the President said:

"Now I'll tell you a story. You have heard of the Irishman who, when a fellow was cutting his throat with a blunt razor, complained that he 'haggled it.' Now if I can't have troops direct through Maryland, and must have them all the way round by water, or marched across out-of-the-way territory, I shall be 'haggled.'

"Now, if you won't hit me, I won't hit you."

Outside the White House, one of the callers from Baltimore lamented: "God have mercy upon us when the government is placed in the hands of a man like that!"

While the anxious president wrestled mentally with the specter of murderous Rebels storming the White House, the panic in Washington, isolated from the North, grew worse. Frederick Seward, son of the secretary of state, heard that forty thousand Virginia volunteers, "armed with bowie knives," would soon come across the Potomac. "Business was at a standstill," he noted. "The railway station was silent, the wharves deserted." The hotels, so recently swarming with office seekers and tipplers in the barrooms, had pitifully few guests now.

Lincoln's obsessive fear of being hanged by the Rebels was confirmed in a dispatch by a *Chicago Tribune* reporter who wrote:

Lincoln and his cabinet and Gen. Scott are marked for hanging. The President yesterday said to Dr. Fuller, of Baltimore, who came to preach peace to him, "that the troops of South Carolina had already crossed the Virginia line for his head."

The secessionists are gathering at Alexandria, lining the banks of the Potomac with batteries, so that the river cannot be used for our troops or supplies. They have Maryland with them to such a degree that no provisions can come to Washington through Baltimore, or by the Relay House.

Today, at a place near Harper's Ferry, I heard a secessionist chuckling over the prospect that "in two weeks the government and the city of Washington would be starved out like Fort Sumter and they would have it."

Nothing can save the city from the Tories but celerity, and nothing can save it from famine but military occupation of the railroad from Wilmington, Delaware, to Washington.

Fears of a food shortage became intense. "The whole country around Washington has been scoured for provisions," one newspaperman reported. "The people over in Virginia will not deal at all with the city—not an ounce of provisions can come from Maryland." The price of bread doubled; flour rose to fifteen dollars a barrel "and all bought up at that." The government seized two thousand barrels of flour in Georgetown and moved them to the Capitol, to feed the troops who had come earlier from Pennsylvania and Massachusetts and were camping out in the halls of Congress. Bread for the soldiers was baked in the Capitol basement. Under General Scott's orders, the Capitol and other public buildings were barricaded and protected by sandbags, braced for the coming Rebel assault.

Lincoln's own secretaries, Nicolay and Hay, confirmed that he suffered severely through nearly a week of isolation from the Northern states, "in a state of nervous tension." The President, they added, feared the "sudden collapse" of his government and this fear "begot in him an anxiety approaching torture."

"The White House is turned into barracks," wrote Hay. For several nights, a band of volunteer guards, armed with revolvers and rifles, protected the President and his family in the mansion and slept on the carpet in the East Room. They were led by Cassius Clay, a Kentucky abolitionist and Lincoln's nominee to be the minister to Russia, and James J. Lane, the roughneck senator from the new state of Kansas. Both were veterans of the Mexican war, and Jim Lane brought along some of his bloodthirsty Jayhawkers who had fought in the Kansas border battles. Senator Lane, wrote Hay, would vow, in a husky, blood-curdling whisper, "Baltimore will be laid in ashes!"

The *New Orleans Delta* quoted a letter from an unidentified Southern woman in Washington, who claimed: "Old Lincoln sleeps with a hundred men in the East Room to protect him from the Southern army. He is expecting them to attack the city every night; and often gets so frightened that he leaves the White House and sleeps out, no one knows where."

While waiting anxiously for the arrival of more soldiers from the North to cope with the phantom "army" of invaders expected from the South, the President seized extraordinary powers and took drastic action so that, in his words, the government would not "fall at once into ruin." On April 21, he summoned all of his cabinet secretaries to meet at the Navy Department, safely away from any possible spies in the White House. "Then and there, with their unanimous concurrence," he later told Congress, he issued a series of orders for national defense.

Without the required authority of Congress, Lincoln directed Treasury Secretary Chase to advance, without security, $2 million to John A. Dix, the former secretary, and George Opdyke and Richard M. Blatchford of New York, to pay for necessary "military and naval measures"—in effect, a blank check. The government departments then had so many "disloyal persons" on their payrolls that Lincoln believed he could not trust official agents alone for duties which he, therefore, confided to "citizens favorably known for their ability, loyalty and patriotism."

He relied upon New York's Republican governor, Edwin D. Morgan—or, in his absence, Blatchford, William M. Evarts, George D. Morgan, and Moses H. Grinnell—to act for the navy in forwarding troops and supplies for the public defense. He also directed that Governor Morgan and Alexander Cummings of New York should arrange for the transportation of troops and munitions of war for the army until the mails and the telegraph lines should be completely restored between Washington and New York. To make sure that the messages and money orders actually went to his trustworthy agents, Lincoln bypassed the post office and sent them by private messengers, who traveled by way of Pittsburgh and Wheeling to New York by "a circuitous way to the seaboard cities," he said.

One example of his unusual mail service appeared in a Philadelphia newspaper story on April 22, which said: "A bearer of dispatches from the President to General Patterson has arrived. The messenger traveled part of the way on foot, passing himself off as a Methodist preacher."

In an especially highhanded move, under the President's orders, United States marshals entered every important telegraph office in the North and seized the originals of all telegrams sent, and copies of all telegrams received, in the previous twelve months. It can only be surmised that, in thus trampling civil liberties and the Bill of Rights, they were looking for evidence that some Northerners had been secretly conniving with the secessionists. Lincoln admitted that his various measures "were without any authority of law," but he believed that, by his actions, "the government was saved from overthrow."

The April days went by and still no more troops had come. One day Lincoln gazed out of a White House window and cried: "Why don't they come?" Visiting the officers and men of the Sixth Massachusetts, some of whom had been wounded in the battle of Baltimore, he sighed: "I don't believe there is any North. The [New York] Seventh Regiment is a myth. Rhode Island is not known in our geography any longer. You are the only Northern realities."

The next day, April 25, a train carrying the New York Seventh Regiment roared into Washington, ending the nerve-racking siege; and soon more regiments from the northeast arrived, to Lincoln's immense relief. They came via a roundabout route from Annapolis, devised by Benjamin F. Butler. This was the same bald, paunchy, cockeyed Massachusetts Democrat of the Breckinridge faction, who had voted for Jefferson Davis for President at the 1860 national convention, but he would soon become a Republican.

Butler became a brigadier general of the Massachusetts militia when Republican Governor John Andrew mobilized the troops in quick response to Lincoln's call. When the Sixth Massachusetts ran into the mob at Baltimore, and the railroad bridges were burned, Butler took his Eighth Massachusetts troops off their train at the head of Chesapeake Bay, seized a steamboat, and conveyed his men to Annapolis, where they landed despite the protests of Governor Hicks. Discovering that the railroad tracks between the Maryland capital and Washington had been ripped up, several mechanics and railroad workers in the ranks of the militia patched up the tracks and repaired a locomotive, thus successfully reopening the line into Washington.

"Washington is safe!" a delighted correspondent reported to the *Chicago Tribune*. "The fearful suspense and apprehension, by which all of the inhabitants, from the President down to the lowliest citizen laborer, have been oppressed, was ended by the safe arrival of the New York Seventh regiment and of the Massachusetts Fifth and Eighth, and the Rhode Island infantry under command of Governor Sprague."

Since the arrival of the Yankee reinforcements made their services no longer necessary, the volunteer White House guards led by Cassius Clay and Jim Lane called in a body and bade farewell to the President. They told him the Northern people demanded that he "crush out the Southern rebellion." Lincoln responded that if he had to choose between maintaining the government and "the liberties of the nation," on the one hand, and the shedding of fraternal blood on the other, "you need not be at a loss which course I will take."

They got the message: Lincoln chose to shed "fraternal blood."

Lincoln now faced a war against, not merely the seven states that originally had plunged into secession, but four more—Virginia, Tennessee, Arkansas, and North Carolina—which joined the Confederacy after his April proclamation calling for the seventy-five thousand troops to crush the rebellion. He also had to worry about a potential revolt in his own state of Illinois. Orville Browning recorded in his diary April 22:

"A scheme has been set on foot, about perfected by traitors in Southern Ills, in confederacy with other traitors in Missouri and Tennessee, to seize Cairo—cut off all the state South of the Ohio and Mississippi Railroad, erect it into a state and join the Southern Confederacy.

"To prevent the execution of so diabolical a plan, it was deemed advisable to anticipate them in the occupation of Cairo and it is now in possession of 1,200 or more of our troops under command of Col. Ben. Prentiss."

Southern Illinois, known as "Egypt" because of its principal town, Cairo, and its fertile lands along the rivers, was a hotbed of Democrats

who sympathized with the South and hated Republicans and abolitionists. Stephen A. Douglas, long a favorite with its voters, found
himself reviled by many as a traitor to his party for upholding Lincoln's
hand in the crisis after the fall of Fort Sumter. Many irate Democrats
could not understand how Douglas, after accusing the radical
Republicans of trying to push Lincoln into a civil war, could suddenly switch and join those same men in backing the President's policy
of armed force against the South. Congressman John Logan, a
typical critic, angrily told the Little Giant: "You have sold out the
Democratic party but, by God, you can't deliver it!"

Alarmed by the reports of pro-secession activity in Illinois,
Douglas hurried home and made a fiery speech to the legislature at
Springfield , calling for all factions to unite in defense of the flag and
the Union. To an applauding audience at Chicago, May 1, representing
all parties, he shouted: "There are but two sides to the question and
every man must be on the side of the United States or against it.
There can be none but patriots or traitors!"

With typical zeal and disregard for his failing health, Douglas
threw himself into a new campaign—this time rallying the people of
Illinois and the Northwest to support the war that he had labored so
hard to avert. Without his herculean efforts, his admirers said, there
could have been civil war in Illinois, "from Cairo north to the door-
steps of Springfield." Douglas, said one, put "five hundred thousand
men into the Union Army and fifty thousand from Illinois alone."

Douglas's exertions proved too much for his body, already weakened by his earlier campaigning and his drinking. He suffered a
severe attack of rheumatism, combined with a liver ailment and com-
plications, and he fell into bed at his hotel suite in Chicago, exhausted.
He had burned himself out.

Shortly after sunrise on the morning of June 3, Douglas cried
out, "Death! Death! Death!" Embracing him, his grief-stricken Adele
asked if he had any words for his two sons. "Tell them," he answered,
"to obey the laws and support the Constitution of the United States."

Four hours later, he died. He was forty-eight.

Orville Browning was appointed to his Senate seat.

Douglas, had he lived, could have had a military career. The *New
York Times* said the valiant warrior was about to don the uniform of a

major general in the Union army, "very properly tendered to him by the President." John W. Forney, in his *Anecdotes of Public Men*, wrote that "the sagacious Lincoln" would have given Douglas "one of the most important commands in the army."

The tragic irony of Douglas's doomed campaign for the presidency became apparent with his death. George Nicholas Sanders, who had been a close friend and thus knew about his weakened health, had feared that Douglas could not live through his term as president, if he had been elected. Sanders made precisely that point in offering second place on the Douglas ticket to—of all men—William Lowndes Yancey.

As this narrative has shown, Sanders's proposed deal with the Alabama firebrand—a last desperate attempt to prevent a Democratic party split and a Lincoln victory—fell through.

But suppose the quarreling Democrats had united on the Douglas-Yancey ticket and suppose, by some miracle, it had won. Then, with President Douglas's death in June 1861, Yancey would have become president of the United States!

29

Lincoln Holds Maryland with Iron Hand

Pro-Confederate feeling raged high in Maryland in the wake of the Baltimore riots. Governor Hicks called it "madness," and he feared the secessionists would exploit it to "strike while the iron was hot." They threatened to call the legislature into session on their own if Hicks still mulishly refused to do it.

"I will call it, and I will carry the state out of the Union," State Senator Coleman Yellott boasted. If the lawmakers had met in Baltimore, under that call, Hicks feared that "they would have passed resolutions of secession, and ... we should have been forced to go with the South."

"To avoid the utter ruin that would follow," the governor finally gave in and called the legislature—but he scheduled the session at Frederick, in the western, pro-Union section of Maryland, forty miles away from the passionate partisans at Baltimore. When Lincoln found out about it, he seriously considered arresting all the legislators to keep them from voting for secession. But, after consulting his cabinet, he decided it would not be a good idea to do that—not yet. He ordered General Scott to watch the lawmakers closely. General Scott thereupon informed General Butler:

"The General-in-chief has received from the President of the United States the following instructions respecting the Maryland legislature:

"It is left to the commanding general to watch and await their action, which, if it shall be to arm their people against the United States, he is to adopt the most prompt and efficient means to counteract—even, if necessary, to the bombardment of their cities, and in the extremest necessity suspension of the writ of habeas corpus."

Lincoln's threat to order "the bombardment of their cities" clearly was designed to have a chilling effect. He did not state what legal authority he claimed to have for bombarding the cities in a state that was still an integral part of the Union. He could not use the excuse that he had vowed to "hold, occupy and protect" federal property, for there was no one menacing Fort McHenry and no federal property was in danger when the legislature met in Frederick.

Lincoln simply was determined to keep his grip on Maryland by military force, whether he could find any constitutional warrant for it or not. To him, it was a simple matter of survival. He feared that he could not safely maintain his government in Washington, otherwise; he would have to take refuge in some city in the North. Lincoln ordered that the Marylanders be told that a vote to secede would be considered an incitement to take up arms against the United States, so he could claim that his harsh reaction would be in self-defense.

Governor Hicks, who had struggled grimly for months against the pressure for secession, told the legislature that the people of Maryland should stand "for Union and peace, and thus preserve our soil from being polluted with the blood of brethren." Taking his advice, and declining to give Lincoln an excuse for "the bombardment of their cities," the legislature voted against secession—unanimously in the State Senate and by 53 to 13 in the House. In an "Address to the People of Maryland," the Senate said it lacked authority to pass an act of secession, but a sovereign convention could be called to do so. No such convention was actually called in Maryland.

In the shadow of the Yankee guns, the Maryland legislators did not dare to vote for secession. Instead, they had to be content with fiery rhetoric. They said:

> Whereas, the war against the Confederate States is unconstitutional and repugnant to civilization, and will result in a bloody and shameful overthrow of our institutions; and, while recognizing the obligations of Maryland to the Union, we sympathize with the South in the struggle for their rights—for the sake of humanity, we are for peace and reconciliation, and solemnly protest against this war, and will take no part in it.
>
> Resolved, that Maryland implores the President, in the name of God, to cease this unholy war, at least until Congress assembles;

that Maryland desires and consents to the recognition of the independence of the Confederate States.

The military occupation of Maryland is unconstitutional and she protests against it, though the violent interference with the transit of Federal troops is discountenanced; that the vindication of her rights be left to time and that a convention, under existing circumstances, is inexpedient.

Still hoping that an all-out war might be averted, the Maryland lawmakers appointed delegations to meet separately with Presidents Lincoln and Davis, in a last-ditch effort for peace. In his reply, the Confederate president said his government "asserts in the most emphatic terms that its sincere and earnest desire is for peace ... peace with all nations and people."

Lincoln received the Maryland commissioners with formal politeness but no sign of conciliation. His troops were tightening their grip on the Maryland railroads and thousands of blue-coated soldiers were pouring into Washington for his defense against the Rebel attack, which, he feared, could come at any time.

The *New York Tribune* made Lincoln's policy perfectly clear: "Beyond the shadow of a doubt," it said, "the policy of the administration, now and henceforth, is war."

The three Maryland commissioners found out directly from Lincoln that his "aggressive measures" were aimed at conquering the South. The trio—Robert McLane, Otho Scott, and William J. Ross—reported back that "the Lincoln government now is abandoning its defensive policy and following a new policy of subjugating the seceding states by force."

"Honorable and true-hearted men," said McLane, "can never again support the administration of Mr. Lincoln, which has abandoned the defensive policy of maintaining the Federal capital." He called upon Governor Hicks to stand for Maryland and leave to Lincoln "only the ruffians and venal portion of our population." Hicks, however, spurned this warning. He pleased Lincoln by raising the four regiments of troops requested from Maryland for the Union army, thereby incurring a new wave of hatred and attacks by those who were frustrated in their efforts to pull Maryland into the Confederacy.

Typical was an editorial in *The South* regretting that the legislature had failed to impeach the governor for his "treason." "By his refusal to call the legislature together six months or even one month ago, he prevented the adoption of timely measures for the defense of the state," the pro-secessionist paper said.

"By his intrigues with the administration, he prepared the way for the military occupation of this city."

Again, *The South* aimed its shafts of ridicule at the hapless governor, saying: "'Old Caesar,' as his friends delight to call Governor Hicks—probably in honor of some dog—certainly not after the great Roman—appears to have a hard time of it generally. Like his canine prototype he gets nothing but kicks all around. Nobody believes him—everybody despises him—there are none sunk so low as to do him honor."

Angry secessionists also vented their hatred against the Blair family, which strongly influenced Lincoln in the direction of war. "Frank Blair says Maryland shall be a free state if every white man has to be destroyed," D. G. Duncan told Confederate Secretary of War Walker in a message from Richmond. Duncan also lamented that, "Maryland is crushed and lost to us, although her people are undoubtedly with us, simply because they cannot resist Federal power." The patriarch, Francis Preston Blair, Sr., according to one newspaper story, received a threat that his Maryland country home at Silver Spring would be burned down if he did not leave it immediately. "The plucky old gentleman ... at once removed his family to the city," the dispatch continued, "and prepared for a vigorous defense, by arming his servants to the teeth."

Blair's daughter, the former Elizabeth (Lizzie) Blair, was the sister of Postmaster General Montgomery Blair and the wife of Samuel Phillips Lee, a naval officer who would command the ships of the Union blockade against his native state, Virginia. Lee built the brick mansion adjoining the Blairs' townhouse on Pennsylvania Avenue, across from the White House.

The intensely pro-Southern wife of Philip Phillips, a former Alabama congressman who had remained in Washington to take care of his law practice, sent more news about the Blairs in a gossipy letter to her dear friend, the wife of former Senator Clement C. Clay, Jr., now back home in Alabama:

You would not know this God-forsaken city, our beautiful capital, with all its artistic wealth, desecrated, disgraced with Lincoln's low soldiery. ... There are thirty thousand troops here. Think of it! They go about the avenue insulting women and taking property without paying for it. ...

I was told that those *giant* intellects, the Blairs, are at the bottom of all this war policy. Old Blair's country place was threatened, and his family, including the fanatical Mrs. Lee, had to fly into the city. This lady was the one who said to me that "she wished the North to be deluged with the blood of the South ere Lincoln should yield one iota!"

Mrs. Phillips's open criticism of Lincoln and her advocacy of the South brought her much grief. She was arrested on trumped-up charges that she was a Confederate spy, and she suffered many months of brutal mistreatment in prison. The Lincoln administration's iron-fisted treatment of its critics frightened many of them into silence. The most militant Maryland secessionists, young enough for combat, went South and joined the Confederate army. The noisiest secessionists were thrown into jail.

General Butler, hailed as a hero for bringing his Massachusetts troops to lift the siege of Washington, scored another coup in Baltimore. He seized the Relay House, southwest of the city, a key junction point where the railroad to Washington from the north met the Baltimore & Ohio's main track from the west. From the Relay House, on May 13, Butler marched the men of the Sixth Massachusetts back into Baltimore, whence they had been driven by the rock-throwing mob on April 19. This time the troops were unhurt and they did not kill any more civilians, for there was no angry mob, only docile citizens. The soldiers seized the fortified Federal Hill, with its commanding view of the harbor and the downtown business district—an ideal site for emplacing a cannon aimed at the heart of Baltimore. Butler showed that Lincoln had not been telling another funny joke when he ordered the possible "bombardment" of Maryland cities.

General Scott, who had not personally authorized Butler's coup, sent him a stinging rebuke, saying "it is a godsend that it is without conflict of arms." Butler was relieved of his command May 15, and transferred to Fortress Monroe in Virginia. His successor at Baltimore,

Major General George Cadwalader, soon became involved in the notorious case of John Merryman, which challenged Lincoln's power to throw opponents into prison without trial.

Merryman, a leader of the Baltimore County Horse Guards, was accused of "treason" for his part in burning the railroad bridges after the Baltimore riots. At two o'clock in the morning of May 25, federal troops broke into Merryman's home near Cockeyville, aroused him from his bed, and hauled him off to Fort McHenry. This is the famous Baltimore fort where the Stars and Stripes waved all night during the British attack in 1814 and inspired Francis Scott Key to write "The Star-Spangled Banner."

Merryman's arrest stirred up a storm of outrage among the people of Baltimore, who denounced it as illegal. Chief Justice Roger B. Taney, a Marylander presiding over the circuit, issued a writ of habeas corpus and commanded General Cadwalader to appear before him, bringing "the body of John Merryman."

Cadwalader refused, saying that President Lincoln had authorized him to suspend the writ in cases of "treason." Taney cited the general for contempt and ordered the U.S. marshal to bring him into court. But the marshal, sent to serve an attachment on the army officer, found himself blocked by soldiers.

In a crowded Baltimore courtroom on May 28, the chief justice read his opinion, to become famous as *Ex parte Merryman*. He charged that Lincoln had usurped the power of Congress by suspending the writ of habeas corpus and had violated the Constitution, which guarantees the accused the right of a speedy public trial by an impartial jury and to have compulsory process for obtaining witnesses in his favor. In an even worse violation of the Constitution, the chief justice charged, a military officer had accused the defendant of "treason" without evidence and had thrown him into prison without a hearing, to be locked up indefinitely.

The President, Taney said, "does not faithfully execute the laws if he takes upon himself the legislative power by suspending the writ of habeas corpus and the judicial power also, by arresting and imprisoning a person without due process of law." Taney said he knew that he, himself, was in danger of being imprisoned by the Lincoln administration. The abolitionists hated him for his Dred Scott decision. Lincoln did not go so far as to arrest the aged jurist, but he refused to free Merryman. Finally, on July 13, after seven weeks of illegal detention in Fort McHenry, Merryman was freed on bail following a grand jury indictment. He was never brought to trial.

Former President Franklin Pierce, who abhorred Lincoln's war as unnecessary, sent the chief justice a letter warmly praising his actions in the Merryman case. Taney replied, on June 12:

> The paroxysm of passion into which the country has suddenly been thrown appears to me to amount almost to delirium.
>
> I hope that it is too violent to last long, and that calmer and more sober thoughts will soon take its place, and that the North, as well as the South, will see that a peaceful separation with free institutions in each section, is far better than the union of all the present states under a military government, and a reign of terror preceded too by a civil war with all its horrors, and which, end as it may, will prove ruinous to the victors as well as the vanquished.
>
> But at present I grieve to say passion and hate sway everything before them.

Many more Maryland men, including Baltimore officials and prominent businessmen, would be thrown into prison to languish there for months without trial, even though their state never joined the Confederacy. Governor Hicks, after being elevated to the United States Senate, said he approved of the arrests and the suspension of the writ of habeas corpus.

"I believe that arrests, and arrests alone, saved the state of Maryland not only from greater degradation than she suffered, but everlasting destruction," Hicks later told the Senate. He only regretted that the Lincoln administration "let some of these men out."

"If the President had had forty of these men hung, I would have voted for exonerating him," Hicks declared.

Incidentally, Coleman Yellott, the state senator who had led the drive to go over the governor's head and call the legislature into session for a vote in favor of secession, later wound up in a madhouse, Hicks said. "If a great many more of these rebels were to be confined in madhouses, it would not surprise me," he said. "I think they are all mad, anyway."

Lincoln told Congress that the Constitution provided for the writ of habeas corpus to be suspended in cases of "rebellion or invasion" and the government had decided that "we have a case of rebellion and that the public safety does require" suspensions. Although Taney maintained that the Constitution intended that only Congress had the right of suspension, Lincoln contended that he could do it, too, so he did.

"Are all the laws, but one, to go unexecuted and the government itself go to pieces lest that one be violated?" he asked. Would the government really have "gone to pieces" if Merryman and other accused men had not been imprisoned? Lincoln implied that it would. The President's claim showed how desperately he feared that the government was falling apart around him when he resorted to obviously illegal acts in an effort to save it. His critics, however, could logically ask how he could "preserve, protect and defend" the Constitution by repeatedly violating it.

Isaac Toucey, Buchanan's secretary of the navy, condemned the long list of extralegal actions that Lincoln took in "carrying on, without authority, the most disastrous war this country was ever engaged in." Toucey, an able constitutional lawyer, former U.S. attorney general, U.S. senator, and governor of Connecticut, blistered Lincoln verbally with a series of questions in a letter to Buchanan. He asked:

> What right has a Prest. of the U.S. to enlist for three years an army of 100 to 150,000 men without the authority of Congress?
>
> What right has he to blockade half our ports & to suspend our commercial treaties with England, France & the other countries? ...
>
> What right has he to seize the city of Alexandria & occupy it by force which he had no authority to enlist, to arrest citizens for alleged offences against the laws & shut them up in camp, proclaim martial law & suspend the Habeas Corpus?
>
> What right has he, by the order of the Atty. Gen., to invade the sanctity of private correspondence & seize summarily and simultaneously the private papers of all the Northern telegraphic offices?
>
> What right has he to plunge the country unto a hundred millions of debt to be followed immediately by an immensely larger one?

Toucey's questions amounted to an indictment of Lincoln on charges of "atrocious usurpations" worthy of impeachment.

Lincoln's plea that he had to break the laws in order to save the government from "ruin" could not provide a satisfactory answer. Nor was it totally convincing for him to say that he had to do arbitrary things out of "military necessity." Claiming "military necessity" was the excuse of tyrants throughout history, his critics said. They branded Lincoln a "tyrant," a "usurper," and worse, but he ruled ruthlessly, all the time saying that events had ruled him. He did not say, with the French monarch, "L'etat, c'est moi." But he wielded just as much power.

When Congress convened on the Fourth of July, in response to his call, Lincoln sought ex post facto approval of the actions he had taken in the previous months—all necessary, he said, to save the nation from crumbling to pieces. Everyone knew that the Constitution gave Congress alone the power to raise armies, appropriate money, and wage war. The President had done all these things, and more; but since he called them essential to crush the Southern "insurrection," the lawmakers had no choice but to give him their stamp of approval.

In his message to Congress, Lincoln said that, if he had given up Fort Sumter out of military necessity, it would have been misunderstood as voluntary, and therefore would have been "ruinous ... our national destruction consummated." So he told again the familiar story of his attempt to send some "bread to the few brave and hungry men of the garrison" who were there "to preserve the Union from actual, and immediate, dissolution." By bombarding and reducing the fort, he charged, "the assailants of the Government began the conflict of arms. They have forced upon the country the distinct issue: 'Immediate dissolution or blood.'"

This issue, he said, was far larger: "It presents to the whole family of man, the question whether a constitutional republic, or democracy— a government of the people, by the same people—can, or cannot, maintain its territorial integrity against its own domestic foes." So, he argued, "no choice was left but to call out the war power of the Government; and so to resist force, employed for its destruction, by force for its preservation." Lincoln's powerful argument—a foretaste of his Gettysburg Address—thus elevated the contest to an enormous significance, involving, in his view, "an end to free government on the earth."

This was his answer to Jefferson Davis's charge that Lincoln's call for seventy-five thousand troops was "a plain declaration of war." Davis, in addressing the Confederate Congress, had ridiculed the idea that the Union army was really just a "posse comitatus" to enforce the orders of federal courts being flouted by the "combinations" of the five million people making up the states of the new republic. Lincoln's intention "to invade our soil, capture our forts, blockade our ports and wage war against us," Davis said, made it necessary for the Confederacy to raise an army of one hundred thousand men, or more. "We protest solemnly," he said, "in the face of mankind, that we desire peace at any sacrifice except that of honor and independence; we seek no conquest, no aggrandizement, no concession of any kind. ... all we ask is to be let alone."

Lincoln was "incorrect," Davis said, years later, in asserting that the Confederates used force "for the destruction of the Government of the United States." "On the contrary," he said, "we wished to leave it alone. Our separation did not involve its destruction. To such fiction was Mr. Lincoln compelled to resort to give even apparent justice to his case." Also fictitious, Davis said, was Lincoln's claim that the Confederates were engaged in an insurrection.

Even if there had been an insurrection, Davis argued, the President could not lawfully have used military force against another state, because that was making war, and the U. S. Constitution gave Congress alone the "power to declare war" and "to raise and support armies."

Lincoln astutely got around that inconvenient problem by winning Congress's approval of all the things he had done, outside the law, while he was running the government entirely on his own for nearly four months before the special session began. "These measures, whether strictly legal or not, were ventured upon, under what appeared to be a popular demand, and a public necessity," Lincoln stated, "trusting, then as now, that Congress would readily ratify them."

Lincoln had no trouble winning everything he asked from the members of Congress. Their constituents, intoxicated by visions of quick and easy victory, with glory for every gallant soldier, were calling for an early offensive to smash the Confederacy in its new capital at Richmond. In the glorious days of early July 1861, with most of the people in the North clamoring for war, their President called upon Congress to give him "the legal means for making this contest a short and a decisive one." He asked for 400,000 men; Congress gave him 500,000; he asked for $400 million, he received $500 million.

Orville Browning, in his new role as Douglas's successor in the Senate, spent two and a half hours with Lincoln on July 8, and found him eager for a quick victory: "He is for the most vigorous and active measures to bring the war to a speedy close, and totally opposed to any compromise of any kind or character. We also discussed the negro question and agreed upon this as upon other things, that the government neither should nor would send back into bondage such as came into our armies, but that we could not have them in camp, and that they must take care of themselves till the war is over, and then colonize & c." Lincoln then favored colonizing many blacks by sending them to Africa or Central America.

Amid the clamor for war, however, there were a few men calling for peace. Congressman Clement L. Vallandigham said Lincoln had followed a mistaken policy "which has precipitated us into a terrible and bloody revolution."

"He has totally and wholly underestimated the magnitude and character of the revolution," the Ohio Democrat said, "or surely he never would have ventured upon the wicked and hazardous experiment of calling thirty millions of people to arms among themselves, without the counsel and authority of Congress."

The secession of Virginia, North Carolina, Tennessee, and Arkansas, after his call for the seventy-five thousand troops, waked up the President and his advisers to the frightening realization that they had aroused "the slumbering demon of civil war," Vallandigham said. "I am for *peace*—speedy, immediate, honorable *peace* with all its blessings. Others may have changed; I have not."

In the Senate, James Asheton Bayard, Jr., presented a stinging indictment of Lincoln for plunging into a civil war after the fall of Fort Sumter without making a single move toward conciliation and peace. Bayard, a figure of dignity with brown, curly hair and a superior intellect, commanded respect as the heir to a distinguished family. His father had been a senator; his son and grandson would also become senators; the clan traced its ancestry back to the famed Chevalier Bayard.

Although Lincoln claimed that he was forced to fight to keep the United States government from crumbling to ruin, the Delaware Democrat said the withdrawal of the seven Gulf States really "did not subvert the Government but left us a great and powerful nation." Bayard called for peaceful separation as preferable to "the greatest curse ... civil war." He had warned that coercion would drive other states into the Confederacy, and that prophecy had proved correct; now it had eleven states. Bayard said he would cheerfully have made "any sacrifice ... of property or even life itself," to restore the Union. But the passions of the nation had become excited, and the cry now was "unconditional submission and the crushing out of rebellion, without the first step having been taken for the purpose of conciliation. ... Even a servile insurrection is threatened." With great emotion, the Delaware Senator further said:

"When I think of the blood that must flow in this contest, this unnatural contest, of the devastation that must ensue, of the human lives that must be sacrificed, a shudder runs through my frame and my heart sickens with despair. I am for peace, and armistice and negotiation ... I would, by compromise, restore ... the Union if possible." If not, he said, he would part with the seceding states in peace.

Bayard aimed his sharpest shafts against Lincoln's suspension of the writ of habeas corpus at his own discretion, and Congress's decision not only approving his extralegal acts but giving him carte blanche to keep on throwing Americans into prison without warrant, or evidence, on the whim of some official or army officer, with no hope of early trial or release.

As Bayard had expected, the Republican majority in both houses of Congress rode roughshod over all opposition and gave Lincoln all the power he demanded to win the war, by any means, at any cost. "Our president is now dictator, imperator, what you will," Senator Sumner told Dr. Francis Lieber of Columbia College on September 17. But the Massachusetts Republican complained that Lincoln was not yet using his "power of a god" to free all the slaves by invoking martial law. Eventually, though, Sumner and the other "iron-backs" would pull the President over to their side, and he would issue the Emancipation Proclamation as a military measure to weaken the South and thus hasten the triumph of the cause of freedom.

EPILOGUE

Lincoln called himself a man of peace; then why did he turn his back on peace and make no move for conciliation to avert a bloody war? Historians have been puzzling over this question for many years, ever since objective scholars began rejecting the popular nineteenth-century panegyrics that depicted the war as a wicked plot by the "Slave Power," and Lincoln as the savior divinely anointed to restore the Union and free the slaves.

One explanation lies in Lincoln's iron determination to enforce the federal laws in all the states, including those that claimed they had seceded. With such a mind-set, viewing the Union as some mystical being that even preceded the states, he followed the old Federalist doctrine of Alexander Hamilton while quoting Thomas Jefferson's Declaration of Independence.

Lincoln also aspired to show the strength and firmness of George Washington and Andrew Jackson. Repeatedly, as this narrative has shown, he evinced a morbid dread of appearing weak, timid, or cowardly, and he feared that he would look that way if he even made a conciliatory speech. He would not give those "bad men" any concessions; he would show them he was the boss.

In fact, however, Lincoln was not really as decisive as he wished to appear. He knew that sending any ships to resupply or to reinforce Fort Sumter would inevitably result in armed conflict. General Scott told him so; every member of his cabinet, except one, warned him against it; statesmen from the upper South pleaded with him to refrain from any form of "coercion" that would cause the Unionists in their states to be overrun by the secessionists.

The evidence indicates that General Scott and Secretary Seward, with the backing of nearly all the cabinet, had persuaded him by March

11 to give up Fort Sumter on the grounds of "military necessity." Major Anderson wanted to go, if he could honorably leave without a fight. Even Republican newspapers went along with the explanation that evacuation was unavoidable, and it was all the fault of Buchanan and the Democrats. Lincoln dreaded the war that would ensue from coercion; he worried himself sick over it.

Then came the tidal wave of outrage from Northern governors, Republicans in Congress, and party leaders in the provinces, all demanding that the fort must be held, even at the cost of war. Then the Blairs, father and son, grimly warned him that it would be "treason" to give up Sumter. Lincoln buckled under all these angry demands, and took the easy way out by sending the fleet with "bread" for the hungry troops.

His plan turned out to be a master stroke, worthy of a man who played a strictly defensive game of chess. Lincoln knew that, if he let Major Anderson and his men leave the fort because they had run out of food, the administration would have looked weak and even heartless. Poor old Buchanan hadn't given up Sumter, so how could the brave new president be so weak?

If the Confederates could be finagled into forcing the surrender of the fort, then they could be accused of firing the first shot. The Northern people would become enraged against the Southerners and intoxicated with patriotic fervor, and furious enough to cry for war. That is exactly what happened, as Lincoln reassured Captain Fox in his consoling letter; Sumter fell, and thereby did more good than expected.

Now Lincoln had an overwhelming majority of the Northern people waving flags and calling for a war to crush the "rebellion." In July 1861, he was assembling the largest army ever seen in the United States, to attack the Confederates in northern Virginia, to win one glorious victory and then "On to Richmond!" to crush the Rebel regime there. Lincoln could not imagine that it would take four years of mass slaughter to achieve that goal, at a cost of six hundred thousand lives.

The appalling loss of life, and the monetary cost, of the Civil War would far exceed the toll of the Mexican war, which freshman Congressman Lincoln blamed on President Polk. Lincoln charged in 1847–1848 that the earlier conflict had been "unnecessarily and unconstitutionally begun" by the Democratic president, who had expected an easy triumph. As the war dragged on, according to the young House member, Polk was sorely troubled by feeling that "the blood of this war, like the blood of Abel, is crying from the ground against him."

Lincoln even insinuated that Polk's war guilt was driving him insane: "His mind, taxed beyond its power, is running hither and thither, like an ant on a hot stove." Now, in the summer of 1861, Lincoln occupied Polk's old office in the White House; he could not know that the time would come when the ocean of blood, spilled unnecessarily in the brothers' war, would drive his own mind to the verge of despair.

Congress, almost unanimously, in July 1861, passed a resolution declaring that the war was waged "to defend and maintain the supremacy of the Constitution and to preserve the Union," and not to interfere with slavery or to subjugate the South. But as the carnage ground on, the war aims of the North were changed to unconditional surrender and the abolition of slavery.

Lincoln employed his great powers, not to restore the old Union of the states, but to create an entirely new nation, with more authority concentrated in the federal government and a new economic order dominated by the great industries and financial institutions of the North.

Historians no longer agree with the old thesis that the Civil War was "inevitable" or an "irrepressible conflict." It could have been averted if Lincoln, instead of viewing secession as an illegal affront to his right to rule the entire United States, had simply left the seven Cotton States alone for the first several months of his administration.

He would never, of course, recognize the Confederacy as a separate republic. But a policy of quiet forbearance, and of conversations with the Union leaders in the South, could have reassured the other slave states that it was safe for them to remain in the old Union. Thus the Confederacy would have been restricted to the original seven states. They might have prospered in their isolation for a while, but not indefinitely. They were too weak to survive without Virginia and the rest of the upper South. A little league of seven states, against a mighty nation of twenty-seven states, would have faced a hopeless contest over a long period of time, so the new republic could hardly have maintained its independence forever.

Slavery would have remained for a long time in the Deep South, where it formed the basis of the economy and the social order. But it was already on the way out in Delaware, Maryland, Missouri, east Tennessee, and western Virginia. Undoubtedly, the Civil War hastened the end of slavery, but at a tremendous price. Gradual emancipation, through political and economic pressures and the force of world opinion, could have succeeded in attaining that most desirable goal in time; and if the Civil War had been avoided, six hundred thousand Americans would not have had their lives cut short, a needless sacrifice to political stupidity and pride.

NOTES

ABBREVIATIONS

CWL   *The Collected Works of Abraham Lincoln*, Roy Basler, ed., New Brunswick, N.J.: Rutgers University Press, 1953.

DAB   *The Dictionary of American Biography*. Allen Johnson and Dumas Malone, eds., New York: Charles Scribner's Sons, 1936.

LC   Library of Congress.

OR   U.S. War Department. *The War of the Rebellion: A Compilation of the Official Records of the Union and Confederate Armies*. 128 vols. Washington, D.C.: Government Printing Office, 1880–1901.

ORN   U.S. Naval Records Office. *Official Records of the Union and Confederate Navies in the War of the Rebellion*. 31 Vols. Washington, D.C.: Government Printing Office, 1894–1922.

Chapter 1

1   Descriptions of Lincoln: William H. Herndon and Jesse W. Weik: *Abraham Lincoln: The True Story of a Great Life*, New York: D. Appleton and Co., 1892. New edition edited by Paul Angle, Cleveland: World Publishing Co., 1949. Also, *A Short Life of Abraham Lincoln*, by John G. Nicolay, New York: The Century Co., 1902; and *The Lincoln Nobody Knows*, by Richard N. Current, New York: McGraw-Hill Book Co. Inc., 1958, pp. 1–6. "His eyebrows cropped out": *Lincoln*, by David Herbert Donald, New York: Simon & Schuster, 1995, p. 115.

1   Lincoln's storytelling at the Capitol: Carl Sandburg, *Abraham Lincoln: The Prairie Years*, New York: Harcourt, Brace & World, 1926, I, pp. 356–357.

2   Lincoln's "spot" resolutions: *Congressional Globe*, Thirtieth Congress, First Session, December 22, 1847, p. 64.

2   House approval of Whig measure declaring the Mexican war "unnecessarily and unconstitutionally begun by the President of the United States": Ibid., January 3, 1848. Roll call, p. 95.

3   Lincoln's speech, blaming Polk for "the blood of this war": Ibid., January 12, 1848, pp. 154–156.

3   "Ant on a hot stove": Lincoln Papers, LC. The printed version in the *Globe* was changed to "a man on a hot shovel." See also *The Collected Works of Abraham Lincoln*, Roy Basler, ed., New Brunswick, N.J.: Rutgers University Press, 1953, (hereafter, *CWL*) I, pp. 139–142.

3   Lincoln-Herndon letters about the Mexican War: CWL., I, pp. 446–452.

4   "Died of Spotted Fever": Benjamin P. Thomas, *Abraham Lincoln: A Biography*, New York: Alfred A. Knopf, 1952, p. 120.

4   "Ranchero Spotty of one term": Donald W. Riddle, *Congressman Abraham Lincoln*, Urbana: University of Illinois Press, 1957, pp. 35–39.

4   Lincoln's depression: Dwight G. Anderson, *Abraham Lincoln, the Quest for Immortality*, New York: Alfred A. Knopf, 1982, pp. 110–112. Albert J. Beveridge, *Abraham Lincoln, 1809–1858*, Boston: Houghton Mifflin, 1928, I, p. 493.

5   Lincoln's defeat for the Senate in 1855: Thomas, pp. 154–155.

5–6   Lincoln's meeting with Henry Villard in the railroad freight car: *The Lincoln Reader*, Paul M. Angle, ed., New Brunswick, N.J.: Rutgers University Press, 1947, p. 255.

6   "Just think of such a sucker." Ibid.

6   "Though I now sink out of sight and shall be forgotten": Lincoln to Anson G. Henry, Springfield, Ill., Nov. 19, 1858. CWL, III, p. 339.

7   "I am absolutely without money": Lincoln to Norman B. Judd, November 16, 1858. CWL, III, p. 337.

7   Lincoln's conversations with Jesse W. Fell: Thomas, pp. 194–195.

7   "I must, in candor, say": Lincoln to Thomas J. Pickett, Springfield, Ill., April 16, 1859. CWL, III, p. 377.

8   "There is not much of it": CWL, III, pp. 511–512.

8–9   Noah Brooks's eyewitness account of Lincoln's Cooper Union speech: Noah Brooks, *Abraham Lincoln and the Downfall of American Slavery*. New York: G. P. Putnam's Sons, 1894, pp. 185–189. Text of speech: CWL, III, pp. 522–550; *New York Tribune*, February 28, 1860.

9   "The taste *is* in my mouth a little": Lincoln to Lyman Trumbull, April 29, 1860. CWL, IV, pp. 45–46.

10   "I think the Illinois delegation": Lincoln to Richard N. Corwine, May 2, 1860. CWL, IV, pp. 47–48.

10   "If I have any chance": Lincoln to Samuel Galloway, CWL, IV, p. 434.

10   "Abraham Lincoln, the Rail Candidate": Richard J. Oglesby's account of the Illinois Republicans' 1860 convention. CWL, IV, pp. 48–49.

Chapter 2

13   "Tonight, there was a jolly time at the ranche": *New York Herald*, April 17, 1860.

13   "Much of the Douglas fever is the result of poor whiskey": Ibid., April 16, 1860.

14   Douglas "held their hearts in his hand": Sen. Jacob Collamer, Vermont Republican, in tribute after Douglas's death. *Congressional Globe*, Thirty-seventh Congress, First Session, July 9, 1861, p. 29.

14   "There are at least fifty runners": *Washington Evening Star*, April 11, 1860.

15–16   "Their arms thrown about his neck": Andrew Johnson to David Patterson, Greeneville, Tenn., from Washington, April 4, 1852: Andrew Johnson Papers, LC. Also, *The Papers of Andrew Johnson*, Leroy P. Graf and Ralph W. Haskins, eds., Knoxville: University of Tennessee Press, 1970, vol. II, pp. 30–31.

18   "Nothing but money": Anna J. Sanders's Journal, August 2, 1855, George Nicholas Sanders Papers, LC. For Sanders's profile, see DAB, XVI, pp. 334–335.

18   "Mr. Sanders feels that it is a crisis": Anna J. Sanders's Journal, May 31, 1856, LC.

19   "Today Mr. Sanders triumphed": Ibid., June 5, 1856.

19   "His father generaled the first men": Ibid., November 17, 1856.

20   Buchanan and "his wife": Aaron V. Brown to Mrs. James K. Polk, January 14, 1844. Polk Papers, LC. Quoted by Elbert B. Smith, *Francis Preston Blair*, New York: The Free Press, 1980, p. 238.

20–21 "That damned old wry-necked": Benjamin Brown French, *Witness to the Young Republic: A Yankee's Journal*, Donald B. Cole and John J. McDonough, eds., Hanover, N.H., and London: University Press of New England, 1989, p. 329.

21   "That poor, almost imbecilic man!": Maria Lydig Daly in her *Diary of a Union Lady*, Harold Earl Hammond, ed., New York: Funk & Wagnalls, 1962, p. 7.

21   "Mr. Buchanan was ... very malicious": Sen. Thomas Lanier Clingman in *Selections from the Speeches and Writings of Hon. Thomas L. Clingman of North Carolina*. Raleigh N.C.: J. Nichols, 1877, p. 508.

21   "He likes to have people deceived": Sen. Douglas in *Mystery of "A Public Man"* by Frank Maloy Anderson, Minneapolis: University of Minnesota Press, 1948, p. 197.

21   "By God, sir, I made Mr. James Buchanan": Sen. Douglas quoted in George Fort Milton, *The Eve of Conflict: Stephen A. Douglas and the Needless War*, Boston and New York: Houghton Mifflin, 1934, p. 273.

21   Sanders's offer of the Kansas governorship to Robert J. Walker: George Nicholas Sanders Papers, LC, March 17, 1857.

22   "I will denounce it": Milton, p. 273.

22   "General Jackson is dead": Ibid., p. 273.

23   "Douglas will be laid up in lavender": *New York Herald*, April 21, 1860.

23–24 "The old fogies in the Senate": Sen. Robert Toombs to Alexander H. Stephens, December 26, 1859, in Ulrich B. Phillips, ed., *The Correspondence of Robert Toombs, Alexander H. Stephens, and Howell Cobb*, annual report, American Historical Association, 1911, vol. II, pp. 451–452. Also March 16, 1860, pp. 464–465.

24   "This clique first began its operations": *New York Herald*, April 21, 1860.

24   Slidell as a "matchless wire-worker": Murat Halstead, *Caucuses of 1860*, Columbus, Ohio: Follett, Foster & Co., 1860, p. 7. Also, the *New York Tribune*, April 14, 1860, called Slidell "the cogitating brain and the animating soul" of the anti-Douglas cabal.

24   "An infamous lie": *Washington Evening Star*, April 24, 1860. Also, the *New York Tribune*, April 23, 1860, said: "Messrs. Slidell, Bright, and Banker Corcoran have gone to Charleston, determined to defeat Mr. Douglas, if money will do it."

Chapter 3

25   "Great portly fellows": Halstead, p. 6.

25–26 "Imagine a crowded barroom": *New York Herald*, April 23, 1860.

26   "With a proper appreciation": *New York Tribune*, April 23, 1860.

27   "Stop Douglas" men in the King Street mansion: Halstead, pp. 11–13; *New York Tribune*, April 25, 1860.

27   "I court and defy": Sen. Bright to Allen Hamilton, December 1858, Allen Hamilton Papers, Indiana State Library, Indianapolis.

28   Slidell's early life: Burton J. Hendrick, *Statesmen of the Lost Cause*, Boston: Little, Brown & Co., 1939. p. 286.

28   "Build up and consolidate": Slidell to Buchanan in Louis M. Sears, *John Slidell*, Durham, N.C.: Duke University Press, 1925, p. 151.

29   "The candidate of the pothouse politicians": *New York Herald*, April 23, 1860.

29   "Hunkers": George Stimpson, *A Book About American Politics*, New York: Harper and Brothers, 1952, p. 149.

30   Profile of Dean Richmond: De Alva Alexander, *A Political History of the State of New York*, 4 vols., New York: H. Holt and Co., 1906, reissued in 1969, vol. II, pp. 271–272. Also, *New York Times*, April 27, 1860, and DAB, XV, pp. 582–583.

30   "Dean Richmond is as potent at Albany": *New York Herald*, May 31, 1860.

30   "As a politician": De Alva Alexander, II, p. 271.

30–31   Syracuse convention riot: Ibid., II, pp. 257–258.

31   Daniel S. Dickinson profile: *New York Times*, March 17, 1859, and July 4, 1860. *New York Herald*, April 11, 1860. De Alva Alexander, II, pp. 256–257.

31   "We've got that damned fool": *New York Herald*, April 11, 1860.

32   "We've got to start, first, to toss that damned smart fellow": *New York Herald*, April 25, 1860.

32   "Richmond had the delegation in his pocket": Ibid.

32   Profiles of Richardson, Logan, and McClernand. Halstead, pp. 9 and 20.

33   "The hell hounds are on my back": Douglas to Linder, Usher F. Linder, *Reminiscences of the Early Bench and Bar of Illinois*, Chicago: The Chicago Legal News Company, 1879, p. 78.

33   "Tittlebat Titmouse": *New York Herald*, April 17, 1860.

33   "Came here like a gang of wolves": Alfred Huger to William Porcher Miles, May 7, 1860. Miles Papers, Southern Historical Collections, University of North Carolina.

34   "Now, then, you may depend upon it": *New York Herald*, April 21, 1860.

34   "Douglas dodge": Halstead, p. 25.

34   "Dysentery and diarrhea": *Washington Evening Star*, April 25, 1860.

35   W. W. Avery's speech: *New York Herald* and *New York Tribune*, April 28, 1860. John Witherspoon Du Bose, *The Life of William Lowndes Yancey*, Birmingham: Roberts and Son, 1892, p. 456.

35   "We never will recede from that doctrine, sir": *New York Times*, April 28, 1860. Robert W. Johannsen, *Stephen A. Douglas*, New York: Oxford University Press, 1973, p. 754; Halstead, pp. 45–46.

36   "Hi-hi's and cock crows": *New York Times*, April 28, 1860.

36   "Yancey burst into tears": *New York Herald*, April 28, 1860.

36   "Ours is the property invaded": Allan Nevins, *The Emergence of Lincoln*, New York: Charles Scribner's Sons, 1950, vol. II, p. 217.

36   "Gentlemen of the South": Halstead, pp. 49–50; Johannsen, p. 754.

37   George Nicholas Sanders's telegram to Buchanan: *Washington Evening Star*, April 28, 1860; *New York Times*, May 9, 1860.

37   "Mr. Slidell, who is an imperious man": Ibid., April 28, 1860.

37   "Cochrane denounced Richmond": *New York Herald*, May 1, 1860.

37–38   "Richmond retorted with curses": Ibid.

38   "What the hell do we care about the South?": Ibid.

38   "Lightning might strike": Senator Hammond to M.C.M. Hammond, March 9, 1860, and Hammond to Simms, April 18, 1860, Hammond Papers, LC. Quoted by Johannsen, p. 754.

38   "The vice-presidency has been held out as bait": *New York Tribune*, April 20, 1860.

38 "Slidell & Co.": Halstead, p. 69.

39 "Wears a Southern aspect": Ibid., p. 62.

39 Spitting from the galleries: Ibid., p. 62.

39 Yancey "smiling as a bridegroom": Ibid., p. 70.

39 "round, bald head": Ibid., p. 72.

39 "the very citadel and heart": Ibid., p. 66.

40 "His face pale as ashes": Ibid., p. 73.

40 "The pen of the historian is nibbed": Ibid., p. 75.

40 Sen. Bayard's charge of New York double-cross: *New York Times* and *New York Tribune*, May 2, 1860.

40 "In God's name": Milton, p. 444.

40 "Clods falling on Douglas' coffin": De Alva Alexander, II, p. 278.

41 "Knocked into the middle of next week": *Washington Evening Star*, May 3, 1860.

41 "Guthrie would be a very strong candidate": *New York Times*, May 2, 1860. "New York was ready to take Mr. Guthrie": *New York Tribune*, May 2, 1860. "But some Southerners opposed Guthrie, a personal enemy of Slidell": De Alva Alexander, II, p. 276.

41 "Caleb Cushing and Jefferson Davis": *New York Herald*, May 2, 1860.

42 "The Douglas men were caught in a trap": *Washington Evening Star*, May 1, 1860.

42 "The Douglas leaders feared": *New York Herald*, May 2, 1860. "The New England delegations are preparing to abandon him": *New York Tribune*, May 2, 1860.

43 "Bloodhounds after his life," Senator Latham's interview with Douglas: Edgar Eugene Robinson, ed., "The Day Journal of Milton Latham," *Quarterly of the California Historical Society* XI: p. 18.

43 "Bite a pin in two": Halstead, p. 102.

43 Delegate G. A. Henry's remarks: *New York Times*, May 11, 1860.

43 "Even burnt brandy wouldn't save me now": *New York Times*, May 11, 1860; Halstead, p. 117.

Chapter 4

44 "How are you, hoss?" Halstead, p. 140. Gin cocktails: Ibid., p. 122.

47 Jesse K. Dubois's telegram to Lincoln from Chicago, May 13, 1860: *The Lincoln Papers*, David C. Mearns, editor, Garden City, N.Y.: Doubleday & Co., 1948, I, p. 233.

47–48 N. M. Knapp's telegram to Lincoln, May 14, 1860: Ibid., p. 234.

48 Telegrams to Lincoln from Davis and Dubois, May 15, 1860: Ibid., p. 235.

48 "We're going to have Indiana for Old Abe, sure!": James Monaghan, *The Man Who Elected Lincoln*, Indianapolis: The Bobbs-Merrill Company, 1956, p. 162.

49 "I authorize no bargain": Lincoln to Davis, Henry C. Whitney, *Lincoln the Citizen*, vol. I of *A Life of Lincoln*, New York: The Baker and Taylor Company, 1908, p. 289; see also Benjamin P. Thomas, *Abraham Lincoln: A Biography*, New York: Alfred A. Knopf, 1952, p. 210.

49 "Make no contracts that will bind me": CWL, IV, p. 50; Herndon and Weik, pp. 373–374; William E. Baringer, *A House Dividing: Lincoln as President-Elect*, Springfield, Ill.: The Abraham Lincoln Association, 1945, p. 24.

49 "Lincoln ain't here": Monaghan, p. 168; Whitney, p. 289; Thomas, p. 210.

49   "Am very hopeful": Davis to Lincoln, May 17, 1860: Mearns, I, p. 236.

50   "Damned if we haven't got them": Monaghan, pp. 168–169, relaying a story attributed to Joe Medill.

51   D. K. Cartter's speech: Halstead, p. 149.

51   Congratulatory telegrams to Lincoln: Mearns, I, p. 237; Thomas, p. 214.

51   "They have gambled on me all around": O. J. Hollister, *Life of Schuyler Colfax*, New York: Funk & Wagnalls, 1886, p. 147.

52   "Don't come here for God's sake": Davis to Lincoln, Lincoln Papers, LC.

52   "The lines upon his face": Angle, ed., pp. 278–280.

52   "Lincoln was known as 'Old Abe'": *New York Herald*, May 19 and 22, 1860.

52   "I knew Hamlin twenty years ago": Ibid.

53   "Vulgar village politician": Ibid., May 30, 1860.

53   "We deem it highly important": Mearns, I, p. 261.

53   Rep. Horace Maynard's speech about polyglot Republican factions, united beneath a blanket of "African wool," February 6, 1861: *Congressional Globe*, Thirty-sixth Congress, Second session, Appendix, pp. 164–165.

Chapter 5

54   Douglas managers' delight over Lincoln's nomination: Milton, p. 458.

54   "The mist of the morning": Jefferson Davis's speech, May 7, 1860. *Congressional Globe*, Thirty-sixth Congress, First session, p. 1939.

54–55   Douglas's debate with Davis, May 16–19, 1860: Ibid., pp. 2143–2156; also Appendix, pp. 309–313.

55   Sen. Benjamin's denunciation of Douglas, May 22, 1860: Ibid., pp. 2233–2241.

56   "The friends of the plucky little man": *New York Herald*, June 2, 1860.

56   Ellen Douglas' death: Johannsen, p. 767.

56   Douglas's avowal of friendship with Yancey, "We are old personal friends": *Congressional Globe*, Thirty-sixth Congress, First Session, Appendix, p. 304.

57   "This visit set all sorts of rumors afloat": *New York Times*, June 19, 1860.

57–59   The detailed account of George Nicholas Sanders's offer to Yancey, of second place on the Douglas ticket, is in John Witherspoon Du Bose's biography of Yancey.

59   Comment on the offer to Yancey: Dwight L. Dumond, *The Secession Movement, 1860–61*. New York: The Macmillan Company, 1931, pp. 75–76.

59–60   Presidential boom for Horatio Seymour: See his biography, *Horatio Seymour of New York*, by Stewart Mitchell, New York: Da Capo Press, 1970. Also see De Alva Alexander, II, pp. 299–300, and *New York Tribune*, June 20–21, 1860.

59   "To destroy the United States because of slavery": Mitchell, p. 206.

60   "Genial and fascinating": *New York Herald*, June 4, 1859.

60   "Considering the effect of Seward's humiliation": *New York Herald*, May 29, 1860. "We get this information": Ibid.

60   "The Regency in the New York delegation is split": *New York Herald*, June 20, 1860.

61   "This is my stand point": Ibid.

61   Republicans say "Pooh! Pooh!": *New York Herald*, June 3, 1860.

62   Four factions in New York delegation: *New York Times*, June 22, 1860.

62   Dickinson "dropped like a hot poker": Ibid., June 19, 1860.

62   Years later, John Cochrane: Mitchell, p. 213.

62   "All during his life": Ibid., p. 158.

62   "It is now concluded": *New York Herald*, June 19, 1860.

62–63 "The united New England and Southern delegations": *New York Times*, June 22, 1860.

63   "To lift Seymour out of the mire": *New York Herald*, June 22, 1860.

63   "A two-man contest between": Mitchell, p. 212

63   "Just how much blood": Ibid., p. 229.

Chapter 6

64   For an account of the Democrats' breakup at Baltimore, see *The Disruption of American Democracy*, by Roy Franklin Nichols, New York: The Macmillan Company, 1948, pp. 306–322. See also Halstead, pp. 159–230.

64   "Mr. Whiteley of Delaware": *New York Herald*, June 19, 1860.

64   "the days of the demoralized Democratic party": Ibid.

64   "The worst temper prevails": Strong, June 21, 1860, III, p. 35.

65   "To break down the oligarchy of the Senate": Ibid., June 19, 1860.

65–66 Douglas's withdrawal letter: Milton, p. 473; *New York Times*, June 23, 1860.

66   He "stood up, straight as a ramrod": *New York Times*, June 23, 1860.

68   "told her the governor would be ruined": J. Henly Smith to Alexander Stephens, Stephens Papers, LC.

68   Fitzpatrick's withdrawal: *Philadelphia Press*, June 25, 1860.

68   Yancey's tale of Herschel V. Johnson's selection for the vice-presidency is in a Memphis speech August 14, 1860, printed in the *New York Times*, August 21, 1860.

68   "Would carry the whole South": Smith to Stephens, August 18, 1860. Stephens Papers, LC.

68–69 Jefferson Davis's proposal for three candidates to withdraw and unite to beat Lincoln: Jefferson Davis, *The Rise and Fall of the Confederate Government*, New York: Thomas Yoseloff, 1958, I, p. 52; also *Breckinridge: Statesman, Soldier, Symbol*, by William C. Davis, Baton Rouge and London: Louisiana State University Press, 1974, pp. 225–226.

69   "The Albany Regency has slaughtered Dickinson. ... Like harlots, they glory in their shame": *New York Herald*, June 27, 1860.

69   Buchanan's "cold and clammy nature": *New York Times*, June 25, 1860.

69   Buchanan fires Sanders: *New York Times*, June 28, 1860.

69   Sanders strikes back: Ibid., July 31, 1860.

69   "He is fighting a political ghost": Ibid.

69–70 Buchanan snubs New York's Mayor Wood: *New York Times*, June 30, 1860.

70   Dickinson's attack on Dean Richmond: Ibid., July 19, 1860.

71   "Every Fillmore paper in the Northwest": Ibid, July 9, 1860.

71   Congressman Covode's corruption charges: Ibid., June 27, 1860. "Douglas is so short he can't split rails": Ibid.

72   Republicans' song ridiculing Douglas: *Congressional Globe*, Thirty-sixth Congress, First Session, June 19, 1860, Appendix, p. 462.

72–73 Congressman Isaac Morris's doggerel in reply: Ibid., pp. 461–468.

73   "He had the biggest mouth": *New York Times*, October 4, 1860.

73 "Today, it looks as if": Lincoln to Dr. A. G. Henry, July 4, 1860. CWL, IV, p. 82.

Chapter 7

74 Douglas' claim that he could have beaten Lincoln in every state except Vermont and Massachusetts is in his Baltimore speech September 6, 1860, in the *New York Times*, September 7, 1860.

74 "Madness and folly": Stephens to S. J. Anderson, New York, from Crawfordville, Ga., July 1, 1860; in OR, series II, vol. 2, p. 606.

74 "Anyone who has got sense enough": Stephens to J. Henly Smith, Washington, D.C., from Crawfordville, Ga., July 2, 1860, Stephens Papers, LC. Also, Toombs, II, p. 484.

74–75 "It can only be": Dickinson speech at Baltimore, August 2, 1860, in the *New York Times*, August 4, 1860.

75 "Old Dean Richmond rolls round": Ibid., August 17, 1860.

75 Douglas's trip to Vermont: Ibid., August 2, 1860.

76–77 "He cares nothing about his own personal success": *New York Times*, August 16, 1860.

78 "The Patriotic National Union Democracy": *Louisville Journal*, quoted in the *New York Times*, August 14, 1860.

78–79 Douglas's remarks at Norfolk: *New York Herald*, August 27, 1860; *New York Times*, August 29, 1860.

79 "I tell them, No, never on earth!": *New York Times*, August 29, 1860.

79 "He was roughly dressed": Ibid., September 5, 1860.

79 "This man calls himself a Democrat!": *Charleston Mercury*, quoted in the *New York Times*, September 7, 1860.

79 "It is the culmination of his treachery": *Natchez Mississippian*, quoted by the *New York Times*, September 12, 1860.

79 *Richmond Enquirer* letter printed in the *New York Times*, September 12, 1860.

79–80 Douglas, a "traveling mountebank": Isaac Stevens in the *New York Times*, August 17, 1860.

80 "grand political carnival and ox roast": Ibid., September 13, 1860.

80 "There's plenty of rope in New York": Ibid.

80–81 "A BOY LOST!" handbill: Johannsen, p. 781.

81 Douglas finds his mother: *New York Times*, September 17, 1860.

82 Artemus Ward in the *Cleveland Plain Dealer*, reprinted in Emerson David Fite, *The Presidential Campaign of 1860*, New York: The Macmillan Company, 1911, pp. 207–209.

83 "Mr. Lincoln is the next President": Sen. Henry Wilson in *The History of the Rise and Fall of the Slave Power in America*, Boston: J. R. Osgood and Company, 1872–1877, vol. II, pp. 699–700. Also Milton, p. 496, and Johannsen, p. 798.

83–85 "Wide Awake" parade: *New York Times*, October 4, 1860.

Chapter 8

86 Southern newspapers' despair after Republicans' victories in October elections: *New York Times*, October 17, 1860.

86 "Abe Lincoln must be our next President": Ibid.

86 "We believe now that the Union will be dissolved": Ibid.

86 "If a financial pressure": Ibid.

86   Texas plots: Ibid., August 4, 1860. Antiabolition violence in Southern states: Ibid., September 4, 1860.

87–88   Congressman Reagan's speech confirming Texas town burnings: *Congressional Globe*, Thirty-sixth Congress, Second Session, January 15, 1861, pp. 391–395.

88   "the incendiary torch": Orr's comments, *New York Times*, September 20, 1860.

88   Hamlin is a "mulatto" charge: Strong, III, p. 139, May 3, 1861. Congressman Emerson Etheridge's speech, January 23, 1861: *Congressional Globe*, Thirty-sixth Congress, Second Session, Appendix, vol. III.

88   South Carolina Minutemen: *Charleston Mercury*, reprinted in the *New York Times*, October 18, 1860. Also *New York Herald*, November 5, 1860.

88   "restless and idle vagabonds": *New York Times*, September 22, 1860.

89   John Minor Botts's speech: Ibid., October 2, 1860.

89   "Gov. Wise and his co-workers": Ibid., September 28, 1860.

89–90   Douglas's charge of proposed coup to place Breckinridge in the White House: Browning *The Diary of Orville H. Browning*, I, 1860–1864, edited by Theodore Calvin Pease and James G. Randall, Springfield, Ill.: The Trustees of the Illinois State Historical Library, 1927, p. 466, entry of April 26, 1861. Browning wrote:

"Douglas told me that prior to the Nov. election a deliberate contract was entered into between Buchanan, Davis, Floyd, Toombs and others, that, if they could carry all the slave states & Oregon & California for Breckinridge, that Buchanan should hand the government, army, navy, and all over to him, that he should be inaugurated—seize upon the government and complete the revolution by deposing Lincoln, or rather by preventing his inauguration. Douglas says he *knows* this to be a *fact.*"

John W. Forney in his *Anecdotes of Public Men*, (New York: Harper and Brothers, 1970, reprint of the 1873 edition) on p. 226, quoted Douglas as saying in May 1861: "If the Disunion candidate in the late presidential contest had carried the united South, their scheme was ... to seize the capital ... and, by a united South and a divided North, hold it. Their scheme was defeated in the defeat of the Disunion candidate in several of the Southern states."

90   Douglas's report of the same plot to Charles Francis Adams: Allan Nevins, *The Emergence of Lincoln*, New York: Charles Scribner's Sons, 1950, II, p. 293.

91   "The plan of the seceders": *Philadelphia Press*, reprinted in the *New York Times*, November 1, 1860.

91   Scheme in the Treasury Department, "Treason at Washington": *Louisville Journal*, reprinted in the *New York Times*, October 18, 1860. Further details, Ibid., October 26 and 31 and November 2, 1860.

92   Stock market slump: Strong, October 24, 1860, III, p. 54.

92   Washington Hunt's plea for Sen. Crittenden to aid New York fusion effort, September 3, 1860; Crittenden Papers, LC. Hunt profile: De Alva Alexander, II, pp. 326–327.

92   "By God, sir, the election shall never go into the House": Douglas to Rep. Edward McPherson of Pennsylvania, *New York Weekly Tribune*, October 20, 1860. Nevins, *Emergence of Lincoln*, II, p. 285.

On October 17, 1860, the *New York Times* printed the following item:

MR. DOUGLAS WILLING TO GIVE
THE ELECTION TO MR. LINCOLN

The Raleigh, N.C., *Standard* publishes the following note. The writer is
a nephew of Ex-Chief Justice Lewis of Philadelphia:

Philadelphia, July 23, 1860
Dear Sir: Your favor has been placed in my hands. The words of
Judge Douglas, as nearly as I can at this moment recall them, as repeated
to me by the honorable gentlemen I have named, were as follows:
"By God, sir, the election shall never go into the House. Before it
shall go into the House, I will throw it to Lincoln." The words thus used
were accompanied by a violent gesture, and perhaps an additional oath.
I am very truly yours,
Alfred E. Lewis.

93 "Every year the Southerners": *New York Times*, September 6, 1860.

93 "They are reduced": Ibid., October 25, 1860.

93 "Did you ever see an old hen": Ibid., October 30, 1860.

93–94 Don Piatt's comments about Lincoln: Angle, ed., pp. 198–300.

94 Douglas in Alabama: Milton, pp. 498–500; Johannsen, pp. 800–803.

94–95 Lincoln on election day: Angle, ed., pp. 292–294. Also David Herbert
Donald, *Lincoln*, New York: Simon & Schuster, 1995, pp. 255–256.

96 August Belmont's letter to John Forsyth: *New York Times*, January 10,
1861.

97 Sen. George Pugh: "I do not believe": *Congressional Globe*, Thirty-sixth
Congress, Second Session, December 10, 1860, p. 51.

97 Francis Granger, "seventy-five thousand good Old Line Whigs": Lucius
E. Chittenden, *Report of the Debates and Proceedings of the Secret Sessions of
the Conference Convention for Proposing Amendments to the Constitution of
the United States*, New York: D. Appleton and Company, 1864, pp. 120–
125.

Further evidence that the Republicans' victories in 1860 did not
amount to the voters' solid endorsement of the party's antislavery platform can be found in this *New York Times* editorial, October 12, 1860,
interpreting the Republicans' success in the October elections as a sure
sign of Lincoln's coming triumph:

The Slavery question has *much less* to do with this
canvass and its probable result than is generally supposed.
Indeed, so far as Pennsylvania and portions of this state are
concerned, we have serious doubts whether it is not an
element of weakness rather than strength. ...

There is a very wide and effective, though vague,
distrust of Republicans in the public mind. ... The truth is
that the people have become utterly disgusted with Democratic sway, on general principles. It has become selfish,
narrow, meanly partisan and utterly and hopelessly corrupt.

The people have become thoroughly convinced that the
country needs a change, and we have very little doubt that
the change would have taken place quite as certainly if the
subject of Slavery had never been introduced.

Chapter 9

99 "Lincoln elected. Hooray!": Strong, III, p. 60, November 7, 1860.

99 "I thought Magrath": Sen. Hammond to Marcellus Hammond, November 12, 1860. Hammond Papers, LC.

99 Buchanan "pledged to secession": Milton, p. 506; *New York Times*, November 14, 1860.

100 Buchanan's cabinet meeting on November 9, 1860: *New York Times*, November 10, 1860; Milton, p. 507.

100 "My associates considered me 'too slow'": Davis, I, pp. 58–59.

101 Judge Woodward's letter to Atty. Gen. Black, November 18, 1860: Black Papers, LC, quoted by Milton, p. 505.

101 Horace Greeley's editorial proposing that the seceding states "go in peace": *New York Tribune*, November 9, 1860.

101 "I would rather be at the bottom of the Potomac": Floyd's account of his interview with President Buchanan appeared in a speech given by the former secretary at Richmond and published in the *New York Herald*, January 17, 1861.

101–102 "South Carolina will certainly secede": Senator Hammond's letter to a committee of Georgians, November 21, 1860, published in the *New York Times*, December 1, 1860.

102 "the mortal dread of negro insurrection": Ibid.

102 Alabama plot for slave uprising: Ibid., January 12, 1861.

102 "I *knew* he was a *damned* Yankee!": Ibid., December 1, 1860.

102 "The negroes have already heard of Lincoln's election": Ibid. See also *New York Tribune* dispatch, December 28, 1860, in *Chicago Tribune*, January 7, 1861.

103 Ex-Senator Clemens's letter to Crittenden, November 24, 1860: Crittenden Papers, LC.

104 "Will you be the tail to the chivalry kite?": *Raleigh Standard*, November 24, 1860.

105 The "thirty million dollar men": J. S. Pike in *New York Tribune* dispatch February 21, 1859.

105 Congressman Perry's exposé of Democrats' expansionist foreign policies, May 29, 1860: *Congressional Globe*, Thirty-sixth Congress, First Session, Appendix, pp. 380–384.

107 "The secession movement is founded": *Louisville Democrat* editorial, reprinted in the *New York Times*, November 27, 1860.

Chapter 10

108 Many newsmen's accounts of Lincoln at Springfield after his election appeared in the *New York Herald*, *Tribune*, and *Times*, the *Chicago Tribune*, and other newspapers in November and December 1860. Henry Villard provided some of the best in the *Herald*, starting with his November 11 dispatch.

See also Angle, ed., pp. 295–304.

108 "These are men with rough clothes": *New York Times*, November 15, 1860.

109 Lincoln's cautious chess game: Ibid.

109 "in no probable event": Lincoln to John B. Fry of New York, August 15, 1860, CWL, IV, p. 96.

109 "I should have no objection": Lincoln to George T. M. Davis, October 27, 1860, CWL, IV, pp. 132–133.

110   "The Union is at the mercy of the President": Gen. Winfield Scott to Sen. Crittenden, November 12, 1860, Crittenden Papers, LC.

110   "I am rather glad of this military preparation in the South": Lincoln to Sen. Lyman Trumbull, November 20, 1860, CWL, IV, pp. 141–142.

110   "consummate folly": David M. Potter, *Lincoln and His Party in the Secession Crisis*, New Haven, Conn.: Yale University Press, 1942, p. 141.

111   Lincoln's disappointment over reaction to Trumbull's speech: Letter to Henry J. Raymond, November 28, 1860, CWL, IV, pp. 145–146.

111   "gentleman who talked with him": *Chicago Tribune*, November 21, 1860.

112   "We must not deceive ourselves": Thurlow Weed, *Albany Evening Journal*, November 30, 1860, quoted by Greeley, I, pp. 360–361.

112–113   Buchanan's message: *Congressional Globe*, Thirty-sixth Congress, Second Session, December 3, 1860, Appendix, pp. 1–7.

113   "The message shows conclusively": Milton, p. 508.

113   "eccentricities": *New York Times*, December 5, 1860.

113–114   Senator Clingman's speech: *Congressional Globe*, Thirty-sixth Congress, Second Session, December 4, 1860, pp. 3–5.

114   Lincoln "known to be a dangerous man": Ibid., p. 3.

114   Southerners "must submit": Sen. Hale, Ibid., p. 10.

114   "Where is this war to come from?": Sen. Brown, December 5, 1860, Ibid., p. 10.

114   "some Texas Brutus will arise": Sen. Iverson, December 5, 1860, Ibid., p. 11.

114   "I have no apprehension, sir": Sen. Wigfall, Ibid., p. 13.

115   "the greatest murderer": Sen. Lane: December 5, 1860, Ibid., p. 14.

115   "If Maryland secedes": Sen. Iverson, December 11, 1860, Ibid., p. 51.

115   "habitations of the bats and the owls": Ibid.

115   "there is no doubt about the eventual secession": *New York Times*, December 3, 1860.

115   "You cannot save this Union": Sen. Wigfall, *Congressional Globe*, Thirty-sixth Congress, Second Session, December 12, 1860, p. 71.

115   "Senators laugh in my face": Ibid., p. 72.

116   "I say that you shall not excite your citizens": Ibid., p. 73.

116   "The senator from New York may laugh on": Ibid., p. 85. Also, *New York Times*, December 13–14, 1860.

Chapter 11

117   Buchanan and the South Carolina congressmen: Edward A. Pollard, *The Lost Cause*, New York: E. B. Treat & Co., 1867, pp. 96–97. Pollard says Buchanan gave "a distinct and solemn pledge" not to change the status quo of the Charleston forts.

117   Buchanan would be "arraigned at our bar": Sen. Pugh, December 10, 1860. *Congressional Globe*, Thirty-sixth Congress, Second Session, p. 34.

117   Senator Hale's reply, "Buchanan is on his knees": Ibid.

118   Cobb's letter of December 6, 1860, published as a sixteen-page pamphlet. Text is in Toombs, II, pp. 505–516.

118   "There is nothing to *shell*": *Chicago Tribune*, January 4, 1861.

118   "Secretary Cass has left the scuttled Ship of State": *Congressional Globe*, Thirty-sixth Congress, Second Session, January 16, 1861, Appendix, p. 54.

119   Rumors of Buchanan's resignation: *New York Times*, December 4, 1860.

119   Stanton originally a "secession sympathizer": S. S. Cox, *Three Decades of Federal Legislation, 1855–1885*, Providence, R. I.: J. A. and R. A. Reid, Publishers, 1886, p. 200.

120   Rep. Dan Sickles blames Republicans for disunion: *Congressional Globe*, Thirty-sixth Congress, Second Session, December 10, 1860, pp. 40–41.

120   Rep. George S. Hawkins blames Lincoln: Ibid., p. 37.

120   "Let the sealed lips of the Medusa head at Springfield": Rep. Sickles, December 10, 1860, Ibid., p. 40.

120   "Let there be no compromise": Lincoln to Trumbull, December 10, 1860, CWL, IV, pp. 149–150.

121   "Entertain no proposition": Lincoln to Rep. William Kellogg, December 11, 1860, CWL, IV, p. 150.

121   "Prevent, as far as possible": Lincoln to Rep. E. B. Washburne, December 13, 1860, CWL, IV, p. 151.

121   "you judge from my speeches": Lincoln to Thurlow Weed, December 17, 1860, CWL, IV, p. 154.

122   "Does any man think": George Robertson to Crittenden, December 16, 1860, Crittenden Papers, LC.

122   "I feel perfectly confident": Horatio Seymour to Crittenden, from Buffalo, N.Y., January 18, 1861. In Ann Mary Butler Coleman, *John J. Crittenden*, 1970 edition, New York: Da Capo Press, II, pp. 254–255.

122   "I am satisfied": John Brodhead to Crittenden, January 1861, Crittenden Papers, LC.

123   "God save our country": Maj. Robert Anderson to Crittenden, January 12, 1861, Coleman, II, pp. 253–254.

124   "no prospect remains": Benjamin's letter, December 8, 1860, published in the *New Orleans Delta*, December 23, 1860. See Pierce Butler, *Judah P. Benjamin*, Philadelphia: G. W. Jacobs, 1907, pp. 203–204.

124   "All hope of relief": *Washington Constitution*, December 15, 1860.

124   "eight states are certain to secede": *New York Times*, December 14, 1860.

125   "I didn't know you had resigned": Dialogue between Jacob Thompson and Sen. Clingman is in *Selections from the Speeches and Writings of Hon. Thomas L. Clingman of North Carolina*, Raleigh, N.C.: J. Nichols, 1877, pp. 526–527.

126   "The President approves the visit": Mrs. Thompson to Mrs. Cobb, December 15, 1860. In Toombs, p. 523. "My heart goes *pit-a-pat*": Ibid., p. 524.

126   "If the President has not become imbecile": *New York Times*, December 17, 1860.

126   "You own the cabinet": Sen. Benjamin F. Wade, December 17, 1860, *Congressional Globe*, Thirty-sixth Congress, Second Session, pp. 99–104.

127   "A bevy of conspirators": Sen. Andrew Johnson's Senate speech, January 31, 1862, *Congressional Globe*, Thirty-seventh Congress, Second Session, pp. 584–589.

128   "Did I hear someone hiss?" Johnson speech at Nashville, Tenn., March 25, 1862, Johnson Papers, LC.

128   "Andrew Johnson was born and reared in this city": The Raleigh, N.C., *Confederate*, June 29, 1864.

128   "Prick louse": House of Representatives Report No. 104 on "The Assassination of President Lincoln." Thirty-ninth Congress, First Session, July 28, 1866, p. 34: "General Carroll, of Tennessee, when in Canada discussing the proposed assassination of Lincoln, insisted that Vice President Johnson also be killed, saying: "If the damned prick-louse is not killed by somebody, I'll kill him myself." *Webster's New International Dictionary*, unabridged, p. 1962: "'Prick-louse'—also 'prick-the-louse'—A tailor, so-called in contempt."

128–129   Andrew Johnson's Senate speech, December 19, 1860: *Congressional Globe*, Thirty-sixth Congress, Second Session, pp. 134–143.

129   Senator Lane's reply to Johnson: Ibid., pp. 142–145.

129   "I presume you have heard": George Fort Milton, *The Age of Hate: Andrew Johnson and the Radicals*, New York: Coward-McCann, Inc., 1930, p. 102.

130   "Sir, your strength has failed to satisfy the country": Johnson's speech at Nashville, and Breckinridge's replies, March 25, 1862, Johnson Papers, LC.

130–131   Buchanan at wedding reception, startled by the news of South Carolina's secession: Mrs. Roger Pryor, *Reminiscences of Peace and War*, New York: The Macmillan Company, 1905, pp. 110–113.

Chapter 12

132   "That termagant little South Carolina": Strong, III, p. 79, December 21, 1860.

132   "The Cotton States *are going*": Horace Greeley to Lincoln, December 22, 1860. Mearns, ed., II, pp. 349–350.

133   John Minor Botts's predictions: Botts, *The Great Rebellion: Its Secret History, Rise, Progress, and Disastrous Failure*, New York: Harper and Brothers, 1866, pp. 113–114 and 181–182.

133   "white-livered Black Republicans": Sen. Solomon Foot quoted by Chittenden in *Recollections of President Lincoln*, pp. 20–22.

133–134   a secret organization: Joseph Medill to Lincoln, December 26, 1860. Mearns, ed., II, pp. 355–357.

134   He thinks the Southern plan now is: Leonard Swett to Lincoln, December 31, 1860, Ibid., II, pp. 363–365.

135   "The White House is abandoned": Seward to his wife, December 31, 1860. Frederick W. Seward, *William H. Seward*, New York: Derby and Miller, 1891, II, pp. 488 and 497.

136   "Yours giving an account": Lincoln to Francis Preston Blair, Sr., December 21, 1860, CWL, IV, pp. 157–158.

137   "When the struggle was at its height": Sen. Bigler quoted by Cox, p. 80.

138   Lincoln's resolutions for Seward: CWL, IV, pp. 156–157.

138   Duff Green's mission: Philip Shriver Klein, *President James Buchanan*, University Park: University of Pennsylvania Press, 1962, pp. 385–386.

138   "our discreet friends": Lincoln to Trumbull, December 28, 1860, CWL, IV, p. 163.

138   "I do not desire any amendment": Lincoln to Duff Green, December 28, 1860, CWL, IV, pp. 162–163.

139   "We recommend to the people": Ibid.

139   Wigfall, "His face was not one to be forgotten": William Russell, *My Diary North and South*, New York: Harper and Brothers, 1863, vol. I, p. 155.

139   "His speech was half crazy": Daly, p. 8.

140   "He has a profusion of hair": *Philadelphia Bulletin* reprinted in the *Chicago Tribune*, March 14, 1861.

140   Anecdotes of Wigfall by his daughter, Mrs. D. Giraud Wright, in *A Southern Girl in '61*, New York: Doubleday Page, 1905, pp. 30–32.

141–142   Wigfall's plot to kidnap Buchanan: See *The Mystery of "A Public Man"* by Frank Maloy Anderson, Minneapolis: University of Minnesota, 1948. Text of original diary, pp. 197–198. See also Alvy L. King, *Louis T. Wigfall*,

Southern Fire-Eater, Baton Rouge: Louisiana State University Press, 1970, p. 105. Philip Klein, in his biography of Buchanan, accepts Wigfall's kidnapping plot as a fact. So does Ward Hill Lamon in his *Recollections of Abraham Lincoln, 1847–1865,* edited by his daughter, Dorothy Lamon Teillard, Washington, D.C.: privately published, 1911, pp. 264–265.

142 "This Bailey is a South Carolinian": *Chicago Weekly Tribune,* January 3, 1861. December 25, 1860, dispatch.

143 "Had Lincoln been defeated": Ibid.

Chapter 13

144 For the dramatic White House scene on December 27, 1860, see William Henry Trescot's eyewitness account, "Narrative and Letter," edited by Gaillard Hunt in the *American Historical Review* XIII, April 1908: pp. 528–556.

144 "Now, Mr. President, you are surrounded": Ibid., p. 544.

144 "My God!" cried Buchanan: Ibid., p. 544.

144–145 "emotions of rage and panic": George C. Gorham, *Life and Public Services of Edwin M. Stanton,* Boston: Houghton Mifflin, 1899, I, p. 135.

145 Black flourishes December 11 order to Anderson: Klein, p. 279.

145 Anderson had no "tangible evidence" of impending attack: Benjamin P. Thomas and Harold M. Hyman, *Stanton: The Life and Times of Lincoln's Secretary of War,* New York: Alfred A. Knopf, 1962, p. 95.

145 "the solemn pledge": Gorham, I, p. 136.

145 Stanton-Buchanan clash: "Oh, no! Not so bad as that!" Gorham, I, pp. 158–159.

146 "private gentlemen": Buchanan's reply to the South Carolina Commissioners, *Chicago Tribune,* January 10, 1861.

146 "determined to trust to your honor": Ibid.

146 "Mr. Barnwell, you are pressing me too importunately": Gorham, I, p. 143.

146 "No administration, much less this one": Nichols, p. 431. Also, Thomas and Hyman, p. 97.

146–147 The *Chicago Tribune's* account of two cabinet meetings: Issue of January 3, 1861.

147 "because I can no longer hold it," text of Floyd's letter to Buchanan resigning as secretary of war: Gorham, I, p. 155.

147 "The decent people of the city": *Chicago Tribune,* January 3, 1861.

148 "They are lawbreakers, traitors": Thomas and Hyman, p. 98.

148 "This I cannot do; this I will not do": *Congressional Globe,* Thirty-sixth Congress, Second Session, January 9, 1861, p. 288.

149 "Though he admitted the obligation," and "they will burn his house at Wheatland": Clingman, p. 528.

149 "President Buchanan has forfeited": Jefferson Davis to Gov. J. J. Pettus: Jefferson Davis, *Jefferson Davis, Constitutionalist: His Letters, Papers, and Speeches,* Dunbar Rowland, ed., Jackson: Mississippi Department of Archives and History, 1923, IV, p. 565.

149 "alternately praying and cursing": *Chicago Tribune,* February 4, 1861.

149–151 Sen. Benjamin's speech: *Congressional Globe,* Thirty-sixth Congress, Second Session, December 31, 1860, pp. 212–217.

151 Senate spectators' comments: *New York Times,* January 1, 1861.

Chapter 14

152–153   Text of South Carolinians' reply to Buchanan, January 1, 1861, is in the *Congressional Globe*, Thirty-sixth Congress, Second Session, January 9, 1861, pp. 288–289.

153   South Carolinians "packed up their duds": *Chicago Tribune*, January 4, 1861. The *New York Post*, January 4, 1861, said the commissioners considered Buchanan's statements "grossly insulting" and "a declaration of war."

153   "the President has ordered reinforcements": "Diary of a Public Man," January 1, 1861, p. 199 of Anderson.

153   Gen. Scott's note of December 30, 1860: OR, series I, vol. IV, p. 114.

154   "The meanest trick": Jacob Thompson to Howell Cobb, Washington, D.C., January 16, 1861, in Milton, p. 514. In Toombs, p. 532.

   Wigfall found out about it and telegraphed Gov. Pickens, January 8, 1861: "The Star of the West sailed from New York on Sunday with government troops and provisions. It is said her destination is Charleston. If so, she may be hourly expected off the harbor of Charleston." OR, series I, vol. I, p. 253.

154   "He convinced Holt": Thompson to Cobb, January 16, 1861, in Toombs, p. 532.

155   "Now you can guess what I think of the President's heart": Mrs. Kate Thompson to Mrs. Howell Cobb, Washington, D.C., January 13, 1861. Cobb Papers, University of Georgia.

155   "Another traitor has left the cabinet!": *Chicago Tribune*, January 12, 1861.

155   "snake in the grass": Ibid., January 17, 1861.

155   "It is to be presumed that in his prayers": Ibid., January 6, 1861.

156–157   Sen. Douglas's speech: *Congressional Globe*, Thirty-sixth Congress, Second Session, January 3, 1861, Appendix, p. 35 et. seq.

157   "Douglas' speech yesterday was infamous": Rep. E. B. Washburne to Lincoln, Washington, D.C., January 4, 1861; in Mearns, ed., II, pp. 378–379.

Chapter 15

158   Deep South senators' caucus, January 5, 1861: *New York Times*, January 7, 1861; *Chicago Tribune* and *Washington Evening Star*, both January 11, 1861. Sen. C. C. Clay, Jr.'s report to Alabama Gov. A. B. Moore, Washington, January 7, 1861, lists the resolutions. OR, series IV, vol. I, pp. 28–29. Sen. David Yulee's report to Florida authorities, OR, series I, vol. I, pp. 442–446.

159   "We are advancing rapidly": Jefferson Davis to E. De Leon. De Leon Papers, South Caroliniana Library, quoted by Nevins, *Emergence of Lincoln*, II, p. 398.

159   "Thousands of Bell men": Crittenden Papers, LC.

159   "ascertained": *Cincinnati Gazette* dispatch in *Chicago Tribune*, January 12, 1861.

160   Gov. Hicks's January 3, 1861, message to the people of Maryland: Text is in U.S. House of Representatives, *Report of the House Select Committee Investigating Alleged Hostile Organization Against the Government Within the District of Columbia*, Thirty-sixth Congress, Second Session, Report No. 79, February 14, 1861. Hicks's message, p. 100.

160   "Taunts were used, my personal safety was threatened": Ibid., Gov. Hicks's testimony before the select committee, Rep. W. A. Howard (R-Michigan) chairman, covers pp. 166–178 of its report.

161   "I know what they desired": Hicks's speech to U.S. Senate, February 28, 1863, *Congressional Globe*, Thirty-seventh Congress, Third Session, pp. 1371–1382. J.L.M. Curry's plea to Hicks as Alabama commissioner: OR, series IV, vol. I, pp. 38–42.

161–162   Judge A. H. Handy's remarks about pushing quick secession: See George L. P. Radcliffe, *Governor Thomas H. Hicks of Maryland and the Civil War*, Johns Hopkins University Studies of Historical and Political Science, series XIX, numbers 11 and 12, Baltimore: Johns Hopkins University Press, 1901, p. 26.

162   "The plans of the Secessionists are settled": Lord Lyons to Lord Russell, January 15, 1861. British Foreign Office, five, vol. 757, number 15, quoted in *Robert Barnwell Rhett, Father of Secession*, by Laura A. White, Gloucester, Mass.: P. Smith, 1965, p. 193.

162   Senator Hunter's speech for "reconstructing" the Union: *Congressional Globe*, Thirty-sixth Congress, Second Session, January 11, 1861, pp. 328–332. Also *Chicago Tribune*, January 16, 1861.

163   Congressman Garnett's speech: *Congressional Globe*, Thirty-sixth Congress, Second Session, January 16, 1861, pp. 411–416.

163   "We shall all be back here in two months": Sen. Benjamin to Judge Daly, February 4, 1861, in Daly, p. 6.

163–164   Gen. Scott learns secessionists' plans: Ibid., pp. 162–163.

164   Southerners expect to absorb some free states: *New York Times*, January 19, 1861.

164   Horace Greeley says Seymour and Gov. Price favor a new Confederacy: Greeley, 1, pp. 390–391.

164   Horatio King confirms Southerners' plans to take Washington: Horatio King, *Turning on the Light*, Philadelphia: J. B. Lippincott, 1895, pp. 27, 33, 34, 56, and 57.

164–165   Gov. Hicks's appeals to Sen. Crittenden: December 13, 1860, January 9, 19, and 25, 1861, Crittenden Papers, LC.

165   "The disunionists have despaired": *Chicago Tribune*, January 16, 1861.

165   "The next step ... is to deed it to the Southern Confederacy": Ibid.

165   "Maryland is to be forced into the disunion lines," and "We are sleeping upon the verge of a volcano": Congressman Morris's speech, January 16, 1861. *Congressional Globe*, Thirty-sixth Congress, Second Session, Appendix, p. 55.

Chapter 16

166   "We are out; we have bid adieu": ex-senator Jeremiah Clemens, January, 1861, Crittenden Papers, LC.

166–167   Sen. Seward's speech, January 12, 1861: *Congressional Globe*, Thirty-sixth Congress, Second Session, pp. 341–344.

167   "Let none be deceived": Sen. James M. Mason to Lewis E. Harvie, Richmond, Va., from Washington, January 13, 1861, OR, series I, vol. 51, part 2, p. 5. Confederate Correspondence.

167   Sen. Bragg's telegram: January 12, 1861, Ibid.

167   Sen. Toombs's speech, January 7, 1861: *Congressional Globe*, Thirty-sixth Congress, Second Session, pp. 267–271.

168   "Imagine a big, obese": *Chicago Tribune*, January 11, 1861.

168   "dragooned and bullied": The *Southern Confederacy*, Atlanta, a newspaper quoted in the *Chicago Tribune*, January 11, 1861.

169   Sen. Clark's amendment passed by the Senate, 25 to 23, January 16, 1861: *Congressional Globe*, Thirty-sixth Congress, Second Session, p. 409. *New York Times*, January 17, 1861.

169   "Why do you not vote?" Andrew Johnson's challenge to Benjamin: Johnson's speech at Nashville, March 25, 1862. He called Sen. Benjamin "a sneaking, Jewish, unconscionable traitor." See also Johnson's Senate speech, January 31, 1862, *Congressional Globe*, Thirty-seventh Congress, Second Session, p. 587.

James Ford Rhodes, in his *History of the United States from the Compromise of 1850 to the Restoration of Home Rule in the South in 1877*, New York: The Macmillan Company, 1909–1919, charged in vol. II, pp. 41–42, that the Republicans were chiefly to blame for blocking the Crittenden Compromise in the Senate Committee of Thirteen in December 1860.

Rhodes wrote: "No fact is clearer than that the Republicans in December defeated the Crittenden Compromise. Few historic probabilities have better evidence to support them than the one which asserts that the adoption of this measure would have prevented the secession of the Cotton States, other than South Carolina, and the beginning of the Civil War in 1861.

"It seems to be likewise clear that, of all the influences tending to the result, the influence of Lincoln was the most potent."

Senator George Pugh, retiring from the Senate, said this on March 2, 1861, for the sake of the historical record, about the defeat of the Crittenden amendment: "At any time before the first of January, a two-thirds vote for the Crittenden resolution in this chamber would have saved every state in the Union but South Carolina." Georgia and Louisiana, the Ohio Democrat said, would not have seceded—they "would have broken the whole column of secession." Source: *Congressional Globe*, Thirty-sixth Congress, Second Session, pp. 1390 and 1391.

169–170   "Could not this Union have been made permanent?": Cox, pp. 78–80.

170   Herschel V. Johnson "never felt so sad before": Percy S. Flippin, *Herschel V. Johnson, of Georgia, States Rights Unionist*, Richmond: Press of the Dietz Printing Co., 1931, p. 192.

170   "Women grew hysterical": Virginia Clay-Clopton, *A Belle of the Fifties*, New York: Doubleday, Page & Co., 1905, p. 147.

170   Sen. Mallory "wept as he spoke": *Chicago Tribune*, January 28, 1861.

171   "it seemed as if the blood within me congealed": Clay-Clopton, p. 147.

171   Jefferson Davis gazed "with the reluctant look": Mrs. Varina Howell Davis, *Jefferson Davis: A Memoir by His Wife*, New York: Freeport, N.Y., Books for Libraries Press, 1971, I, p. 697.

171   "We have piped and they would not dance": Davis to Clay, January 19, 1861, Clay-Clopton, p. 146.

171   "I have for many years advocated," January 21, 1861: *Congressional Globe*, Thirty-sixth Congress, Second Session, p. 487.

171   "Jefferson Davis has gone South": *New York Times*, January 23, 1861.

172   "The thread of the conspiracy": Washburne to Lincoln, January 13, 1861, Mearns, ed., II, pp. 401–402.

172   "It appears to be well understood": Washburne to Lincoln, January 4, 1861, Ibid., pp. 378–379.

172   "Things look more threatening": Washburne to Lincoln, January 10, 1861. Ibid., pp. 398–399.

172   "scandalous painting": Villard, p. 52.

172–173   Former Senator Ewing's meeting with General Scott: Ewing revealed this in a speech at Circleville, Ohio, November 3, 1864, urging Lincoln's reelection. The speech appeared in the *Cincinnati Commercial*. Ewing's biography is in DAB, vol. VI, pp. 237–238.

173   "My country extends from Maine": *New York Times*, January 3, 1861.

173–174   Gen. Scott's testimony before the Howard investigating committee: U.S. House of Representatives, p. 52 et seq.

174   Senator Foot on "the plot to seize the Capital": Chittenden, pp. 28 29.

174   "Our adversaries have us": Lincoln to Seward, January 3, 1861, CWL, IV, p. 170.

174   "Some proposed that it should be done": Secretary Thompson to the Howard Committee, pp. 87 and 88 of U.S. House of Representatives, *Report of the House Select Committee*.

174   "disaffected persons": Ibid., pp. 1–2.

175   "I have said that any man" and "A few drunken rowdies": Chittenden, p. 38.

Chapter 17

176   "Going through the city": Hicks's Senate speech, *Congressional Globe*, Thirty-seventh Congress, Third Session, February 28, 1863, p. 1372.

176   "If you send your sergeant-at-arms": U.S. House of Representatives, p. 151.

176   "Mississippi has seceded and gone to the devil": Radcliffe, p. 35.

176   "struck a melancholy blow": *New York Times*, January 21, 1861.

177   Virginia Congressman John S. Millson's Union speech: *Congressional Globe*, Thirty-sixth Congress, Second Session, January 21, 1861, Appendix, pp. 76–80.

177–178   Virginia Congressman Sherrod Clemens's antisecession speech and resulting House dispute: January 22 and 25, 1861, Ibid., Appendix, pp. 103–106. *Chicago Tribune* dispatch, January 23, 1861.

178   "if the North will do anything": *New York Times*, February 1861.

179   North Carolina Congressman John A. Gilmer's plea for peace, January 26, 1861: *Congressional Globe*, Thirty-sixth Congress, Second Session, pp. 580–583.

179   Tennessee Congressman Emerson Etheridge, "Sambo game," January 23, 1861: *Congressional Globe*, Thirty-sixth Congress, Second Session, Appendix, pp. 111–116.

180   Tennessee Congressman Horace Maynard, "Go to your Clerk's desk," February 6, 1861: Ibid., pp. 164–167. Maynard described: Cox, p. 73.

180–181   "Appeals from the Union men": Seward to Lincoln, January 27, 1861, in Mearns, ed., II, pp. 422–423.

181   Salmon P. Chase's letter to Lincoln: Ibid., pp. 424–425. The Springfield, Ill., *Journal*, January 29, 1861, printed an authorized declaration that Lincoln "stands immovably on the Chicago platform" of the Republican Party.

181–182   New York workingmen's anti-Lincoln rally: *New York Times*, January 16, 1861.

182–183   New York Democrats' peace assembly of January 31, 1861: *New York Times*, February 1, 1861.

183   Lincoln's tough talk to Browning is in Browning, I, p. 453.

184 *"there are very few submissionists"*. Richmond dispatch in *Chicago Tribune*, February 8, 1861.

184 "I am inflexible": Lincoln to Seward, February 1, 1861, CWL, IV, p. 183.

184 "We will welcome you with bloody hands": Carl Sandburg: *Abraham Lincoln: The War Years*, New York: Review of Reviews Corp., 1939, vol. I, p. 26.

184 "If the states are no more harmonious": Congressman Tom Corwin to Lincoln. Lincoln Papers, LC. Quoted in Nevins, *The Emergence of Lincoln*, II, p. 410.

184–185 "I will suffer death": *New York Herald*, January 28, 1861. CWL, IV, pp. 175–176.

185 Kellogg's compromise bill and McClernand's response: *Congressional Globe*, Thirty-sixth Congress, Second Session, February 8, 1861, Appendix, pp. 192–196.

185 Kellogg "has sold himself to the Slave Power": *Illinois State Journal*, reprinted in the *Chicago Tribune*, February 18, 1861.

185 Editorial attacks on Kellogg: *Chicago Tribune*, February 13, 16, 18, and 19, 1861.

186 Kellogg's assault on *Chicago Tribune* editor: Ibid., Feb. 18, 19, and 21, 1861.

186 Kellogg "a ruffian and a bully": *New York Tribune*, February 19, 1861, reprinted in *Chicago Tribune*, February 23, 1861.

186 "sucked egg", Sen. Sumner to F. W. Ballard, January 26, 1861: Edward L. Pierce, *Memoir and Letters of Charles Sumner*, New York: Arno Press, 1969 reprint edition, IV, p. 14.

Chapter 18

188 "The separation is perfect, complete and perpetual": *New York Times*, February 5, 1861.

188 "No stronger pair of men could have been selected": Nevins, *The Emergence of Lincoln*, II, p. 434.

However, Burton J. Hendrick, in *Statesmen of the Lost Cause*, p. 96, quoted Alexander Stephens as saying: "Had the Montgomery Convention really exercised a free choice, he insisted, it would have unanimously elevated Robert Toombs. That he was a far more attractive man than Davis, a far more brilliant orator, far more human, and probably abler as a statesman, most commentators agree."

189 "Why, that is the face of a corpse": Halstead, p. 103.

189 Thomas R. R. Cobb to his wife, February 4 and 15 and March 6, 1861, T.R.R. Cobb Correspondence, edited by A. R. Hull, the Southern Historical Society's papers, vol. XXVII, and Proceedings of the Southern History Association, vol. XI (1907), pp. 161, 166, 178, and 255.

189 "Our separation from the old Union is complete": Nevins, *The Emergence of Lincoln*, II, p. 435.

190 "The man and the hour have met": Shelby Foote, *The Civil War: A Narrative*, New York: Random House, 1958–1974, I, p. 17. Hudson Strode, *Jefferson Davis: American Patriot 1808–1861*, New York: Harcourt, Brace & Co., 1955, p. 407.

190 "We have entered upon the career of independence": Davis, *The Rise and Fall*, I, pp. 232–236, provides text of inaugural address. See also OR, series IV, vol. I, pp. 104–106; Strode, p. 410.

190 "The audience was large and brilliant": Davis to his wife, in Varina Howell Davis, II, pp. 32–33. Also Foote, I, p. 41, and Strode, p. 413.

191 "I found out yesterday why George Sanders was here": T.R.R. Cobb Correspondence. See also Bruce Catton, *The Coming Fury*, Garden City, N.Y.: Doubleday & Co., 1961, p. 256, for Sanders's lobbying at Montgomery for "reconstruction."

192 "we at the North have been the quiet and unsuspecting dupes": *New York Times*, February 5, 1861.

193 Sen. Slidell's farewell speech, February 4, 1861: *Congressional Globe*, Thirty-sixth Congress, Second Session, pp. 720–721.

193 "A senile executive": Sen. Benjamin's speech, February 4, 1861, Ibid., p. 722.

194 "There's another Jew!": Sen. Andrew Johnson to Rep. Charles Francis Adams: C. F. Adams, *Charles Francis Adams, 1835–1915: An Autobiography*, Boston and New York: Houghton Mifflin, 1916, pp. 94–95. Also Eli N. Evans, *Judah P. Benjamin, the Jewish Confederate*, New York: The Free Press, 1988, p. 306.

194 "The cotton states are out forever": Sen. William M. Gwin to Calhoun Benham, February 8, 1861, in OR, series II, vol. II, pp. 1009 and 1015. See also Lately Thomas, *Between Two Empires: The Life Story of California's First Senator, William McKendree Gwin*, Boston: Houghton Mifflin, 1969, pp. 232–233.

194 Blowing up the Capitol feared: *Chicago Tribune*, February 14, 1861.

195 "There were jeers": Chittenden, *Recollections of President Lincoln*, pp. 40–46.

195 Seizing Washington "was certainly on the conspirators' programme": Strong, III, p. 90.

Chapter 19

196 For press accounts of Lincoln's farewell speech at Springfield, see *New York Times*, *Chicago Tribune*, and other newspapers of February 12, 1861.

196 For text of Lincoln's remarks, see CWL, IV, pp. 190–191.

196 "We will pray for you": *New York Times*, February 12, 1861.

197 Lincoln's Indianapolis speech: CWL, IV, pp. 194–196.

197 "There is nothing going wrong": Ibid., pp. 205–206.

198 "There is no crisis": Ibid., pp. 208–215.

198 "twaddling puerilities": *New York Herald*, March 14, 1861.

198 Lincoln kisses Grace Bedell: CWL, IV, p. 218; *Philadelphia Inquirer*, February 20, 1861.

198 Mayor Wood's remarks: CWL, IV, pp. 232–233.

198 "put the foot down firmly": Ibid., p. 237.

199 For details of Lincoln's undercover trip to Washington to avoid assassination plot, see: Norma B. Cuthbert, ed., *Lincoln and the Baltimore Plot 1861*, San Marino, Calif.: Huntington Library, 1949. Also Forney, *Anecdotes of Public Men*, and Lamon, *Recollections of Abraham Lincoln, 1847–1865*.

199–200 Warning messages to Lincoln from Seward and Gen. Scott: Mearns, ed., II, pp. 441–443. Also Frederick W. Seward, *Reminiscences of a War-Time Statesman and Diplomat, 1830–1915*, New York: G. P. Putnam's Sons, 1916, pp. 134–139.

200–201 Chittenden's confirmation of the plot is in his *Recollections*, pp. 58–64.

201 Lincoln's speech at Independence Hall: CWL, IV, pp. 241–242.

201 "Abe, you can't play that on me": Cuthbert, p. 82.
202 "How the devil did he get through Baltimore?": Chittenden, *Recollections of President Lincoln*, p. 66.
202 "the moment the train arrived": *Chicago Tribune*, February 26, 1861.
202 Shouts by Baltimore crowd: *New York Times* and *Chicago Tribune*, February 26, 1861.
203 "Scotch plaid cap": *New York Times*, reprinted in the *Chicago Tribune*, February 26, 1861.
203 "Mr. Lincoln soon learned": Lamon, *Recollections of Abraham Lincoln*, pp. 46–47.
     Benjamin Brown French, chief marshal of Lincoln's inaugural parade, wrote in his own diary that General Scott said these were the assassins' aims: "That all who could act as President of the U.S. should be got out of the way, thus leaving the U.S. Govt. without any head, when the Southern Confederation was to step in and assume the Government of the whole country." French, p 343.
203 "His kindly eyes looked out": Chittenden, *Recollections of President Lincoln*, pp. 68–69.
203 & 205 Details of Lincoln's conversations with Peace Convention delegates: Ibid., pp. 68–78.
205–208 Former Kentucky Governor Charles S. Morehead detailed the spirited encounter between Lincoln and the Border State men in a letter to Sen. Crittenden, February 23, 1862, published in Mrs. A.M.B. Coleman's book, *John J. Crittenden*, New York: Da Capo Press, 1970 edition, II, pp. 336–338.
     "I took occasion to write down the entire conversation soon after it occurred," Morehead wrote. A longer account by Morehead appeared in the Liverpool, Ohio, *Mercury*, October 13, 1862, republished by David R. Barbee and Milledge L. Bonham, Jr., ed., "Fort Sumter Again," in *Mississippi Valley Historical Review* XXVIII (1941): pp. 63–73.
     In October, 1861, Lincoln, his secretary, John Hay, and others met at Seward's home one evening. Hay wrote in his diary that Lincoln spoke of a committee of "Southern pseudo-unionists" coming to him before the inauguration. Hay wrote: "He promised to evacuate Sumter if they would break up their convention, without any row or nonsense. They demurred." The diary of John Hay, October 22, 1861, in Tyler Dennett, ed., *Lincoln and the Civil War in the Diaries and Letters of John Hay*, New York: Da Capo Press, 1939, p. 30.
208 "A state for a fort is no bad business": See "Rudolf Mathias Schleiden and the Visit to Richmond April 25, 1861," by Ralph Haswell Lutz, *Annual Report of the American Historical Association for 1915*. Washington, D.C., 1917, pp. 210 et seq.
208 "you will have to make up for it in *war*": Ibid.
208 Francis Granger's impassioned warning against war is in Chittenden's account of the Peace Convention, Chittenden, *Recollections of President Lincoln*, pp. 121–125.
209 Tyler a "disunionist": *Chicago Tribune*, February 9, 1861.
209 "a bottle of gin" and "screaming brats with sugar": Ibid., February 16, 1861.
209 "Clay, the end has come": Clay-Clopton, p. 144.
209–210 A. R. Wright's report of his unsuccessful attempt to sell secession to Gov. Hicks: OR, series IV, vol. I, pp. 151–160.
210 "The General told him to stand firm": Daly, p. 163.

210 "Indeed, a formidable organization": Botts, quoting *Richmond Sentinel*, November 2, 1863, in his book, *The Great Rebellion*, pp. 113–114. "If the plot had succeeded," Botts wrote, "Lincoln would have been assassinated in 1861 instead of 1865."

Chapter 20

211 Profile of Seward: DAB, XVI, pp. 615–621.

212 Thurlow Weed's editorial calling for conciliation, and Senator King's rebuke: King to Weed, December 7, 1860, in Weed, *The Life of Thurlow Weed: Memoir*, edited by his grandson, Thurlow Weed Barnes, Boston: Houghton Mifflin, 1883–1884. p. 309.

212 Weed's Southern candidates for Lincoln's cabinet: Weed, *Autobiography of Thurlow Weed*, edited by his daughter, Harriet A. Weed, Boston: Houghton Mifflin, 1883, pp. 603–614. "White crows": Ibid., p. 606. Montgomery Blair "obnoxious": Ibid., p. 608.

213 Lincoln's letter to Gilmer, December 15, 1860: CWL, IV, pp. 151–153. See also Albert Shaw, *Abraham Lincoln: The Year of His Election*, New York: Review of Reviews Corporation, 1929, II, pp. 211–212.

214 "Since seeing you," Lincoln to Cameron January 3, 1861: CWL, IV, pp. 169–170.

214–215 Struggle over Cameron: Shaw, II, p. 215. McClure, pp. 134–154.

215 "I can't afford to let Seward take the first trick": John G. Nicolay and John Hay, *Abraham Lincoln: A History*, New York: The Century Co., 1890, III, pp. 370–371.

215 "I did not dare go home": William H. Seward, *The Works of William H. Seward*, Boston: Houghton Mifflin, 1884, II, p. 518.

216 Lincoln "intends to make war on the South," Rep. Garnett's speech: *New York Times*, February 26, 1861.

216 Clingman to James W. Osborne, February 18, 1861: Clingman, p. 554.

216 Verbal duel between Sen. Lane and Sen. Andrew Johnson, March 2, 1861: *Congressional Globe*, Thirty-sixth Congress, Second Session, pp. 1370–1372.

216 Senator Chandler's "whiskey insurrection": Ibid., p. 1373.

217 "God forbid!" Wigfall's retort on "Comanches": Ibid., p. 1372.

217 "Tomorrow is the day": Halsey Wigfall to Louise Wigfall, March 3, 1861, Wigfall Papers, LC.

217–219 Lincoln's inauguration is described in *Chicago Tribune*, March 5, 1861, and in Chittenden's *Recollections of President Lincoln*, pp. 84–92. Text of inaugural address, CWL, IV, pp. 249–271, and *Congressional Globe*, Thirty-sixth Congress, Senate special session, March 4, 1861, pp. 1433–1435.

218 Story of Douglas holding Lincoln's hat first appeared in the *Cincinnati Commercial*, on the authority of an Ohio congressman, then was reprinted in the *New York Times*, March 15, 1861. "Public Man" also said he witnessed this symbolic gesture. See Anderson, p. 231.

219 Douglas's favorable remarks about Lincoln's inaugural address: *Chicago Tribune*, March 6, 1861.

219–220 Lincoln's first levee: *New York Times*, March 11, 1861; *Chicago Tribune*, March 12, 1861; *Philadelphia Press* dispatch March 10, 1861.

221 "The Southern secession papers": *Chicago Tribune*, March 12, 1861.

221 "damned set of humbugs": Strong, March 7, 1861, III, p. 107.

221 "Inaugural means war": Wigfall to Gov. Pickens, March 4, 1861, OR, series I, vol. I, p. 261.

Chapter 21

222 "with a force of less than twenty thousand": Richard N. Current, *Lincoln and the First Shot*, Philadelphia: J. B. Lippincott & Co., 1963, p. 45.

222 Plague of office seekers: *Chicago Tribune*, March 14, 1861.

222–223 Gen. Scott's advice to Lincoln: Mearns, ed., II, pp. 456–457; Also Winfield Scott, *Memoirs of Lieut. General Scott, L.L.B., Written by Himself*, New York: Sheldon and Company, 1864, II, pp. 625–627.

224 Douglas's speech, March 6, 1861: *Congressional Globe*, Thirty-sixth Congress, Senate special session, pp. 1436–1439.

224 "Mr. Douglas says that the President": Anderson, March 11, 1861, p. 245.

224–225 Douglas and Mason speeches March 7, 1861: *Congressional Globe*, Thirty-sixth Congress, Senate special session, pp. 1442 to 1446. Mason described, *Chicago Tribune*, February 5, 1861.

225 "Mr. Douglas has passed out of politics": *Chicago Tribune*, February 5, 1861.

225 "We all agreed": Confederate commissioners' report to Montgomery. L. Q. Washington to Secretary of War Walker, March 5, 1861: "Inaugural undoubtedly means war, and that right off": OR, series I, vol. I, p. 263.

225–226 Bell's warning to Lincoln in Crawford's letter to Toombs: Nevins, *The Emergence of Lincoln*, II, p. 462.

226 Forsyth's letter to Toombs: Allan Nevins, *The War for the Union*, New York: Charles Scribner's Sons, 1959–1971, I, p. 38.

226–227 Sen. Gwin's letter to "a gentleman of Jackson": March 1, 1861, in *Vicksburg Whig*, quoted in *Chicago Tribune*, March 23, 1861.

227 Sam Ward's report to Seward on visit to Gwin: Lately Thomas, *Sam Ward, King of the Lobby*, Boston: Houghton Mifflin, 1965, pp. 243–255.

227 Benjamin to Barlow—Confederates would not "await events": Ibid., p. 259; also Anderson, p. 165.

228 *New York Herald*'s criticism of Lincoln for snubbing Confederate Commissioners: *Herald*, March 13, 1861.

229 "If Jefferson Davis had known": Samuel W. Crawford, *The Genesis of the Civil War*, New York: n. p., 1887, p. 328.

229 "Before that letter could reach him": Henry G. Connor, *John Archibald Campbell*, Boston: Houghton Mifflin, 1920, pp. 123–124.

229 "Seward had, several times": Browning, I, p. 467. Wigfall to Davis: OR, series I, vol. I, p. 273.

229 "I was astonished": Edward Bates, *The Diary of Edward Bates, 1859–1866*, edited by Howard K. Beale, New York: Da Capo Press, 1971, p. 177—reprint of the original publication in vol. IV of the *Annual Report of the American Historical Association*, 1930.

229–230 "Mr. Lincoln has assured Mr. Douglas": Anderson, March 12, 1861, p. 248.

230 Seward's warnings against reinforcing Fort Sumter: CWL, IV, p. 285.

230 Gen. Scott's order of March 11, 1861, to Major Anderson, to evacuate Fort Sumter: Mearns, ed., II, p. 476.

231 Scott had convinced "a great many Republican senators": Cincinnati newspapers' predictions that troops would soon leave Fort Sumter, quoted in *Chicago Tribune*, March 13 and 16, 1861.

231 Certain "gentlemen in prominent positions": Ibid., March 12, 1861.

231 "humiliating": Ibid.

231 "The fort has no strategic importance": Ibid.

231 Keep Virginia out of "Cotton Confederacy": *New York Post*, March 10, 1861, dispatch.

232 "There is no doubt": Stanton to Buchanan, March 14, 1861. Fletcher Pratt, *Stanton, Lincoln's Secretary of War*, New York: W. W. Norton, 1953, p. 117. "Low, cunning clown": Ibid., p. 210.

232 Charleston dispatch March 15, 1861: *Chicago Tribune*, March 20, 1861.

232 "assurances, from high sources": Ibid.

232 "I confidently believe": Forsyth to Beauregard, March 14, 1861, OR, series I, vol. I, p. 275.

232 "a terrific fight in the cabinet": Forsyth to Secretary of War Walker, March 14, 1861, OR, series IV, vol. I, p. 165.

233 "Assuming it to be possible ... is it wise?": Lincoln's inquiry to his cabinet March 15, 1861, CWL, IV, pp. 284–285.

233 Chase privately favored allowing the seven original secession states to go "rather than incur the evils of a bloody war": Chase to Elihu Burritt, October 6, 1862, in Chase Papers, Historical Society of Pennsylvania, quoted by James G. Randall in *Lincoln the President*, New York: Dodd, Mead & Company, 1945, I, p. 321.

233 Cameron's advocacy of giving up Sumter: OR, series I, vol. I, pp. 196–198.

233–234 Cabinet members' replies: CWL, IV, p. 285. Three-hour cabinet debate was reported in dispatch to the *New York Tribune*, March 15, 1861.

234 Bates's opposition to a "social war": Bates, March 16, 1861, p. 179.

234 Montgomery Blair's opposition to giving up Fort Sumter: Elbert B. Smith, *Francis Preston Blair*, New York: The Free Press, 1980, pp. 276–277.

234 Francis Preston Blair, Sr.'s tough talk to Lincoln: Ibid., pp. 275–277. Gideon Welles's diary, *The Diary of Gideon Welles*, John T. Morse, ed., Boston: Houghton Mifflin, 1909–1911; revised edition, Howard Beale, ed., New York: W. W. Norton, 1960, I, p. 13, says Montgomery Blair threatened to resign from Lincoln's cabinet if Fort Sumter were given up.

234 "His earnestness and indignation": Welles, Howard Beale, ed., I, pp. 13–14.

234 "Frank P. Blair talked some backbone": *New York Herald*, April 6, 1861.

235 Douglas's criticism of the Blairs: Anderson, p. 209.

235–236 Douglas's attack on Republican "war wing," March 15, 1861: *Congressional Globe*, Thirty-sixth Congress, special Senate session, pp. 1457–1462.

236 Sen. Clingman's remarks: Ibid., March 19, 1861, p. 1477.

236–237 "I propose three tugs": Gustavus Vasa Fox letters, OR, series I, vol. IV, pp. 224–225. "Finding that there was great opposition": Ibid., p. 247.

237 Major Anderson's anticipation of orders to leave Fort Sumter: *Cincinnati Gazette*, March 23, 1861.

237 Lamon's escape: Lamon, *Recollections of Abraham Lincoln*, privately published, pp. 76-77.

238 "Let your President attempt": Ibid., p. 74.

238 "South Carolina is too small for a republic but too large for an insane asylum": James Petigru to Benjamin F. Perry, December 8, 1860, quoted in Lacy K. Ford, Jr., *Origins of Southern Radicalism: The South Carolina Upcountry, 1800–1860*, New York: Oxford University Press, 1988, p. 371.

238–239 Stephen Hurlbut's report to Lincoln on March 26, 1861: The Lincoln Papers, LC.

Chapter 22

240 "The advocates of ... administration weakness": *Chicago Tribune*, April 13, 1861.

240 Republican senators "violently and bitterly opposed" giving up Fort Sumter: Confederate commissioners' report to Toombs, March 22, 1861, in Allan Nevins, *The War for the Union*, vol. I: *The Improvised War*, New York: Charles Scribner's Sons, 1959, footnote, p. 55.

240 Members of Congress protest to Lincoln: *Chicago Tribune*, April 5, 1861.

241 "indignant surprise": *New York Herald*, March 19, 1861.

241 "I voted for you": The Lincoln Papers, LC.

241 "You have not only run": Ibid.

241 "Are you the commander-in-chief?": Ibid.

242 "The reinforcement of Fort Sumter": Ibid.

242 "If it be possible": Ibid.

242 "Forces are here ready": Rep. Sherrod Clemens to Lincoln, Ibid.

243 Gen. Scott's proposal to give up both Sumter and Pickens: OR, series I, vol. I, pp. 200–201.

243 Gen. Scott "is playing ... politician": Crawford, p. 333; Smith, p. 278; Current, p. 78.

243 Lincoln "in the dumps": Sam Ward to S.L.M. Barlow, March 31, 1861, Barlow papers, Huntington Library, quoted by Nevins, *The War for the Union*, vol. I, *The Improvised War*, I footnote, p. 56.

243 "Though perhaps not averse to a small war": Clingman, p. 564.

244 "The dispatch of an expedition": Cabinet memoranda in Lincoln Papers, LC.

244 "Steamers Pocahontas at Norfolk": CWL, IV, pp. 301–302.

246 "Sir: I desire that an expedition": OR, series I, vol. I, pp. 226–227.

246 Lincoln's disavowal of Lamon as his agent: the *Chicago Tribune*, April 4, 1861, said: "All the talk about the 'armistice' between the administration and the three representatives of the abortive cotton republic is simply 'bosh.'

    "The statement that Col. Lamon called on Gov. Pickens and Gen. Beauregard, as the representative of the President of the United States, is equally unfounded." This comment, apparently authorized by the White House, raises the question: Did Lincoln send Lamon, as a false agent, to fool the Confederates at Charleston into thinking the evacuation of Fort Sumter was imminent?

246–247 "The President may desire to supply Fort Sumter": Connor, pp. 127–128. Glyndon G. Van Deusen, *William Henry Seward*, New York: Oxford University Press, 1967, pp. 277–280.

247 "My opinion is that the President": Crawford to Walker, April 1, 1861, OR, series I, vol. I, pp. 283–284.

247 "Fort Sumter to be Reinforced": the *New York Tribune* headlined its March 31 dispatch from Washington revealing the drastic turnabout in Lincoln's policy.

247 "The war wing presses on the President": Crawford and Roman to Toombs, April 2, 1861, OR, series I, vol. I, p. 284.

248 "The President ... is working early and late": *Chicago Tribune*, March 14, 1861.

248 "Why don't you disperse the selfish, mercenary crowds?": Orville Browning to Lincoln, March 26, 1861, Lincoln Papers, LC.

248–249 Lincoln's angry clash with California Republicans, March 30, 1861: Lincoln Papers, LC; CWL, IV, p. 302; *Chicago Tribune*, April 4, 1861, reprinting correspondence of the *Philadelphia Press*, March 31, 1861.

249 "Some Thoughts for the President's Consideration": CWL, IV, pp. 316–318; also, Van Deusen, pp. 281–284.

249 "dispatched it by private hand": Seward, *Reminiscences*, pp. 148–150.

250 "It is argued in high official circles": *New York Herald*, April 4, 1861.

Chapter 23

252 Seward's plan to relieve Fort Pickens: Welles, I, pp. 16–32; Current, *Lincoln and the First Shot*, pp. 82–86; W. A. Swanberg, *First Blood: The Story of Fort Sumter*, New York: Scribners, 1957, pp. 255–260, 263–269.

252 Lincoln's order to Lt. David D. Porter, April 1, 1861: CWL, IV, p. 315.

252 Lincoln's order to Captain Andrew H. Foote: Ibid., p. 314.

252–253 Seward's order to Lt. Porter and his response: Current, *Lincoln and the First Shot*, p. 106; Swanberg, pp. 267–268. Secretary Welles's complaints against Seward: Welles, I, pp. 16–32.

253 "Positively determined": April 6, 1861, OR, series I, vol. I, p. 287.

254 "Faith as to Sumter fully kept": Catton, p. 300; Welles, I, p. 28.

254 "Southern men have been flattered": *New York Herald*, April 7, 1861.

255 John B. Baldwin's interview with Lincoln April 4, 1861: Baldwin's testimony is in the report of the Joint Committee on Reconstruction, Thirty-ninth Congress, First Session, pp. 102–106. Baldwin said he was introduced to nine Northern governors who met with Lincoln on April 4. The Republican governors pressured Lincoln to relieve Fort Sumter even at the risk of war, and he complied.

255–256 Virginia legislators' plea to Lincoln: *Cincinnati Commercial*, April 6 dispatch reprinted in the *Chicago Tribune*, April 9, 1861.

256 "Sumter and Pickens are both to be reinforced": *Chicago Tribune*, April 6, 1861.

256 Northern governors meet Lincoln: Dispatch to *Cincinnati Gazette*, April 4, 1861.

256 "blood would be spilled": *Cincinnati Commercial* dispatch, April 5, 1861.

256 Washington excited over war: *Cincinnati Gazette* dispatch, April 5, 1861.

256–257 Lincoln and governors agree upon defense plan: *Chicago Tribune*, April 18, 1861.

257–258 John Minor Botts's account of his meeting with Lincoln is in Botts, pp. 195–196.

258 Lincoln's April 6, 1861, order to Robert Chew: CWL, IV, pp. 323–324.

259 "he did not want it known in the North": Botts, p. 197.

259 "ready to raise the banner of revolt": *New York Times*, April 8, 1861.

259 Roger A. Pryor's "strike a blow" speech: *Charleston Mercury*, reprinted by the Loyal Publication Society, New York, 1864, Pamphlet No. 40, "How the War Was Commenced." Also *Chicago Tribune*, April 20, 1861.

260 "Oh, they all say the same thing": C. Vann Woodward, ed., *Mary Chesnut's Civil War*, New Haven: Yale University Press, 1981, p. 47.

260 "The truth is that the sooner we are out ... the better": Major Anderson to the War Department, April 6, 1861, OR, series I, vol. I, p. 245.

260 "an attempt will be made": CWL, IV, pp. 323–324.

261 "Madame, your country is invaded": Woodward, p. 43. The *New York Herald* reported April 9 that "a fleet of seven Government vessels is reported off the bar," at Charleston.

261 "Hoping that you will be able": OR, series I, vol. I, p. 235; also, CWL, IV, pp. 321–322.

262 "I ought to have been informed": OR, series I, vol. I, p. 294.

262 Major Anderson blamed the war on the Lincoln administration: Strode, II, pp. 35–36. Strode observes on page 31 that Blair pulled Welles and Chase over to the Fox resupply plan, "which the Captain was already implementing at the New York Navy Yard."
"Without majority cabinet support," Strode wrote, "Lincoln made his decision, and penned the fateful order that was to cause the most bitter tragedy the American people have ever suffered."

262 "No one now doubts that Lincoln intends war," Wigfall to Davis, April 10, 1861: Current, *Lincoln and the First Shot*, p. 151.

262 "The 'Tribune' of today," Confederate commissioners to Gen. Beauregard, April 11, 1861: OR, series I, vol. I, p. 301. Also, Davis, *The Rise and Fall*, I, p. 278.

263 The text of Seward's memorandum to the Confederate commissioners appears on pages 676–679 of Davis, vol. I.

263 The commissioners' reply: Ibid., pp. 679–682.

263 Justice Campbell's charge of "systematic duplicity" is in his letter to Seward: Ibid., pp. 683–685.
"The last assurances to me 'that the Govt. will not undertake to supply Sumter without giving notice to Gov. Pickens' I have in writing & I know that it came from the President." Justice John A. Campbell to Jefferson Davis, from Washington, April 3, 1861. In Davis, *The Papers of Jefferson Davis*, Linda Crist, ed., Baton Rouge and London: Louisiana State University Press, 1991, VII, p. 88.
"But the President is light, inconstant and variable. His ear is open to everyone—and his resolutions are easily bent—his inaugural is a great stumbling block for notwithstanding the characteristics I have mentioned, he is conscientious and tenacious of his word, and easily affected when he supposes *that* will be called into question." Ibid.

263 "The crooked paths of diplomacy": Jefferson Davis to the Confederate Congress, April 29, 1861, in Davis, *Rise and Fall*, I, p. 280. Also, OR, series I, vol. 53, pp. 161–164.

264 Lincoln's "fatal mistake": *New York Herald*, April 10, 1861.

264 Gov. Wise's resolution: *Chicago Tribune*, April 11, 1861.

264 "Are we going to have war in Washington?": Ibid., April 12, 1861.

264–265 Lincoln warns Gov. Curtin of "design to attack ... Washington": Ibid., April 10 and 12, 1861. Lincoln telegraphed the Pennsylvania governor on April 8, 1861: "I think the necessity of being *ready* increases. Look to it." CWL, IV, p. 324.

265 Reluctant D. C. militia stricken from the rolls: *Chicago Tribune*, April 12, 1861.

265 "the prospect of civil war": *Cincinnati Gazette* dispatch in the *Chicago Tribune*, April 12, 1861.

265 "Abraham Perpetrates Another Joke": *Cincinnati Commercial*, April 10, 1861, reprinted in *Chicago Tribune*, April 12, 1861.

265 Lincoln limits his time with office seekers: *Chicago Tribune*, April 4, 1861.

265 Lincoln visits the "city of the dead": Ibid., April 10, 1861.

266 "see whether they dare to fire": *New York Herald*, April 11, 1861.

Chapter 24

268   "Sir, unless you sprinkle blood": Sen. Clemens's speech at a Huntsville, Alabama, peace meeting, March 13, 1864, quoted in Cox, p. 150.

268   "suicide, murder": Pleasant Stovall, *Robert Toombs*, New York: Cassell Publishing Company, 1892, p. 26.

268   "If you have no doubt": Walker to Beauregard April 10, 1861, OR, series I, vol. I, p. 297.

268   "I am ordered by the government": OR, series I, vol. I, p. 13.

268   "I have the honor to acknowledge": Ibid.

269   "I shall await the first shot": Ibid, p. 59. Capt. Lee's version, in Robert Underwood Johnson and Clarence Clough Buel, eds., *Battles and Leaders of the Civil War*, New York: Thomas Yoseloff, 1956, I, p. 75.

269   "Do not desire needlessly": OR, series I, vol. I, p. 301.

269   Anderson "made every possible effort": Johnson and Buel, eds., I, p. 75.

269   Anderson's reply: OR, series I, vol. I, p. 14.

269   "Inasmuch as any attempt": Davis, *Rise and Fall*, I, pp. 288–289.

270   "Sir: By authority": Ibid., I, p. 288.

270   "If we never meet in this world": Johnson and Buel, eds., I, p. 76.

270   "I could not fire": Ibid.

270   "a flash as of distant lightning": Ibid., p. 66.

270   "and shot and shell went screaming": Ibid., p. 66.

271   Stanton to Buchanan, April 12, 1861: Pratt, p. 120.

271   "Major Anderson's only hope": *New York Herald*, April 12, 1861.

272   "I am not going in there to begin civil war": Fox Report, ORN, series I, vol. IV, p. 249.

272   "Vessels cannot get in": *New York Herald*, April 12, 1861.

272   Confederate soldiers jeered at idle Northern ships: Strode, II, p. 46.

272   "There is a furious fire": April 13, 1861, dispatch from Richmond published in the *Chicago Tribune*, April 15, 1861.

272   "Civil war has at last begun": *New York Herald*, April 13, 1861.

273   Sen. Wigfall's adventure: Crawford, pp. 439–441; OR, series I, vol. I, pp. 23 and 37–39; *A Southern Girl in '61* by Wigfall's daughter, Mrs. D. Giraud Wright, pp. 41–46; and Mrs. Wigfall to her son, Halsey, April 15, 1861, Wigfall Papers, LC.

273   "the embodiment of Southern chivalry": *New York Tribune*, April 23, 1861.

274   Beauregard's message to Anderson offering surrender terms at five minutes till 6 P.M. April 13, 1861: OR, series I, vol. I, p. 15.

274   "the fort was like an oven": *New York Herald*, April 15, 1861.

274   "Had the surrender not taken place": Ibid.

274   Walker's prophecy: *Chicago Tribune*, April 15, 1861.

274–275   "I hope, my dear boy": Mrs. Wigfall to her son, Halsey, from Charleston, April 15, 1861, Wigfall Papers, LC.

275   "An old slave passed through": *New York Herald*, April 15, 1861.

276   "Sir: Having defended": OR, series I, vol. I, p. 12.

Chapter 25

277   "You cannot imagine": *Chicago Tribune*, April 13, 1861.

277   "I knew they would do it": Rep. Alexander Long, D-Ohio, April 8, 1864, *Congressional Globe*, Thirty-eighth Congress, First session, p. 1499. The motion to expel Long won a majority, 84 to 58, but fell short of the required two-thirds: Ibid., p. 1518.

278　"The supply vessels could not reach him": *New York Evening Post* quoted by *Chicago Tribune*, April 18, 1861.

279　"The plan succeeded": Browning, I, p. 476.

279　Lincoln's letter of consolation to Captain Fox, May 1, 1861: OR, series I, vol. IV, p. 248. CWL, IV, pp. 350–351. Fox's complaint to Secretary Cameron, April 19, 1861, OR, series I, vol. I, p. 11.

279　"the states which claim to have seceded": Lincoln's reply to the Virginia legislators April 13, 1861, CWL, IV, pp. 329–331.

280　Lincoln's April 14 proclamation: Ibid., pp. 331–333.

280　"Some time ago": Carl Schurz to Lincoln, April 5, 1861, Lincoln Papers, LC.

281　Douglas has "drawn the dagger": *Chicago Tribune*, March 21, 1861.

281　"I don't know as he wants my advice": Johannsen, p. 859.

281　"I concur in every word": Milton, pp. 559–60; Nicolay and Hay, IV, p. 80; *Chicago Tribune*, April 16, 1861.

282　"Fifteen hundred, sir": An eyewitness account of Lincoln's April 15, 1861, war conference is in A. K. McClure's book, *Abraham Lincoln and Men of War-Times*, Philadelphia: The Times Publishing Co., 1892, pp. 57–62.

282　Charles P. Stone, quoting a "lady recently arrived from Montgomery": Mearns, ed., I, p. 527.

282　"leading spirits of the Confederacy": *New York Times*, reprinted in *Chicago Tribune*, April 24, 1861.

283　Southerners wild with excitement: *New York Tribune* dispatch April 19, 1861.

283　Philadelphia patriots: *Chicago Tribune*, April 16–17, 1861.

283–284　Rep. Clement Vallandigham's opposition to civil war: *Cincinnati Enquirer*, April 20, 1861, quoted by Wood Gray, *The Hidden Civil War: The Story of the Copperheads*, New York: The Viking Press, 1942, p. 57.

　　　Also see *A Life of Clement L. Vallandigham*, by his brother, the Rev. James L. Vallandigham, Baltimore: Turnbull Brothers, 1872. Rep. Vallandigham's speech for peace, January 14, 1863, in *Congressional Globe*, Thirty-seventh Congress, Third Session, pp. 52–60.

285　Sen. Breckinridge's call for a united South: *Chicago Tribune*, April 18, 1861.

Chapter 26

286–287　Southern governors' replies to Lincoln's call for troops: OR, series III, vol. I, pp. 70, 72, 76, 81, 82, and 83.

287　Laughter at Montgomery: *Chicago Tribune*, April 17, 1861.

287–288　"Spontaneous People's Convention": Jones, *A Rebel War Clerk's Diary*, I, pp. 20–24.

288　"This cruel, needless, *corrupt betrayal*": T. H. Gilmer to Douglas, April 17, 1861, Douglas Papers, University of Chicago Library, quoted by Johannsen, p. 861.

289　Federals wreck their own Gosport Navy Yard at Norfolk: Greeley, I, pp. 473–477.

289　"As for Harper's Ferry," Vallandigham's speech, July 10, 1861: *Congressional Globe*, Thirty-seventh Congress, First Session, p. 58.

289　"I would have put three thousand": Gov. Pickens to Gen. John B. Floyd, August 4, 1861, OR, series I, vol. 51, part 2, pp. 212–213.

290　"I declined the offer": Douglas S. Freeman, *R.E. Lee: A Biography*, New York: Charles Scribner's Sons, 1934, I, pp. 437–441.

290　"Awful times!": French, p. 351.

290–291   Zebulon Baird Vance's pleas for the Border States to stay in the Union: Clement Dowd, *The Life of Zebulon B. Vance*, Charlotte, N.C.: Observer Printing and Publishing House, 1897, pp. 440–443.

291–292   North Carolina Unionists' betrayal: James G. de Roulhac Hamilton, ed., *The Correspondence of Jonathan Worth*, Raleigh, N.C.: Edwards and Broughton Printing Co., 1902, I, pp. 143–144 and 150–151.
Also, *Jonathan Worth: A Biography of a Southern Unionist*, by Richard L. Zuber, Chapel Hill: University of North Carolina Press, 1965, pp. 120–125. "The hotspurs": Worth to T. C. and B. G. Worth, Asheboro, N.C., April 26, 1861, Worth Papers, University of North Carolina.

292   Whigs' denunciation of Lincoln: *Carolina Watchman*, Salisbury, N.C., April 23, 1861.

292   "the stupid, treacherous administration": Fayetteville, N.C., *Observer*, April 15, 1861.

292   "A gentleman just arrived here": *Chicago Tribune*, May 1, 1861.

292   "the streets were alive with soldiers": reprinted by the Loyal Publication Society, New York, 1864, no. 40, pp. 10–12.

292   "The first fruits": *New Orleans Picayune*. Ibid.

292   "With independent Virginia": Ibid.

292–293   "From the mountain-tops": Greeley, I, p. 470, quoting *Richmond Examiner*.
Bruce Catton, in *The Coming Fury*, p. 330, wrote:
Lincoln's proclamation "knocked Virginia straight out of the Union and turned the war into a life-or-death affair for the whole nation."
John Minor Botts said Lincoln's proclamation, with its call for armed forces against the South, was "the most unfortunate state paper that ever issued from any Executive since the establishment of the government." Instead of going to war, Lincoln should have made a public appeal that could have "retained the support of the Union party of the South, which seemed to be all paralyzed by the simple dash of his pen," Botts contended. See Botts, pp. 195–196.

Chapter 27

294   "Civil war has commenced!": *Chicago Tribune*, April 20, 1861.

294–301   *The South*, a Baltimore newspaper, provides colorful details of "the Battle of Baltimore," in its issues immediately after the April 19, 1861, riot. See also Sprague, pp. 1–56.

297   "The blood which has this day been spilt": *The South*, April 22, 1861.

297   "A collision between the citizens and the Northern": Ibid.

297   "If the blood of your fellow citizens": Ibid.

298   "Why didn't you choke him?": Ibid.

298   "Because he gave me reason to respect him": Ibid.

298   "But, if otherwise, I bow in submission to the mandate of the people": Ibid.

298   "I am a Marylander!": Sprague, pp. 10–11.

298   "Baltimore was a secession volcano": Greeley, I, pp. 462–472.

299   "He pleaded sickness and fatigue": *The South*, April 22, 1861.

299   "Streets red with Maryland blood": Sprague, p. 11.

299   "a stalwart company, well mounted": *The South*, April 22, 1861.

299   "as a unit in defense of the South": Ibid.

300   "Parties of men": *Chicago Tribune*, April 20, 1861. For more details of the Baltimore conflict, see OR, series I, vol. II, pp. 7–21 and Nicolay and Hay, IV, pp. 111–132.
For Gov. Hicks's remarks see Radcliffe, p. 35.

300   "a few nights since, gathered together": *The South*, April 22, 1861.
300   "The office of *The Wecker*": Ibid.
300   "A respectably attired man from New York": Ibid.
300   "It is to Maryland, after all": Ibid.
301   James Ryder Randall writes "Maryland, My Maryland": Harold R. Manakee, in *Maryland in the Civil War*, Baltimore: Maryland Historical Society, 1961, provides a detailed account on pages 44–46. Text is on pages 155–157.

Chapter 28

302   "Women and children were sent away": Stanton to Buchanan, May 11, 1861, Pratt, p. 123.
302   "imbecility of Lincoln": June 6, 1861, Ibid., p. 124.
303   "declaring that no more troops": *The South*, April 22, 1861.
303   "President Lincoln Scared": Ibid.
303   "My God, Mr. Harris": Ibid.
       "I had better go out and hang myself": Ibid.
       "die like rats in a trap!": Ibid.
303   "On top of that hill is a battery": Ibid.
304   "Mrs. Lincoln Alarmed": Ibid., April 23, 1861.
304   "Lincoln is in a trap": H. D. Bird to Confederate Secretary of War Walker, April 20, 1861, OR, series I, vol. II, pp. 771–772.
305   "reduce the city of Baltimore to ashes": *Chicago Tribune*, April 26, 1861.
305   "Mr. Brown, I am not a learned man!": *The South*, April 23, 1861.
305   "Three thousand Northern troops": John W. Garrett to Baltimore Mayor Brown, Ibid.
306   "Lest there be the slightest": Ibid.
306   "Union men are fleeing for their lives": April 21, 1861, dispatch to the *New York Times*.
306 & 308   Lincoln meets Baltimore YMCA delegation and asks, "what am I to do?": *The South*, April 23, 1861. "those Carolinians are crossing Virginia to ... hang me": Ibid.
308   "Business was at a standstill": Seward, *Reminiscences*, pp. 155–157.
308   Lincoln and his cabinet "marked for hanging": *Chicago Tribune*, April 29, 1861.
309   "The whole country around Washington": Ibid.
309   Lincoln "in a state of nervous tension": Nicolay and Hay, IV, p. 151.
309   "The White House is turned into barracks": Hay, p. 1, diary entry of April 18, 1861. Also see Nicolay and Hay, II, pp. 106–107.
310   "Baltimore will be laid in ashes!": Hay, p. 9.
310   "Old Lincoln sleeps with a hundred men": *New Orleans Delta* quoted by *Chicago Tribune*, April 23, 1861.
310–311   Lincoln's extralegal actions: He reported them to Congress on May 26 of the following year: CWL, V, pp. 240–243. Nicolay and Hay, IV, pp. 136–138.
311   Messenger poses as preacher: *Chicago Tribune*, April 23, 1861.
311   "the government was saved from overthrow": CWL, V, p. 242. Also , OR, series III, vol. II, pp. 73–75.
311   "Why don't they come?": Nicolay and Hay, IV, p. 152.
311   "I don't believe there is any North": Hay, p. 11.
312   "Washington is safe!": *Chicago Tribune*, April 29, 1861.
312   Lincoln chooses to shed "fraternal blood": Ibid, April 30, 1861.

312 "A scheme has been set on foot": Browning, April 22, 1861, I, 465.

313 "You have sold out the Democratic party": Milton, *Eve*, p. 565. Congressman Logan later had a change of heart, became a Union general, and was the Republican nominee for vice-president in 1884, the running mate of James G. Blaine, who narrowly lost the presidency to Grover Cleveland.

313 "patriots or traitors!": *Chicago Tribune*, May 2, 1861.

313 "from Cairo north": Milton, *Eve*, p. 566.

313 Details of Douglas's death are narrated by Johannsen, pp. 870–874.

313–314 Douglas could have become a Union army general: *New York Times*, June 4, 1861; Forney, I, pp. 121 and 226.

Chapter 29

One of the best accounts of the struggle for and against secession in Maryland is George L. P. Radcliffe's book, *Governor Thomas H. Hicks of Maryland and the Civil War*. Also valuable is J. Thomas Scharf's three-volume *History of Maryland from the Earliest Period to the Present Day*, Baltimore: J. B. Piet, 1879. See vol. III, pp. 336–450.

315 Gov. Hicks's account of his struggle to block secession, and his final decision to call the legislature, is in his February 28, 1863, speech to the U.S. Senate: *Congressional Globe*, Thirty-seventh Congress, Third Session, pp. 1371–1381. See Radcliffe, pp. 63–88 and Scharf, III, pp. 348–350, 361–371, and 424–429.

315 "The General-in-chief": Gen. Scott to Gen. Butler, April 26, 1861, OR, series II, vol. I, pp. 675–676. See also OR, series II, vol. I, pp. 563–748, "Union Policy of Repression in Maryland," for details of the army's crackdown on civilians.

316 Maryland legislature's call for Lincoln "in the name of God, to cease this unholy war": Greeley, I, pp. 471–472.

317 Jefferson Davis's assertion that the Confederacy wanted peace: Davis, *Rise and Fall*, I, p. 333.

317 Lincoln's policy "is war": *New York Tribune* dispatch, May 1, 1861.

317 "The Lincoln government now is abandoning": *The South*, May 1, 1861.

318 Hicks accused of "treason": Ibid.

318 "'Old Caesar'": Ibid.

318 "Frank Blair says Maryland shall be a free state": D. G. Duncan to L. P. Walker, from Richmond, April 27 and May 5, 1861, OR, series I, vol. 51, part 2, pp. 47 and 55.

318 "The plucky old gentleman": *Chicago Tribune*, May 6, 1861.

319 "You would not know this God-forsaken city": Mrs. Phillips to Mrs. Clay in Clay-Clopton, pp. 151–152.

320–321 The Merryman case is discussed in detail in *Freedom Under Lincoln* by Dean Sprague, pp. 39-44. See also William Safire, *Freedom*, Garden City, N.Y.: Doubleday, 1987, pp. 978–980, and Edward McPherson, *The Political History of the United States of America During the Great Rebellion*, Washington, D. C.: Philp and Solomons, 1865, pp. 151–158. OR, series II, vol. I, covers the Merryman case, p. 571 et seq. Chief Justice Taney's statement about the Merryman case, pp. 577–585.

321 "The paroxysm of passion": Taney to Pierce, Washington, D.C., June 12, 1861. *American Historical Review* X, nos. 1 and 2, October 1904–January 1905, p. 368.

321　"I believe that arrests". Hicks to U.S. Senate, February 28, 1863, *Congressional Globe*, Thirty-seventh Congress, Third Session, pp. 1371–1376.

322　Toucey's arraignment of Lincoln: Toucey to Buchanan, June 5, 1861, Buchanan Papers, Historical Society of Pennsylvania; quoted by Philip Gerald Auchampaugh, in *James Buchanan and His Cabinet on the Eve of Secession*, Lancaster, Pa.: privately printed, 1926, pp. 87–88.

323　Lincoln's message to Congress, July 4, 1861; CWL, IV, pp. 421–444.

324　President Davis's message to the Confederate Congress April 29, 1861: OR, series IV, vol. I, pp. 256–268.

324　"all we ask is to be let alone": Davis, *Rise and Fall*, I, p. 327.

325　Lincoln favors "the most vigorous and active" war measures and opposes all compromise: Browning, July 8, 1861, p. 478.

325　Vallandigham deplores Lincoln's war policy and blames him for the "terrible and bloody revolution": *Congressional Globe*, Thirty-seventh Congress, First Session, July 10, 1861, pp. 56–60.

325–326　Senator Bayard's speech warning Lincoln against the blood bath of civil war: Ibid., July 19, 1861, Appendix, pp. 12–19.

326　"Our president is now dictator": Edward L. Pierce, *Memoir and Letters of Charles Sumner*, New York: Arno Press, 1959, vol. IV, p. 42.

327　John J. Crittenden, having moved from his Senate seat to a new role as a Kentucky Congressman, sponsored the new Crittenden resolution, adopted by Congress in July 1861, narrowly defining the North's war aims at that time. The war, it affirmed, was being waged, not "in any spirit of oppression, or for any purpose of conquest or subjugation, or ... of overthrowing or interfering with the rights or established institutions of those states, but to defend and maintain the supremacy of the Constitution and to preserve the Union with all the dignity, equality and rights of the several states unimpaired; and that as soon as these objects are accomplished the war ought to cease."
The House adopted this statement of war aims July 22, 1861, immediately after the Union army's defeat in the battle of Bull Run. The resolution sailed through, 121 to 2. *Congressional Globe*, Thirty-seventh Congress, First Session, pp. 222–223. The Senate adopted a similar measure July 25, 1861. Ibid., p. 265.

BIBLIOGRAPHY

The primary sources consulted in the several years of research that led to this narrative are the records of the people who played the major roles in the tragic drama that culminated in the breakdown of the American political system and the unnecessary Civil War.

Among the sources are original manuscripts and journals; newspapers; published letters, diaries, and memoirs; and the "OR," the Official Records of the Union and Confederate Armies.

On the pages of the *Congressional Globe* are recorded the often-passionate debates wherein the pleas for conciliation, compromise, and peace were spurned by politicians who were determined to wield power.

MANUSCRIPTS

In the Library of Congress are the papers of many individuals of the Lincoln era.

Most important are the Robert T. Lincoln Papers, a large collection of letters to Abraham Lincoln as well as the President's own papers.

Other collections are those of the following individuals:

Robert Anderson
Edward Bates
August Belmont
Judah P. Benjamin
Jeremiah S. Black
Francis Preston Blair
James Buchanan
Benjamin F. Butler
Simon Cameron
Zachariah Chandler
Salmon P. Chase
Samuel W. Crawford
John J. Crittenden
Caleb Cushing
Thomas Ewing
William Pitt Fessenden
John W. Forney
Benjamin Brown French
Duff Green
Horace Greeley
James H. Hammond
John Hay
Joseph Holt

Andrew Johnson
Reverdy Johnson
Horatio King
John A. Logan
James M. Mason
William Porcher Miles
Eugenia Yates Phillips
Philip Phillips
John Thomas Pickett
James S. Pike
Allen Pinkerton
William Cabell Rives
Anna Sanders
George Nicholas Sanders
William Henry Seward
John Sherman
William T. Sherman
Edwin M. Stanton
Alexander H. Stephens
Thaddeus Stevens
Alexander Hugh Holmes Stuart
Jacob Thompson
Robert Toombs

Lyman Trumbull	Gideon Welles
Benjamin F. Wade	Louis T. Wigfall
Robert John Walker	Levi Woodbury
Elihu B. Washburne	William L. Yancey

The S.L.M. Barlow Papers in the Huntington Library at San Marino, California, are a treasure trove of documents about the politics of the Lincoln era, with special emphasis on Barlow, an influential New York lawyer, railroad promoter, and leader in the Democratic Party.

NEWSPAPERS

Albany, N.Y., *Atlas and Argus*
Albany, N.Y., *Evening Journal*

Baltimore, *The South*
Baltimore Sun

Charleston, S.C., *Courier*
Charleston, S.C., *Mercury*

Chicago Times
Chicago Tribune

Cincinnati Commercial
Cincinnati Enquirer
Cincinnati Gazette

Columbia, S.C., *Guardian*
Columbus, Ga., *Cornerstone*
Eufala, Ala., *Express*
Fayetteville, N.C., *Observer*
Houston, Texas, *Telegraph*

Jackson, Miss., *Mississippian*

Louisville Journal

Mobile, Ala., *Register*

Natchez Mississippian

New Orleans Delta
New Orleans Picayune
New York Express
New York Herald
New York Post
New York Times
New York Tribune

Philadelphia Bulletin
Philadelphia Inquirer
Philadelphia Press

Raleigh: *Confederate*
Raleigh: *Standard*

Richmond Dispatch
Richmond Enquirer
Richmond Examiner
Richmond Sentinel
Richmond Whig

Salisbury, N.C., *Carolina Watchman*

Springfield, Ill., *Journal*

Washington Constitution
Washington Evening Star
Washington: *National Intelligencer*

PUBLISHED LETTERS AND DIARIES

Anderson, Frank Maloy. *The Mystery of "A Public Man,"* including the text of the diary. Minneapolis: University of Minnesota Press, 1948.

Bates, Edward. *The Diary of Edward Bates, 1859–1865.* Howard K. Beale, ed. Washington, D.C.: U.S. Government Printing Office, 1933. Vol. IV of the *Annual Report of the American Historical Association,* 1930. Reprint, New York: Da Capo Press, 1971.

Belmont, August. *Letters, Speeches and Addresses.* New York: privately printed, 1890.

Black, Jeremiah S. *Essays and Speeches of Jeremiah Black.* Chauncey F. Black, ed. New York: D. Appleton and Company, 1885.

Browning, Orville H. *The Diary of Orville H. Browning.* Theodore Calvin Pease and James G. Randall, eds. Springfield, Ill.: The Trustees of the Illinois State Historical Library, 1927.

Buchanan, James. *The Works of James Buchanan.* John Bassett Moore, ed. Twelve vols. Philadelphia: J. B. Lippincott, 1908–1911.

Chase, Samuel Portland. *The Salmon P. Chase Papers.* John Niven, ed. Vol. I, *Journals, 1827–1872.* Kent, Ohio: Kent State University Press, 1993.

Chesnut, Mary. *Mary Chesnut's Civil War.* C. Vann Woodward, ed. New Haven, Conn.: Yale University Press, 1981.

Cobb, Thomas R. R. Extracts from His Letters to His Wife, February 3, 1861, to December 10, 1862. Southern Historical Society papers, Vol. XXVIII. Richmond: Southern Historical Society, 1900.

Daly, Maria Lydig. *The Diary of a Union Lady, 1861–1865.* Harold Earl Hammond, ed. New York: Funk & Wagnalls Company, Inc., 1962.

Davis, Jefferson. *Jefferson Davis, Constitutionalist: His Letters, Papers and Speeches.* Dunbar Rowland, ed. Ten vols. Jackson: Mississippi Department of Archives and History, 1923.

———. *The Papers of Jefferson Davis.* Linda Lasswell Crist, ed. Vol. VI and Vol. VII. Baton Rouge, La., and London: Louisiana State University Press, 1989 and 1991.

Douglas, Stephen A. *The Letters of Stephen A. Douglas.* Robert W. Johannsen, ed. Urbana, Ill.: University of Illinois Press, 1961.

Fox, Gustavus V. *The Confidential Correspondence of Gustavus V. Fox.* Two vols. New York: Naval History Society, 1920.

French, Benjamin Brown. *Witness to the Young Republic: A Yankee's Journal, 1828–1870.* Donald B. Cole and John F. McDonough, eds. Hanover and London: University Press of New England, 1989.

Hay, John. *Lincoln and the Civil War in the Diaries and Letters of John Hay.* Tyler Dennett, ed. New York: Da Capo Press, 1939.

Johnson, Andrew. *The Papers of Andrew Johnson.* Leroy P. Graf and Ralph W. Haskins, eds. Seven vols. Knoxville: University of Tennessee Press, 1967 et seq.

Jones, John Beauchamp. *A Rebel War Clerk's Diary at the Confederate States Capital.* Two vols. Philadelphia: J. B. Lippincott & Co., 1866.

Lincoln, Abraham. *The Collected Works of Abraham Lincoln.* Roy P. Basler, ed. Nine vols. New Brunswick, N.J.: Rutgers University Press, 1953.

Mearns, David C., ed. *The Lincoln Papers.* Two vols. Garden City, N.Y.: Doubleday & Co., 1948.

Seward, William H. *The Works of William H. Seward.* G. E. Baker, ed. Five vols. Boston: Houghton Mifflin, 1884.

Strong, George Templeton. *The Diary of George Templeton Strong.* Allan Nevins and Milton Halsey Thomas, eds. Four vols. New York: Macmillan, 1952.

Toombs, Robert. *The Correspondence of Robert Toombs, Alexander H. Stephens, and Howell Cobb.* Ulrich B. Phillips, ed. The American Historical Association's Annual Report, 1911, Vol. II.

Welles, Gideon. *The Diary of Gideon Welles.* John T. Morse, Jr., ed. Three vols. Boston: Houghton Mifflin, 1909–1911. Revised edition, Howard Beale, ed. Three vols. New York: W. W. Norton, 1960.

Worth, Jonathan. *The Correspondence of Jonathan Worth.* James G. de Roulhac Hamilton, ed. Two vols. Raleigh, N. C.: Edwards and Broughton Printing Company, 1902.

BIOGRAPHIES AND MEMOIRS

Adams, Charles Francis, Jr. *Charles Francis Adams, 1835–1915: An Autobiography*. Boston and New York: Houghton Mifflin, 1916.

———.*Charles Francis Adams, 1807–1886*, American Statesmen Series, Boston and New York: Houghton, Mifflin and Company, 1900.

Anderson, Dwight G. *Abraham Lincoln: The Quest for Immortality*. New York: Alfred A. Knopf, 1982.

Auchampaugh, Philip Gerald. *James Buchanan and His Cabinet on the Eve of Secession*. Lancaster, Pa.: privately printed, 1926.

Bancroft, Frederic. *The Life of William H. Seward*. Two vols. New York: Harper and Brothers, 1900.

Barbee, David R., and Milledge L. Bonham, Jr., eds. "Fort Sumter Again." *Mississippi Valley Historical Review* XXVIII (1941): 63–73.

Benton, Thomas Hart. *Thirty Years View*. Two vols. New York: D. Appleton and Company, 1854–1856.

Beveridge, Albert J. *Abraham Lincoln, 1809–1858*. Two vols. Boston: Houghton Mifflin, 1928.

Blaine, James G. *Twenty Years of Congress: From Lincoln to Garfield*. Two vols. Norwich, Conn.: The Henry Bill Publishing Company, 1884.

Bradley, Erwin Stanley. *Simon Cameron, Lincoln's Secretary of War*. Philadelphia: University of Pennsylvania Press, 1965.

Brooks, Noah. *Abraham Lincoln and the Downfall of American Slavery*. New York: G. P. Putnam's Sons, 1894.

Brown, Charles H. *William Cullen Bryant*. New York: Charles Scribner's Sons, 1971.

Buchanan, James. *Mr. Buchanan's Administration on the Eve of the Rebellion*. Freeport, N.Y.: Books for Libraries Press, 1970 edition.

Butler, Benjamin Franklin. *Butler's Book*. Boston: A. M. Thayer and Company, 1892.

Butler, Pierce. *Judah P. Benjamin*. Philadelphia: G. W. Jacobs, 1907.

Castleman, John B. *Active Service*. Louisville: Courier-Journal Job Printing Company, 1917.

Clay-Clopton, Virginia. *A Belle of the Fifties*. Narrated by Ada Sterling. New York: Doubleday, Page & Company, 1905.

Clingman, Thomas Lanier. *Selections from the Speeches and Writings of Hon. Thomas L. Clingman*. Raleigh, N.C.: J. Nichols, 1877.

Coleman, Mrs. A.M.B. *John J. Crittenden*. Two vols. New York: De Capo Press, 1970.

Connor, Henry G. *John Archibald Campbell*. Boston: Houghton Mifflin, 1920.

Conway, Moncure. *Autobiography*. Boston and New York: Houghton Mifflin and Company, 1904.

Cox, Samuel S. *Three Decades of Federal Legislation, 1855–1885*. Providence, R.I.: J. A. & R. A. Reid, Publishers, 1886.

Craven, John J. *The Prison Life of Jefferson Davis*. New York: George W. Carlton, Publisher, 1866.

Current, Richard N. *The Lincoln Nobody Knows*. New York: McGraw-Hill, 1958.

Curtis, George Ticknor. *Life of James Buchanan*. New York: Harper and Brothers, 1883.

Cuthbert, Norma B., ed. *Lincoln and the Baltimore Plot, 1861*. San Marino, Calif.: Huntington Library, 1949.

Cutting, Elizabeth Brown. *Jefferson Davis, Political Soldier*. NewYork: Dodd, Mead and Company, 1930.

Davis, Jefferson. *The Rise and Fall of the Confederate Government*. Two vols. New York: Thomas Yoseloff, 1958.

Davis, Varina Howell. *Jefferson Davis: A Memoir, by His Wife*. Freeport, N.Y.: Books for Libraries Press, 1971.

Davis, William C. *Jefferson Davis, the Man and His Hour.* New York: HarperCollins, 1991.

———. *Breckinridge: Soldier, Statesman, Symbol.* Baton Rouge and London: Louisiana State University, 1974.

Dickinson, John R. *Daniel Stevens Dickinson.* Two vols. New York: G. P. Putnam and Son, 1867.

Dix, Morgan. *Memoirs of John Adams Dix.* Compiled by his son. Two vols. New York: Harper & Brothers, 1883.

Donald, David Herbert. *Lincoln.* New York: Simon & Schuster, 1995.

———. *Charles Sumner and the Coming of the Civil War.* New York: Alfred A. Knopf, 1970.

———. *Lincoln Reconsidered.* New York: Alfred A. Knopf, 1958.

———. *Lincoln's Herndon.* New York: Alfred A. Knopf, 1948.

Douglas, Henry Kyd. *I Rode with Stonewall.* Chapel Hill, N.C.: University of North Carolina Press, 1939.

Dowd, Clement. *The Life of Zebulon B. Vance.* Charlotte, N.C.: Observer Printing and Publishing House, 1897.

Du Bose, John Witherspoon. *The Life of William Lowndes Yancey.* Birmingham: Roberts and Son, 1892.

Duke, Basil W. *Reminiscences of Basil W. Duke.* Garden City, N.Y.: Doubleday, Page & Company, 1911.

Eaton, Clement. *Jefferson Davis.* New York: The Free Press, 1977.

Eckenrode, Hamilton James. *Jefferson Davis: President of the South.* New York: The Macmillan Company, 1923.

Elliott, Charles Winslow. *Winfield Scott: The Soldier and the Man.* New York: The Macmillan Company, 1937.

Evans, Eli N. *Judah P. Benjamin, the Jewish Confederate.* New York: The Free Press, 1988.

Fehrenbacher, Don E. *Prelude to Greatness: Lincoln in the 1850s.* Palo Alto, Calif.: Stanford University Press, 1962.

Flippin, Percy S. *Herschel V. Johnson, of Georga: States Rights Unionist.* Richmond: Press of the Dietz Printing Co., 1931.

Foote, Henry S. *A Casket of Reminiscences.* Washington, D.C.: Chronicle Publishing Company, 1874.

Foulk, William Dudley. *The Life of Oliver P. Morton.* Two vols. Indianapolis: The Bowen-Merrill Company, 1899.

Gilmore, James R. *Personal Recollections of Abraham Lincoln and the Civil War.* Boston: L. C. Page and Company, 1898.

Gorham, George C. *Life and Public Services of Edwin M. Stanton.* Two vols. Boston: Houghton Mifflin, 1899.

Grant, Ulysses. *Personal Memoirs of U. S. Grant.* Two vols. New York: C. L. Webster & Company, 1886.

Greenhow, Rose O'Neal. *My Imprisonment, and the First Year of Abolition Rule in Washington.* London: R. Bentley, 1863.

Hale, William Harlan. *Horace Greeley, Voice of the People.* New York: Harper and Brothers, 1950.

Hamlin, Charles Eugene. *The Life and Times of Hannibal Hamlin.* Two vols. Cambridge, Mass.: The Riverside Press, 1899.

Henderson, Col. G. F. R. *Stonewall Jackson and the American Civil War.* Two vols. New York and London: Longmans, Green and Company, 1911.

Herndon, William H., and Jesse W. Weik. *Abraham Lincoln: The True Story of a Great Life.* New edition edited by Paul Angle. New York: D. Appleton and Company, 1916.

Hertz, Emanuel. *The Hidden Lincoln: From the Letters and Papers of William Herndon*. New York: Blue Ribbon Books, 1940.

Hesseltine, William B. *Lincoln and the War Governors*. New York: Alfred A. Knopf, 1948.

Holden, W. W. *Memoirs of W. W. Holden*. The John Lawson Monographs of the Trinity College Historical Society. Vol. 11. Durham, N.C.: Seaman Printery, 1911.

Hollister, O. J. *Life of Schuyler Colfax*. New York: Funk & Wagnalls, 1886.

James, Marquis. *The Raven, A Biography of Sam Houston*. Indianapolis: The Bobbs-Merrill Company, 1929.

Johannsen, Robert W. *Stephen A. Douglas*. New York: Oxford University Press, 1973.

Johnson, Allen. *Stephen A. Douglas*. New York: The Macmillan Company, 1908.

Johnston, Joseph E. *Narrative of Military Operations*. New York: D. Appleton and Company, 1874.

Johnston, Richard M., and W. H. Browne. *The Life of Alexander Stephens*. Philadelphia: J. B. Lippincott & Co., 1878.

Jones, J. William. *The Davis Memorial Volume; or Our Dead President Jefferson Davis and the World's Tribute to His Memory*. Atlanta: H. C. Hudgins & Co., 1890.

Julian, George W. *Political Recollections, 1849–1872*. Chicago: Jansen, McClurg and Company,1884.

King, Alvy L. *Louis T. Wigfall: Southern Fire-Eater*. Baton Rouge: Louisiana State University Press, 1970.

King, Horatio. *Turning on the Light*. Philadelphia: J. B. Lippincott & Co., 1895.

King, Willard. *Lincoln's Manager, David Davis*. Cambridge, Mass.: Harvard University Press, 1960.

Klein, Philip Shriver. *President James Buchanan*. University Park: Pennsylvania State University Press, 1962.

Klement, Frank L. *The Limits of Dissent: Clement Vallandigham and the Civil War*. Lexington: University of Kentucky Press, 1970.

Kunhardt, Philip B., Jr., Philip B. Kunhardt III, and Peter W. Kunhardt. *Lincoln: An Illustrated Biography*. New York: Alfred A. Knopf, 1992.

Lamon, Ward Hill. *Recollections of Abraham Lincoln, 1847–1865*. Edited by Dorothy Lamon Teillard. Washington, D.C.: privately published, 1911.

———. *The Life of Abraham Lincoln: His Birth to His Inauguration as President*. Boston: J. R. Osgood and Company, 1872.

Lewis, Lloyd. *Sherman, Fighting Prophet*. New York: Harcourt, Brace and Company, 1932.

Lewis, Walker. *Without Fear or Favor: A Biography of Roger Brooke Taney*. Boston: Houghton Mifflin, 1865.

Linder, Usher F. *Reminiscences of the Early Bench and Bar of Illinois*. Chicago: The Chicago Legal News Company, 1879.

Lorant, Stefan. *Lincoln: A Picture Story of His Life*. New York: Harper and Brothers, 1957.

Lothrop, Thornton Kirkland. *William Henry Seward*. Boston: Houghton Mifflin, 1899.

Luthin, Reinhard H. *The Real Abraham Lincoln*. Englewood Cliffs, N.J.: Prentice-Hall, 1960.

Mayes, Edward. *Lucius Q. C. Lamar: His Life, Times and Speeches, 1825–1893*. Nashville: Publishing House of the Methodist Episcopal Church, South, 1896.

McClellan, George B. *McClellan's Own Story*. New York: C. L. Webster and Company, 1887.

McClure, A. K. *Abraham Lincoln and Men of War-Times*. Philadelphia: The Times Publishing Company, 1892.

Meade, Robert D. *Judah P. Benjamin, Confederate Statesman*. New York: Oxford University Press, 1943.

Merritt, Elizabeth. *James Henry Hammond, 1807–1864*. Baltimore: Johns Hopkins University Press, 1923.

Milton, George Fort. *The Age of Hate: Andrew Johnson and the Radicals*. New York: Coward-McCann Inc., 1930.

———. *The Eve of Conflict: Stephen A. Douglas and the Needless War*. Boston and New York: Houghton Mifflin, 1934.

Mitchell, Stewart. *Horatio Seymour of New York*. New York: De Capo Press, 1970.

Monaghan, James.*The Man Who Elected Lincoln*. Indianapolis: The Bobbs-Merrill Company, 1956.

Nichols, Roy Franklin. *Franklin Pierce: Young Hickory of the Granite Hills*. Second edition. Philadelphia: University of Pennsylvania Press, 1958.

Nicolay, Helen. *Personal Traits of Abraham Lincoln*. New York: The Century Company, 1912.

Nicolay, John G. *A Short Life of Abraham Lincoln*. New York: The Century Company, 1911.

Nicolay, John G., and John Hay. *Abraham Lincoln: A History*. Ten vols. New York: The Century Company, 1890.

Oates, Stephen B. *With Malice Toward None: The Life of Abraham Lincoln*. New York: Harper and Row, 1977.

Parks, Joseph H. *John Bell of Tennessee*. Baton Rouge: Louisiana State University Press, 1950.

Patrick, Rembert Wallace. *Jefferson Davis and His Cabinet*. Baton Rouge: Louisiana State University Press, 1944.

Peterson, Merrill D. *Lincoln in American Memory*. New York: Oxford University Press, 1994.

Pierce, Edward L. *Memoir and Letters of Charles Sumner*. Four vols. Boston: Roberts Brothers, 1877–1892. Reprint, New York: Arno Press, 1959.

Pollard, Edward A. *Life of Jefferson Davis, With a Secret History of the Confederacy*. Philadelphia: National Publishing Company, 1869.

Poore, Benjamin Perley. *Perley's Reminiscences of Sixty Years in the National Metropolis*. Two vols.: New York: AMS Press, 1971.

Pratt, Fletcher. *Stanton, Lincoln's Secretary of War*. New York: W. W. Norton, 1953.

Pryor, Mrs. Roger. *Reminiscences of Peace and War*. New York: The Macmillan Company, 1905.

Radcliffe, George L. P. *Governor Thomas H. Hicks of Maryland and the Civil War*. Johns Hopkins University Studies in Historical and Political Science. Series XIX, Nos. 11 and 12. Baltimore: Johns Hopkins University Press, 1901.

Randall, James G. *Lincoln the President*. Four vols. New York: Dodd, Mead & Company, 1945–1955. The final volume, *The Last Full Measure*, was completed by Richard N. Current.

Randall, Mary Painter. *Lincoln's Sons*. Boston: Little, Brown & Co., 1955.

Reagan, John H. *Memoirs, with Special Reference to Secession and Civil War*. New York: The Heale Publishing Company, 1906.

Richardson, Leon Burr. *William E. Chandler, Republican*. New York: Dodd, Mead & Company, 1940.

Riddle Donald W. *Congressman Abraham Lincoln*. Urbana: University of Illinois Press, 1957.

Robinson, Alexander. *Alexander Hugh Holmes Stuart*. Richmond, Va.: n.p., 1925.

Sandburg, Carl. *Abraham Lincoln: The Prairie Years*. Two volumes. New York: Harcourt, Brace & World, 1926.

————. *Abraham Lincoln. The War Years.* Four volumes. New York: Review of Reviews Corporation, 1939.

Schurz, Carl. *The Autobiography of Carl Schurz.* Wayne Andrews, ed. New York: Scribner, 1961.

————. *The Reminiscences of Carl Schurz.* Three vols. Garden City, N.Y.: Doubleday & Co., 1913.

Scott, Winfield. *Memoirs of Lieut. General Scott, LLB., Written by Himself.* Two vols. New York: Sheldon and Company, 1864.

Sears, Louis Martin. *John Slidell.* Durham, N.C.: Duke University Press, 1925.

Seward, Frederick W. *Seward at Washington.* New York: Derby and Miller, 1891.

————. *Reminiscences of a War-Time Statesman and Diplomat, 1830–1915.* New York: G. P. Putnam's Sons, 1916.

Shaw, Albert. *Abraham Lincoln: His Path to the Presidency.* New York: Review of Reviews Corporation, 1929.

————. *Abraham Lincoln: The Year of His Election.* New York: Review of Reviews Corporation, 1929.

Shenton, James P. *Robert John Walker: A Politician from Jackson to Lincoln.* New York and London: Columbia University Press, 1961.

Sherman, John. *Recollections of Forty Years in the House, Senate and Cabinet.* Two vols. Chicago and New York: Werner, 1895.

Sherman, William T. *Memoirs.* Bloomington: Indiana University Press, 1875.

Smith, Elbert B. *Francis Preston Blair.* New York: The Free Press, 1980.

Smith, William Ernest. *The Francis Preston Blair Family in Politics.* Two vols. New York: The Macmillan Company, 1933.

Stephens, Robert Grier, Jr. *Intrepid Warrior, Clement Anselm Evans.* Dayton, Ohio: Morningside House, 1992.

Stillwell, Lucille. *Born to Be a Statesman: John Cabell Breckinridge.* Caldwell, Idaho: The Caxton Printers, 1936.

Stone, Irving. "Horatio Seymour," biography. In *They Also Ran.* New York: Garden City, N.Y.: Doubleday & Co., 1966.

Stovall, Pleasant. *Robert Toombs.* New York: Cassell Publishing Company, 1892.

Strode, Hudson. *Jefferson Davis.* Three vols. New York: Harcourt, Brace & Co., 1955–1964.

Tate, Allen. *Jefferson Davis, His Rise and Fall: A Biographical Narrative.* New York: Minton, Balch and Company, 1929.

Taylor, Richard. *Destruction and Reconstruction.* Richard B. Harwell, ed. Waltham, Mass.: Blaisdell Publishing Co., 1968.

Thayer, William Roscoe. *The Life and Letters of John Hay.* Two vols. Boston and New York: Houghton Mifflin, 1916.

Thomas, Benjamin P. *Abraham Lincoln: A Biography.* New York: Alfred A. Knopf, 1952.

Thomas, Benjamin P., and Harold Hyman. *Stanton: The Life and Times of Lincoln's Secretary of War.* New York: Alfred A. Knopf, 1962.

Thomas, Lately. *Between Two Empires: The Life Story of California's First Senator, William McKendree Gwin.* Boston: Houghton Mifflin, 1969.

————. *Sam Ward: King of the Lobby.* Boston: Houghton Mifflin, 1965.

————. *The First President Johnson.* New York: William Morrow and Company, 1968.

Trefousse, Hans Louis. *Benjamin Franklin Wade, Radical Republican from Ohio.* New York: Twayne Publishers, 1963.

Tucker, Glenn. *Zeb Vance: Champion of Personal Freedom.* Indianapolis: The Bobbs-Merrill Company, 1965.

Vallandigham, James L. *A Life of Clement L. Vallandigham.* Baltimore: Turnbull Brothers, 1872.

Van Deusen, Glyndon G. *William Henry Seward.* New York: Oxford University Press, 1967.

———. *Thurlow Weed: Wizard of the Lobby.* New York: Boston: Little, Brown & Co., 1947.

Vandiver, Frank. *Mighty Stonewall.* New York: McGraw-Hill, 1957.

Villard, Henry. *Memories of Lincoln on the Eve of '61.* Harold G. and Oswald Garrison Villard, eds. New York: Alfred A. Knopf, 1941.

———. *Memoirs of Henry Villard, Journalist and Financier, 1835–1900.* Two vols. Boston: Houghton Mifflin, 1904.

Von Abele, Rudolph. *Alexander H. Stephens.* New York: Alfred A. Knopf, 1946.

Wall, Joseph Frazier. *Henry Watterson, Reconstructed Rebel.* New York: Oxford University Press, 1956.

Weed, Thurlow. *The Life of Thurlow Weed* and *Autobiography of Thurlow Weed.* Thurlow Weed Barnes and Harriet A. Weed, eds. Two vols. Boston: Houghton Mifflin, 1883–1884.

Wells, Damon. *Stephen Douglas: The Last Years, 1857–1861.* Austin: University of Texas Press, 1971.

White, Horace. *The Life of Lyman Trumbull.* Boston: Houghton Mifflin, 1913.

White, Laura A. *Robert Barnwell Rhett, Father of Secession.* Gloucester, Mass.: P. Smith, 1965.

Whitney, Henry Clay. *Lincoln the Citizen.* Vol. I of *A Life of Lincoln.* New York: The Baker and Taylor Company, 1908.

Williams, T. Harry. *Beauregard, Napoleon in Gray.* Baton Rouge: Louisiana State University Press, 1954.

Willson, Beckles. *John Slidell and the Confederates in Paris, 1862–1865.* New York: Minton, Balch and Company, 1932.

Wise, Barton Haxall. *The Life of Henry A. Wise.* New York: The Macmillan Company, 1899.

Wise, Henry Alexander. *Seven Decades of the Union.* New York: J. B. Lippincott & Company, 1881.

Wise, John S. *The End of an Era.* Boston: Houghton Mifflin, 1901.

Wright, Mrs. D. Giraud (nee Louise Wigfall). *A Southern Girl in '61.* New York: Doubleday, Page & Co., 1905.

Wyatt-Brown, Bertram. *Lewis Tappan and the Evangelical War Against Slavery.* Cleveland: Press of Case Western University, 1969.

Zuber, Richard L. *Jonathan Worth: A Biography of a Southern Unionist.* Chapel Hill: University of North Carolina Press, 1965.

OFFICIAL PUBLICATIONS

Biographical Directory of the American Congress. Washington, D.C. 1971.

Congressional Globe, thirty-fifth, thirty-sixth, thirty-seventh, and thirty-eighth Congresses, 1857–1865. Washington, D.C.

Reconstruction. House Report No. 30, Part 2, thirty-ninth Congress, First Session. Washington, 1866.

Richardson, James D., comp. *A Compilation of the Messages and Papers of the Presidents, 1789–1897.* Washington, D.C., 1897.

U.S. Naval War Records Office. *Official Records of the Union and Confederate Navies in the War of the Rebellion.* 31 vols. Washington, D.C., 1894–1922.

U.S. House of Representatives. *Report of the House Select Committee Investigating Alleged Hostile Organization Against the Government Within the District of Columbia.* Report number 79, February 14, 1861. Thirty-sixth Congress, Second Session.

U.S. War Department. *The War of the Rebellion: A Compilation of the Official Records of the Union and Confederate Armies.* 128 vols. Washington, D.C., 1880–1901.

OTHER PUBLICATIONS

Adams, Henry. *The Great Secession Winter of 1860–61.* Proceedings of the Massachusetts Historical Society, Vol. XLII. Boston: n.p., 1910. Reprinted by Sagamore Press, New York, 1958.

Alexander, De Alva S. *A Political History of the State of New York.* Four vols. New York: H. Holt and Company, 1906–1909.

Angle, Paul M., ed. *The Lincoln Reader.* New Brunswick, N.J.: Rutgers University Press, 1947.

Angle, Paul M., and Earl Schenck Miers. *Tragic Years, 1860–1865.* Two vols. New York: Simon & Schuster, 1960.

Baringer, William E. *A House Dividing: Lincoln as President-Elect.* Springfield, Ill.: The Abraham Lincoln Association, 1945.

———. *Lincoln's Rise to Power.* Boston: Little, Brown & Co., 1937.

Basler, Roy. *Abraham Lincoln: His Speeches and Writings.* Cleveland: The World Publishing Company, 1946.

Belden, Thomas, and Marva Robins Belden. *So Fell the Angels.* Boston: Little, Brown & Co., 1956.

Bill, Alfred Hoyt. *The Beleaguered City.* New York: Alfred A. Knopf, 1946.

Binkley, Wilfred E. *American Political Parties, Their Natural History.* New York: Alfred A. Knopf, 1951.

Botts, John Minor. *The Great Rebellion: Its Secret History, Rise, Progress, and Disastrous Failure.* New York: Harper and Brothers, 1866.

Bowers, Claude. *The Tragic Era: The Revolution After Lincoln.* Boston: Houghton Mifflin, 1929.

Boyd, William K. "North Carolina on the Eve of Secession." American Historical Association Reports, 1910.

Brooks, Noah. *Washington, D.C., in Lincoln's Time.* New York: The Century Company, 1895.

Brownlow, William Gannaway. *Sketches of the Rise, Progress and Decline of Secession.* Philadelphia: G. W. Childs, 1862.

Burgess, John W. *The Civil War and the Constitution.* Two vols. New York: Charles Scribner's Sons, 1901.

The Campaign of 1860. Collected pamphlets containing speeches by Abraham Lincoln, William H. Seward, Henry Wilson, Benjamin F. Wade, Carl Schurz, Charles Sumner, William Evarts, and others. Albany, N.Y.: Weed, Parsons & Company, 1860.

Carman, Harry J., and Reinhard H. Luthin. *Lincoln and the Patronage.* New York: Columbia University Press, 1943.

Carter, Hodding. *The Angry Scar: The Story of Reconstruction.* Garden City, N.Y.: Doubleday & Co., 1959.

Catton, Bruce. *The Coming Fury.* Vol. I of *The Centennial History of the Civil War.* Garden City, N.Y.: Doubleday & Co., 1961.

Channing, Steven A. *Crisis of Fear: Secession in South Carolina.* New York: Simon & Schuster, 1970.

Chittenden, Lucius E. *Recollections of President Lincoln and His Administration.* New York: Harper and Brothers, 1891.

———. *A Report of the Debates and Proceedings in the Secret Sessions of the Conference Convention, for Proposing Amendments to the Constitution of the United States, Held in Washington, D.C. in February 1861.* New York: D. Appleton and Company, 1864. Reprinted in New York: De Capo Press, 1971, under the title, *Report of the Debates and Proceedings of the Peace Convention.*

Cochran, William C. *The Dream of a Northwestern Confederacy.* Madison: The State Historical Society of Wisconsin, 1916.

Craven, Avery. *The Coming of the Civil War.* New York: Charles Scribner's Sons, 1942.

———. *The Repressible Conflict.* Baton Rouge: Louisiana State University, 1939.

Crawford, Samuel Wylie. *The Genesis of the Civil War: The Story of Fort Sumter, 1860–1861.* New York: n.p., 1887.

Crenshaw, Ollinger. *The Slave States in the Presidential Election of 1860. John Hopkins University Studies in Historical and Political Science.* Series 63, No. 3. Baltimore: Johns Hopkins University Press, 1945.

Crofts, Daniel W. *Reluctant Confederates: Upper South Unionists in the Secession Crisis.* Chapel Hill: University of North Carolina Press, 1989.

Current, Richard N. *Lincoln and the First Shot.* Philadelphia: J. B. Lippincott & Co., 1963.

Dell, Christopher. *Lincoln and the War Democrats: The Grand Erosion of Conservative Tradition.* Rutherford, N.J.: Fairleigh Dickinson University Press, 1975.

Dictionary of American Biography. 22 vols. New York: n.p., 1946.

Dictionary of American History. Six vols. New York: n.p., 1941.

Dowdey, Clifford. *Experiment in Rebellion.* Garden City: N.Y.: Doubleday & Co., 1946.

Dumond, Dwight L. *The Secession Movement 1860–61.* New York: The Macmillan Company, 1931.

Eaton, Clement. *A History of the Southern Confederacy.* New York: The Macmillan Company, 1954.

———. *The Mind of the Old South.* Baton Rouge: Louisiana State University Press, 1967.

Eisenschiml, Otto. *Why the Civil War?* Indianapolis: The Bobbs-Merrill Company, 1958.

Fehrenbacher, Don E. *Prelude to Greatness: Lincoln in the 1850s.* Stanford, Calif.: Stanford University Press, 1962.

Fite, Emerson D. *The Presidential Election of 1860.* New York: The Macmillan Company, 1911.

Foote, Henry S. *The War of the Rebellion.* New York: Harper and Brothers, 1866.

Foote, Shelby. *The Civil War: A Narrative.* Three vols. New York: Random House, 1958–1974.

Ford, Lacey K., Jr. *The Origins of Southern Radicalism: The South Carolina Upcountry, 1800–1860.* New York: Oxford University Press, 1988.

Forney, John W. *Anecdotes of Public Men.* Two vols. New York: 1970,Harper and Brothers, 1873.

Freeman, Douglas Southall. *Lee's Lieutenants: A Study in Command.* Three vols. New York: Charles Scribner's Sons, 1942.

———. *R. E. Lee: A Biography.* Four vols. New York: Charles Scribner's Sons, 1934–1935.

Furnas, J. C. *The Road to Harper's Ferry.* New York: William Sloan Associates, 1959.

Gray, Wood. *The Hidden Civil War: The Story of the Copperheads.* New York: The Viking Press, 1942.

Greeley, Horace. *The American Conflict.* Two vols. Hartford, Conn.: O. D. Case & Company, 1865–1866.

Halstead, Murat. *Caucuses of 1860.* Columbus, Ohio: Follett, Foster and Company, 1860.

Hart, Albert Bushnell. *Slavery and Abolition, 1831–1841.* Vol. 16 of *The American Nation: A History.* New York: Harper and Brothers, 1906.

Helper, Hinton Rowan. *The Impending Crisis of the South: How to Meet It.* New York: Burdick Brothers, 1857.

Hendrick, Burton J. *Lincoln's War Cabinet.* Boston: Little, Brown & Co., 1946.

———. *Statesmen of the Lost Cause.* Boston: Little, Brown & Co., 1939.

Henry, Robert Selph. *The Story of the Confederacy.* Indianapolis: The Bobbs-Merrill Company, 1943.

Huston, James L. *The Panic of 1857 and the Coming of the Civil War.* Baton Rouge: Lousiana State University, 1987.

Johnson, Robert Underwood, and Clarence Clough Buel, eds. *Battles and Leaders of the Civil War.* Four vols. New York: The Century Company, 1887. New edition, New York: Thomas Yoseloff, 1956.

Kunhardt, Dorothy Meserve, and Philip B. Kunhardt, Jr. *Twenty Days.* New York: Harper and Row, 1965.

Latham, Sen. Milton S. "The Day Journal of Milton S. Latham, January 1 to May 6, 1860." Edgar Eugene Robinson, ed. *Quarterly of the California Historical Society,* Vol. XI, No. One, pp. 18–35, March 1932.

Leech, Margaret. *Reveille in Washington.* New York: Harper and Brothers, 1941.

Long, E. B., with Barbara Long. *The Civil War Day by Day, 1861–1865.* Garden City, N.Y.: Doubleday & Co., 1971.

Luthin, Reinhard H. *The First Lincoln Campaign.* Cambridge, Mass.: Harvard University Press, 1944.

Lutz, Ralph Haswell. "Rudolf Mathias Schleiden and the Visit to Richmond April 25." *Annual Report of the American Historical Association for 1915.* Washington, D.C.: American Historical Association, 1917.

McPherson, Edward. *The Political History of the United States of America During the Great Rebellion.* Washington, D. C.: Philp and Solomons, 1865.

McPherson, James M. *Battle City of Freedom: The Civil War Era.* New York: Oxford University Press, 1988.

———. *Abraham Lincoln and the Second American Revolution.* New York: Oxford University Press, 1991.

Manakee, Harold R. *Maryland in the Civil War.* Baltimore: Maryland Historical Society, 1961.

Marshall, John A. *American Bastile: A History of the Illegal Arrests and Imprisonment of Americans During the Late Civil War.* Philadelphia: Thomas W. Hartley, 1878.

Meredith, Roy. *Storm Over Sumter.* New York: Simon & Schuster, 1957.

Miers, Earl Schenck. *The Great Rebellion.* Cleveland: World Publishing Company, 1958.

Miller, Francis Trevelyan. *The Photographic History of the Civil War.* Ten vols. New York: The Review of Reviews Company, 1911.

Moore, Frank. *The Rebellion Record: A Diary of American Events.* Eleven vols. and supplement. New York: Putnam and Van Nostrand, 1861–1868.

Myers, Robert M. ed. *The Children of Pride: A True Story of Georgia and the Civil War.* New Haven, Conn.: Yale University Press, 1972.

Nevins, Allan. *The Ordeal of the Union.* Vols. I and II. New York: Charles Scribner's Sons, 1947.

———. *The Emergence of Lincoln.* Vols. I and II. New York: Charles Scribner's Sons, 1950.

———. *The War for the Union.* Four vols. New York: Charles Scribner's Sons, 1959–1971.

Nichols, Roy Franklin. *The Democratic Machine, 1850–1854.* New York: Columbia University, 1923.

———. *The Disruption of American Democracy*. New York: The Macmillan Company, 1948.

O'Connor, Thomas H. *Lords of the Loom: The Cotton Whigs and the Coming of the Civil War.* New York: Charles Scribner's Sons, 1968.

Oldroyd, Osborn H. *Lincoln's Campaign, or the Political Revolution of 1860.* Chicago: Laird & Lee, 1896.

Owsley, Frank. *King Cotton Diplomacy.* Chicago: University of Chicago Press, 1931.

Parrington, Vernon Louis. *Main Currents in American Thought.* Three vols. New York: Harcourt, Brace & Company, 1927.

Phillips, Ulrich Bonnell. *The Course of the South to Secession.* New York: D. Appleton: Century Company, 1939.

Piatt, Don. *Memories of the Men Who Saved the Union.* Chicago and New York: Belford Clarke, 1887.

Pike, James S. *First Blows of the Civil War.* New York: The American News Company, 1987.

Pollard, Edward A. *The Lost Cause.* New York: E. B. Treat & Co., 1879.

Potter, David M. *Lincoln and His Party in the Secession Crisis.* New Haven, Conn.: Yale University Press, 1942.

———. *The Impending Crisis, 1848–1861.* Completed by Don Fehrenbacher. New York: Harper and Row, 1976.

Procter, Addison G. *Lincoln and the Convention of 1860.* Chicago Historical Society, 1918.

Ramsdell, Charles W. "The Changing Interpretation of the Civil War." *The Journal of Southern History,* August 1937.

Randall, James G. *Constitutional Problems Under Lincoln.* Urbana: University of Illinois Press, 1951.

Rhodes, James Ford. *History of the United States from the Compromise of 1850 to the Final Restoration of Home Rule in the South in 1877.* Eight vols. New York: The Macmillan Company, 1909–1919.

Rice, Allen Thorndike. *Reminiscences of Abraham Lincoln by Distinguished Men of His Time.* New York: North American Publishing Company, 1886.

Richardson, Albert D. *The Secret Service: The Field, the Dungeon, and the Escape.* Hartford, Conn.: American Publishing Company, 1866.

Russell, William. *My Diary North and South.* New York: Harper and Brothers, 1863.

Safire, William. *Freedom.* Garden City, N.Y.: Doubleday & Co., 1987.

Scharf, J. Thomas. *History of Maryland from the Earliest Period to the Present Day.* Three vols. Baltimore: J. B. Piet, 1879.

Schouler, James. *History of the United States Under the Constitution.* Seven vols. New York: Dodd, Mead & Company, 1894–1913.

Scrugham, Mary. *The Peaceable Americans from 1860–61.* New York: Columbia University Press, 1921.

Shanks, Henry T. *The Secession Movement in Virginia.* Richmond: Garrett and Massie, 1934.

Sitterson, Joseph Carlyle. *The Secession Movement in North Carolina.* The James Sprant Studies in History and Political Science. Vol. 23, No. 2. Chapel Hill: University of North Carolina Press, 1939.

Sprague, Dean. *Freedom Under Lincoln: Federal Power and Personal Liberty Under the Strain of Civil War.* Boston: Houghton Mifflin, 1965.

Stampp, Kenneth M. *And the War Came: The North and the Secession Crisis, 1860–61.* Baton Rouge: Louisiana State University Press, 1950.

———. *Indiana Politics During the Civil War.* Indiana Historical Collections, Vol. XXXI. Indianapolis: Indiana Historical Bureau, 1949.

———. *America in 1857: A Nation on the Brink.* New York: Oxford University Press, 1990.

Stanwood, Edward. *A History of the Presidency from 1788 to 1897.* Two vols. Boston: Houghton Mifflin, 1898.

Stephens, Alexander H. *A Constitutional View of the Late War Between the States.* Two vols. Philadelphia: National Publishing Company, 1870.

Stimpson, George. *A Book About American Politics.* New York: Harper and Brothers, 1952.

Swanberg, W. A. *First Blood: The Story of Fort Sumter.* New York: Scribners, 1957.

Tidwell, William A. *April '65—Confederate Covert Action in the American Civil War.* Kent, Ohio: Kent State University Press, 1995.

Tidwell, William A., with James O. Hall and David Winfred Gaddy. *Come Retribution: The Confederate Secret Service and the Assassination of Lincoln.* Jackson: University Press of Mississippi, 1988.

Tilley, John Shipley. *Lincoln Takes Command.* Chapel Hill: University of North Carolina Press, 1941.

Trescot, William Henry. "Narrative Letter," *American Historical Review* XIII, No. 3 (April 1908): 528–556.

Whitridge, Arnold. *No Compromise! The Story of the Fanatics Who Paved the Way to the Civil War.* New York: Farrar, Straus and Cudahy, 1960.

Williams, Kenneth P. *Lincoln Finds a General.* Five vols. New York: The Macmillan Company, 1949–1952.

Williams, T. Harry. *Lincoln and the Radicals.* Madison: University of Wisconsin Press, 1941.

———. *Lincoln and His Generals.* New York: Alfred A. Knopf, 1952.

———. *Beauregard: Napoleon in Gray.* Baton Rouge: Louisiana State University Press, 1954.

Wilson, Henry. *The Rise and Fall of the Slave Power in America.* Three vols. Boston: J. R. Osgood and Company, 1872–1877.

Wilson, Woodrow. *Division and Reunion.* New York: Longmans, Green and Co., 1893.

Zornow, William Frank. *Lincoln and the Party Divided.* Norman: University of Oklahoma Press, 1954.

INDEX